Intelligent Information Systems 2001

# Advances in Soft Computing

**Editor-in-chief**
Prof. Janusz Kacprzyk
Systems Research Institute
Polish Academy of Sciences
ul. Newelska 6
01-447 Warsaw, Poland
E-mail: kacprzyk@ibspan.waw.pl
http://www.springer.de/cgi-bin/search-bock.pl?series=4240

---

Esko Turunen
*Mathematics Behind Fuzzy Logic*
1999. ISBN 3-7908-1221-8

Robert Fullér
*Introduction to Neuro-Fuzzy Systems*
2000. ISBN 3-7908-1256-0

Robert John and Ralph Birkenhead (Eds.)
*Soft Computing Techniques and Applications*
2000. ISBN 3-7908-1257-9

Mieczysław Kłopotek, Maciej Michalewicz and Sławomir T. Wierzchoń (Eds.)
*Intelligent Information Systems*
2000. ISBN 3-7908-1309-5

Peter Sinčák, Ján Vaščák, Vladimír Kvasnička and Radko Mesiar (Eds.)
*The State of the Art in Computational Intelligence*
2000. ISBN 3-7908-1322-2

Bernd Reusch, Karl-Heinz Temme (Eds.)
*Computational Intelligence in Theory and Practice*
2001. ISBN 3-7908-1357-5

Robert John, Ralph Birkenhead (Eds.)
*Developments in Soft Computing*
2001. ISBN 3-7908-1361-3

Mieczysław A. Kłopotek
Maciej Michalewicz
Sławomir T. Wierzchoń
Editors

# Intelligent Information Systems 2001

Proceedings of the International Symposium "Intelligent Information Systems X", June 18–22, 2001, Zakopane, Poland

With 71 Figures
and 55 Tables

Springer-Verlag Berlin Heidelberg GmbH

Assoc. Prof. Dr.-Eng. Mieczysław A. Kłopotek
Dr.-Eng. Maciej Michalewicz
Assoc. Prof. Dr.-Eng. Sławomir T. Wierzchoń
Polish Academy of Sciences
ul. Ordona 21
01-237 Warsaw
Poland
klopotek@ipipan.waw.pl
michalew@ipipan.waw.pl
stw@ipipan.waw.pl

ISSN 1615-3871
ISBN 978-3-7908-1407-1

Cataloging-in-Publication Data applied for
Die Deutsche Bibliothek – CIP-Einheitsaufnahme
Intelligent information systems 2001: proceedings of the International Symposium "Intelligent Information Systems 10", Zakopane, Poland, June 18–22, 2001; with 55 tables / Mieczysław A. Kłopotek ... ed. – Heidelberg; New York: Physica-Verl., 2001
(Advances in soft computing)
ISBN 978-3-7908-1407-1 ISBN 978-3-7908-1813-0 (eBook)
DOI 10.1007/978-3-7908-1813-0



Originally published by Physica-Verlag Heidelberg New York in 2001



Hardcover Design: Erich Kirchner, Heidelberg

SPIN 10838803 88/2202-5 4 3 2 1 0 – Printed on acid-free paper

# Preface

This volume contains articles accepted for presentation during The Intelligent Information Systems Symposium IIS'2001 which was held in Zakopane, Poland, on June 18-22, 2001. This is tenth, in the order, symposium organized by the Institute of Computer Science of Polish Academy of Sciences and devoted to new trends in (broadly understood) Artificial Intelligence.

The idea of organizing such meetings dates back to 1992. Our main intention guided the first, rather small-audience, workshop in the series was to resume the results gained in Polish scientific centers as well as contrast them with the research performed by Polish scientists working at the universities in Europe and USA. This idea proved to be attractive enough that we decided to continue such meetings. As the years went by, the workshops has transformed into regular symposia devoted to such fields like Machine Learning, Knowledge Discovery, Natural Language Processing, Knowledge Based Systems and Reasoning, and Soft Computing (i.e. Fuzzy and Rough Sets, Bayesian Networks, Neural Networks and Evolutionary Algorithms). At present, about 50 papers prepared by researches from Poland and other countries are usually presented. Besides, for several years now, the symposia are accompanied by a number of tutorials, given by the outstanding scientists in their domain.

Up to this year the proceedings were published as our local publication and they were distributed among the scientific libraries. We feel however, that the subject matter as well as the quality of papers is sufficient to present the proceedings to a broader scientific audience.

The main topics of this year symposium included:

- Logical and Methodological Foundations of AI
- Unsupervised Learning
- Rules and Decision Trees Acquisition
- Handling of Uncertainty
- AI for Database Systems
- Rough Sets
- Neural Networks and Evolutionary Algorithms

Out of a large number of submissions, the Program Committee has selected only 28 full papers for presentation. The remaining papers qualified as communications, will appear in the associated volume, edited by the local publishing house.

We were pleased to see the continuation of the last year trend towards an increase in the number of co-operative contributions and in the number and diversity of practical applications of theoretical research.

Application areas of presented methods and systems included medical and mechanical diagnosis, decision making. Practical issues were investigated from various theoretical points of view like automated and semi-automated learning procedures, evolutionary and rough set theoretic approaches to learning and knowledge representation, agent technology. As a result, interesting practical solutions were proposed and challenging new research issues were suggested. Questions of efficiency of proposed and existing algorithms were studied by means of logical analysis and simulation studies. Overlapping of diverse branches of AI research was strikingly visible.

On behalf of the Program Committee and of the Organizing Committee we would like to thank all participants: computer scientists mathematicians, engineers, logicians and other interested researchers who found excitement in advancing the area of intelligent systems. We hope that this volume of IIS'2001 Proceeding will be a valuable reference work in your further research.

Warsaw,
June, 2001

*Mieczysław A. Kłopotek*
*Maciej Michalewicz*
*Sławomir T. Wierzchoń*

# Contents

## Rule and Decision Tree Learning



## Unsupervised Learning

## Biologically Motivated Methods



## Learning and Reasoning Under Uncertainty

# Logical Foundations of AI

# IIS'2001 Programme Committee

- Prof. Dr. hab. Zdzisław Bubnicki, Instytut Sterowania i Techniki Systemów Politechniki Wrocławskiej
- Prof. Dr. hab. Eng. Ryszard Choraś, Akademia Techniczno-Rolnicza w Bydgoszczy
- Prof. Dr. hab. Piotr Dembiński, Instytut Podstaw Informatyki PAN - chairman
- Prof. Dr. hab. Ludosław Drelichowski, Akademia Techniczno-Rolnicza w Bydgoszczy
- Płk Dr. hab. Eng. Czesław Flanek, Akademia Obrony Narodowej
- Prof. Dr. hab. Eng. Zdzisław Hippe, Politechnika Rzeszowska
- Prof. Dr. hab. Eng. Olgierd Hryniewicz,Instytut Badań Systemowych PAN
- Prof. Dr. hab. Eng. Józef Korbicz, Politechnika Zielonogórska
- Prof. Dr. hab. Jacek Koronacki, Instytut Podstaw Informatyki PAN
- Prof. Dr. hab. Witold Kosiński, Polsko-Japońska Wyższa Szkoła Technik Komputerowych
- Dr Eng. Maciej Michalewicz, Instytut Podstaw Informatyki PAN - scientific secretary
- Prof. Dr. hab. Zbigniew Michalewicz, University of North Carolina, Instytut Podstaw Informatyki PAN
- Prof. Dr. Ryszard S. Michalski, George Mason University, Instytut Podstaw Informatyki PAN
- Dr Eng. Paweł Nowacki, Polsko-Japońska Wyższa Szkoła Technik Komputerowych
- Prof. Dr. hab. Eng. Zdzisław Pawlak, Komitet Badań Naukowych
- Prof. Dr. Zbigniew Raś, University of North Carolina, Instytut Podstaw Informatyki PAN
- Prof. Dr. hab. Henryk Rybiński, Instytut Informatyki Politechniki Warszawskiej
- Prof. Dr. hab. Andrzej Skowron, Instytut Matematyki, Uniwersytet Warszawski
- Prof. Dr. hab. Eng. Ryszard Tadeusiewicz, Akademia Górniczo-Hutnicza w Krakowie
- Prof. Dr. hab. Eng. Alicja Wakulicz-Deja, Instytut Informatyki Stosowanej, Uniwersytetu Śląskiego
- Prof. Dr. hab. Jan Węglarz, Instytut Informatyki Politechniki Poznanskiej
- Prof. Dr. hab. Eng. Stefan Węgrzyn, Instytut Informatyki Teoretycznej i Stosowanej PAN

- Doc. Dr. hab. Sławomir Wierzchoń, Instytut Podstaw Informatyki PAN
- Prof. Dr. hab.Eng. Krzysztof Zieliński, Akademia Górniczo Hutnicza w Krakowie
- Prof. Dr. hab. Jan Żytkow, University of North Carolina, Instytut Podstaw Informatyki PAN

We would like to thank the Programme Commmittee Members for careful reviewing of the submitted papers.

Proceedings Editors

# Identification of Rules for Brain Metastases and Survival Time Prediction for Small Cell Lung Cancer Patients

Kwei Aryeetey[1], Wojciech Ziarko[1], Patricia Tai[2], and Casely Ago[2]

[1] Computer Science Department
University of Regina, Regina, Saskatchewan, S4S 0A2 Canada
[2] Allan Blair Cancer Center, Regina, Saskatchewan, S4T 7T1 Canada

**Abstract.** This paper presents experiments with the application of rough set-based data mining methodology to discover predictive rules in small cell lung cancer patient data. The specific prediction targets are the occurrence of the spread of cancer to the brain and the prediction of patient survival time. The obtained results have been derived from patient data supplied by cancer researchers from the Allan Blair Cancer Center, Regina, Saskatchewan, Canada who also provided all the necessary background information and conducted medical evaluation of the results.

## 1 Introduction

Metastases is the spread, or the extension of cancerous cells from a tumor to distant parts of the body. The brain is a common site for metastases, and small cell lung cancers (SCLC) are both chemo-sensitive and radio-sensitive. Chemotherapy cannot reach the lipid-rich parts of brain and so unfortunately the brain does not achieve tumoricidal doses of this form of drugs. Some patients achieve complete response (CR) in the chest, only to develop brain metastasis later. Researchers have suggested that patients with CR might benefit from prophylactic cranial irradiation (PCI) [12]. PCI patient metastases rate was significantly lower than those who did not. Only a few randomized trails have tested the efficacy of PCI in patients with limited stage SCLC who have achieved a complete response after combined chemotherapy and thoracic radiation. A retrospective study from Memorial Sloan-Kettering Cancer Center found a statistically significant survival benefit for PCI, with five year survivors only occurring in the PCI group. This paper presents an alternative approach to the patient-data analysis aimed at understanding the effects of PCI treatment in conjunction with other factors such as patient's age, sex etc. The approach is derived from methods of rough set theory [1] and is applied here to predict the occurrence of the spread of cancer to the brain and the prediction of SCLC patients' survival time. The theory of rough sets have been successfully applied in a number of clinical data analysis problems in the past (for example [2-10]). One of the key issues in the applications of rough set methodology in medicine and other areas is constructing predictive models from data in the form of series of

**if** <conditions> **then** <predictions>

rules with attached prediction confidence probabilities.

The major step when constructing predictive models from data in this approach is building the classification of objects of interest into disjoint categories. These categories are then used to generate predictive rules by a rule discovery program. In this medical application, the objects are patients, represented in terms of measured parameters. More specifically, the project involves the analysis of patient data accumulated over the period from 1987 -1998 at the Alan Blair Cancer Center, in Regina, Saskatchewan, Canada. The data that was used for this project, was collected from 144 patients with small cell lung cancer. The main objective of the rough-set based analysis of the data was to determine how different combinations of symptoms, patients' age, health status factors and treatments affect the likelihood of occurrence of brain metastases and survival time within different time ranges (one year, two years etc.). In the analysis, the techniques of rule generation based on a probabilistic extension of the rough set model, called the Variable Precision Rough Set (VPRS) model were used [11]. The VPRS model is an extension of the original Pawlak's rough set model aimed at constructing probabilistic rule-based decision and predictive models from data. In the presented project, a UNIX-based KDD-R data-mining tool based on the VPRS model, was utilized to generate predictive rules to aid in the identification of patients who are likely to develop brain metastases, and who are likely to survive longer periods of time. The resulting predictive model could then be used to identify only patients who would benefit from PCI. This would spare those who would not benefit the side effects of PCI treatment and consequently preserve costly resources.

## 2 Data Preparation

As indicated earlier, the data collection consisted of 144 patient records. These records are described by the following 42 attributes, that is, factors describing available information about patients. The attributes are:

| | Field Name | Description |
|---|---|---|
| 1 | GENDER | Sex of patient |
| 2 | DOB | Date of Birth |
| 3 | SITE | Primary site of metastases |
| 4 | SIDE | Side of lung |
| 5 | DIM | Maximum dimension of primary tumor |

| | | |
|---|---|---|
| 6 | LNDX | Any lymph node disease |
| 7 | HILAR | Hilar lymph node disease |
| 8 | SIZEHIL | Size of HILAR |
| 9 | MEDIA | Mediastinal lymph node |
| 10 | SIZEMED | Size of MEDIA |
| 11 | IPSIL | Ipsilateral supraclavicular lymph node |
| 12 | SIZEIP | Size of IPSIL |
| 13 | CONTRA | Contralateral supraclavicular lymph node |
| 14 | SIZECON | Size of CONTRA |
| 15 | PERIEFF | Pericardial effusion |
| 16 | PLEUREF | Pleural effusion |
| 17 | BRONOBS | Bronchial obstruction |
| 18 | SVDCOBS | Superior vena cava obstruction |
| 19 | PATH | Pathology |
| 20 | STAGE | Stage |
| 21 | SURGRES | Surgical resection |
| 22 | STATPRES | Performance status at presentation |
| 23 | NFCP | Neuro-functional class |
| 24 | WEIGHTP | Weight loss $\geq$5% in the last 3 months |
| 25 | LDHP | Lactic dehydrogenase level at presentation |
| 26 | HEMP | Hemoglobin level around time of presentation given or on first day of chemotherapy i.e. before chemotherapy is given |
| 27 | RSTEQ | Sequence of radiotherapy with chemotherapy |
| 28 | RSTDT | Start date of radio therapy to lung |
| 29 | RSEDT | End date of radiotherapy to lung |
| 30 | RTDOSE | Total radiation dose |
| 31 | PCI | PCI Treatment |
| 32 | SYMPDT | Diagnosis of brain metastases, date symptoms started to occur |
| 33 | METSDT | Proven date of diagnosis of brain metastases (strongly suspected on history and physical or confirmed by imaging) |
| 34 | BRCHRT | Best response after chemo-radiation completion |
| 35 | LFUDT | Date of last known status (last follow-up or death) |
| 36 | PS1 | Pattern of spread. Local recurrence |
| 37 | PS2 | Pattern of spread. Lymph node spread ever occur within patient's lifetime |
| 38 | PS3 | Pattern of spread. Lymph node recurrence in previous site |
| 39 | PS4 | Pattern of spread. Distant metastases |
| 40 | LASTSTAT | Last known status (i.e. Last Follow-up or death) |
| 41 | BMETS | Diagnosis of brain metastases within patient's lifetime |
| 42 | STIME | Survival time - Date of diagnosis (i.e. LFUDT - DODX) |

The attributes have been divided into two categories: condition attributes, to represent the state of the patient and other prognostic factors, and the decision attributes, to represent the prediction targets. Attributes 1 - 40 were selected by the medical specialists, as condition attributes, and attributes 41 42 i.e. BMETS and STIME (Survival Time), were categorized as the only decision attributes. Next, with the help of the medical experts, the decision attributes were reduced from 40 to the most significant 7. The following seven were then used for predicting the occurrence of BMETS in this particular project: SEX (gender of patient), AGE (age of patient, in years), IPSIL (ipsilateral supraclavicular lymph node), PLEUREF (pleuref effusion), CHDOSE (duration of of chemotherapy, in days), BED (biologically effective radiation dose), and PCI (prophylactic cranial irradiation) After determining the condition and decision attributes the next major step in data preprocessing was data discretization. Data discretization involves converting high precision numeric values into meaningful coarse qualitative ranges. This conversion helps in uncovering data regularities and extends the scope (the generality) of the classification of patients produced based on the sample data. In our case, this was done with the cooperation of the cancer specialists, our domain experts. With their aid the original exact attribute values were translated into intervals of values represented by symbols 1, 2, 3, and 4. The adopted discretization definition (norms) is shown in the Table 1.

**Table 1.** Table of norms

| | Attribute | | | Domain(code) | | |
|---|---|---|---|---|---|---|
| | (symbol) | 0 | 1 | 2 | 3 | 4 |
| 1. | SEX | M | F | | | |
| 2. | AGE (Years) | | <50 | ≥50,<60 | ≥60,<70 | ≥70 |
| 3. | IPSIL (Binary) | 0 | 1 | | | |
| 4. | PLEUREF (Binary) | 0 | 1 | | | |
| 5. | CHDOSE (Days) | | <75 | ≤75,<125 | ≥125 | |
| 6. | BED (cGy) | | <40 | ≤40, <50 | ≥50,< 60 | ≥60 |
| 7. | PCI (Binary) | 0 | 1 | | | |
| 8. | BMETS (Binary) | 0 | 1 | | | |
| 9. | STIME (Years) | | <1 | ≥1,<2 | ≥2,<5 | ≥5 |

After applying the values from the discretization definition table to the original data collection, the decision table [1], Table 2, was obtained (the symbol "-" means unknown value).

This decision table represents a classification of patients corresponding to combinations of discretized condition and decision attributes occurring in the data. At this stage, the table is incomplete because it does not include some other possible medical cases. These are yet to be observed. As the table gets saturated, with growth in size, over time, it will come to include the unobserved cases and consequently lead to more accurate conclusions and predictions about the nature, treatments and progress of the disease.

**Table 2.** Decision Table

| CLASS | SEX | AGE | IPSIL | PLEUREF | CHDOSE | BED | PCI | BMETS | STIME |
|---|---|---|---|---|---|---|---|---|---|
| 1 | F | 3 | 0 | 0 | 3 | 3 | 0 | 0 | 2 |
| 2 | M | 4 | 0 | 1 | 3 | 1 | 0 | 0 | 2 |
| .. | .. | .. | | | | | | | |
| 143 | M | 4 | 1 | 0 | 2 | - | 1 | 1 | 2 |
| 144 | F | 4 | 1 | 1 | 3 | 3 | 1 | 1 | 2 |

## 3 The Rough Set-based Methodology of Decision Table Analysis

The main objective of the next analytical stage was constructing and analyzing a decision table, consisting of the above seven condition attributes, to develop a predictive model for the two target attribute values i.e. BMETS (Brain Metastases) and STIME (Survival Time). The model will enable the prediction, with acceptable confidence, of whether an object matching a combination of attribute values occurring in the decision table belongs to the target set, in this case whether brain metastases occurs i.e. BMETS = Y, or its complement i.e. BMETS = N. The predictive model will also predict survival time defined as:

(STIME) = Last Known Status Date (LFUDT) - Diagnosis Date (DOX)

The data analysis methodology used in this project is based on the variable precision (VPRS) model of rough sets [3], as implemented in the KDD-R system. The original RS model-based analysis involves detection of functional or partial functional dependencies and subsequent dependency-preserving reduction of condition attributes. The VPRS model extends the capability of the RS model to allow handling of probabilistic information given in the form of frequency distributions. In the VPRS model, the definitions of set approximations are based on real-valued approximation precision control parameters called lower ($l$) and upper ($u$) limits respectively, such that $0 \leq l < u \leq 1$. Let $U$ represent the universe of objects of interest, the cancer patients in our case, and let $R$ be an equivalence relation on $U$ representing the classification of objects into disjoint categories. In terms of this application, the equivalence relation $R$ represents the partitioning of patients into identity classes denoted as $E$ with respect to discretized attributes SEX, AGE, IPSIL, PLEUREF, CHDOSE, BED, and PCI. For any subset $X \in U$, and $R^*$, a set of equivalence classes of relation $R$, the following three approximation regions are defined as follows (in the context of the cancer patient data, the $X$ represents the current prediction target, such as, the set of all those cases for which BMETS = "Y"). The $u$-positive region, or $u$-lower approximation of $X$ is given by

$$POS_u(X) = \bigcup\{E \in R^* : P(X/E) \geq u\}$$

where $P(X/E)$ is a conditional probability estimate of $X$ given $E$, typically calculated using ratios of data frequency distributions. This region of $X$ represents an area in the universe where the predictions concerning the membership in $X$ can be made with acceptable error rate, where the acceptability level is defined by the value of the parameter $u$.

The $l$-$u$-boundary region defines the area in the universe $U$ where the predictions about object membership in $X$, or its complement $-X$, cannot be made with acceptable error rate. The parameter $l$ (lower limit) represents the acceptability level for the complement $-X$ of the set $X$. In detail,

$$BNR_{l,u}(X) = \bigcup\{E \in R^* : l < P(X/E) < u\}$$

In other words, this region represents objects which cannot be classified with sufficiently high confidence (represented by $u$) into set $X$ and which also cannot be excluded from $X$ with sufficiently high confidence (represented by $l$).

The third important approximation region of the set $X$ is the $l$-negative region. The $l$-negative region is formally defined as

$$NEG_l(X) = \bigcup\{E \in R^* : P(X/E) \leq l\}$$

This region represents objects of the universe for which it is known, based on their relation $R$ equivalence class membership, that it is relatively unlikely that they would belong to $X$.

## 4 The System KDD-R

The system KDD-R implements the essential elements of the VPRS model. It is focused on the generation of strong, i.e. supported by sufficient (as defined by the user) number of data cases, predictive rules from data. The rule in this context is a conditional statement in the form

***If*** <conjunction of conditions > **then** < prediction > with probability ***p***

The conditions appearing on the left hand-side of the rule (rule antecedent ) are specifications of values of some of the discretized attributes from among SEX, AGE, IPSIL, PLEUREF, CHDOSE, BED, PCI, whereas the prediction is statement regarding the value of the selected decision attribute, for example, BMETS = Y. For instance, the following rule to predict BMETS = Y has been obtained from the available cancer data:

***If*** Bed > 1 And Pleuref = 0 And Age ≤ 3 And Pci = 0
**then** BMETS = "Y" with the predictive probability 0.377.

The medical interpretation of the above and other data-acquired rules are given in the section 5. The rules produced by KDD-R are based on equivalence classes of the $l$-positive region of the target set $X$ (corresponding to BMETS = Y) in the classification of the available data collection according to discretized values of the attributes appearing in the rule antecedent. The system KDD-R is performing bounded search for such rules satisfying user-defined strength and probability requirements. In this process, multiple approximation regions, as defined in the previous section, are constructed, from which the rules, meeting the user-imposed quality criteria, eventually are extracted. For the search process, we will skip the theory and focus only on the user perspective. The KDD-R system data mining process can be divided into the following major stages:

**Stage 1.***Data discretization using the table of norms*
The discretization stage was conducted with the help of medical experts who defined significant value ranges for the selected attributes. This discretization definition is shown in Table 1. However, automatic discretization option also exists in KDD-R where the original data can be first discretized into n ranges followed by automatic selection of best discretization points for the final data translation using system-defined statistical criteria. Our experience in this, and other projects demonstrates that the best results are achieved when the discretization is done by domain experts. The discretization definition along with attribute type definition is contained in the systems format file, as presented below:

<X 0 CASE I 1 144 D 10>
<C 0 SEX S 2 F M>
<C 0 AGE I 1 4 M 1.5 2.5 3.5>
<C 0 IPSIL S 2 0 1>
<C 0 PLEUREF S 2 0 1>
<C 0 CHDOSE I 1 3 M 1.5 2.5>
<C 0 BED I 1 4 M 1.5 2.5 3.5>
<C 0 PCI S 2 0 1>
<X 0 BMETS S 2 0 1>
<D 0 STIME S 4 1 2 3 4>

Each row of that file represents one column of the original data. Letters X, C or D in the first column control the inclusion and category of the attribute, that is X means exclusion, C means conditional attribute, D stands for decision (prediction target) attribute. The other parameters of the format file entry are attribute weight, name, type (integer, real, string), attribute value range for numeric attributes or the listing of values for string attributes, and the discretization specification:

**Stage 2.** *Preprocessing of the Original Data*
In this stage the actual data is discretized and a decision table according to to user-defined size constraints is created. During discretization, each discretization point is converted to a binary attribute, resulting in a binary decision table. A partial listing of the resulting discretized (binarized) file is shown below. The only non-binary target attribute is placed in the last column.

0 1 1 0 0 0 1 1 1 1 0 0 1
1 1 1 1 0 1 1 1 0 0 0 0 1
0 1 0 0 0 0 1 1 1 0 0 1 1
0 1 1 1 0 0 1 1 1 0 0 1 2

..
1 1 1 0 0 0 1 1 1 0 0 1 1

The corresponding format file is partially shown below:
<C 0 SEX_0 S 2 0 1>
<C 3 AGE_0 S 2 0 1>
<C 8 AGE_1 S 2 0 1>
<C 16 AGE_2 S 2 0 1>
<C 11 IPSIL_0 S 2 0 1>
<C 2 PLEUREF_0 S 2 0 1>
<C 15 CHDOSE_0 S 2 0 1>
<C 22 CHDOSE_1 S 2 0 1>

**Stage 3.** *Selection of k-best bits for the final binary representation of the decision table*
At this stage the binarized decision table is restricted to k-best binary attributes (k is user-defined), using a statistical criterion in evaluating the quality of each binary attribute.

**Stage 4.** *Rule Search*
At this stage bounded search for the satisfactory rules is performed. The form of branch-and-bound algorithm is adopted to conduct the task. The following constraints are imposed on the search process by the user:

- a. Maximum number of attributes to appear in the rule conditions
- b. Minimum number of supporting cases e.g. only rules with more than 10 cases would qualify
- c. Minimum rule predictive probability i.e. only rules that guarantee equal or greater predictive probability greater than the prior probability would be selected.

This process results in a set of binary rules with associated strength figures and rule predictive probabilities. Table 3 shows a partial sample of this.

**Table 3.** Binary rules with associated probabilities

| Aa | Ab | Ac | Ad | Ae | Af | Ag | Ah | Ai | Aj | Ak | Al | |
|---|---|---|---|---|---|---|---|---|---|---|---|---|
| - | - | - | - | - | - | 1 | 0 | 1 | - | - | 0 | (26 0.42) |
| - | - | - | - | - | - | 0 | 1 | - | 1 | - | 0 | (22 0.45) |
| - | - | - | - | - | 1 | 0 | - | - | - | 0 | 0 | (18 0.50) |
| .. | | | | | | | | | | | | |
| - | - | - | - | - | 1 | 0 | - | - | - | 1 | 0 | (14 0.43) |

**Stage 5.** *Rule Minimization and Translation*

Some of the generated binary rules are already contained in other more general rules hence are redundant. The optional minimization stage therefore allows the user to retain only the most general (i.e. strongest) rules. Following the minimization, the rule has to be translated into human-readable form. This involves replacing the binary conditions with their definitions as specified in the norms table. A typical rule obtained at this stage looks as follows:

$$\textbf{If } \textit{Bed} \leq 3 \textit{ And Pleuref} = 0 \textit{ AND Age} \leq 3 \textit{ And Pci} = 0$$
$$\textbf{then } \textit{BMETS} = \text{"}Y\text{"} \ (20,\ 0.75)$$

The above rule is supported by 20 cases and its predictive probability is 0.75 which is about twice the prior probability for this target.

**Stage 6.** In this optional step the rules can be visualized in a graphical form resembling a bar chart. The sizes of the bars are proportional to the number of cases that support the rule, and their heights are in line with rule probabilities. Generally, thicker and higher bar means the better rule.

## 5 Results and their Medical Interpretation

Space limitation prevents us from showing all the generated predictive rules for brain metastases and survival time after initial diagnosis. For brain metastases (BMETS) 22 rules were generated with the prior probability of its occurrence equal to 0.3777 . The predictive rules guarantee probabilities in the range 0.70 to 0.80 which is about twice the prior probability. For survival time, 415 rules were generated in total, for different survival ranges. In more detail, for each survival time category, the following results were obtained.

For the survival time category STIME=A, i.e. STIME $<$ 1 year, 320 predictive rules were generated. The prior probability was 0.195. The rules correct prediction probabilities are in the range 0.67 to 0.82. This is three times the prior probability. In the survival time category STIME=B, i.e. STIME $<$ 2 years, 16 rules were generated. The prior probability in this category was 0.517. The rules correct prediction probabilities are in the range 0.82 to 0.87. This is about one and a half times the prior probability. In the category STIME=C, i.e. STIME $<$ 5 years, 23 rules were computed. The prior probability was 0.223. The rules correct prediction probabilities fall in the range 0.45 to 0.60. This is about two-to-three times the prior probability. Lastly, in the category STIME=D, i.e. STIME $\geq$ 5 years, 59 rules were computed. The prior probability in this case was 0.063. The rules correct prediction probabilities were in the range 0.45 to 0.60. This is about three-to-five times the prior probability.

The following is a sample of the rules which were judged by medical professionals as interesting:

**If** *Pleuref = 0 And Age ≥ 3 And Ipsil = 0 And Pci = 0*
**then** *BMETS = "Yes" (8, 0.72)*

This rule in words states that:

*If patient is younger than 70 years of age (Age 3) and has no pleural effusion (Pleuref = 0) and there is no supraclavicular lymph node (Ipsil = 0) and no PCI (Pci=0), his or her chance of brain metastases is 0.72*

That rule is supported by 8 cases. It confirms that for the brain metastases prediction, younger patients with adequate biological effective dose (BED) to the chest but without PCI tend to be at highest risk.

The following for predicting BMETS is also considered interesting, and reveals some more SCLC and brain metastases:

*If* Bed ≤ 2 And Chdose > 1 And Ipsil = 0 And Pci = 0
*then* BMETS="Yes" (14, 0.71)

which, in words state that:

*If a patient has adequate dose of radiation to the chest, 40 to 50 cGy (Bed < 2) and has no supraclavicular lymph node (Ipsil=0), his or her chance of brain metastases is 0.71, if no Pci was given (Pci=0)*

This is supported by 14 cases. In predicting BMETS, the PCI attribute appears in all the 22 predictive rules. In terms of clinical utility, PCI is the most important factor in determining or predicting the chances of brain metastases. PCI overrides all the other prognostic factors since it always appear in the rules, indicating the strong dependence of BMETS on PCI. This agrees with Cox-Regression analysis [13]. For STIME = A (survival time less than 1 year), the shortest survival time it can be deduced from the rule patterns that with poor risk factors like ipsilateral pleural effusion (Ipsil = 1, Pleuref = 1), and no PCI (Pci = 0), most patients die earlier than other survival time ranges such as STIME = B (survival time less than 2 years but more than 1 year), or STIME = C (survival time more than 2 years but less than 5 years), or STIME = D (survival time more than 5 years). For STIME = D (survival time more than 5 years) the following 10 rules were considered interesting from medical perspective. All of them are supported by 10 cases and have the predictive probability equal to 0.20.

***If*** *Pleulef=1 And Age>1 And Sex=F And Pci=1*
***then*** *STIME=D (10, 0.20)*

***If*** *Pleuref=1 And Chdose>1 And Sex=1*
***then*** *STIME=D (10, 0.20)*

***If*** *Pleuref=1 And Bed≤2 And Chdose>1*
***then*** *STIME=D (10, 0.20)*

***If*** *Pleuref=1 And Sex=1 And Pci=1*
***then*** *STIME=D (10, 0.20)*

***If*** *Bed≤3* And Pleuref=1 And Sex=F And Pci=1
***then*** *STIME=D (10, 0.20)*

*If* Pleuref=1 And Bed≤2 And Sex=F
**then** STIME=D (10, 0.20)

*If* Bed≤3 And Pleuref=1 And Bed≤2 And Sex=F
**then** STIME=D (10, 0.20)

*If* Age≥ And Pleuref=1 And Age>1 And Bed≤2
**then** STIME=D (10, 0.20)

*If* Bed≤3 And Age>3 And Pleuref=1 And Bed ≤2
**then** STIME=D (10, 0.20)

*If* Age>3 And Pleuref=1 And Bed≤2
**then** STIME=D (10, 0.20)

It means that even with fluid in their pleural space (Pleuref = 1) patients can still survive beyond 5 years. Furthermore, the rules for STIME = D have relatively low predictive probabilities, ranging from 0.20 to 0.30. Even though this is larger than the prior probability of 0.063, it is still low. This makes the point that only very few SCLC patients would be able to survive beyond 5 years.

## 6 Final Remarks

On the basis of the analysis work done in this project, we could recommend some combinations of attributes of SCLC patients for the approximate determination of their likelihood of developing brain metastases, and their level of survival. However, this assessment will never be complete and error-free without precise knowledge of small cell lung cancers. The combination of the attributes, with the extent of the small cell lung cancer, will enable the physician to determine or predict the likelihood of metastases occurring, and a patient's survivability of the disease, with a high degree of certainty. Future work on this subject will involve further development of probabilistic decision tables, which include a greater number of attributes and larger number of patient cases, for a rapid determination of the likelihood of brain metastases, in patients with small cell lung cancer. One problem which will have to be addressed is the accumulation of significantly larger number of training cases for the produced rules as current 144 observations do not provide credible evidence for the estimation of conditional probabilities.

## 7 Acknowledgment

The research reported in this article was partially supported by a research grant awarded by Natural Sciences and Engineering Research Council of Canada to the second author.

## References


1. Pawlak, Z. (1991) *Rough Sets: Theoretical Aspects of Reasoning About Data,* Kluver Academic Publishers, Dordrecht.
2. Grzymala-Busse, J. Goodwin L. (1997) *Predicting Preterm Birth Risk Using Machine Learning from Data with Missing Values,* Bulletin of International Rough Set Society, Vol. 1, No. 1, 17-21.
3. Cheshenchuk, S. Ziarko, W. (1999) *Mining Patient Data for Predictive Rules to Determine Maturity Status of Newborn Children,* Bulletin of International Rough Set Society, Vol. 3, No 1-2, 23-26.
4. Slowinski, K. Sharif E. (1994) *Rough Sets Approach to Analysis of Data of Diagnostic Peritoneal Lavage Applied for Multiple Injuries Patients. In Ziarko, W. ed. Rough Sets, Fuzzy Sets and Knowledge Discover,* Springer Verlag , 420-425.
5. Slowinski, K. (1992) *Rough Classification of HSV Patients. In Slowinski, R. ed. Intelligent Decision Support,* Kluwer Academic Publishers, 77-94.
6. Grace I. Paterson (1994) *Rough Classification of Pneumonia Patients Using a Clinical Database. In Ziarko, W. ed. Rough Sets, Fuzzy Sets and Knowledge Discover,* Springer Verlag, 412-419.
7. Tsumoto, S. (1999) *Discovery of rules about complications. In Proc. of the 7th International Workshop on Rough Sets, Fuzzy Sets, Data Mining and Granular-Soft Computing, Lecture Notes in Artificial Intelligence 1711,* Springer–Verlag, 29-37.
8. Tsumoto, S. (1998) *Extraction of expert's decision rules from clinical databases using rough set model,* J. Intelligent data Analysis 2(3).
9. Tsumoto, S. (1998) *Automated induction of medical expert system rules from clinical databases based on rough set theory,* Information Sciences 112, 67-84.
10. Tsumoto, S. Ziarko, W. (1996) *The application of rough sets-based data mining technique to differential diagnosis of meningoencephaliti. Proc. of the Int. Conference on Methodologies for Intelligent Systems, Lecture Notes in Artificial Intelligence, vol. 1079,* Springer Verlag, 438-447.
11. Ziarko, W. (1993) *Variable precision rough sets model,* Journal of Computer and Systems Sciences, vol. 46, no. 1, 39-59.
12. Rosen S. T., Makuch R. W., Lichter A. S., et al. (1983) *Role of prophylactic cranial irradiation in prevention of central nervous system metastases in small cell lung cancer. Potential benefit resyticted to patients with complete response,* Am. J. Med 74:615-624.
13. Cox DR. (1972) *Regression models and life-tables,* J. R. Stat. Soc. B 34: 187-220.

# The Development of the AQ20 Learning System and Initial Experiments

**Guido Cervone**
**Liviu Panait**
**Ryszard Michalski***

Machine Learning and Inference Laboratory, George Mason University, Fairfax, VA

* Also Institute of Computer Science, Polish Academy of Sciences, Warsaw, Poland

e-mail: {cervone,panait,michalski}@mli.gmu.edu

***Abstract**: Research on a new system implementing the AQ learning methodology, called AQ20, is briefly described, and illustrated by initial results from an experimental version. Like its predecessors, AQ20 is a multi-purpose learning system for inducing general concepts descriptions from concept examples and counter-examples. AQ20 is viewed as a natural induction system because it aims at producing descriptions that are not only accurate but also easy to understand and interpret. This feature is achieved by representing descriptions in the form of attributional rulesets that have a higher representation power than decision trees or conventional decision rules. Among new features implemented in AQ20 are the ability to handle continuous variables without prior discretization, to control the degree of generality of rules by a continuous parameter, and to generate more than one rule from a star. Initial experimental results from applying AQ20 to selected problems in the UCI repository demonstrate a high utility of the new system.*

*Keywords: Symbolic Learning, Natural Induction, learning from examples.*

## 1. Introduction

The AQ learning methodology traces its origin to the $A^q$ algorithm for solving general covering problems of high complexity (Michalski, 1969a, 1969b). An implementation the $A^q$ algorithm in combination with the *variable-valued logic* representation produced the first AQ learning program, AQVAL/1, which pioneered research on general-purpose inductive learning systems (Michalski, 1975). Subsequent implementations, developed over the span of many years, added many new features to the original system, and produced highly versatile learning methodology, able to tackle complex and diverse learning problems.

One of the recently added features is pattern discovery mode, which allows the program to generate rulesets representing strong patterns in large volumes of noisy data (Michalski and Kaufman, 2000b). The pattern discovery mode complements the original theory formation mode that determines complete and consistent data generalizations.

Due to a wide range of features and a highly expressive representation language, recent members of the AQ family of learning programs arguably belong to the most advanced symbolic learning systems. They have been used in a wide range of domains, including medicine, agriculture, engineering, image processing, economy, sociology, music, geology, and others. An early application of AQ to soybean disease diagnosis was considered one of the most significant achievements of machine learning (Michalski and Chilausky, 1980).

The rapid development of computer technology and high-level programming languages often stimulated researchers to port existing versions of the methodology to new programming environments. AQ programs have been written in Pascal, Fortran, InterLisp, CommonLisp, C and now C++, and for a variety of platforms, including IBM 360, Symbolics, Next/Step, Digital Vax, Digital Ultrix, SunOS 1.0 and 2.0, MacOS, MS-DOS, Windows and recently Linux. These developments were done in an academic environment and primarily for educational purposes. Consequently, they often lacked stability and reliability required by outside users who were most interested in practical applications and the simplicity of program's use rather than in research ideas. As a result, despite of their conceptual advantages, AQ programs met so far a rather limited use.

Before undertaking the task of developing a new AQ program, we analyzed some of the most stable programs, such as AQ15 (Michalski et al., 1986), and AQ18 (Kaufman and Michalski, 2000a) in order to identify parts of the code that needed restructuring. This analysis indicated that the above implementations were optimized for speed, rather than for the extendibility or comprehensibility of the code. As the last two concerns were of great interest to us, we decided to give AQ20 a fresh new start.

Using knowledge acquired from the analysis of the previous codes, a new design aims at making AQ20 reliable, easy to use, easy to modify and extend, while including features previously implemented in AQ rule learning systems. The aim of AQ20 is to become a machine learning environment that supports users in conducting machine learning experiments.

## 2. A Brief Review of the AQ Methodology

To make the paper self-contained, this section reviews very briefly some of the basic features of AQ learning. A detailed description of various aspects of the methodology can be found in (Michalski, 1969a; Michalski, 1974; Michalski, 1983; Michalski, 2001).

AQ pioneered the progressive covering (a.k.a. "separate and conquer") approach to concept learning. It is based on an algorithm for determining quasi-optimal (optimal or sub-optimal) solutions to general covering problems of high complexity (Michalski, 1969b). The central concept of the algorithm is a star, defined as a set of alternative general descriptions of a particular event (a "seed") that satisfy given constraints, e.g., do not cover negative examples, do not contradict prior knowledge, etc. In its simplified version, the algorithm starts by randomly selecting a "seed" from among concept examples, and then creates a *star* for that example. A member (a rule) of the star that satisfies a given preference criterion is selected, and examples covered by it are removed from the set of concept examples. A new seed is selected from the uncovered-so-far examples, and the process repeats until there are no more examples to be covered.

In AQ20, the condition of selecting only one rule from a star has been relaxed and more than one rule can be selected, which speeds up the learning process. The seed generalization process takes into consideration the type of variables in the training data. AQ20 distinguishes between the following types of variables: binary, nominal, linear, continuous, and structured (Kaufman and Michalski, 1996).

Previous versions of AQ dealt with continuous variables by discretizing them into a number of discrete units, and then treating them as ordinal variables. AQ20 does not require such discretization, as it automatically determines ranges of continuous values for each variable occurrence in a rule.

The AQ learning process can proceed in one of two modes: (1) the *theory formation mode* (TF), and (2) the *pattern discovery mode* (PD). In the TF mode, AQ learns rules that are complete and consistent with regard to the data. This mode is mainly used when the training data can be assumed to contain no errors. The PD mode is used for determining strong patterns in the data. Such patterns may partially inconsistent or incomplete with regard to the training data. The PD mode is particularly useful for mining very large and noisy databases.

The core of the AQ algorithm is the star generation, which is done in two different ways, depending on the mode of operation (TF or PD. In TF mode, the star generation proceeds by selecting a random positive example (called seed) and then generalizing it in various ways to create a set of consistent generalizations (that cover the positive example and do not cover any of the negative examples). In PD mode, rules are generated similarly, but the program seeks strong patterns (that may be partially inconsistent) rather than fully consistent rules.

The star generation is an iterative process. First, the seed is *extended-against* each negative example (this is a pair-wise generalization operation). These extensions are then logically multiplied out to form a star, and the best rule (or rules) according to a given multi-criterion functional (LEF) is selected. LEF is composed from elementary criteria and their tolerances so that it best reflects the needs of the problem at hand. The program uses beam search to speed-up this process. The beam width is defined by the *maxstar* parameter. For details, see e.g., (Michalski et al. 1986).

In the original version of the methodology, only one rule, the best according to LEF, was selected. In AQ20, one or more rules may be selected from a star, depending on the degree of intersection between rules. The procedure for selecting rules from a star works as follows:

1 Sort the rules in the star according to LEF, from the best to the worst.

2 Select the first rule, and compute the number of examples it covers. Select the next rule, and compute the number of new training examples it covers.

3 If the number of new examples covered exceeds a *new_examples_threshold*, then the rule is selected, otherwise it is discarded. Continue the process until all rules are inspected.

The result of this procedure is a set of rules selected from a star. The list of positive_events_to_cover is updated by deleting all those events that are covered by these rules. A new seed is selected, and the entire process is repeated. It continuous until there the list positive_events_to_cover becomes empty.

## 3. A Simple Illustration of an AQ Execution

This section illustrates how AQ20 learns rules that characterize a class of events in Theory Formation mode. It also shows the format of an AQ20 input file. Various program parameters and options were omitted due to the space limitation. These are explained in the AQ20 Users' Guide.

The input consists of a set of events, in which each event is classified either as a member of the target class (positive event) or not a member (negative event). Let's assume that an event is defined by values of four nominal variables: X, Y, Z and GROUP. The first step in preparing an input to the program consists of defining attributes and their domains. Each attribute must be assigned a well-defined domain. A domain may be shared, however, by one or more attributes.

Since in our example variables are nominal, their domains are unordered sets. Let's assume that the domain of X, denoted domain_x, is a set {0, 1, 2}, the domain of Y and Z, denoted domain_yz is a set {0, 1}, and the domain of GROUP, denoted domain_group, is a set {good, bad}. The above information is communicated to AQ20 by an input shown below:

```
Generic Domains
{
   domain_x nominal { 0, 1, 2 }
   domain_yz nominal { 0, 1 }
   domain_group  nominal { good, bad }
}
Attributes
{
```

```
    X        domain_x
    Y        domain_yz
    Z        domain_yz
    GROUP  domain_group
}
```

In addition to attributes and their domains, a user may define various control parameters, or allow the system use their default values. An AQ run corresponds to a learning session. The following section illustrates how to set the output variable(s) to define the target class (GROUP is good), and how to set the maxstar parameter (in this case it is equal to 1, that is only one rule is maintained during the star generation). The LEF for this experiment is MaxPositiveCoverage with tolerance 0% and MinNegativeCoverage with tolerance 0%. This means that AQ will prefer rules with have high positive coverage and low negative coverage.

```
Runs
{
  run1_simple_example_of_AQ20 {
     output [GROUP = good ]
     maxstar = 1
     LEF { (MaxPositiveCoverage, 0), ( MinNegativeCoverage, 0 ) }
  }
}
Events
{
         X, Y, Z, GROUP
          0, 0, 0,  good
          2, 0, 1,  good
          1, 1, 1,  good
          1, 1, 0,  bad
          2, 1, 0,  bad
          0, 1, 1,  bad
}
```

The algorithm starts by creating two classes of events, one called positive, and one called negative. The positive events are those with GROUP=good, and remaining are negative events. The algorithm selects a random positive seed, say, the first event on the list (0,0,0), which can be represented as a condition [X=0][Y=0][Z=0]. This seed is used to generate the first star. Elementary partial stars are generated by applying the *extension against operator* to the seed and each negative example (see Section 6.3 for an explanation). The first elementary partial star is obtained be extending the seed (0,0,0) against the first negative example (1,1,0). This operation produces two alternative, maximally general rules that cover the seed and do not cover the negative event:

{[X=0, 2] (p=2, n=2), [Y=0] (p=2, n=0)}

In the first rule (read: X takes value 0 or 2), p=2 means that the rule covers 2 positive events (one is the seed), and n=2 means that it also covers 2 negative events. Let's us assume that LEF selects only one rule [Y=0], because it has the same positive coverage as the first rule, but lower negative coverage. The obtained rule constitutes a reduced elementary partial star {[Y=0]}. By extending the seed against the second negative example, another elementary partial star is generated :

{[X=0,1] (p=2, n=2), [Y=0] (p=2, n=0)}

The obtained star is logically multiplied by the previous partial elementary star, which produces a *partial star* {[X=0,1][Y=0], [Y=0]}. The positive and negative coverage is calculated again for each of the rules. [X=0,1][Y=0] covers 1 positive and 0 negative events, while [Y=0] covers 2 positives and 0 negatives. According to LEF, the second rule is better. Since the parameter maxstar is 1, only one rule can be selected, so the resulting partial star is

{[Y=0]}.

A partial star obtained from extending the seed against the third negative example is:

{[Y=0] (p=2, n=0), [Z=0] (p=2, n=1)}

By multiplying the two elementary partial stars, and using absorption laws, the following partial star is created:

{[Y=0] (p=2, n=0), [Y=0][Z=0] (p=1, n=0)}.

It contains two rules, one covering 2 positive events and the other one covering only 1 positive event. None of the rules covers any negatives. As the second rule is subsumed by the first one, it deleted from the star.

In general, after a partial star (the "star-generated-so-far") is determined, all rules that are subsumed by other rules are deleted. When this process is completed for the last negative example, a star of the given seed is obtained. AQ20 then selects from it one or more rules, as described above. In our case, the algorithm produces just one rule [Y=0].

Because this rule does not cover all positives example (in this case, the third positive event), the above process is repeated for another randomly selected seed from the examples uncovered by the selected rule/s. This is the event (1,1,1,good). The second star generation process gives the rule: {[X=1][Z=1] (p=1,n=0)}, which completes the learning process.

The above two rules constitute a complete and consistent description of the good GROUP, which AQ20 outputs in the form:

[GROUP = good] <- [Y=0]
[GROUP = good] <- [X=1][Z=1]

# 4. New Features in AQ20

AQ20 is not just a reimplementation of the AQ methodology, but it comes along with several new features not present in previous versions. One of the concerns of the authors was the ease of extending the program in the future. For this reason, AQ20 employs an object-oriented architecture. The architecture of the classes (which underwent a few redesign processes) provides, through polymorphism, an easy mechanism for adding new features. Adding binary attributes to AQ20 was a matter of minutes, while adding the linear ones took less than half an hour.

One of the most important new features in AQ20 is handling of continuous variables without prior discretization. This feature was implemented in such a way that it provides the user with an ability to control the level of rule generalization. Another new feature in AQ20, already mentioned earlier, is the possibility of selecting more than one rule from a star, which helps to speed up the learning process.

## 4.1 Handling of Continuous Variables

Previous versions of AQ handle continuous attributes through discretization. The domain of continuous variables is split into several ranges, usually using the $\chi^2$ method, or by hand. This way continuous variables are turned into discrete ones, and AQ works as described above. This method has the advantage that the search space is reduced from infinite to finite.

One disadvantage of this approach is a limited accuracy of the representation, since ranges cannot be modified by the AQ algorithm. Such a limitation may be particularly undesirable in incremental learning, because it limits the locations of concept boundaries to places specified by the predefined ranges. Another weakness is the growth of the memory requirements with the accuracy of discretization. In the AQ representation of discrete variables, one bit is used for one discrete unit. Thus, when a variable is discretized to a larger number of discrete units, the memory allocated for its representation also grows. The latter feature slows down the star generation process.

In contrast to the above, AQ20 represents conditions with continuous variables are by ranges of continuous values. All the operations on conditions with continuous variables are operations on ranges, represented by two real values. By moving the boundaries of the ranges, a condition can be easily specialized or generalized. For example, the condition

[ X = 2 .. 7 ]

can be specialized by narrowing the range to:

[ X = 3.5 .. 4.2 ]

or generalized by widening the range to:

[ X = 1.8 .. 7.5 ].

Such operations can be done only approximately when a variable is discretized into a fixed number of units.

## 4.2 Adjustable Level of Generality

The level of generality of the rules can be controlled through a parameter called *epsilon*, associated to each attribute. This means that in the same rule, some attributes may be more specific than others.

The epsilon parameter ranges between 0 and 1. When epsilon is set to 1 (0), the learned condition with this attribute will be maximally specific (general). Setting epsilon to a value between 0 and 1 defines an intermediate level of specificity. The meaning of the specificity level depends on the attribute type. For continuous and linear attributes, the epsilon parameter determines the location of the boundary within the distance between the negative and the positive examples that lead to this condition; for structured attributes, it determines a position of the boundary within the structure of the attribute domain. For nominal attributes, the epsilon parameter is assumed to have only values 0 and 1. Any value smaller than 0.5 is rounded to 0, and any value greater or equal to 0.5 is rounded to 1.

The default value of epsilon in AQ20 is 0.5. Thus, if a positive example has value of X equal 4, and a negative examples has value of X equal 10, the extension against operation will create a condition [X=0.. 7], since (4+10)/2=7. The value of epsilon is fixed for a given run. A more flexible way of implementing epsilon would be to adjust it dynamically, so that some criterion related to the description quality is optimized.

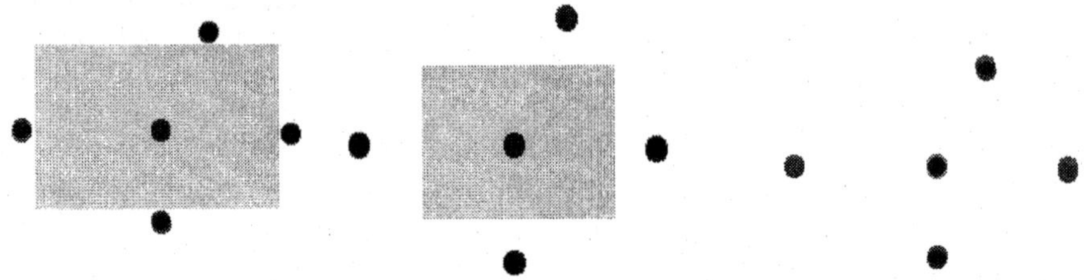

*Fig 1,2,3* Rule generalization for different values of epsilon

Figures 1, 2 and 3 illustrate rule generation with different epsilon values. The number of attributes is two, so the representation space is a plane. The five examples are represented by dots. In each figure, the central dot represents the seed, and the other four dots represent negative examples. Generated rules are represented by darkened rectangles. Recall that epsilon equal to 0 means maximum generalization, and epsilon equal to 1 means maximum specialization.

As shown in the Figures 1, 2, and 3, when epsilon takes a small value, the learned rule is more general, and when it takes a higher value, the rule is more specific.

## 4.3 Implementation of the Extension Operators

The star generation process is governed by the *extension-against* and extension-within operators (Michalski, 1975). This process can also be decomposed in the extension against and within at the attribute level. This paragraph illustrates how this is done in the case of continuous attributes. For details on how it works for other types of attributes, consult (Michalski, 1975). In the remaining of this section, we will refer to the extension-against operator applied with a single variable.

The *extension-against operator* applied to conditions with a single variable has as input two conditions, one covering a positive event and the second covering a negative event. The result of the operator is an epsilon-controlled generalization of the condition for the positive event that does not cover the negative event.

The *extension-within operator* applied to conditions with a single variable receives as input a condition covering of a positive example, and a general condition that may or may not subsume the first condition. If the former is the case, the result of extension-within is an epsilon-controlled generalization of the first condition that is subsumed by the second condition.

To illustrate how AQ20 implements these operators with the control parameter epsilon, suppose that the value of a continuous attribute X for the positive event is 4, and for the negative event is 10. In the first step, the result of the extension-against is the maximally general hypothesis [X < 10], that is, as if epsilon=0.

After performing all the logical intersections, the result are maximally general hypotheses. In order to introduce the epsilon-adjustable levels of generality, a post-processing is applied. AQ20 determines the maximally specific hypothesis that covers all positive examples covered the maximally general hypothesis (by an operation called *refunion,* which is computationally quite simple). Subsequently, the epsilon parameter is applied for each attribute within the maximally specific and the maximally general hypotheses.

## 4.4 Selecting Multiple Rules from a Star

In the rule generation process, the AQ algorithm creates a series of stars in order to cover all positive events. Each star contains a set of rules, all covering the seed of the star. In previous versions of AQ, only one (best according to LEF) rule was selected from the star.

AQ20 can select more than one rule from a star. This leads to the possibility of covering more positive events while generating only one star. Rules in a star have usually have high logical intersection, but not always. Keeping two or more rules that have a small logical intersection can speed-up the learning process, because the number of star generated can be reduced. A potential problem is that the rules may be less optimal, since two rules generated from the same star are never disjoint. AQ20 uses a simple method to calculate the 'gain' obtained by each rule, defined as the number of new positives covered, if the rule were selected from the star.

# 5 Experiments

This section presents selected results from experiments in which AQ20 was applied to two datasets from the UCI repository, *mushroom* and *wine*, and to one synthetic dataset. Results from AQ20 were compared in terms of predictive accuracy with C4.5 and with AQ18.

The datasets were split into training and testing events using different ratios in order to monitor the dependence of the predictive accuracy on the number of training events.

Testing was done using the ATEST module that can execute a flexible and strict matching of events with rules. Flexible matching is a technique for calculating the degree of confidence (a degree of match) that an event belongs to a class. In the case that the event does not match any of the rules constituting the class description, the confidence is 0. If the event matches one or more rules, the confidence is non-zero, and can range from 1 (strict match) to values close to 0 (Michalski et al. 1986).

## 5.1 Mushroom Database

The mushroom database contains the descriptions of more than 8000 different species of mushrooms, classified as poisonous or edible. Each mushroom is described in terms of 23 attributes, out of which 22 are discrete (some are nominal and some are linear), plus 1 nominal attribute representing the decision class. The database was randomly split into training and testing events. The number of training events was increased gradually to analyze how the predictive accuracy increases.

In the experiments relative to the mushroom database the LEF was *MinNumSelector* with tolerance 30% and *MaxNewPositives* with tolerance 10%. This is the standard LEF for AQ20 and for AQ18, and results in a faster execution of the algorithm.

The results are presented in confusion matrices below, in which:

- the first row and column contain the names of the classes used in the experiment
- the element a[i,j] (i and j different than 1) contains the number of elements that belong to class a[i, 1] and were classified as belonging to class a[1, j].
- the classes may not cover the whole space, therefore a new class (called "unknown") is automatically added

Thus, high predictive accuracy is manifested by numbers equal or close to 1 in the main diagonal, and 0s or small values outside the main diagonal. The *accuracy* of a classification is defined in the experiments below as the ratio of the total number of correct classifications (the sum of the elements on the main diagonal in the table) over the total number of classifications (the sum of all the elements in the table). For a training-testing examples ratio of 0.02, AQ20 obtained the following results (Accuracy = 98.3%):

| Predictions | Edible | Poisonous | Unknown |
|---|---|---|---|
| Edible | 4061 | 48 | 0 |
| Poisonous | 84 | 3765 | 0 |
| Unknown | 0 | 0 | 0 |

Table 1 AQ20 rule predictions when the training set included 0.02% of examples from the Mushroom dataset.

For a training-testing examples ratio of 0.10, AQ20 obtained the following results (Accuracy = 100%):

| Predictions | Edible | Poisonous | Unknown |
|---|---|---|---|
| Edible | 3780 | 0 | 0 |
| Poisonous | 0 | 3532 | 0 |
| Unknown | 0 | 0 | 0 |

Table 2 Results of AQ20 with 0.1% learning on the Mushroom database

In addition to the high predictive accuracy, the rules learned by AQ20 were typically quite simple and had high coverage. For example, when learning from only 10% of the examples, AQ20 found the following rules :

Rule 1: [class = p] ← [odor = c, y, f, m, p, s]

that covers 3796 from 3916 poisonous mushrooms described in the repository and none of the edible mushroom, and

Rule 2: [class = p]
← [cap-color = n,b,p,e,w,y] & [gill-color = b, g, r, w] &
[spore-print-color = r,w ] & [ population = c,v ] & [habitat = g,l,m,d]

that covers 471 positive (poisonous) and 0 negative (edible).

Predictive accuracy of AQ20 rules was compared with that of rules obtained from AQ18 and C4.5. The two AQ programs extracted very similar rules, and their predictive accuracy is almost identical. The rules generated by C4.5 are different from AQ20's rules, since the program uses a different representation language. For example C4.5 finds the following rules, all relative to the odor attribute.

R1: [class = p] ← [odor = c ]
R2: [class = p] ← [odor = y ]
R3: [class = p] ← [odor = f ]
R4: [class = p] ← [odor = m]
R5: [class = p] ← [odor = p]
R6: [class = p] ← [odor = s]
R7: [class = p] ← [cap-color = n] & [ring-number = 0 ] & [spore-print-color = w ]

Because of C4.5 does not have the internal disjunction operator in its language, it generated six rules that correspond to one AQ20 rule [odor = c,y,f,m,p,s]. The C4.5 Rule 7 was quite different from AQ20 Rule 2.

The following table summarizes the results of the experiments.

| | AQ18 | AQ20 | C4.5 |
|---|---|---|---|
| 2% training | 97% | 98% | 98.7 |
| 10% training | 99.7% | 100% | 99.7 |
| 30% training | 100% | 100% | 98.7 |

Table 3 Comparison of the Predictive Accuracy of AQ20, AQ19, and C4.5 on the Mushroom dataset

**5.2 Wine Database**

The second experiment concerned the application of AQ20 to the *wine* dataset. This dataset contains 178 events of different Italian wines, divided into three classes. Each event is defined by 14 attributes, 13 continuous attributes, plus 1 nominal attribute for the class. AQ20 generated the following rules:

**First class**:

[group = class1]
← [Alcohol ≥ 12.79] & [Alcalinity_of_ash ≤ 27.495]
[Total_phenols ≥ 2.095] & [Flavanoids ≥ 1.805]
[Color_intensity ≥ 3.4] & [Proline ≥ 679.005]

The rule covers all 59 events described in the dataset as belonging to this class.

**Second class:**

[group = class2]
← [Color_intensity ≤ 4.015] & [Proline ≤ 718.995]
← [Alcohol ≤ 13.12] & [Ash ≤ 3.065] &
[Color_intensity ≤ 4.855] & [Hue ≥ 0.785] &
[OD280_OD315_of_diluted_wines = 1.485..3.505]&
[Proline ≤ 1002.5]
← [Malic_acid ≤ 1.615] & [OD280_OD315 of
diluted_wines ≥ 1.575] & [Proline ≤ 975.995]
←[Alcohol ≤ 12.75] & [Flavanoids ≥ 1.27] & [Proline ≤ 975.995]

All four rules represent strong but intersecting patterns for the second class, covering 56, 58, 36, and 56, events respectively. The total number of training events in class 2 was 71.

**Third class**:

[group = class3]
← [Hue <= 0.825] & [OD280_OD315 of diluted_wines
≤ 2.055]
[group = class3]

← [Malic_acid ≥ 2.135] &
[Proanthocyanins ≤ 1.585] &
[Color_intensity ≥ 4.32][Hue ≤ 0.995] &
[Proline ≤ 979.995]

The first rule covers 40 and the second one 39 events (out of the total of 48 total events in class 3), and they are also highly intersecting (31 events).

AQ20 generated rules that are very easy to understand by human. When using 50% of randomly chosen training events and 50% for testing, the following results were obtained (Table 4).

| Predictions → | Class 1 | Class 2 | Class 3 | Unknown |
|---|---|---|---|---|
| Class 1 | 28 | 0 | 2 | 0 |
| Class 2 | 1 | 17 | 0 | 0 |
| Class 3 | 0 | 1 | 37 | 4 |
| Unknown | 0 | 0 | 0 | 0 |

Table 4 Results from the Wine database with 50% testing

This means that 82 out of 90 events were classified correctly (91.1% accuracy). Rules with different levels of generality were tested on the wine dataset. The tests used 10% events for training and the remaining 90% percent for testing. Results were obtained for three different values of epsilon: 0.1 (very general rules), 0.5 (medium) and 0.9 (highly specific). The results for the experiments are presented in the next 3 tables.

| Predictions → | Class 1 | Class 2 | Class 3 | Unknown |
|---|---|---|---|---|
| Class 1 | 40 | 4 | 0 | 6 |
| Class 2 | 3 | 32 | 6 | 2 |
| Class 3 | 5 | 1 | 44 | 14 |
| Unknown | 0 | 0 | 0 | 0 |

Table 5 Confusion matrix for highly general rules (epsilon=0.1). The accuracy is 73.9%.

| Predictions → | Class 1 | Class 2 | Class 3 | Unknown |
|---|---|---|---|---|
| Class 1 | 37 | 0 | 0 | 12 |
| Class 2 | 2 | 30 | 3 | 5 |
| Class 3 | 4 | 1 | 38 | 19 |
| Unknown | 0 | 0 | 0 | 0 |

Table 6 Confusion matrix for rules of medium generality (epsilon=0.5). The accuracy is 69.5%.

| Predictions → | Class 1 | Class 2 | Class 3 | Unknown |
|---|---|---|---|---|
| Class 1 | 28 | 0 | 0 | 21 |
| Class 2 | 1 | 26 | 2 | 10 |
| Class 3 | 2 | 1 | 36 | 22 |
| Unknown | 0 | 0 | 0 | 0 |

Table 7 Confusion rules for highly specific rules (epsilon=0.9). The predictive accuracy is 60.4%.

The number of events classified as "unknown" (last column) when the rules are highly specific (Table 7) is relatively large compared to the other tests. When the description of the classes becomes more and more general (epsilon=0.5; Table 6, and epsilon=0.1; the Table 5), the number of events classified as "unknown" decreases and the number of events classified correctly increases. On the other hand, number of events from one class incorrectly classified as belonging to another class also increases with the increase of generalization for the rules. This is, of course, an expected behavior.

Although the predictive accuracy increased with the rule generalization level, in this problem, it is preferable to classify an event as "unknown" than to misclassify it (it is clearly better to classify a poisonous mushroom as unknown than as edible). Therefore, it is better to keep the rules for edible mushrooms more specialized.

The results of AQ20 on the wine dataset were also compared with those from AQ18. The wine dataset was split in 50% training, 50% testing. The following table summarizes the results of the experiment with the default epsilon equal 0.5.

| | AQ18 | AQ20 |
|---|---|---|
| 50% training | 71% | 91.1% |

Table 8 Comparison of AQ18 and AQ20 on the Wine database with 50% training

As shown in the table, AQ18' rules did not work as well as they did in the previous experiment. This result can be attributed either to an internal bug of AQ18 that could not be verified, or to the incapacity of AQ18 to find appropriate concept boundaries due to prior discretization. This result suggests that direct handling of continuous variables in AQ20 can significantly improve the predictive accuracy of the learned rules (in the case, 20%). Further experiments are needed to confirm this hypothesis.

It should be noted, however, that the AQ20's method of handling continuous variables is more prone to over-fitting the training dataset due to a more powerful representation language. Thus, choosing an appropriate epsilon is an important problem.

More experiment will be done to investigate this further, trying to discretized the variables in a larger number of intervals, and see how this affects the quality of the rules.

### 5.3 Synthetic Database

The last experiment involved a designed dataset to test the ability of AQ20 to select more than one rule from a star whenever it is desirable. A dataset containing 80 events belonging to two classes was generated using a general logic diagram. The events were arranged in a such a way that there existed a star that have highly disjoint rules. Out of 80 events, 57 were used as training and 23 as testing.

In the experiment, AQ20 was run with and without the capability of generating more than one rule form a star. The number of star generated and the time required for learning in both cases was recorded. The results are presented in the table below:

| | 1 rule only | More than 1 rule |
|---|---|---|
| Number of stars | 2 | 1 |
| Time required | .6 sec | .4 sec |

Table 9 Time spent by AQ20 learning rules keeping more than a rule from a star versus learning rules by keeping only one rule from a star

The learned hypotheses were identical in both runs, but, as shown in Table 9, learning with multiple rule selection from a star decreased the execution time by 50%.

## 6 Future Work

Among topics for future work are testing the program on a variety of problems, determining its advantages and disadvantages in comparison to other learning methods, such as Ripper (Cohen, 95), CN2 (Clark and Niblett, 89), C4.5 (Quinlan, 93), those employing rough set theory (e.g., Pawlak, 91), and previous implementations of AQ learning. It is planned to make these comparisons in terms of both the predictive accuracy and the simplicity and understandability of the learned rules.

Future work includes also an integration of AQ20 with supporting modules, such as Knowledge Visualizer that facilitates a visual validation of the learned rules (KV; Zhang, 1997), and ALPE for automatically executing and testing AQ learning programs (Lee and Michalski, 1997).

Among important features implemented in some AQ programs is constructive induction, which is the capacity of the algorithm to automatically improve the representation space for learning (e.g., Bloedorn and Michalski, 1998). Future work will also include the employment of AQ20 in the Learnable Evolution Model (LEM) methodology for non-Darwinian Evolutionary Computation (Cervone et al, 2000).

## 7 Conclusion

This paper described a new implementation of the AQ methodology called AQ20. AQ20 tries to encompass in one place many features previously found in several programs. It includes new features such as the capacity of keeping more than one rule from a star, that may greatly increase the speed of the algorithm, the capacity of dealing with continuous attributes without a fixed discretization, and the introduction of a new parameter called epsilon, that allows each attribute to be learned with a different level of generality. AQ20 can be freely downloaded from the website: www.mli.gmu.edu/aq20

## Acknowledgements

The authors wish to thank Dr. Ken Kaufman for his help in understanding the methodology and his continuous support throughout the development of AQ20. His help was crucial in comparing with AQ18, and solve problems with the previous program. This research has been supported in part by the National Science Foundation under grant IIS-9906858 and by a UMBC Grant under LUCITE Task #32.

## References

1. Cervone, G., Michalski, R.S., Kaufman, K. and Panait, L., "Combining Machine Learning with Evolutionary Computation: Recent Results on LEM," *Proceedings of the Fifth International Workshop on Multistrategy Learning (MSL-2000)*, Guimarães, Portugal, pp. 41-58, June, 2000.

2. Clark, P. and Niblett, T., "The CN2 Induction Algorithm," *Machine Learning* 3, pp. 261-283, 1989.

3. Cohen, W., "Fast Effective Rule Induction," *Proceedings of the Twelfth International Conference on Machine Learning*, Lake Tahoe, CA, 1995.

4. Kaufman, K.A. and Michalski, R.S., "Learning in an Inconsistent World: Rule Selection in STAR," *Reports of the Machine Learning and Inference Laboratory*, George Mason University, Fairfax, VA, 2000a (to appear).

5. Kaufman, K.A. and Michalski, R.S., "An Adjustable Rule Learner for Pattern Discovery Using the AQ Methodology," Journal of Intelligent Information Systems, 14, pp. 199-216, 2000b.

6. Lee, S.W. and Michalski, R.S., "ALPE: A System for Automatic Learning Performance Evaluation The Method and User's Guide," Reports of the Machine Learning and Inference Laboratory, MLI 97-6, George Mason University, Fairfax, VA, 1997

7. Michalski, R.S., "Recognition of Total or Partial Symmetry in a Completely or Incompletely Specified Switching Function," *Proceedings of the IV Congress of the International Federation on Automatic Control (IFAC)*, Vol. 27 (Finite Automata and Switching Systems), pp. 109-129, Warsaw, June 16-21, 1969a.

8. Michalski, R.S., "On the Quasi-Optimal Solution of the General Covering Problem," *Proceedings of the V International Symposium on Information Processing (FCIP 69)*, Bled, Yugoslavia Vol. A3 (Switching Circuits), pp. 125-128, 1969b.

9. Michalski, R.S., "Synthesis of Optimal and Quasi-Optimal Variable-Valued Logic Formulas," *Proceedings of the 1975 International*

*Symposium on Multiple-Valued Logic*, pp. 76-87. Bloomington, Indiana, May 13-16, 1975.

10. Michalski, R.S, "A Theory and Methodology of Machine Learning, in Michalski, R.S, Carbonell, J.G. and Mitchell, T.M. (Eds.), *Machine Learning: An Artificial Intelligence Approach*, Tioga Publishing Company, 1983, pp. 83-134.

11. Michalski, R.S., "Inferential Theory of Learning: Developing Foundations for Multistrategy Learning," in Michalski, R.S. and . Tecuci, G. (eds.), *Machine Learning: A Multistrategy Approach, Vol. IV*, Morgan Kaufmann, San Mateo, CA, 1994.

12. Michalski, R.S., "Natural Induction: A Theory and Methodology," *Reports of the Machine Learning and Inference Laboratory*, George Mason University, Fairfax, VA, 2000 (to appear).

13. Michalski, R.S., and Chilausky, R.L., "Learning By Being Told and Learning From Examples: An Experimental Comparison of the Two Methods of Knowledge Acqusition in the Context of Developing an Expert System for Soybean Disease Diagnosis," *Policy Analysis and Information Systems,* Vol. 4, No. 2, 1980.

14. Pawlak, Z., *Rough Sets: Theoretical Aspects of Reasoning about Data*, Kluwer Academic Publishers, 1991.

15. Quinlan, J.R., *C4.5: Programs for Machine Learning*, Morgan Kaufmann, Los Angeles, CA, 1993.

16. Zhang, Q., "Knowledge Visualizer: A Software System for Visualizing Data, Patterns and Their Relationships," *Reports of the Machine Learning and Inference Laboratory* , MLI 97-14, George Mason University, Fairfax, VA, September, 1997.

# Discovering Multi-head Attributional Rules in Large Databases

**Cezary Głowiński, Ryszard S. Michalski***

Machine Learning and Inference Laboratory, School of Computational Sciences, George Mason University, Fairfax, VA

*Also with the Institute of Computer Science, Polish Academy of Sciences, Warsaw, Poland

*Abstract: A method for discovering multi-head attributional rules in large databases is presented and illustrated by results from an implemented program. Attributional rules (a.k.a. attributional dependencies) can be viewed as generalizations of standard association rules, because they use more general and expressive conditions than those in the latter ones, and by that can express more concisely inter-attribute relations in a database. Multi-head rules have multiple conditions/statements in their conclusion. The presented method applies AQ learning to create single-head characteristic rules, and then seeks conditions (selectors) that can be transferred to the conclusion part of the rule. Experiments with the program MAR1 (Multi-head Attributional Rules), implementing the developed method, has produced highly encouraging results.*

*Keywords: attributional rules*

## 1. Introduction

The problem of discovering unknown relations among groups of attributes in a large database is one of the most challenging and practically important problems in the field of data mining. A popular form of expressing such relations in data mining are association rules [1]. In the original formulation, such rules were in the form in which a conclusion consists of only one transaction item (literal). Subsequently, this form was extended to many items in the conclusion [2].

This paper is concerned with discovering more general relations in the data, called attributional rules (or attributional dependencies). An attributional rule is a relation between conjunctions of attributional conditions, expressed as an implicative or equivalence expression in attributional calculus [9]. An elementary form of an attributional condition is a relation between an attribute and a set of values. A more general form can represent a simple relation between attributes (see Section 2).

The concept of attributional rule, as well as of an association rule, can be viewed as a special case of a more general relational structure, called *parametric association rule* or, briefly, PAR, introduced in [7]. An advantage of using attributional rules in data mining is that they allow the system to express succinctly implicative or equivalence relations among statements involving discrete and/or continuous variables.

Among important problems in data mining are the determination of characteristic rules and rules with low support. Solving them is typically a time consuming task. The method proposed in this paper addresses both problems. It can generate characteristic descriptions as well as attributional dependencies with low support too. A characteristic rule for a class (or concept) is a logic-style description that specifies features that are common to all objects in the class (defined by a specific value of the output attribute). Such rules introduce a approach to characterizing classes of entities, different from statistical methods (e.g., [3]).

In many cases rules with high confidence and low support are very interesting for analysts. Our method differs from other algorithms generating association rules because it allows discover weak patterns with high confidence. Mentioned algorithms discover only strong patterns in practice. Using characteristic rules our algorithm can discover such kind of a relationship easily. The presented method is very efficient. During each iteration a database is scanned only once. Moreover this method does not generate new selectors or numerical intervals but use only these generated during learning of characteristic rules. This speeds up generation of attributional dependencies.

## 2. Attributional dependencies

This section describes the concept of multihead attributional rule, and defines closely related terms.

### 2.1. Formal model of attributional dependencies

The basic element used to describe dependencies in data is called *attributional condition* (or simply selector). First time it was introduced in [4] and later in [5]. There are two main types of attributional conditions: nominal and continuous. Attributional condition nominal describes dependency between attribute and a nominal value or a disjunction of values. There are two relations, which can be used inside such condition: equal and not equal. Attributional condition continuous describes dependency between attribute and a value or an interval of values.

The basic form of an attributional condition for attributes with a nominal domain is:

$$[\,\boldsymbol{A}\ rel\ \boldsymbol{V}\,],$$

where *rel* is a relation symbol from the set {=,!=}, ***A*** is an attribute, ***V*** is a value or an disjunction of values.

The basic forms of an attributional condition for attributes with a continuous (or numerical) domain are:

$$[\,\boldsymbol{A}\ rel\ \boldsymbol{V}\,]$$

or

$$[\,\boldsymbol{A} = \boldsymbol{I}\,],$$

where *rel* is a relation symbol from the set {=,!=,<,>,<=,>=}, ***A*** is an attribute, ***V*** is a value and ***I*** is a range describing interval between two values.

Attributional condition [ **A** *rel* **V** ] is satisfied by the example (or is true) if for this example the value of attribute ***A*** is in relation *rel* to ***V***.

A conjunction of attributional conditions is called a complex. We say that a complex is satisfied by an example if all attributional conditions in the complex are satisfied.

An attributional dependency is a rule in implicate form *X=>Y* or in equivalence form *X<=>Y*, where *X* and *Y* are complexes. In other words, an attributional dependency describes relationship between conjunctions of attributional conditions. The rule is satisfied by an example if both a condition and a conclusion, which are complexes, are satisfied.

To select most significant dependencies we use coefficients well known in data mining and statistics like *support*, *confidence* and *lift*. We also introduce a coefficient called *concept coverage*, shortly *cover*.

### 2.2. Definitions and interpretation of coefficients

#### Support

Support is the base coefficient used to make a rule assessment. It says how strong is a dependency. We say that support is equal *s* if *s%* of examples from database satisfy dependency. It's mean that if support is high then dependency is satisfied by many examples from a database. In particular we define support for a complex and a rule. A value of this coefficient belongs to the interval [0,1].

Support for a complex $C_i$ is defined as follows:

$$supp(C_i) = \#\ examples\ satisfying\ C_i\,/\,N,$$

where $N$ is a number of all examples in a database.

Support for a rule $R$ is defined as follows:

$$supp(R) = supp(X{=>}Y) = \#\ examples\ satisfying\ X\ and\ Y / N.$$

**Confidence**

Confidence describes the probability of dependency. We say that confidence is equal $c$ if $c\%$ of examples that satisfy condition also satisfy conclusion of a rule. High confidence means that if condition is true then is high probability that also conclusion is true. A value of this coefficient belongs to the interval [0,1].

Confidence for a rule $R$ is defined as follows:

$$conf(R) = conf(X{=>}Y) = supp(X\ and\ Y) / supp(X).$$

**Lift**

Lift describes the interestingness of the rule. It says how strong is the association between a condition and a conclusion of the rule. Based on statistical independence we can say that if lift is equal 1 then the condition and the conclusion are independent. If lift is greater than 1 then the condition is associated with the conclusion. If lift of a rule is between 0 and 1 then a condition is negatively associated with a conclusion.

Lift for a rule $R$ is defined as follows:

$$lift(R) = lift(X{=>}Y) = N\ conf(X{=>}Y) / supp(Y) = N\ supp(X\ and\ Y) / supp(X)\ supp(Y).$$

This coefficient has only informative character and isn't used to prune rules during a mining process.

**Concept coverage**

Concept coverage describes the importance of dependency. We say that concept coverage is equal $c$ if $c\%$ of examples that satisfy conclusion also satisfy condition of a rule. High concept coverage means that dependency highly covers chosen concept. A value of this coefficient belongs to the interval [0,1].

Concept coverage for a rule $R$ is defined as follows:

$$cover(R) = cover(X{=>}Y) = supp(X\ and\ Y) / supp(Y).$$

If $cover(R)$ is equal 1 we can say that the rule $R$ covers whole a concept $Y$. If $cover(R)$ is equal to 0 then we can say that the rule $R$ doesn't cover a concept $Y$. The rule $R$ with higher *cover* is more general. The advantage of concept coverage is that it can be used to rules pruning during mining process.

**Equivalence tolerance**

The MAR1 algorithm can generate attributional dependencies in the form of implicate rules and equivalence rules. Equivalence rule says that two complexes are equivalent. Theoretically this situation comes when confidence is equal 1 and concept coverage is equal 1. Introducing of equivalence tolerance coefficient allow us to generate approximate (or fuzzy) equivalence rules. Using this parameter we can treat all dependencies which meet the following condition as equivalence:

*conf(R) >= (1-equivalence tolerance) and cover(R) >= (1-equivalence tolerance),*

where equivalence tolerance is in [0,1]. In practice, the value of equivalence tolerance parameter should be low. If the value of equivalence tolerance parameter is equal 0 we get real equivalence rules.

## 2.3. Methodology and theoretical framework

The methodology of discovering attributional dependencies assume that the process is consists of two steps. In the first step we learn characteristic rules (description) for given attribute or set of attributes using machine learning program, i.e. AQ or INLEN. In the second step, we generate attributional dependencies based on learned rules.

Let's assume we have characteristic rule in the following form:

$$a_1 \;\&\; a_2 \;\&\; a_3 \;\&\; a_4 \;\&\; \ldots \&\; a_i \;\&\; \ldots \;\&\; a_n \Rightarrow b_1$$

Based on inferential theory of learning [8] if we want to move selector *ai* from the condition to the conclusion we have to check support of two relationships:

$$R_1\!: \; a_1 \;\&\; a_2 \;\&\; a_3 \;\&\; a_4 \;\&\; \ldots \;\&\; a_n \Rightarrow a_i$$

and

$$R_2\!: \; a_1 \;\&\; a_2 \;\&\; a_3 \;\&\; a_4 \;\&\; \ldots \;\&\; a_n \Rightarrow \textbf{not}\; a_i$$

The support of the first rule is denoted as $supp(R_1)$ and the second rule is denoted as $supp(R_2)$. If the $supp(R_1)$ is high in compare to $supp(R_2)$ then we can suppose that it is possible to move attributional condition (selector) $a_i$ to the conclusion. In other case we can't do it. To describe difference between $supp(R_1)$ and $supp(R_2)$ we compute coefficient *trans*. This coefficient expresses relative relation between supports of both rules in percents and is defined as follows:

$$trans(a_i) = supp(R_1) \,/\, (supp(R_1) + supp(R_2))$$

The coefficient *trans* belongs to the interval [0,1] from definition.

To decide if we can move selector from a condition to a conclusion we use input threshold parameter called *mintrans*. If $trans(a_i) > mintrans$ we can generate new rule in the following form:

$$a_1 \,\&\, a_2 \,\&\, a_3 \,\&\, a_4 \,\&\, \ldots \,\&\, a_n \Rightarrow b_1 \,\&\, a_i$$

Usually the value of *mintrans* parameter should be close to 1, then the process of new rules generation is most efficient.

This methodology allows discovering attributional dependencies for both nominal and continuous values.

## 2.4. Algorithm MAR1

In previous section we described the methodology of attributional dependencies generation. Now, we will show the new algorithm, called MAR1 (*Multi-head Attributional Rules*), which implements presented ideas in practice. This algorithm consists of three phases:

- reading and analyzing characteristic rules,
- selecting rules,
- generating attributional dependencies.

In the first phase algorithm reads characteristic rules (procedure `ParseRules()`) form a ruleset. Next, we generate simple rules with single conjunction (procedure `AnalizeRules()`) from complex rules (which have alternative of conjunctions in a condition part). In second phase we prune these characteristic rules, which have support less than *minsup* (procedure `SelectRules()`). The most interesting is third phase, where the algorithm generates attributional dependencies (procedure `Generate Dependencies()`).

```
algorithm MAR1(minsup, minconf, mincover, mintrans)
begin
  ruleset=0
  ParseRules(ruleset);
  AnalizeRules(ruleset);
  SelectRules(ruleset, minsup);
  GenerateDependencies(ruleset, minconf, mincover, mintrans);
end
```

Fig. 1 Pseudo-code of the MAR1 algorithm

Procedure for generating attributional dependencies takes a ruleset and a database. At the beginning this procedure scans a database and check if selectors are satisfied by examples. With each selector in a rule there is associated vector of flags. The value of the flag *i* is 1 if an attributional condition is satisfied by *i*th example in a database. Otherwise the value is 0. The advantage of this solution is that we scan database only once during iteration. In the next step, procedure computes the coefficient *trans* for all selectors in the condition of the rule. If `trans(s)` is greater than *mintrans* then procedure may generate a new rule. We transfer selected attributional condition from the condition to the conclusion. Then we compute confidence and cover coefficients for new rule. If both are greater than minimal threshold values we add the rule to new ruleset. If new ruleset is not empty we continue starting next iteration.

```
procedure GenerateDependencies(ruleset, minconf, mincover,
mintrans)
while ruleset<>0
begin
  newruleset=0;
  ScanDatabase(ruleset);
  for all r in ruleset
  begin
    for all selectors s in r
    begin
      Compute(trans(s));
      if trans(s)>=mintrans then
        begin
          newr=Transfer(r,s);
          Compute(conf(newr) and cover(newr));
          if conf(r)>=minconf and cover(r)>=mincover then
            newruleset=newruleset+newr;
        end
    end
  end
  ruleset=newruleset;
end
```

Fig. 2 Procedure for generating dependencies

## 3. An example and other experiments

In this paper we present results from our algorithm for database zoo. It contains data about animals (17 attributes and 108 examples). We set input parameters as follow: number of iterations = 3, trans threshold = 0.9, support threshold = 0.2, confidence threshold = 0.2, cover threshold = 0.8 and equivalence tolerance = 0.05. Using INLEN we found 8 characteristic rules for attribute airborne. According to threshold values MAR1 selected 2 rules:

```
IF [type != 2 or 6] and [feathers = 0] THEN [airborne = 0]      {
supp=0.72    conf=0.90    cover=0.95    lift=1.18 }
IF [legs = 2 or 6] and [catsize = 0] and [type = 1 or 2 or 6] and
[breathes = 1] and [fins = 0] THEN [airborne = 1]      { supp=0.21
conf=0.84    cover=0.88    lift=3.54 }
Rules #2
```

Based on above characteristic rules MAR1 generated 4 rules in first iteration, 6 rules in second iteration and 6 rules in third iteration. We present rules obtained in second:

```
Iteration=2
IF [legs = 2 or 6] and [catsize = 0] and [fins = 0] THEN [airborne =
1] and [type = 1 or 2 or 6] and [breathes = 1]      { supp=0.21
conf=0.78    cover=0.88    lift=3.27    trans=0.92 }
IF [legs = 2 or 6] and [catsize = 0] and [breathes = 1] THEN
[airborne = 1] and [type = 1 or 2 or 6] and [fins = 0]      {
supp=0.21    conf=0.84    cover=0.88    lift=3.54    trans=1.00 }
IF [legs = 2 or 6] and [catsize = 0] and [fins = 0] THEN [airborne =
1] and [breathes = 1] and [type = 1 or 2 or 6]      { supp=0.21
conf=0.78    cover=0.88    lift=3.27    trans=0.92 }
IF [legs = 2 or 6] and [catsize = 0] and [type = 1 or 2 or 6] THEN
[airborne = 1] and [breathes = 1] and [fins = 0]      { supp=0.21
conf=0.84    cover=0.88    lift=3.54    trans=1.00 }
IF [legs = 2 or 6] and [catsize = 0] and [breathes = 1] THEN
[airborne = 1] and [fins = 0] and [type = 1 or 2 or 6]      {
supp=0.21    conf=0.84    cover=0.88    lift=3.54    trans=1.00 }
IF [legs = 2 or 6] and [catsize = 0] and [type = 1 or 2 or 6] THEN
[airborne = 1] and [fins = 0] and [breathes = 1]      { supp=0.21
conf=0.84    cover=0.88    lift=3.54    trans=1.00 }
Rules #6
```

and third iteration:

```
Iteration=3
IF [legs = 2 or 6] and [catsize = 0] THEN [airborne = 1] and [type =
1 or 2 or 6] and [breathes = 1] and [fins = 0]      { supp=0.21
conf=0.78    cover=0.88    lift=3.27    trans=1.00 }
IF [legs = 2 or 6] and [catsize = 0] THEN [airborne = 1] and [type =
1 or 2 or 6] and [fins = 0] and [breathes = 1]      { supp=0.21
conf=0.78    cover=0.88    lift=3.27    trans=0.92 }
IF [legs = 2 or 6] and [catsize = 0] THEN [airborne = 1] and
[breathes = 1] and [type = 1 or 2 or 6] and [fins = 0]      {
supp=0.21    conf=0.78    cover=0.88    lift=3.27    trans=1.00 }
IF [legs = 2 or 6] and [catsize = 0] THEN [airborne = 1] and
[breathes = 1] and [fins = 0] and [type = 1 or 2 or 6]      {
supp=0.21    conf=0.78    cover=0.88    lift=3.27    trans=0.92 }
IF [legs = 2 or 6] and [catsize = 0] THEN [airborne = 1] and [fins =
0] and [type = 1 or 2 or 6] and [breathes = 1]      { supp=0.21
conf=0.78    cover=0.88    lift=3.27    trans=0.92 }
```

```
IF [legs = 2 or 6] and [catsize = 0] THEN [airborne = 1] and [fins =
0] and [breathes = 1] and [type = 1 or 2 or 6]      { supp=0.21
conf=0.78   cover=0.88   lift=3.27   trans=0.92 }
Rules #6
```

Results for mushroom database. It contains data about mushrooms (23 attributes and 8124 examples). We set input parameters as follow: number of iterations = 3, trans threshold = 0.9, support threshold = 0.2, confidence threshold = 0.9, cover threshold = 0.9 and equivalence tolerance = 0.05. Using INLEN we found 2 characteristic rules for attribute A0. Below we show example rule generated by MAR1:

```
IF [odor = a or l or n] and [cap-shape = b or x or f or s] and [cap-
surface != g] and [cap-color = n or y or w or g or e] and [gill-
attachment = f] and [gill-spacing = c or w] and [gill-color = k or n
or h or g or p or u or w] and [stalk-root = b or c or e or r] and
[stalk-surface-above-ring = f or s] and [stalk-surface-below-ring !=
k] and [stalk-color-above-ring = g or p or w] and [stalk-color-below-
ring = g or p or w] and [veil-type = p] and [veil-color = w] and
[ring-number = o] and [ring-type = e or p] and [spore-print-color = k
or n or u] and [population != c] and [habitat != l or w] THEN
[mushroom = e]
```

from original characteristic rule:

```
IF [odor = a or l or n] and [gill-attachment = f] and [gill-spacing =
c or w] and [gill-color = k or n or h or g or p or u or w] and
[stalk-root = b or c or e or r] and [stalk-surface-above-ring = f or
s] and [stalk-surface-below-ring != k] and [stalk-color-above-ring =
g or p or w] and [stalk-color-below-ring = g or p or w] and [veil-
type = p] and [veil-color = w] and [ring-number = o] and [ring-type =
e or p] and [spore-print-color = k or n or u] and [population != c]
and [habitat != l or w] THEN [mushroom = e] and [cap-shape = b or x
or f or s] and [cap-surface != g] and [cap-color = n or y or w or g
or e] { supp=0.42   conf=1.00   cover=0.85   lift=2.04   trans=1.00 }
```

We carried out several experiments with MAR1 using benchmark databases from UCI Repository. Then we compared our results with result from Apriori algorithm [2] for finding association rules. In most cases additional rules were discovered that were not discovered by Apriori.

Comparing a rulesets obtained from MAR1 and Apriori algorithms we can say that Apriori algorithm usually generates more rules. However, rules generated by MAR1 are more interesting because most of them have high confidence and high cover (even if support is low). Apriori especially prefers rules with high support. To generate rules with particular attribute in a conclusion part users need additional rules filtering in Apriori. Summarizing, the most general difference between algorithms is that Apriori focuses on rule generation directly from data, while MAR1 generates multi-head rules from other single-head rules.

## 4. Related works, conclusions and future research

The concept of an attributional dependency is a generalization of an association rule. An association rule is an implication of the form *X*=>*Y*, where *X* and *Y* are sets of items [1], where items are binary attributes. Our definition of attributional dependency says that a condition and a conclusion are conjunction of attributional conditions. Moreover we can formulae dependencies in either implicative or equivalence form. Known algorithms for discovery rules use only data to formulae rules. In this paper we presented new methodology to formulae rules from other rules especially we propose use of characteristic rules because they are most informative. Based on them and a database we discover attributional dependencies. In practice miners are interested in finding dependencies consist of selected feature because discovering all rules in database is very complex task. The advantage of our method is this that we generate only most characteristic dependencies for chosen attributes. Moreover, there are many interesting and useful dependencies with low support but with high confidence. Known algorithms need a lot of time to discover association rules with low support. Proposed methodology allows discover either strong or weak relationships without additional computation. To find most interesting association rules there are used statistical measures based on rules occurrence frequency in the database. We also proposed coefficient (called concept coverage) as one of measure of interestingness of dependency. This coefficient is used to prune rules during process of generation. Coverage says how a rule covers a concept interested for us.

This research was completed but we see some opportunities for future work. In our method may be introduced better selection procedure, which will help to select more interesting rules. Currently select procedure is based on coefficients (like support, confidence, cover, lift and trans). It is also possible to select rules according to the content of the condition and the conclusion. It means that user can describe what attribute or set of attributes should be in the head and/or body of the rule interesting for him.

Moreover, MAR1 algorithm can be implemented as new operator in KGL language (*Knowledge Generation Language*). In the future MAR1 module can be invoked by KGL using operator ADGEN with proper parameters. Implementing this feature will require a modification of the KGL parser.

## Acknowledgements

This research has been conducted in Machine Learning and Inference Laboratory at George Mason University. Cezary Głowiński has been supported by Kosciuszko Foundation in New York, in part by the National Science Foundation

Grant IIS 9906858, and in part by the UMBC/MPO/Lucite #32 grant. The authors especially thank Guido Cervone for his great help during our research.

## References

1. Agrawal R., Imielinski T., Swami A.: Mining Association Rules between Sets of Items in Large Databases, *Proceedings of VLBD-93*, 1993
2. Agrawal R., Srikant R.: Fast Algorithms for Mining Association Rules, *Proceedings of VLBD-94*, 1994
3. Bayardo R.J., Agrawal R.: Mining the Most Interesting Rules, *Proceedings of the Fifth International Conference on Knowledge Discovery and Data Mining*, 1999
4. Michalski R.S.: AQVAL/1-Computer Implementation of a Variable-Valued Logic System VL1, *Proceedings of the Third International Joint Conference on Artificial Intelligence*, Stanford, 1973
5. Michalski R.S.: Variable-Valued Logic and Its Applications to Pattern Recognition and Machine Learning, chapter in *Computer Science and Multiple-Valued Logic Theory and Applications* Rine D.C. (ed.), North-Holland Publishing, 1975
6. Michalski R.S.: A Theory and Methodology of Inductive Learning, *Artificial Intelligence*, 1983
7. Michalski R.S.: Toward a Unified Theory of Learning: Multistrategy Task-adaptive Learning, in *Readings in Knowledge Acquisition and Learning* Buchanan B.G., Wilkins D.C., 1991
8. Michalski R.S.: Inferential Theory of Learning: Developing Foundations for Multistrategy Learning, chapter in *Machine Learning A Multistrategy Approach Volume IV* Michalski R.S., Tecuci G. (eds.), Morgan Kaufman Publishers, 1994
9. Michalski, R.S.: Natural Induction and Concept Learning: The AQ Methodology and Its Application to Machine Learning and Knowledge Mining, 2001, to appear.

# Melanoma Prediction Using k-Nearest Neighbor and LEM2 Algorithms

**Jerzy W. Grzymala-Busse**
Department of Electrical Engineering and Computer Science, University of Kansas, Lawrence, KS 66045, USA
E-mail: Jerzy@eecs.ukans.edu

and

**Zdzislaw S. Hippe**
Department of Expert Systems and Artificial Intelligence, University of Information Technology and Management, 35-225 Rzeszow, Poland
E-mail: zhippe@wenus.wsiz.rzeszow.pl

***ABSTRACT***: *Two melanoma data sets, with and without an important attribute called TDS, were studied. The index TDS is a valuable diagnostic parameter used in the diagnosis of melanoma. Both data sets were partitioned into training data sets (250 cases) and testing (26 cases). Two classifiers were used: the well-known k-th Nearest Neighbor (KNN) algorithm and the algorithm LEM2, a part of the data mining system LERS. KNN algorithm is a typical statistical method based on voting among k training cases that are as close to the tested case as possible. On the other hand, LEM2 induces rules, and then classification is based on voting among all rules that match the case. Surprisingly, both methods yield similar results. However, the KNN algorithm may produce a smaller error rate, but LEM2 offers explanation of its results.*

*Keywords: Melanoma, nevi pigmentosi, TDS index, classification rules, k-Nearest Neighbor algorithm, LERS system, LEM2 algorithm.*

## 1 Introduction

Our data sets describing melanoma were collected in the Outpatient Center of Dermatology in Rzeszow, Poland [3, 6]. Both data sets were partitioned into training data sets (250 cases) and testing (26 cases). One of the important tools used in diagnosis of melanoma is TDS (Total Dermatoscopic Score). The TDS index is computed on the basis of the so called ABCD formula, where four variables are used: *Asymmetry*, *Border, Color* and *Diversity*. Variable *Asymmetry* has three different values: *symmetric spot*, *one axial symmetry*, and *two axial symmetry*. *Border* is a numerical attribute, with values from 0 to 8. *Asymmetry* and *Border* are single-values attributes. The remaining two attributes, *Color* and *Diversity*, are many-values attributes. *Color* has six possible values: *white*, *blue*, *black*, *red*, *light brown*, and *dark brown*. Similarly, *Diversity* has five values: *pigment globules*, *pigment dots*, *branched stricks*, *structureless areas* and *pigment network*. We introduced six single-valued variables describing color: *Color_white*, *Color_blue*, *Color_black*, *Color_red*, *Color_light_brown*, *Color_dark_brown* and five single-valued variables describing diversity: *Diversity_pigment_globules*, *Diversity_pigment_dots*, *Diversity_branched_stricks*, *Diversity_structureless_areas*, *Diversity_pigment_network*. In all of these 11 attributes the values are 0 or 1, 0 meaning lack of the corresponding property and 1 meaning the occurrence of the property. Thus, every case was characterized by values of 13 attributes. On the basis of those 13 attributes the index TDS was computed using the following formula (known as the ABCD formula):

$$\text{TDS} = 1.3 * \text{Asymmetry} + 0.1 * \text{Border} + 0.5 * \Sigma \text{ Colors} + 0.5 * \Sigma \text{ Diversities},$$

where for *Asymmetry* the value *symmetric spot* counts as 0, *one axial symmetry* counts as 1, and *two axial symmetry* counts as 2, Σ Colors means the sum of all values of the six color attributes and Σ Diversities means the sum of all values of the five diversity attributes. For example, for a case described by

*symmetric spot*, 0, 0, 0, 1, 1, 1, 1, 1, 0, 1, 1, 1,

the value of TDS is

$$1.3 * 0 + 0.1 * 0 + 0.5 * (0 + 0 + 1 + 1 + 1 + 1) + 0.5 * (1 + 0 + 1 + 1 + 1) = 4.0.$$

We conducted experiments with original data, containing 13 attributes, and, separately, with an additional data set, containing 13 original attributes and the TDS index as the fourteenth attribute. Including TDS to the original data set is an example of a constructive generalization [10]. Each of the cases was diagnosed as belonging to one of four classes of the decision *Melanoma*: *benign*, *blue*, *suspicious*, or *malignant* .

## 2 Classification

The first classifier used for our experiments was a KNN (k-Nearest Neighbor) algorithm, implemented as a module MLC (Multi-strategy Learning Classifier) of the system SCANKEE [4–8]. For every unseen case, k nearest training cases are found, and the class indicated by voting is selected. The nearness was evaluated as the Euclidean distance. An odd number of training cases are used to make voting decisive.

We also used rule induction and classification based on a rule set. Our rule induction system was LERS (Learning from Examples based on Rough Sets) [1, 2]. LERS has two rule induction algorithms belonging to machine learning approaches: LEM1 and LEM2 [1]. In our experiments we used LEM2.

The process of classification used in LERS has four factors: *Strength*, *Specificity*, *Matching_factor*, and *Support*. The original approach is known under the name *bucket brigade algorithm* [9]. In this approach, the classification of a case is based on three factors: strength, specificity, and support. The additional factor, used for partial matching, was added to LERS. These four factors are defined as following:

*Strength* is a measure of how well the rule performed during training. It is the number of cases correctly classified by the rule in training data. The bigger the strength, the better.

*Specificity* is a measure of completeness of a rule. It is the number of conditions (attribute-value pairs) of a rule. It means a rule with a bigger number of attribute-value pairs is more specific. Specificity may or may not be used to classify cases.

For a specific case, if complete matching (where all attribute-value pairs of at least one rule match all attribute-value pairs of a case) is impossible, LERS tries partial matching. During partial matching all rules with at least one match between the attribute-value pairs of a rule and the attribute-value pairs of a case are identified. *Matching_factor* is a measure of matching of a case and a rule. Matching_factor is defined as the ratio of the number of matched attribute-value pairs of a rule with a case to the total number of attribute-value pairs of the rule.

*Support* is related to a class *C*. It is the sum of scores of all matching rules from *C*. The class *C* for which the support, defined as follows:

$$\sum_{\text{partially matching rules } R \text{ describing } C} \text{Matching\_factor}(R) * \text{Strength}(R)$$

is the largest is a winner and the case is classified as being a member of *C*. Classification algorithm of LERS was run without specificity (i.e., in computing support, specificity was always equal to one).

## 3 Experiments

The rules sets induced from the two melanoma data sets by LEM2 algorithm are described in the Table 1.

**Table 1** Rule sets induced by LEM2 algorithm

| | Data set with 13 attributes (without TDS) | Data set with 14 attributes. (with TDS) |
|---|---|---|
| Total number of rules | 44 | 21 |
| Total number of conditions | 188 | 81 |

Rules induced from the data set with 14 attributes (including TDS) are more general. In the sequel we cite all 21 rules induced from the melanoma data set with TDS:

62

(TDS, 1..4.9) & (Color_blue, 0) -> (Melanoma, benign)

64

(Color_blue, 1) & (TDS, 1..4.9) -> (Melanoma, blue)

16

(TDS, 4.9..8) & (Diversity_pigment_globules, 1) & (Diversity_branched_stricks, 1) & (Diversity_structureless_areas, 1) & (Diversity_pigment_network, 1) & (Asymmetry, one_axial_symmetry) & (Color_red, 1) -> (Melanoma, malignant)

16

(Diversity_pigment_dots, 1) & (Diversity_pigment_network, 1) & (Color_black, 1) & (Border, 2..6) -> (Melanoma, malignant)

21

(Diversity_branched_stricks, 1) & (Asymmetry, 2) -> (Melanoma, malignant)

15

(TDS, 4.9..8) & (Diversity_branched_stricks, 1) & (Diversity_pigment_dots, 1) & (Color_white, 1) & (Border, 2..6) -> (Melanoma, malignant)

13

(Color_black, 1) & (Asymmetry, one_axial_symmetry) & (Border, 6..8) & (Diversity_pigment_dots, 1) -> (Melanoma, malignant)

6

(Color_black, 1) & (Border, 6..8) & (Color_white, 1) & (Diversity_pigment_network, 1) -> (Melanoma, malignant)

10

(Color_light_brown, 0) & (TDS, 4.9..8) -> (Melanoma, malignant)

15

(TDS, 4.9..8) & (Asymmetry, one_axial_symmetry) & (Color_red, 0) & (Border, 0..2) -> (Melanoma, suspicious)

10

(TDS, 4.9..8) & (Asymmetry, one_axial_symmetry) & (Color_black, 0) & (Diversity_pigment_dots, 0) -> (Melanoma, suspicious)

7

(TDS, 4.9..8) & (Border, 0..2) & (Diversity_structureless_areas, 0) -> (Melanoma, suspicious)

7

(TDS, 4.9..8) & (Asymmetry, one_axial_symmetry) & (Color_white, 0) & (Border, 2..6) & (Color_black, 0) -> (Melanoma, suspicious)

8

(TDS, 4.9..8) & (Color_blue, 0) & (Diversity_pigment_network, 0) & (Color_white, 0) -> (Melanoma, suspicious)

10

(TDS, 4.9..8) & (Color_blue, 0) & (Diversity_structureless_areas, 1) & (Color_red, 0) & (Diversity_pigment_dots, 0) & (Diversity_branched_stricks, 1) -> (Melanoma, suspicious)

3

(TDS, 4.9..8) & (Asymmetry, 0) -> (Melanoma, suspicious)

9

(TDS, 4.9..8) & (Asymmetry, one_axial_symmetry) & (Diversity_pigment_dots, 1) & (Diversity_branched_stricks, 0) -> (Melanoma, suspicious)

4

(TDS, 4.9..8) & (Diversity_pigment_globules, 0) -> (Melanoma, suspicious)

1

(Border, 6..8) & (TDS, 4.9..8) & (Diversity_structureless_areas, 0) -> (Melanoma, suspicious)

1

(Border, 6..8) & (Color_white, 1) & (Diversity_pigment_dots, 0) & (Diversity_pigment_network, 0) -> (Melanoma, suspicious)

1

(Border, 6..8) & (Color_black, 0) & (Diversity_branched_stricks, 1) & (Asymmetry, one_axial_symmetry) & (Diversity_pigment_network, 1) & (Diversity_pigment_dots, 1) & (Diversity_structureless_areas, 1) & (Diversity_pigment_globules, 1) -> (Melanoma, suspicious)

Every rule is preceded by its strength. Note, that the first two rules completely describe two classes; the first rule completely describes all 62 cases of benign melanoma and the second rule complete describes all 64 cases of blue melanoma. Both rules are very general. It is much easier to recognize benign and blue melanomas than to recognize malignant or suspicious melanomas.

Results of diagnosis for 26 testing cases are presented in Tables 2–6. Note that the same case (twelfth):

one_axial_symmetry, 5, 0, 0, 1, 0, 1, 1, 1, 1, 1, 0, 1, 5.3, suspicious

was the only example that was not diagnosed correctly by both algorithms, KNN and LEM2, even with k = 1 and with the use of the TDS index. The KNN algorithm classified this case as benign in spite of the fact that the case was suspicious. Thus, the KNN algorithm was too optimistic. Obviously, the KNN algorithm does not provide any explanation for its decision, it may show only the training case to which the testing case is the nearest. The system LERS classified the same case as malignant, so LEM2 is more pessimistic. However, full explanation, offered by LERS, shows that exactly two rules match the case, the first rule:

16

(Diversity_pigment_dots, 1) & (Diversity_pigment_network, 1) & (Color_black, 1) & (Border, 2..6) ->

(Melanoma, malignant)

indicates malignant melanoma, and the second rule:

9

(TDS, 4.9..8) & (Asymmetry, one_axial_symmetry) & (Diversity_pigment_dots, 1) & (Diversity_branched_stricks, 0) -> (Melanoma, suspicious)

indicates suspicious melanoma. There is no mentioning of benign melanoma. The class malignant melanoma was selected because the corresponding rule is stronger. Thus, LERS suggests two solutions, correct and incorrect, and chooses incorrect.

**Table 2** Melanoma diagnosis using the k-th Nearest Neighbor algorithm, data set does not contain the TDS index

| | | Diagnosed disease using KNN algorithm with | |
|---|---|---|---|
| No | Actual disease | **k = 1** | **k = 3** |
| 1 | Benign melanoma | Benign melanoma | Benign melanoma |
| 2 | Benign melanoma | Malignant melanoma | Malignant melanoma |
| 3 | Benign melanoma | Benign melanoma | Suspicious melanoma |
| 4 | Benign melanoma | Benign melanoma | Benign melanoma |
| 5 | Blue melanoma | Blue melanoma | Blue melanoma |
| 6 | Blue melanoma | Blue melanoma | Blue melanoma |
| 7 | Blue melanoma | Blue melanoma | Blue melanoma |
| 8 | Blue melanoma | Blue melanoma | Blue melanoma |
| 9 | Suspicious melanoma | Suspicious melanoma | Suspicious melanoma |
| 10 | Suspicious melanoma | Suspicious melanoma | Suspicious melanoma |
| 11 | Suspicious melanoma | Malignant melanoma | Malignant melanoma |
| 12 | Suspicious melanoma | Benign melanoma | Benign melanoma |
| 13 | Malignant melanoma | Malignant melanoma | Malignant melanoma |
| 14 | Malignant melanoma | Malignant melanoma | Malignant melanoma |
| 15 | Malignant melanoma | Malignant melanoma | Malignant melanoma |
| 16 | Malignant melanoma | Malignant melanoma | Malignant melanoma |
| 17 | Benign melanoma | Benign melanoma | Suspicious melanoma |
| 18 | Benign melanoma | Benign melanoma | Benign melanoma |
| 19 | Blue melanoma | Blue melanoma | Blue melanoma |
| 20 | Blue melanoma | Blue melanoma | Blue melanoma |
| 21 | Blue melanoma | Blue melanoma | Blue melanoma |
| 22 | Suspicious melanoma | Suspicious melanoma | Suspicious melanoma |
| 23 | Suspicious melanoma | Suspicious melanoma | Suspicious melanoma |
| 24 | Malignant melanoma | Suspicious melanoma | Suspicious melanoma |
| 25 | Malignant melanoma | Malignant melanoma | Malignant melanoma |
| 26 | Malignant melanoma | Malignant melanoma | Malignant melanoma |
| | Classification error | 15.4% | 23.1% |

**Table 3** Melanoma diagnosis using the k-th Nearest Neighbor algorithm, data set does not contain the TDS index

| | | Diagnosed disease using KNN algorithm with |
|---|---|---|
| No | Actual disease | **k = 5** |
| 1 | Benign melanoma | Benign melanoma |
| 2 | Benign melanoma | Suspicious melanoma |
| 3 | Benign melanoma | Suspicious melanoma |
| 4 | Benign melanoma | Suspicious melanoma |
| 5 | Blue melanoma | Blue melanoma |
| 6 | Blue melanoma | Blue melanoma |
| 7 | Blue melanoma | Blue melanoma |
| 8 | Blue melanoma | Blue melanoma |
| 9 | Suspicious melanoma | Benign melanoma |
| 10 | Suspicious melanoma | Benign melanoma |
| 11 | Suspicious melanoma | Suspicious melanoma |
| 12 | Suspicious melanoma | Benign melanoma |
| 13 | Malignant melanoma | Suspicious melanoma |
| 14 | Malignant melanoma | Malignant melanoma |
| 15 | Malignant melanoma | Malignant melanoma |
| 16 | Malignant melanoma | Malignant melanoma |
| 17 | Benign melanoma | Suspicious melanoma |
| 18 | Benign melanoma | Benign melanoma |
| 19 | Blue melanoma | Blue melanoma |
| 20 | Blue melanoma | Blue melanoma |
| 21 | Blue melanoma | Blue melanoma |
| 22 | Suspicious melanoma | Malignant melanoma |
| 23 | Suspicious melanoma | Suspicious melanoma |
| 24 | Malignant melanoma | Suspicious melanoma |
| 25 | Malignant melanoma | Malignant melanoma |
| 26 | Malignant melanoma | Malignant melanoma |
| | Classification error | 38.5% |

**Table 4** Melanoma diagnosis using the KNN algorithm, data set contains the TDS index

| | | Diagnosed disease using KNN algorithm with | |
|---|---|---|---|
| No | Actual disease | **k = 1** | **k = 3** |
| 1 | Benign melanoma | Benign melanoma | Benign melanoma |
| 2 | Benign melanoma | Benign melanoma | Benign melanoma |
| 3 | Benign melanoma | Benign melanoma | Suspicious melanoma |
| 4 | Benign melanoma | Benign melanoma | Suspicious melanoma |
| 5 | Blue melanoma | Blue melanoma | Blue melanoma |
| 6 | Blue melanoma | Blue melanoma | Blue melanoma |
| 7 | Blue melanoma | Blue melanoma | Blue melanoma |
| 8 | Blue melanoma | Blue melanoma | Blue melanoma |
| 9 | Suspicious melanoma | Suspicious melanoma | Suspicious melanoma |
| 10 | Suspicious melanoma | Suspicious melanoma | Suspicious melanoma |
| 11 | Suspicious melanoma | Suspicious melanoma | Suspicious melanoma |
| 12 | Suspicious melanoma | Benign melanoma | Malignant melanoma |
| 13 | Malignant melanoma | Malignant melanoma | Malignant melanoma |
| 14 | Malignant melanoma | Malignant melanoma | Malignant melanoma |
| 15 | Malignant melanoma | Malignant melanoma | Malignant melanoma |
| 16 | Malignant melanoma | Malignant melanoma | Malignant melanoma |
| 17 | Benign melanoma | Benign melanoma | Suspicious melanoma |
| 18 | Benign melanoma | Benign melanoma | Benign melanoma |
| 19 | Blue melanoma | Blue melanoma | Blue melanoma |
| 20 | Blue melanoma | Blue melanoma | Blue melanoma |
| 21 | Blue melanoma | Blue melanoma | Blue melanoma |
| 22 | Suspicious melanoma | Suspicious melanoma | Suspicious melanoma |
| 23 | Suspicious melanoma | Suspicious melanoma | Suspicious melanoma |
| 24 | Malignant melanoma | Malignant melanoma | Malignant melanoma |
| 25 | Malignant melanoma | Malignant melanoma | Malignant melanoma |
| 26 | Malignant melanoma | Malignant melanoma | Malignant melanoma |
| | Classification error | 3.8% | 11.5% |

**Table 5** Melanoma diagnosis using the KNN algorithm, data set contains the TDS index

| No | Actual disease | Diagnosed disease using KNN algorithm with **k = 5** |
|---|---|---|
| 1 | Benign melanoma | Benign melanoma |
| 2 | Benign melanoma | Benign melanoma |
| 3 | Benign melanoma | Benign melanoma |
| 4 | Benign melanoma | Suspicious melanoma |
| 5 | Blue melanoma | Blue melanoma |
| 6 | Blue melanoma | Blue melanoma |
| 7 | Blue melanoma | Blue melanoma |
| 8 | Blue melanoma | Blue melanoma |
| 9 | Suspicious melanoma | Suspicious melanoma |
| 10 | Suspicious melanoma | Suspicious melanoma |
| 11 | Suspicious melanoma | Suspicious melanoma |
| 12 | Suspicious melanoma | Malignant melanoma |
| 13 | Malignant melanoma | Suspicious melanoma |
| 14 | Malignant melanoma | Malignant melanoma |
| 15 | Malignant melanoma | Malignant melanoma |
| 16 | Malignant melanoma | Malignant melanoma |
| 17 | Benign melanoma | Benign melanoma |
| 18 | Benign melanoma | Benign melanoma |
| 19 | Blue melanoma | Blue melanoma |
| 20 | Blue melanoma | Blue melanoma |
| 21 | Blue melanoma | Blue melanoma |
| 22 | Suspicious melanoma | Malignant melanoma |
| 23 | Suspicious melanoma | Suspicious melanoma |
| 24 | Malignant melanoma | Malignant melanoma |
| 25 | Malignant melanoma | Malignant melanoma |
| 26 | Malignant melanoma | Malignant melanoma |
| | Classification error | 15.4% |

**Table 6** Melanoma diagnosis using the LEM2 algorithm

| | | Diagnosed disease using LEM2 algorithm | |
|---|---|---|---|
| No | Actual disease | **without TDS index** | **with TDS index** |
| 1 | Benign melanoma | Benign melanoma | Benign melanoma |
| 2 | Benign melanoma | Malignant melanoma | Benign melanoma |
| 3 | Benign melanoma | Suspicious melanoma | Benign melanoma |
| 4 | Benign melanoma | Benign melanoma | Benign melanoma |
| 5 | Blue melanoma | Blue melanoma | Blue melanoma |
| 6 | Blue melanoma | Blue melanoma | Blue melanoma |
| 7 | Blue melanoma | Blue melanoma | Blue melanoma |
| 8 | Blue melanoma | Blue melanoma | Blue melanoma |
| 9 | Suspicious melanoma | Malignant melanoma | Suspicious melanoma |
| 10 | Suspicious melanoma | Malignant melanoma | Suspicious melanoma |
| 11 | Suspicious melanoma | Suspicious melanoma | Suspicious melanoma |
| 12 | Suspicious melanoma | Malignant melanoma | Malignant melanoma |
| 13 | Malignant melanoma | Malignant melanoma | Malignant melanoma |
| 14 | Malignant melanoma | Malignant melanoma | Malignant melanoma |
| 15 | Malignant melanoma | Malignant melanoma | Malignant melanoma |
| 16 | Malignant melanoma | Suspicious melanoma | Malignant melanoma |
| 17 | Benign melanoma | Benign melanoma | Benign melanoma |
| 18 | Benign melanoma | Benign melanoma | Benign melanoma |
| 19 | Blue melanoma | Blue melanoma | Blue melanoma |
| 20 | Blue melanoma | Blue melanoma | Blue melanoma |
| 21 | Blue melanoma | Blue melanoma | Blue melanoma |
| 22 | Suspicious melanoma | Suspicious melanoma | Suspicious melanoma |
| 23 | Suspicious melanoma | Suspicious melanoma | Suspicious melanoma |
| 24 | Malignant melanoma | Malignant melanoma | Malignant melanoma |
| 25 | Malignant melanoma | Malignant melanoma | Malignant melanoma |
| 26 | Malignant melanoma | Malignant melanoma | Malignant melanoma |
| | Classification error | 23.1% | 3.8% |

## Conclusions

In general, the melanoma data set with the TDS index enables much better results than the melanoma data set without the TDS index. The index TDS is a valuable parameter helping with diagnosis. For both melanoma data sets, with and without TDS index, the KNN algorithm produces the best result (the smallest error rate on testing data) for k = 1. It is surprising because normally the greater k the better results. Secondly, for the melanoma data sets with the TDS index, the k-Nearest Neighbor algorithm, diagnosed the testing cases with the same error rate as the LEM2 algorithm. The difference is that LEM2 supplies explanation and thus the diagnostician is provided with more information and , consequently, may decide what should be the final outcome. Finally, for the melanoma data set without the TDS index, the KNN algorithm provides more accurate results for k = 1, the same quality results for k = 3, and worse results for k = 5 than the LEM2 algorithm.

## References

1. Grzymala-Busse, J. W.: LERS—A system for learning from examples based on rough sets. In Intelligent Decision Support. Handbook of Applications and Advances of the Rough Sets Theory. R. Slowinski (ed.), Kluwer Academic Publishers, 1992, 3–18.

2. Jerzy W. Grzymala-Busse, J. W.: LERS—A knowledge discovery system. In Rough Sets in Knowledge Discovery 2, Applications, Case Studies and Software Systems, L. Polkowski and A. Skowron (eds.), Physica-Verlag, 1998, 562–565.

3. Grzymala-Busse, J. W. and Hippe, Z.: Data mining experiments for a melanoma data set. Proc. of the Ninth International Symposium on Intelligent Information Systems, Bystra k/Bielska Biala, Poland, June 12–16, 2000. Advances in Soft Computing. M. Klopotek, M. Michalewicz, S. T. Wierzchon (eds.), Physica-Verlag, 2000, 27–34.

4. Hippe Z. S.: Multiple type reasoning expert system of open architecture. System Science **23** (1997) 29–38.

5. Hippe Z. S.: Design and application of an intelligent information system SCANKEE for solving selected chemical problems. Computer Chem. **22** (1998) 133–140.

6. Hippe, Z. S.: Data mining in medical diagnosis. In Computers in Medicine. E. Kacki (ed.), Polish Society of Medical Informatics, Lodz, 1999, vol. 1, 25–34.

7. Hippe Z. S. and Hippe T. M.: Decision-support system for engineering sciences. In: K. E. Oczos (ed.) CAE Techniques, Rzeszow University of Technology Press, Rzeszów 1997, 42–51.

8. Hippe Z. S. and Mazur M.: Algorithm "look-ahead-and-back" in pattern recognition and prediction of their properties (in Polish). In M. Kurzynski , E. Puchala , M. Wozniak (eds.), Pattern Recognition Systems, Wroclaw University of Technology Press, 1999, 117–122.

9. Holland, J. H., Holyoak K. J., and Nisbett, R. E.: Induction. Processes of Inference, Learning, and Discovery. The MIT Press, 1986.

10. Michalski, R. S.: A theory and methodology of inductive learning. In Machine Learning. An Artificial Intelligence Approach, R. S. Michalski, J. G. Carbonell, T. M. Mitchell (eds.), Morgan Kauffman, 1983, 83–134.

# Technologies for Sound Database Indexing: Musical Instrument Classification Methods

**Alicja A. Wieczorkowska**

Polish – Japanese Institute of Information Technology, Warsaw, Poland

e-mail: alicja@pjwstk.waw.pl or awieczor@uncc.edu

***Abstract***: *Description of various types of multimedia content, including audio tracks, is the main objective of MPEG-7 standard, which is being currently developed. Automatic extraction of features (descriptors) is indispensable to fully exploit this standard. In this paper, we revue and compare main techniques used for automatic classification of musical instrument sounds. These techniques usually require selection of singular sounds as a preprocessing; therefore, segmentation techniques for audio data are also necessary.*

*Keywords: multimedia databases, sound classification*

## 1. Introduction

Automatic content description is probably the main area of interest in multimedia database domain. Researchers aim to extract various types of multimedia information, including video [4] and audio data [3], [13], [14]. The automatic classification of sounds is needed in many areas, for example in banking, military applications, medicine and so on. However, the largest area of interest for most users is automatic classification of musical data. The musical patterns searched for include melodic patterns, rhythm, chords and timbres [2], [8], [13].

The processing of any audio data requires (but is not limited to) the following steps:

- sound analysis,
- data segmentation and feature extraction,
- classification.

Sound analysis can be performed in time domain, frequency domain or time-frequency domain [9], [10], [13]. Time domain analysis is quite simple and takes into account such features as zero crossing density for the analyzed signal, energy for the analyzed frame and amplitude characteristics. The spectrum of the sound is described using frequency analysis. This analysis allows one to extract pitch and harmonics or noise present in the sound. The most popular frequency analyzers are filters and FFT (Fast Fourier Transform). Time-frequency analysis is usually performed using wavelets, which are especially useful for musical sound [14].

Feature extraction is based on the analysis performed and allows one to create descriptors of sound. More detailed discussion of description production is provided in the next section of this paper. Data segmentation is performed determining the times of sound transitions and provides reference points for search purposes [6]. Techniques of data segmentation are behind the scope of this paper.

Classification of audio data, if performed for descriptors calculated on the basis of sound analysis, can be done using many existing classifiers. Classification techniques used for audio descriptors are discussed in details in the fourth section of the presented paper.

## 2. Description production

Sound descriptors are calculated on the basis of sound analysis, which includes time domain analysis, spectrum analysis (frequency domain) and time-frequency analysis. Comparison of these analysis methods is presented in Fig. 1.

Feature extraction procedures allow one to create a vector of descriptors for each sound. Descriptors necessary to characterize sound properly depend on the purpose of final sound classification. In case of timbre classification, as it happens for musical instrument recognition, time-domain descriptors usually are some reference points, frequently used for normalization of other features. Time-domain descriptors for instrument classification include the length of the whole sound and the lengths of particular phases of sound (transitions and steady state), velocity of transients, amplitude and energy functions etc. Time-domain features are also essential to distinguish between very short and long sounds – this way the classifier can easily recognize string instruments played pizzicato [13].

Frequency analysis is usually performed for the steady state of sounds, for some short time frame. However, long time average spectrum is also sometimes calculated to characterize the audio fragment. Since the spectrum changes with the evolution of the sound and is quite different for the steady state and for transients, frequency analysis should be performed for various stages of the sound to fully describe sound properties [3], [13]. The feature extraction for the steady state only usually is not sufficient for correct classification – also human experts need transients (especially starting transient) to recognize musical instrument. Frequency-based descriptors include pitch, statistical properties of the spectrum (central and normalized moments, average amplitude of partials, correlation and cross-correlation) and contents of the selected groups of partials in the spectrum (even/odd partials, low/middle/high frequency partials).

Additionally, many others descriptors, such as brightness of the sound, formants, irregularity of the spectrum, frequency deviation of partials, are also used [3], [10], [12], [13].

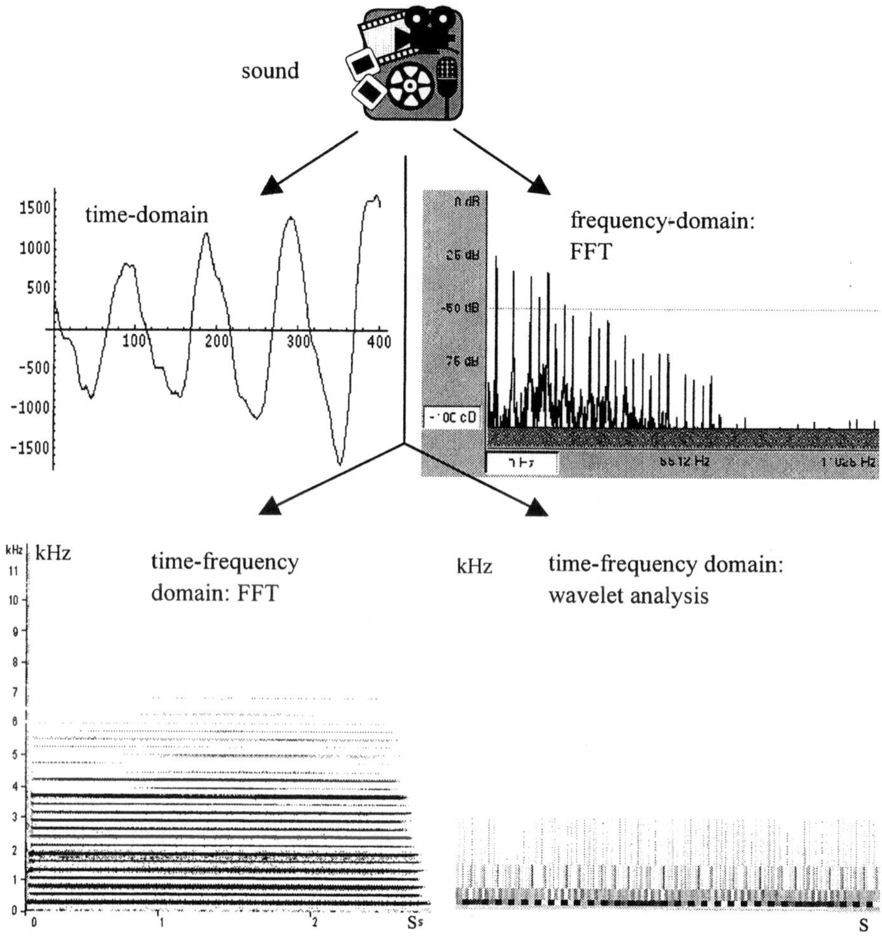


Fig. 1 Exemplary methods of sound analysis

Time-frequency based descriptors are most frequently based on wavelet analysis, although other analysis methods are also used, for example McAulay-Quatieri analysis. Even wavelet transform can be calculated in many different ways, depending on the mother wavelet and scaling function chosen [1], [14]. Basically, wavelet analysis is a multiresolution analysis, in musical research usually octave-based or 1/3-octave-based one. There is trade off between time-domain and frequency-domain precision: the better time resolution (usually for higher frequencies), the worse frequency resolution and vice versa. The most common wavelets used in wavelet analysis are Daubechies filters (of various orders), Coifman, Morlet, Shannon, Haar, Meyer, Mexican hat and others. Some of these functions are depicted in Fig. 2.

Fig. 2 Wavelets: a) Coiflet mother wavelet (order 2),

b) Morlet wavelet (real part),

c) Daubechies mother wavelet (order 2)

Wavelet-based sound descriptors may characterize any features of time-frequency diagram of the described sound. For example, the set of descriptors may consist of energy coefficients for the selected part of the diagram, normalized to the whole energy [14].

Standardization of the audio and any multimedia data description is in the scope of MPEG-7 works [5] – see Fig. 3. This standard will not cover methods of description production nor consumption. The MPEG-7 standard (Multimedia Content Description Interface standard) is currently under development, expected in September 2001.

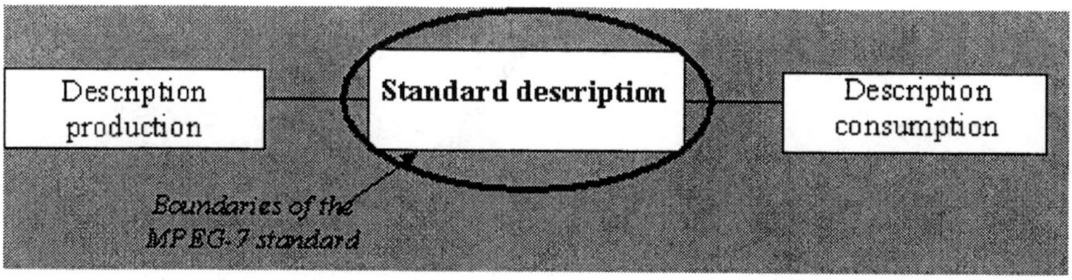


Fig. 3 Scope of MPEG-7 [5]

## 3. Classification techniques

Researchers investigating automatic musical instrument classification have already experimented with many techniques used in supervised learning, including [3], [7], [10], [13], [14]:

- k-nearest neighbors,
- artificial neural networks,
- binary trees,
- rough sets,
- naïve Bayesian classifiers,
- discriminant analysis,
- higher order statistics,
- hidden Markov models,
- AQ strategy, and
- support vector machines.

The most successful methods are k-nearest neighbors and artificial neural networks the latter for very limited set of data (4 - 5 instruments, for full musical range), but other methods also yield promising results. Great part of all instrument investigation mentioned above have been performed on the musical instrument sound data taken form CD library, prepared by McGill University [11]. Researchers not only test the automatic recognition of particular instruments, but also the recognition of families of instruments. Of course, better results are obtained for instrument families – this task is also easier for human. People usually recognize that an instrument belongs, for instance, to the string family, before they can tell whether it is a violin or viola. The scheme of hierarchical instrument recognition is presented in Fig. 4 [10].

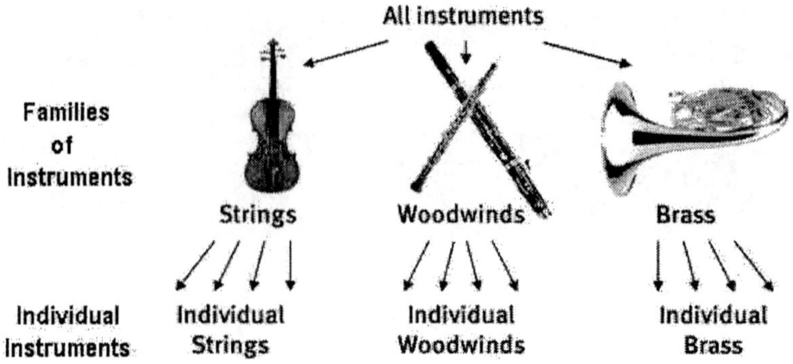


Fig. 4 Hierarchical recognition of musical instruments

The most popular algorithm for instance-based learning for any data is k-Nearest Neighbors (k-NN) method, which is easy to implement. However, this algorithm requires storing all training examples and computing distance to all of them, since for each new example a set of k nearest training objects has to be found and the new example is assigned to a class that has more examples in this set. In experiments with 4 instruments (and selected notes only), the classification was totally correct, but such a database is too small to draw general conclusions. In experiments with 15 instruments (1023 sounds, 31 descriptors), 87% accuracy at the instrument families level and 61% at the instrument level was achieved. With hierarchical procedure of classification, i.e. discriminating pizzicato vs. other sounds first, the accuracy at the instrument level reached 79%, but the accuracy at the family level decreased to 79% [10]. Similar hierarchical architecture for a combination of Gaussian classifier, used for discrimination between pizzicato and sustained sounds, and k-NN classifier for database with 1498 samples, resulted in 75% correctness at instrument level and 94% for family classification.

Another, very successful classification, was obtained using artificial neural networks. The feedforward network with backpropagation training algorithm and 3-5-4 architecture classified piano, marimba, accordion and guitar with 97% accuracy. Also very high results, reaching 97-100% accuracy, were obtained for feedforward networks with one hidden layer when classifying another 4 instruments (tenor trombone, bass trombone, English horn and contrabassoon) using 14 descriptors [7]. Another experiment with 10 classes (but with only 40 sounds), with a multiplayer perceptron, a time-delay network and hybrid of self-organizing network and radial basis function, ended up with the accuracy ranging from 94% (hybrid network) through 97% (perceptron) and 100% (time-delay network). In yet another experiment with self-organizing map, 98% accuracy for 5 instruments and 10 descriptors was obtained. Since the training phase in experiments with neural networks is time-consuming, the data sets used in neural experiments were always very small. Therefore, one should not compare these results with other experiments.

Binary trees have also been used in experiments with musical instrument sound recognition and with other audio data [3]. There are reports about experiments with audio data (but not specifically with musical data) using binary trees and descriptors based on energy and cepstral coefficients in Mel scale, presented in Fig. 5, and experiments with musical instrument sounds (results expected soon). In tests with 14 and 62 descriptors based on FFT and 152 descriptors based on wavelet transform, the accuracy for 11 instruments with up to 1358 objects reached about 70% at instrument level and about 90% for FFT-based descriptors (about 80% for wavelet-based ones) at family level [13], [14]. The same data sets were also used in experiments with AQ strategy and with rough set based classifiers, yielding up to 78% accuracy (for 14 descriptors, rough set classifier) in training/testing using 90%/10% of the data.

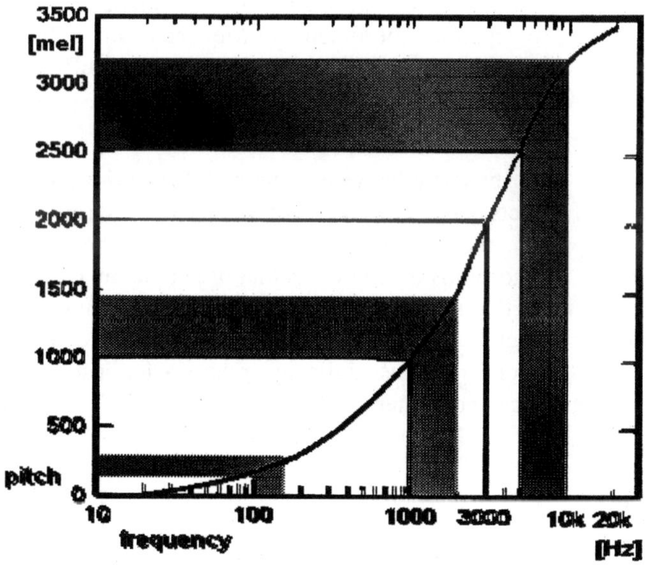


Fig. 5 Mel scale

Naïve Bayesian classifiers were used in experiments with 18 cepstrum coefficients in Mel scale, classifying 30 short sounds of oboe and saxophone with 85% accuracy. In experiments with a larger database (15 instruments, 1023 sounds, 31 descriptors), 71% accuracy was reached at instrument level and 85% at family level [10]. The same data were also used in discrimination analysis, which attempts to minimize the ratio of within-class scatter to the between-class scatter and builds the appropriate decision regions. In experiments with another data set, with 120 sounds from 8 classes and 3 families, 85% was reached when assigning sounds to the family first and then to a specific instrument class.

Some authors claim that since musical sounds have been generated through non-linear process, they do not fit Gaussian distribution and higher order statistics should be used to describe these sounds. The experiments have been carried out with 18 instruments, proving that such a classification is also possible. Another technique applied to musical instrument classification is Support Vector Machines (SVMs), developed quite recently. In SVMs, optimal linear hyperplane has to be found, minimizing the expected classification error for unseen test objects. For linearly non-separable data, SVMs can nonlinearly map the data into a high dimensional feature space, where linear hyperplane can be found. Training SVMs is equivalent to solving a quadratic programming task with linear constraints and number of variables equal to the number of objects in the data set [3]. 70% accuracy was obtained in experiments with 0.2s long sound segments of 8 instruments, using 16 cepstrum coefficients in Mel scale, and 83% accuracy for longer segments, with trombone and harpsichord especially difficult to classify correctly. The sounds were taken from commercial recordings, containing pieces of famous composers for solo instruments.

Since the described results were obtained for various data sets, with various numbers of objects and classes, and various sets of descriptors, it is hard to compare precisely the performance of all these algorithms. Anyway, the performance of some algorithms is as good as that of people on average. However, skilled musicians are better in instrument recognition than computers, when we take classification of singular sounds into account. As far as recognition of sounds in the environment is concerned, as violin in orchestra for instance, even small children are still better than computers so far.

## 4. Conclusions

Indispensable step, required before any searching through multimedia database, is preparation of multimedia content descriptors (audio descriptors, in our case). Selection of such descriptors depends on the aim of the search. Descriptors necessary for melody or chords searching will be probably different that ones needed for correct classification of musical instrument, and different sets of properties will be important for different sounds. The aim of the search also determines the way of data segmentation, which is also necessary in this process.

The main interest of this paper is how to perform classification of musical instruments, assuming data segmentation as a preprocessing.

Automatic classification of musical sounds can be based on practically any classifier, assuming that these sounds are represented by the appropriate descriptors. The techniques used in experiments so far yield good results, but this research has been carried out for solo sounds only. Therefore, further work with orchestral and other group sounds from real recordings along with the investigation of sound recognition in musical environment is necessary in the nearest future.

## References

1. Arfib D., Analysis, Transformation, and Resynthesis of Musical Sounds with the Help of a Time-Frequency Representation, in: De Poli G., Piccialli A., Roads C. (ed.), Representations of Musical Signals, MIT Press, Cambridge, Massachusetts, 1991
2. Chen A. L. P., Music Representation, Indexing and retrieval at NTHU, International Symposium on Music Information Retrieval ISMIR 2000, Plymouth, MA, October 23-25, 2000
3. Herrera P., Amatriain X., Batlle E., Serra X., Towards instrument segmentation for music content description: a critical review of instrument classification techniques, International Symposium on Music Information Retrieval ISMIR 2000, October 23-25, Plymouth, MA
4. Hunter J., Ianella R., The Application of Metadata Standards to Video Indexing, Second European Conference on Research and Advanced Technology for Digital Libraries ECDL'98, 19-23 September, 1998, Crete, Greece
5. ISO/IEC JTC1/SC29/WG11, MPEG-7 Overview (version 3.0), International Organisation for Standardisation Organisation Internationale de Normalisation, Coding of Moving Pictures and Audio, N3445, Geneva, May/June 2000
6. Izmirli O., Using a Spectral Flatness Based Feature for Audio Segmentation and Retrieval, International Symposium on Music Information Retrieval ISMIR 2000, October 23-25, Plymouth, MA
7. Kostek B., Krolikowski R., Application of artificial neural networks to the recognition of musical sounds, Archives of Acoustics, 22 (1), pp. 27-50, 1997

8. Kostek B., Szczerba M., Wieczorkowska A., Musical Databases - Construction and Analysis, 19 Tonmeistertagung, Karlsruhe, 1996, pp. 807-812

9. Kronland-Martinet R., Grossmann A., Application of Time-Frequency and Time-Scale Methods (Wavelet Transforms) to the Analysis, Synthesis, and Transformation of Natural Sounds, in: De Poli G., Piccialli A., Roads C. (ed.), Representations of Musical Signals, MIT Press, Cambridge, Massachusetts, 1991, pp. 45-85

10. Martin K. D., Kim Y. E., Musical instrument identification: A pattern-recognition approach, 136 meeting of the Acoustical Society of America, October 13, 1998. Internet: ftp://sound.media.mit.edu/pub/Papers/kdm-asa98.pdf

11. Opolko F., Wapnick J., MUMS – McGill University Master Samples, CDs, McGill University, Montreal, Canada, 1987

12. Pollard H. F., Jansson E. V., A Tristimulus Method for the Specification of Musical Timbre, Acustica, Vol. 51, 1982, 162-171

13. Wieczorkowska A., The recognition efficiency of musical instrument sounds depending on parameterization and type of a classifier (in Polish), Ph.D. Dissertation, Technical University of Gdańsk, 1999

14. Wieczorkowska A., Application of Decision Trees to Wavelet-based Classification of Musical Instrument Sounds, 9th International Symposium on Intelligent Information Systems, Bystra 11-15.06.2000, Proceedings, 45-53.

# Significance Testing in the Grade Correspondence Analysis

**Alicja Ciok**

Institute of Computer Science PAS, 01-237 Warsaw, Ordona 21, Poland
e-mail: alac@ipipan.waw.pl

**Abstract.** Several problems concerning significance testing in the grade correspondence analysis are considered in the paper. A certain method of coping is proposed and tested on an example of real data. (The data describe actual living conditions of physically disabled people in Poland.)

**Key words:** bootstrap, maximal grade correlation coefficient, conditional independence, quantile

## 1 Introduction

The grade correspondence analysis (GCA) belongs to a class of data mining tools (exploratory data analysis). In this class, significance testing is not as straightforward as in classic statistics, where two hypotheses must be formulated: the null $H_0$ and the alternative $H$; the statistician's task is to decide, which of them should be accepted. These hypotheses must be expressed in terms of distributions of a certain test statistic. For every test statistic the critical region is defined. If the value of test statistic obtained for the analysed data belongs to the critical region, the null hypothesis is rejected with probability, which is small enough under $H_0$.

In the GCA (as in most procedures from this class) the situation is much more complicated. Its aim is to find latent structures in two-way data tables. In this context structures are described by pairs of permutations for rows and columns of data table. These permutations define row and column variables of the data table. If these variables are independent, there is no structure in the data table. In other words the structure concept is equivalent to deviation from independence between row and column variables.

If the data table includes values of random discrete variables, they may be treated as frequencies or probabilities but they are restricted to a certain range. Therefore, the conditional independence of row and column variables should be considered as our null hypothesis. Its formal description as well as description of the chosen test statistics are shown in Section 3.

The inference scheme is the classic. A structure in data table is acknowledged significant, if the null hypothesis of the conditional independence has been rejected. The problem is that many significant structures may be found in one data table. These structures may be mixed together or may contain elements, which do not belong to either structure. To make the situation worse, the effects of mixing two strong, different structures, are similar to those where there is no structure at all. On the other hand, if there are two almost equally strong structures, either of them may prevail by chance (depending on the sample). Moreover, as the GCA is a maximization procedure, there is the problem (common to the class of optimization procedures) of finding a local maximum rather than the global. However, it occurs very often (as shown by Szczesny (2000)) that local maxima correspond to situations, in which structures other than the strongest one, dominate. Generally, we have to investigate variability of the GCA solutions simultaneously with the analysis of local maxima. Consequently, a large number of structures should be tested. To diminish the cost, the following steps in the significance testing of the GCA solutions are proposed:

1. analysis of the structure variability with respect to the sampling process, for example, with of bootstrap-like procedures,
2. analysis of the local maxima, which should be performed in parallel to step 1,
3. classic significance testing for chosen revealed structures with an appropriately chosen null hypothesis and a test statistic.

In this paper, the results of the step 1 and the step 3 analyses are presented in Section 5. The analyses were performed on real data, which concern the situation of disabled people in Poland (described in Section 2). The analysis of local maxima for the same data may be found in Szczesny (2000). Section 3 provides the necessary information about the statistical tools used for the testing in the step 3. As the distributions necessary for this significance testing are not analitically derivable, they must be generated by computer intensive methods. The algorithm used for the distribution estimation is described in Section 4.

## 2 Data description

The analysed data characterize the actual situation of physically disabled people in Poland. Information was gathered by The Foundation Supporting Physically Disabled Mathematicians and Computer Specialists. This was done via an Internet survey among users of the Internet Node for the Disabled, run by this fundation for the past four years (c.f. Bulinska et al. (2000)). The data table has 400 rows corresponding to the particular respondents and 10 columns which correspond to answers for particular questions (values of the variables). The responses provide individual evaluations of various aspects of living conditions and are expressed on the same scale, ranging from 1 to 6. A list of survey items is included in Table 1.

**Table 1.** Survey items describing respondent's situation

| Number | Name | Description |
|---|---|---|
| 1 | equip | Equipment (computer related) |
| 2 | skills | Skill level (with computers) |
| 3 | lang | Language skills |
| 4 | prof_exp | Professional experience |
| 5 | pop_size | Population size of city of residence |
| 6 | educ | Education |
| 7 | age | Age |
| 8 | econ | Economic situation |
| 9 | employ | Current employment |
| 10 | func_lev | Functional level of disability |

# 3 Statistical testing framework

The significance testing framework for the grade correspondence analysis is based on the concept of *statistical dependence* and of *conditional tests*. The GCA assumes that a data table is considered as a two-way probability table, after suitable normalization. (Practically every two-dimensional table with nonnegative values may be treated as such). The aim of the GCA is to find a pair of latent traits for rows and for columns, which order them in such a way that similar rows (columns) are placed near each other. When the data table consists of variable values (in columns), this property makes it possible to identify groups of objects (rows) with similar characteristics (profiles). In other words, the GCA tries to reveal structure in the data table. Moreover, it orders the profiles such that large values in the data table tend to be placed along the diagonal (to the extent possible), what is the case of monotone dependence. Therefore, the significance of the revealed structure may be expressed by the strength of the monotone dependence between the row and column latent traits. This dependence is measured by the so called grade correlation coefficient $\rho^*$, given by the following formula (cf. Schriever (1985)):

$$\rho^* = 3\sum_{i=1}^{M}\sum_{j=1}^{K} p_{ij}\left(S_{i-1}^r + S_i^r - 1\right)\left(S_{j-1}^c + S_j^c - 1\right) \tag{1}$$

where $P = (p_{ij})_{M\times K}$ is a probability table and $S_l^r = \sum_{i=1}^{l}\sum_{j=1}^{K} p_{ij}$ and $S_l^c = \sum_{j=1}^{l}\sum_{i=1}^{M} p_{ij}$. GCA maximizes $\rho^*$ in the set of all pairs of orderings of rows and columns. Such a maximized coefficient is called the maximal grade correlation coefficient $\rho^*_{\max}$, and is used as the test statistic.

Lack of structure in the data corresponds to independence of the rows and columns, and to small values of $\rho^*_{\max}$. The higher the observed value of $\rho^*_{\max}$, the stronger the latent structure revealed. However, to decide whether a value is small or not, it is necessary to compare this value with the distribution of the test statistic. Let us note that this distribution is strongly dependent on the marginal distributions of the rows and columns. Therefore, we need the distribution of $\rho^*_{\max}$ under the null hypothesis $H_0$ that the rows and columns of the $M \times K$ table are independent, providing that the row and column totals are fixed. This restriction, although necessary, is not sufficient. As the analyzed variables are categorical with values from the same range we need the distribution calculated for such data tables. Hence, rather than $H_0$, we should consider a modified hypothesis $H_0'$, which postulates rows and columns independence not only when row and column totals are fixed but also when cell ranges are fixed.

The theoretical distribution of a test statistic under $H_0'$ (as well as $H_0$) is usually not derivable and must be estimated from a set of tables drawn according to $H_0'$ for given totals and ranges. Therefore, an efficient algorithm generating such "random" tables is needed. Algorithms which generate tables distributed according to $H_0$ are known in the statistical literature (e.g. Patefield (1981)). To obtain random samples under $H_0'$ a new procedure is needed (c.f. Ciok (1997), which is a modification and an extension of Patefield's algorithm.

# 4 Generation of random tables with row and column totals fixed and cell ranges imposed

A full description of the applied generation algorithm is presented in Ciok (1997), here we will present on a general description. The procedure consists of two parts, the first one may be roughly specified as a modification of Patefield's algorithm of generating random frequency $M \times K$ tables under $H_0$ (independence with given row and column totals). It was observed that the most natural modification of this algorithm - the simulate-and-reject Monte-Carlo procedure is practically infeasible, particularly when $M$ or $K$ are large. It generates a random table with fixed totals according to Patefield's algorithm and rejects the table if any of the cell values are not admissible. Unfortunately, such a small fraction of generated tables usually is admissible, that aquisition of a reasonable sample of tables is practically impossible. This observation is in accord with the experience of other authors who try to cope with similar problems (see Smith and McDonald (1995) and (1994)).

The proposed modification of Patefield's algorithm generates table cells by sampling them successively from the relevant distributions, as in the original algorithm. In our case, however, this distribution must be restricted to the imposed range.

To simplify the calculations, we consider the range $R_a = \{0, 1, ..., r-1\}$ rather than $\{1, ..., r\}$ and consequently all initial totals must be suitably modified (by subtracting $M$ or $K$ from the totals for columns or rows respectively). The addition of 1 to every cell in the generated table will provide a solution for the initial problem.

Let $T = (t_{mk})$ denote a table with fixed row and column totals: $t_{i\bullet} = \sum_{j=1}^{K} t_{ij}$, $t_{\bullet j} = \sum_{i=1}^{M} t_{ij}$. Let $N = \sum_{i=1}^{M} t_{i\bullet} = \sum_{j=1}^{K} t_{\bullet j}$. In Patefield's algorithm the values of $t_{mk}$ are drawn successively according to the conditional distributions $P_{mk} = (P_{mk}(t),\ t = 0, 1, 2, ....)$, where $P_{mk}(t)$ is the probability (calculated under $H_0$) that $t_{mk}$ is equal to $t$ provided that the table values $t_{ij}$ are fixed for all previous rows ($i = 1, ..., m-1; j = 1, ..., K$) and for the preceding cells in row $m$. Consequently, for $m = 1, ..., M-1$; $k = 1, ..., K-1$,

$$\begin{aligned}
P_{mk}(t) = {} & \left(t_{m\bullet} - \sum_{j=1}^{k-1} t_{mj}\right)! \left(N - \sum_{i=1}^{m} t_{i\bullet} - \sum_{j=1}^{k-1} t_{\bullet j} + \sum_{j=1}^{k-1}\sum_{i=1}^{m} t_{ij}\right)! \\
& \times \left(t_{\bullet k} - \sum_{i=1}^{m-1} t_{ik}\right)! \left(\sum_{j=k+1}^{K} \left(t_{\bullet j} - \sum_{i=1}^{m-1} t_{ij}\right)\right)! \\
& \times \left[t! \left(t_{\bullet k} - \sum_{i=1}^{m-1} t_{ik} - t\right)! \left(t_{m\bullet} - \sum_{j=1}^{k-1} t_{mj} - t\right)! \right. \\
& \times \left(N - \sum_{i=1}^{m} t_{i\bullet} - \sum_{j=1}^{k} t_{\bullet j} + \sum_{j=1}^{k-1}\sum_{i=1}^{m} t_{ij} + \sum_{i=1}^{m-1} t_{ik} + t\right)! \\
& \times \left. \left(\sum_{j=k}^{K} \left(t_{\bullet j} - \sum_{i=1}^{m-1} t_{ij}\right)\right)! \right]^{-1}
\end{aligned} \tag{2}$$

if all factors in (2) are nonnegative, and otherwise $P_{mk}(t) = 0$. Moreover, for any $m = 1, ..., M$ each $P_{mK}$ concentrates on a single value $t_{mK}$, where

$$t_{mK} = t_{m\bullet} - \sum_{k=1}^{K-1} t_{mk} \tag{3}$$

and for any $k = 1, ..., K$ each $P_{Mk}$ concentrates on a single value $t_{Mk}$, where

$$t_{Mk} = t_{\bullet k} - \sum_{m=1}^{M-1} t_{mk}. \tag{4}$$

In the modified algorithm the values of $t_{mk}$ are successively drawn according to the modified (conditional) probabilities $Q_{mk}$:

$$Q_{mk}(t) = P_{mk}(t) / \sum_{s \in R_a} P_{mk}(s),\ t \in R_a \tag{5}$$

for $m = 1, ..., M-1$ and $k = 1, ..., K-1$. Therefore these values always belong to the imposed range. The values in the last row and column: $t_{mK}$ for $m = 1, ..., M-1$ and $t_{Mk}$ for $k = 1, ..., K$ are calculated according to formulas (3) and (4), regardless of whether they belong to the admissible range $R_a$ or not. Note that the generated $t_{MK}$ may be negative while $t_{mK}$ $(m = 1, ..., M-1)$ and $t_{Mk}$ $(k = 1, ..., K-1)$ are always nonnegative but may be outside the admissible range

If not all generated values satisfy the imposed restrictions, the second part of the procedure begins. Let us suppose that the generated value of $t_{mk}$ is beyond the range. In consecutive steps of the procedure we move "frequency masses" to the other cells of table $T$ in the following way.

$$\begin{aligned} t_{mk} &:= t_{mk} - \epsilon,\ t_{m_0,k} := t_{m_0,k} + \epsilon, \\ t_{m,k_0} &:= t_{m,k_0} + \epsilon, t_{m_0,k_0} := t_{m_0,k_0} - \epsilon, \end{aligned} \tag{6}$$

where $\epsilon \in \{-1, 1\}$. If the value of $t_{mk}$ is too large, then $\epsilon$ must be positive, otherwise $\epsilon$ must be negative. As values: $t_{m_0,k_0}$, $t_{m_0,k}$ and $t_{m,k_0}$ should remain inside the imposed range, cell $(m_0, k_0)$ must be appropriately chosen. It is clear that modification (6) improves bad cells, but it does not change table totals. Such improvements should be repeated until all cells are correct but sometimes this is not possible. In such a case a bad table is rejected and the procedure is repeated.

As the proposed algorithm is a simulate-and-reject procedure, its efficiency is crucial. Efficiency is defined as the expected number of attempts needed to generate one admissible table. The results of a simulation study in Ciok (1997) confirm that efficiency strongly depends on the chosen totals. Efficiency, in the case of our data, ranges from 1.12 to 1.53.

## 5 Significance testing

As computations are extremely time consuming, it is not possible to apply the full bootstrap methodology. Therefore only six random samples were drawn from the original data table (only rows are drawn, columns always remain exactly as in the original). Four samples were of size 100, and two of size 200. As the ordering of columns in any local solution determines the ordering of rows (and vice versa), we will describe these solutions in terms of columns (survey items) orderings. The optimal column orderings for the larger samples appear to be very similar - only three adjacent columns interchange places (see Table 2). The corresponding values of the test statistic are also very similar (0.208 and 0.206).

Much greater differences occur in the optimal orderings for smaller samples (Table 2), but the common trend is still clearly visible (equip, skills and lang occupy the extreme positions on one side, with employ and func_lev on the other side). Only in the sample 4 this trend is distorted. The suspicion is that it is only a random effect of sample too small. However, an almost identical ordering can be obtained as a local maximum for the much larger sample number 5. Hence, this ordering should not be considered as meaningless. To the contrary, the corresponding value of the test statistic should be

**Table 2.** Positions of the particular survey items in the optimal orderings of columns obtained for six samples

| Survey item | Sample number 1 | 2 | 3 | 4 | 5 | 6 |
|---|---|---|---|---|---|---|
| equip | 1 | 1 | 1 | 2 | 1 | 1 |
| skills | 2 | 2 | 3 | 3 | 2 | 3 |
| lang | 3 | 3 | 2 | 6 | 3 | 2 |
| prof_exp | 4 | 9 | 8 | 5 | 7 | 7 |
| pop_size | 5 | 6 | 4 | 9 | 6 | 5 |
| educ | 6 | 5 | 5 | 7 | 5 | 6 |
| age | 7 | 7 | 6 | 8 | 8 | 8 |
| econ | 8 | 4 | 7 | 4 | 4 | 4 |
| employ | 9 | 10 | 10 | 1 | 9 | 10 |
| func_lev | 10 | 8 | 9 | 10 | 10 | 9 |
| Sample size | 100 | 100 | 100 | 100 | 200 | 200 |

compared with the respective distribution. Finally, the distributions of the test statistics $\rho^{\star}_{\max}$ under hypothesis $H'_0$ of conditional independence were calculated for three samples (number 1, 4 and 5). In all considered cases the quantiles of order 0.95 are significantly smaller than the value of $\rho^{\star}_{\max}$ for the original data table (Table 3). Consequently, there is no reason to reject any of these optimal orderings as random effects. The implication of this statement is that we should expect at least two significant structures, almost equally strong, to be present in the considered data table.

**Table 3.** Quantiles of the test statistic $\rho^{\star}_{\max}$ for three samples

| Sample number | $\rho^{\star}_{\max}$ quantiles of order 0.05 | 0.25 | 0.50 | 0.75 | 0.95 | Real $\rho^{\star}_{\max}$ |
|---|---|---|---|---|---|---|
| 1 | 0.1253 | 0.1311 | 0.1363 | 0.1416 | 0.1500 | 0.212 |
| 4 | 0.1240 | 0.1296 | 0.1343 | 0.1399 | 0.1476 | 0.199 |
| 5 | 0.1316 | 0.1371 | 0.1416 | 0.1459 | 0.1522 | 0.208 |

A more in depth approach to significance testing of GCA results will be possible as technical tools appropriate for these time intensive calculations are developed.

## References

1. Bulinska, J., Markiewicz, K., Pleszczynska, E. (2000) Internet survey on independent living of the disabled in Poland, *AAATE Seminar 2000*, Hatfield, UK 4-5 September 2000.
2. Ciok, A. (1997) Generating random MxK tables when row and column totals and cell ranges are given. *ICS PAS REPORTS*, no 844, 5-18

3. Ciok, A., Kowalczyk, T., Pleszczynska, E., Szczesny W. (1995) Algorithms of grade correspondence-cluster analysis, *The Collected Papers on Theoretical and Applied Computer Science*, vol. 7, no 1-4, 5-22.
4. Patefield, W. M. (1981) Algorithm AS159. An efficient method of generating random RxC tables with given row and column totals. *Applied Statistics*, **30**, 91-97.
5. Schriever, B. F. (1985) *Order dependence*, Ph.D. Dissertation, Free University of Amsterdam, .
6. Smith, P. W. F., McDonald, J. W. (1995) Exact conditional tests for incomplete contingency tables: estimating attained significance levels. *Statistics and Computing*, **5**, 253-256.
7. Smith, P. W. F., McDonald, J. W. (1994) Simulate and reject Monte-Carlo exact conditional tests for quasi-independence. *COMPSTAT'94, Proceedings in Computational Statistics*, Physica-Verlag, 509-514.
8. Szczesny, W. (2000) Grade Correspondence Analysis Applied to Questionaire Data (submitted).

# Ensembles of Similarity-Based Models

Włodzisław Duch and Karol Grudziński

Department of Computer Methods, Nicholas Copernicus University,
Grudziądzka 5, 87-100 Toruń, Poland.
E-mails: {duch,kagru}@phys.uni.torun.pl

**Abstract.** Ensembles of independent classifiers are usually more accurate and show smaller variance than individual classifiers. Methods of selection of Similarity Based Models (SBM) that should be included in an ensemble are discussed. Standard $k$-NN, weighted $k$-NN, ensembles of weighted models and ensembles of averaged weighted models are considered. Ensembles of competent models are introduced. Results of numerical experiments on benchmark and real-world datasets are presented.

## 1 Introduction

A framework for Similarity-Based Methods (SBM) covers all methods based on computing similarity between the new case and cases in the training library [1]. The SBM framework is very rich, it includes such well-known methods as the $k$–Nearest Neighbor ($k$-NN) algorithm and it's extensions, originating mainly from machine learning and pattern recognition fields, as well as neural methods such as the popular multilayer perceptron networks (MLP) and networks based on radial–basis functions (RBF). Methods of the SBM type are based on specific parameterization of the $p(C_i|\mathbf{X};M)$ posterior classification probability, where the model $M$ involves various procedures, parameters and optimization methods. Instead of focusing on improving a single method a search for the best method belonging to the SBM framework should select optimal combination of parameters and procedures for a given problem.

Similarity Based Learner (SBL) is a software system developed in our laboratory that systematically implements methods belonging to the SBM framework [2]. Methods implemented so far provide many similarity functions with different parameters, include several methods of feature selection, methods that weight attributes (based on minimization of the cost function or based on searching in the quantized weight space), methods of selection of interesting prototypes in batch and on-line versions, and methods implementing partial-memory of the evolving system. Currently our research focuses on implementation of network-type realizations of various SBM methods, weighting influence of reference vectors and speeding up the calculations.

A single model that may be developed by combining methods and adding parameters within the SBM framework may be improved further by combining or mixing many models. Mixture of models may not only improve the accuracy but also decrease variance of the model, stabilizing and improving its generalization

[3]. Except for SBL several other programs have been developed in our laboratory. All these programs are at present being integrated into a data-mining software that should allow to create ensembles of quite different methods.

In the next section methods for model combination are briefly discussed and an algorithm for selection of subsets of models that are included in an ensemble described. In the third section modifications of these algorithms suitable for similarity based learning are discussed. Results comparing stand-alone methods to ensembles of similarity based methods are presented for a few benchmark and real-world datsets. Finally some conclusions and plans for further work are given.

## 2 Ensembles of SBM Models

A few definitions are needed first. **An algorithm**, or **a method**, is a certain well-defined computational procedure. For example standard $k$-NN, a variant of the $k$-NN with optimization of weights scaling individual input features performed by search in the weight space, and by minimization of the cost function, are three distinct methods. Methods may have the same or different input and output parameters. **A model** is an instance of a method with specific values of parameters. For example the $k$–NN for $k=1$ and $k=3$ are two distinct models derived from the same method. **Combination, or an ensemble of models**, includes a procedure of selection of a set of models and a decision procedure to compute the final classification probability. Each of the models contributing to the combination should be trained on cases drawn from the same training set. Ensembles may involve models obtained from the same method (in this case adaptive parameters are optimized independently in every model) or from several different methods. Bagged models [3] are created by optimizing models of the same type on different subsets of the training set. Finally **a task or a scheme** is a sequence of one or more models which are added in succession to the ensemble.

In this paper two types of the base classifiers are used: the standard $k$-NN models and weighted $k$-NN models. Weighted $k$-NN uses distance functions:

$$D(\mathbf{X},\mathbf{Y})^{\alpha} = \sum_{i=1}^{n} s_i |X_i - Y_i|^{\alpha} \tag{1}$$

parameterized by the $\alpha$ exponent (for Euclidean distances $\alpha = 2$ is taken) and by the scaling factors $s_i$ that weight the importance of each attribute. These scaling factors are determined by minimization of the number of errors the classifier makes [4]. A multisimplex method or an adaptive simulated annealing minimization [5,6] has been used for this purpose. To reduce the number of numerical experiments only $\alpha = 1$ or 2 is considered here and only the results obtained with the simplex method are reported. Since classification results do not change if all attributes are rescaled by the same factor only $n-1$ attributes should be scaled. Fixing the most important attribute should lead to optimized values of the scaling factors $s_i \leq 1$.

### 2.1 Combining models

Individual models are frequently unstable [3], i.e. quite different models are created as a result of repeated training (if learning algorithms are stochastic) or if the training set is slightly perturbed. The mixture of models allows to approximate complicated probability distributions quite accurately.

With $l = 1..K$ models providing estimation of probabilities $P(C_i|\mathbf{X};M_l)$ an additive combination

$$p(C_i|\mathbf{X};M) = \sum_{l=1}^{K} W_l P(C_i|\mathbf{X};M_l) \tag{2}$$

provides additional $K$ linear parameters for model combination, determined using the standard Least Mean Squares (LMS) procedure. Majority voting is quite frequently used as a decision rule to combine results of multiple models. An empirical comparison of voting algorithms, including bagging and boosting, has been published by Bauer and Kohavi [7]. Tests were made using decision trees and naive Bayes method. The bagging algorithm uses classifiers trained on bootstrap samples, created by randomly drawing a fixed number of training data vectors from the pool which always contains all training vectors (i.e. drawing does not remove them from the pool). Results are aggregated by voting. AdaBoost (Adaptive Boosting) creates a sequence of training sets and determines weights of the training instances, with higher weights for those that are incorrectly classified. The arcing method uses a simplified procedure for weighting of the training vectors. Bauer and Kohavi [7] provided an interesting decomposition of bias and variance components of errors for these algorithms.

Renormalized product of different predictors has been advocated recently by Hinton [8] in context of unsupervised probability density estimation. Each individual model may have rather high variance but the product leads to a sharper probability distribution. Feature weighting or feature selection for different models may constrain different dimensions of the feature space and the product distribution will constrain all features. Each model may specialize in different aspect of the problem and thus instead of trying to generate and make an ensemble of the best models one should diversify them. Unfortunately the best diversification strongly depends on the type of problem analyzed. Renormalized product

$$p(C_i|\mathbf{X};M) = \frac{\prod_{l=1}^{K} P(C_i|\mathbf{X};M_l)}{\sum_{i=1}^{C} \prod_{l=1}^{K} P(C_i|\mathbf{X};M_l)} \tag{3}$$

may be optimized over all parameters of individual models by minimizing the log likelihood on the training data. Hinton's contrastive divergence approach requires minimization of the Kullback-Leibler (K-L) divergence between the data distribution and the Gibbs sampling equilibrium distribution minus the K-L divergence between the "one-step reconstruction" of Gibbs sampling and its equilibrium distribution. Computationally this procedure is very demanding. The product formula may be used for model aggregation without optimization if minimal probability is set to a small, non-zero value.

A novel approach to combination of models is presented below.

## 2.2 Ensembles of Competent Models (ECM)

So far all models selected to the ensemble were allowed to vote on the final result. Krogh and Vedelsby [9] showed that ensemble generalization error is small if highly accurate classifiers disagreeing with each other are used. The SBM models use prototypes and it is relatively easy to determine the areas of the input space in which a given model is highly competent (makes a few errors) and in which it fails. A simple algorithm that includes some information on the competence of different models is presented below.

Parameters of a given model $M_l, l = 1 \dots K$ are optimized on a train set using leave-one-out or cross-validation procedure. Then for each reference case $\mathbf{R}_i$ used in one of the SBM models – the case belonging to the true class $C(\mathbf{R}_i)$ – a list of predicted classes $C_j(\mathbf{R}_i)$ for all $j = 1 \dots m$ models is made. A competence vector $\mathbf{K}_j(\mathbf{R}_i) = \delta(C(\mathbf{R}_i), C_j(\mathbf{R}_i))$ for the area around $\mathbf{R}_i$ is created. In the decision phase nearest neighbor reference vectors are determined and only those classifiers that have been competent for all vectors are included in the voting procedure. If no competent models are found the vector given for classification is probably an outlier and should be left as 'rejected' or 'impossible to classify'.

A more sophisticated way of creating competent ensembles may be introduced if linear combinations are used instead of majority voting. Coefficients of linear combination should depend on the distance between the vector $\mathbf{X}$ and those reference vectors $\mathbf{R}_{l,k}$ of the feature space where model $M_l$ is competent.

$$P(C_i|\mathbf{X};M) = \sum_{l=1}^{K} \sum_{m} W_l D(\mathbf{X}, \mathbf{R}_{l,m}) P(C_i|\mathbf{X};M_l) \tag{4}$$

should be a good choice, where $D(\mathbf{X}, \mathbf{R}_{l,m})$ functions estimate the competence of model $M_l$ around the reference vectors $\mathbf{R}_{l,m}$. After renormalization $p(C_i|\mathbf{X};M) = P(C_i|\mathbf{X};M)/\sum_j P(C_j|\mathbf{X};M)$ gives final probability of classification. Since the problem is linear in $W_l$ least mean squares optimization is sufficient to find the best parameters in this case. In contrast to AdaBoost and similar procedures explicit information about competence, or quality of classifier performance in different feature space areas, is used here.

## 2.3 Selection of $k$-NN models

In the case of the standard $k$-NN, the classifier is used with different values of $k$ on a training partition using leave-one-out algorithm and applied to the test partition. The predicted class is computed on the majority basis. To increase the classification accuracy one may first optimize $k$, $(k_1 \leq k \leq k_2)$ and select $m \leq k_2 - k_1$ best classifiers for an ensemble model. In the case of weighted $k$-NN either $k$ is optimized first and then best models created optimizing all weights, or best models are selected after optimization for a number of $k$ values (a more accurate, but costly procedure).

Selecting a subset of best models that should be included in an ensemble is not an easy task since the number of possibilities grows combinatorially and obviously not all subsets may be checked. A variant of the best-first search (BFS) algorithm has been used for this selection. We have already used the BFS technique for the optimization of weights and for selection of the best attributes [10,11]. BFS algorithm can be used for majority voting of models derived from weighted-NN method based on minimization, or based on standard $k$-NN with different $k$, or for selection of an optimal sequence of any models.

The evaluation function $C(M_l)$ returns the classification accuracy on a validation set; this accuracy refers to a single model or to an ensemble of models selected so far. Let $N$ denote the initial number of models from which selection is made and $K$ the number of models that should be selected. The selection algorithm proceeds as follows:

1. Initialize:
   (a) Create a pool of $N$ models, $\mathcal{M} = \{M_l\}, l = 1 \ldots N$.
   (b) Create an empty set for selected models $\mathcal{F} = \emptyset$.
   (c) Evaluate all models on the validation set, arrange them in a decreasing order $C(M_i) \geq C(M_j)$ for $i > j$.
   (d) Select the best model from the $\mathcal{M}$ pool and move it to the $\mathcal{F}$ pool.
2. Repeat for $L = 2 \ldots K$:
   (a) For $l = 1 \ldots N - L$ models $M_l$ remaining in the pool $\mathcal{M}$ evaluate ensemble $C(\mathcal{F} \cap M_l)$ using majority voting.
   (b) Select the $M_l$ model with highest performance and move it to the $\mathcal{F}$ pool.

At each step $N - L$ sequences consisting of $L$ models are evaluated. If $K = N$ all models are incorporated into a sequence and this algorithm does not differ from the standard 'majority voting' procedure. Frequently the gain in performance may not justify additional complexity of adding a new model to the final pool and new models will be created and evaluated. This algorithm finds a pool of models corresponding to the highest classification accuracy on validation partition. In case of $k$-NN calculations may be done on the training partition in the leave-one-out mode instead of the validation partition.

Although the selection algorithm described above is more computationally expensive than the standard 'majority voter' it has a better chance to work better if a smaller subset of models is selected from a larger pool. Since the SBM scheme allows to add many parameters and procedures new models may also be created on demand if adding models created so far does not improve results. The model optimization (here minimization of the $k$-NN weights) is performed $N$ times at the initialization stage on validation data. Re-optimization of models in the pool may be desirable but it would increase the computational costs significantly, therefore all model parameters are fixed after the initialization step.

## 2.4 Stablization of the weighted models

Maximization of the performance $C(M)$ using the simplex or simulated annealing methods may give quite different sets $\{s_i\}$ of the attribute weighting parameters leading to similar accuracy. In effect the variance of results obtained with weighted $k$-NN methods may be rather high. The stability of standard $k$-NN model [3] is lost.

Perhaps the simplest way to decrease the variance is based on averaging the weights for a few $k$-NN models created on the same data. Weights $s_i$ scaling the components of distance function are obtained by maximization of the number of correct answers using the simplex or multisimplex methods [5]. These methods are stochastic, finding different sets of suboptimal parameters. In principle we could use simulated annealing or search for the best simplex solution obtained from multiple runs, reducing the variance to zero. In such case we would use bootstrap methods to generate different models for the ensemble. Since our goal in these numerical experiments is to investigate the influence of averaging and compare it to majority voted ensembles we have not used yet the sampling techniques to introduce more variability into our models. We have also not used yet the ensembles of competent methods.

Numerical experiments described in the next section include results of 4 methods: single weighted $k$-NN models (designated **WM**), models obtained by averaging weights for several WM models (designated **A-WM**), ensembles of weighted models (**E-WM**), and ensembles of weighted models with averaged weights (**AE-WM**). Performance of these methods depends on the number of models included in the ensemble and the number of models used for weight averaging.

## 3 Numerical experiments

To test some of the ideas presented above we have made a series of calculations using the well-known benchmark datasets taken from UCI repository [12] and real-world medical datasets. The WM symbol designates the single simplex minimization routine model. The A5-WM symbol designates a model that has been obtained from 5 weighted $k$-NN models (WM) independently optimized (differences come only from the stochastic properties of the simplex optimization procedure). The final weights are obtained by averaging over all 5 models. An ensemble of 5 weighted models is called E5-WM, and an ensemble of 10 weighted models, each obtained by averaging weights over 5 models, is called A5E10-WM. In all cases simplexes have been initialized randomly with weights ranging from 0 to 10 except for the ionosphere calculations where weights have been taken from the (0,1) range. A single weight corresponding to a highly-ranked feature is fixed at 1 to establish an absolute scale for distances.

First the ensemble selection method has been used with two artificial datasets, Monk-1 and Monk-3 [13]. These problems are designed for rule-based symbolic machine learning algorithms and the nearest neighbor algorithms usually do not work well in such cases. 6 symbolic features are given as input, 432 cases for testing. Previously we have obtained significant improvements for these datasets using feature selection and weighting [11]; here we are interested in improvements and stabilization of the weighted results due to the ensemble averaging. Calculations were repeated 5-10 times to estimate expected variance of the results.

**Table 1.** Results for the Monk-1 problem

| Method | Accuracy % | Variance % |
|---|---|---|
| $k$-NN | 89.5 | – |
| WM | 94.7 | ± 5.3 |
| A5-WM | 99.6 | ± 0.8 |
| A10-WM | 99.7 | ± 0.8 |
| E5-WM | 98.4 | ± 2.2 |
| E10-WM | 99.7 | ± 0.6 |
| A5E5-WM | 99.7 | ± 0.4 |
| A5E10-WM | 99.98 | ± 0.07 |

For the Monk-1 problem 124 cases are given for training. Euclidean distance with $k$=1 was used; all calculations were repeated 10 times. Weighted $k$-NN does improves the result but the variance is quite high; an ensemble of 5 weighted models (E5-WM) still has quite high variance. Averaging combined with ensemble of 10 models achieves almost always 100% accuracy.

For Monk-3 problem 122 cases are given for training. Features 1 and 3 have been turned off by the initial feature selection procedure, increasing accuracy from 87.3% with all 6 features to 98.6% with 4 features. Weighted models slightly decrease the average accuracy (this decrease shows rather poor performance of the simplex optimization). Averaging over 5 models decreases the variance almost to zero. Results do not improve further because in this case there is some noise in the data and $k$-NN with feature selection achieves the optimal result.

**Table 2.** Results for the Monk-3 problem

| Method | Accuracy % | Variance % |
|---|---|---|
| $k$-NN | 98.6 | – |
| WM | 98.3 | ± 0.6 |
| A2-WM | 98.5 | ± 0.4 |
| A5-WM | 98.6 | ± 0.0 |
| A5E5-WM | 98.6 | ± 0.0 |

The *vowel dataset* is composed of 528 training and 462 test vectors, each with 10 continuous attributes derived from speech samples. The task to identify one of the 11 vowels is rather difficult and the standard $k$-NN with Euclidean function and $k = 1$ obtains only 56.3% correct answers. The best single model with $k = 9$ has only 56.5% accuracy on the test set. An ensemble of 10 $k$-NN models with $k = 1 \ldots 10$ improves this result to 59.1%

The *ionosphere data* has 200 training and 150 test vectors, 2 classes and 34 continuous attributes. In this case significant improvement (4.6%) is obtained by using Manhattan distance function and optimizing $k$. Averaging over 5 weighted models did not improve results. Variance results for this dataset are missing because we performed each test only once (this is due to the high computational cost of the weighted method (34 parameters to optimize).

Poor result of the weighted model is probably due to the overfitting, since the number of parameters (34) is rather high for such small dataset (200 vectors). One of the reasons why averaging of weights may work is that it allows to avoid overfitting. Currently we have no validation test implemented in our software and the test is performed with the best weights found after the convergence of the minimization routine. Difficulty of finding good solutions in this large space may also be important. The simplex method reached accuracy on the training set that is about 5% higher than the multisimplex method (usually finding better solutions) but gave about 2% worse results on the test set.

Unfortunately differences on the training set were not reflected in improvements on the test set and there was no reduction of error using ensembles of 5 or 10 models. Other experiments performed with this dataset also indicate that accuracy on the training and the test set is not correlated. For comparison results of Shang and Breiman [14] obtained with boosted CART decision tree (DB-CART) and the C4.5 results are also provided.

**Table 3.** Results for the ionosphere data

| Method | Accuracy % |
|---|---|
| DB-CART | 91.3 |
| 1-NN, Euclidean | 92.1 |
| $k$-NN E10, Euclidean, $k = 1 \dots 10$ | 92.7 |
| C4.5 | 94.9 |
| 3-NN, Manhattan, | 96.7 |
| WM, Manhattan, $k$=3 | 95.3 |
| WM, Manhattan, $k$=3 (Multisimplex) | 97.3 |
| A5-WM, Manhattan $k$=3 | 96.7 |
| E5-WM,Manhattan $k$=3 | 96.7 |
| A5E10-WM,Manhattan $k$=3 | 96.7 |

The *hepatobiliary disorders* dataset has been obtained from the Tokyo Dental and Medical University. It has 536 cases of which 163 are used as test cases, 9 features (values of biochemical tests) and 4 classes. This data has been used previously by Mitra, De and Pal [15] using a knowledge-based fuzzy MLP system with results on the test set in the range from 33% to 66.3%, depending on the actual fuzzy model used.

$k$-NN with Manhattan distance function reaches 77.9% accuracy for this dataset. This is already much better than many other methods give [16]. For example MLP neural network trained with RPROP gives accuracy that is below 70%. After applying feature selection 4 features were removed (features 2, 5, 6 and 9), increasing accuracy to 80.4%. With ASA optimization the best weighted $k$-NN model achieved

**Table 4.** Results for the hepatobiliary disease data

| Method | Accuracy % | Variance % |
|---|---|---|
| LDA | 65.0 | – |
| C 4.5 | 75.5 | – |
| 1-NN, Manhattan | 77.9 | – |
| WNN, Manhattan, $k$=1 | 80.0 | ± 1.3 |
| A5-WM | 81.2 | ± 1.4 |
| E5-WM | 80.3 | ± 1.1 |
| A5E5-WM | 80.5 | ± 0.3 |
| A5E10-WM | 80.6 | ± 0.6 |

82.8% accuracy on the test set (83.4% on the training set). 5 averaged weighted $k$-NN methods gave better accuracy than ensembles or averaged ensembles, probably indicating that a better minimization should be used. These results are significantly better than those of all other classifiers applied to this data, including IB2-IB4, FOIL, LDA, DLVQ, C4.5, FSM and K* methods [16]. In particular poor results of the linear discrimination analysis should be noted.

**Table 5.** Results for the appendicitis data, using 10-fold stratified crossvalidation

| Method | Accuracy % | Variance % |
|---|---|---|
| 1-NN, Euclidean | 85.8 | ± 1.4 |
| 8-NN, Manhattan | 87.4 | ± 0.4 |
| A5E5-WM, $k$=8 | 86.2 | ± 1.1 |
| A5E10-WM, $k$=8 | 87.0 | ± 1.1 |

Appendicitis data, obtained from S. Weiss contains only 106 cases [18]. Since the data is too small to create separate test partition results given below were obtained from the 10-fold stratified crossvalidation tests. Since parameters of classification models may differ for each partition one could first optimize $k$ and than perform weight optimization. We are aiming at a stable model for the whole data, therefore we have averaged first over the number of neighbors and selected optimal features ($f_2$ and $f_4$ features were removed). Using the value of $k$ which was optimal for the largest number of partitions optimization of weights was performed for each partition and majority voting applied to the ensemble results.

The results of averaging and creating ensembles relatively to the single $k$=8 model have not been improved at all. They are already rather good: for comparison, accuracy of the C4.5 and CART in the leave-one-out tests is only 84.9% [18].

## 4 Conclusions and further work

Ensembles of models offer in some cases significant improvements over single classifiers but in other cases the results on the test set may get worse. The decrease of variance with the number of base classifiers may be slow. Averaging over model parameters - in this paper over feature weights – may help to decrease variance and sometimes gives better results than majority voting ensemble. Although sophisticated genetic-based models have been proposed to evolve the best subsets of models that should be included in ensembles [17] it is doubtful whether the added advantages justify the additional computational costs. Even the simplest majority voting method of combining $k$-NN models may significantly improve accuracy and stabilize results decreasing the variance of the final model.

For several datasets (except for the data described here we have tried sonar and hepatitis datasets from UCI [12]) the improvements have been insignificant. This shows that an ensemble of models of similar types may sometimes fail to improve the results. One reason for this may come from overfitting of the data (Ionosphere), another from poor correlation of results on the training and test sets. Full optimization of all model parameters in crossvalidation tests has not been done here ($k$ was selected first, independently of weights), and that could have contributed to poor results on the appendicitis dataset. On the other hand results on the noisy hepatobiliary disorders data were significantly improved. For all data presented here results of the similarity-based algorithms were much better than results of popular C4.5 and CART decision trees.

Different types of procedures/parameters should be included in the search space for the best classification model [1]. The results could be improved further by employing better global minimization routines such as the multisimplex [5] or ASA (Adaptive Simulated Annealing) [6] but this leads to much higher computational cost of weighted methods which are already very expensive.

A number of other improvements to the ensemble creation algorithm presented here are planned. First, the majority voting scheme should be replaced by a linear combination of models. Combining probabilities of classification for each model $M_l$ and using least square minimization procedure to determine coefficients of the combination may have some advantages. Second, the competence of each model should be included in the voting procedure, as described in the subsection on ensembles of competent models. Third, models of different type should be used in one ensemble. Fourth, boosting, bagging and other procedures [3,19] should help to create better pool of base models. We are currently investigating all these issues.

**Acknowledgments:** Support by the Polish Committee for Scientific Research, grant no. 8 T11E 042 19, is gratefully acknowledged.

## References

1. Duch, W. (1998): A framework for similarity-based classification methods. In: Intelligent Information Systems VII, Malbork, Poland, 288-291

2. Grudziński, K., Duch, W. (2000): SBL-PM: A Simple Algorithm for Selection of Reference Instances for Similarity-Based Methods. In: Intelligent Information Systems IIS'2000. Physica Verlag, Springer, Berlin, Heidelberg, New York, 99-108
3. Breiman, L. (1998): Bias-Variance, regularization, instability and stabilization. In: Bishop, C. (Ed.) Neural Networks and Machine Learning. Springer, Berlin, Heidelberg, New York
4. Wettschereck D., Aha, W., Mohri, T. (1997): A Review and Empirical Evaluation of Feature Weighting Methods for a Class of Lazy Learning Algorithms. Artificial Intelligence Review 11, 273-314
5. Gupta, H.V., Hsu, K., Sorooshian, S. (1997): Superior training of artificial neural networks using weight-space partitioning. In: Proc. of the Intern. Conf. Neural Networks (ICNN'97), Houston, 1919-1923
6. Ingberg, L. (1996): Adaptive simulated annealing (ASA): Lessons learned. J. Control and Cybernetics 25, 33-54
7. Bauer E., Kohavi, R. (1999): An empirical comparison of voting classfication algorithms: Bagging, Boosting and variants. Machine Learning 36, 105-139
8. Hinton, G. (2000): *Training products of experts by minimizing contrastive divergence.* Gatsby Computational Neuroscience Unit Technical Report 2000-004
9. Krogh, A., Vedelsby, J. (1995): Neural Network Ensembles, Cross Validation, and Active Learning. In: Advances in Neural Information Processing Systems 7, 231–238
10. Duch W., Grudziński K. (1999): Weighting and selection of features in Similarity-Based Methods. In: Intelligent Information Systems VIII, Ustroń, Poland, 32-36
11. Duch W., Grudziński K. (1999): Search and global minimization in similarity-based methods. In: Int. Joint Conference on Neural Networks (IJCNN), Washington, July 1999, paper no. 742
12. Mertz, C.J., Murphy, P.M., UCI repository of machine learning datasets, http://www.ics.uci.edu/AI/ML/MLDBRepository.html
13. Thrun S.B. *et al.* (1991): The MONK's problems: a performance comparison of different learning algorithms. Carnegie Mellon University, Technical Report CMU-CS-91-197
14. Shang N., Breiman, L. (1996): Distribution based trees are more accurate. Int. Conf. on Neural Information Processing, Hong Kong, Vol. I, 133-138
15. Mitra S., De R., Pal S. (1997): Knowledge based fuzzy MLP for classification and rule generation. IEEE Transactions on Neural Networks 8, 1338-1350
16. Duch, W., Adamczak, R., Grąbczewski, K., Żal, G., Hayashi, Y. (2000): Fuzzy and crisp logical rule extraction methods in application to medical data. In: P.S. Szczepaniak, P.J.G. Lisboa, J. Kacprzyk (eds.), Fuzzy systems in medicine. Physica - Verlag, Springer, Berlin, Heidelberg, New York, 593-616
17. Yao, X., Liu, Y. (1997): A New Evolutionary System for Evolving Artificial Neural Networks. IEEE Transaction on Neural Networks 8, 694–713
18. Weiss, S.M., Kapouleas, I. (1990): An empirical comparison of pattern recognition, neural nets and machine learning classification methods. In: Shavlik J.W., Dietterich, T.G., Readings in Machine Learning, Morgan Kauffman Publications, California
19. Opitz, D.W., Maclin, R. (1998): Popular ensemble methods: an empirical study, Journal of Artificial Intelligence Research 11, 169-198

# Regression - Yet Another Clustering Method

Piotr Gawrysiak, Michal Okoniewski, and Henryk Rybinski

Institute of Computer Science, Warsaw University of Technology
ul. Nowowiejska 15/19, 00-665 Warsaw, Poland

**Abstract.** The paper contains description of a new clustering methodology that partitions data set into clusters, such that regression indetermination coefficient for data from each cluster is minimized. A clustering algorithm that realizes this methodology with genetic programming approaches, as well as, some experimental results are presented. The application of the algorithm for planning cellular telephone networks is discussed.

**Keywords:** clustering, regression, data mining, cellular networks

## 1 Introduction

Regression is a widely used method for data analysis. Its applications range from assessing experimental data, through mathematical and econometric model building to advanced data mining, mainly as one of the methods of estimating a relationship between some attributes. While being effective and relatively simple method, regression can be applied only for data that are internally consistent. This means that only one function should exists that links attributes, or some of the data set elements have to be removed with residual analysis, if regression is to deliver satisfactory results. To illustrate the problem let us consider the following example:

**Example 1.** Imagine an ichthyology research, in which a population of fish is studied. The fish are indiscernible for the attributes such as shape, size, color etc. so one can assume that they belong to one species. The scientists investigate the effect of water temperature on average swimming speed of the fish. After several measurements they obtain a set of data, as depicted in Figure 1, and would like to build a function that links water temperature with fish speed.

A very rough approach would consist in finding the linear regression function for that data. The function allows us to claim that the speed of fish slowly goes down with the temperature, though the error of the regression is rather high.

There exists however another solution to this problem, namely clustering: after having made a closer look at the measured data one could think of splitting the fish population into two groups. Instead of finding a rough

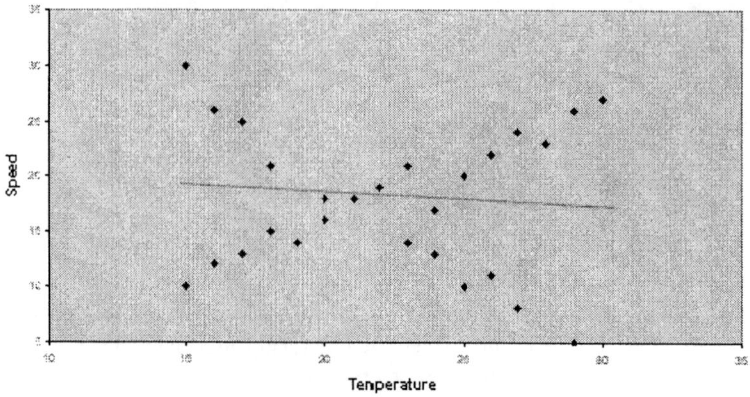


**Fig. 1.** Fish population analysis

regression function for the whole population, we should rather think in this case of applying clustering, which would result in minimizing the regression indetermination coefficient for each cluster separately. Then we should possibly find a new attribute, which would reflect splitting the fish population into two clusters, thus allowing us to classify the population better.

Therefore, if we assume that examined fish belong to two species, that react differently to temperature changes, we can build not one, but two linear regression functions. For each of these functions the indetermination coefficient can be close to zero, which means that these functions constitute a good model for experimental data. In our example the functions that minimize regression error have been depicted in Figure 2.

The solution described in the above example does not create problems, if the data set is small and can be manually processed before finding the regression function. We simply split data into two clusters and then compute the regression function for each cluster separately. Such functions would obviously provide us with much better "relationships" between the water temperature and fish speed attributes. Unfortunately in modern data mining applications it happens very seldom that data are small enough to be able to make the analysis manually. In most cases the whole analysis process must be automated, which makes any human intervention and manual data evaluation impossible.

The goal of the paper is to propose an algorithm, which automatically clusters data set into subsets, so that the regression indetermination coefficients for each subset are minimized. It is not an obvious task, as the regression quality cannot be converted into any kind of distance measure between the elements of the data set, though such a measure is necessary for classical clustering algorithms [1]. Also note that grouping data elements using distance measure (for example Euclidean or Chebyshev) on two-dimensional plane would not help in this case.

We show here how genetic algorithms can be used to solve this problem. We present a simple yet promising genetic clustering algorithm that uses the regression error as a cluster quality measure. The algorithm has been designed for the linear regression based clustering. It has been implemented and tested on data samples, which proved its potential usefulness. Possible extensions and improvements of the algorithm are discussed in the subsequent chapters.

Section 2 of the paper contains basic definitions of statistical concepts. In Section 3 the proposed algorithm together with sample results are overviewed. In Section 4 we discuss possible algorithm extensions for multiple regression., In Section 5 we discuss an application of the algorithm for planning cellular telephone networks. Finally, Section 6 contains conclusion and further research ideas.

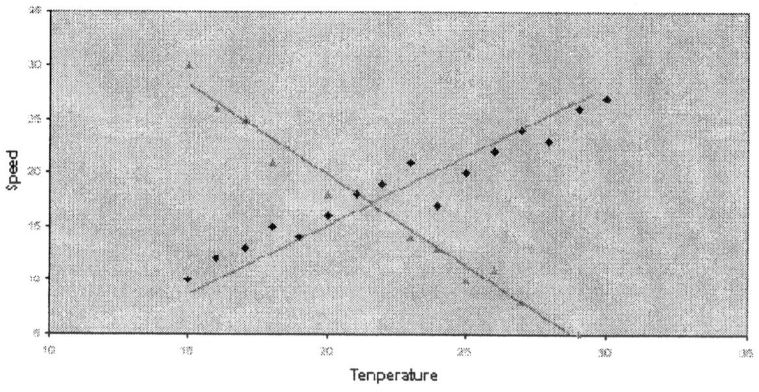


**Fig. 2.** Fish population analysis 2

## 2 Basic definitions

We recall here briefly the basic notions referring to the analysis method based on linear regression. For more detailed description see [2] and [3]. Linear regression is a method commonly used for finding a linear dependency between some attributes. It uses statistical data in a form of set of independent variable and dependent variable pairs $(x_i, y_i)$, to build a function:

$$\hat{y}(x) = ax + b \tag{1}$$

using least squares method.

Finding a linear regression function it is equivalent to finding a solution of two equations:

$$\sum_{i=1}^{n} y_i = a\sum_{i=1}^{n} x_i + nb \tag{2}$$

$$\sum_{i=1}^{n} x_i y_i = a\sum_{i=1}^{n} x_i^2 + b\sum_{i=1}^{n} x_i \tag{3}$$

The solution gives us values for the coefficients $a$ and $b$:

$$a = \frac{n\sum_{i=1}^{n} x_i y_i - \sum_{i=1}^{n} x_i \sum_{i=1}^{n} y_i}{n\sum_{i=1}^{n} x_i^2 - (\sum_{i=1}^{n} x_i)^2} \tag{4}$$

$$b = \frac{\sum_{i=1}^{n} y_i}{n} - \frac{a\sum_{i=1}^{n} x_i}{n} \tag{5}$$

In Example 1 the regression function computed this way has been plotted in Figure 1.

The regression quality is measured by the linear indetermination coefficient:

$$\phi^2 = \frac{\sum_{i=1}^{n}(y_i - \hat{y}_i)^2}{\sum_{i=1}^{n}(y_i - \bar{y})^2}\ ,\ \phi^2 \in \langle 0, 1\rangle \tag{6}$$

Referring to Example 1, the indetermination coefficient for the function as on Figure 1 is equal to 0.9987. It means that the two attributes - temperature and speed - have no linear relation.

## 3 Algorithm proposal and implementation

Humans easily do the analysis performed in Example 1, but for data mining purposes we need an automated system that would perform it. We can not use the regression function parameters as a measure of distance between data set items to perform for example k-means clustering or to build a clustering tree (see [1] for classical clustering methods description). We can however use it to compute cluster quality function, in other words a fit function for clusters. Hence to solve our problem we can apply genetic programming approach (see e.g. [4] and [5]), using cluster quality measure as a fitness function.

Below we present a framework of a clustering algorithm, which splits a data set into a predefined number of clusters. If we do not know a priori the number of clusters, we can use the algorithm repeatedly, as in iterative k-means clustering, to find the most effective solution.

To simplify our considerations let us assume that the input set of data has two attributes, and the number of clusters is two. Let D = {d1, d2, ..., dn} be the data set containing objects d=(x,y) to be clustered. Let U be the binary vector [u1, u2, ..., un] representing the distribution of the objects from D into two sets C1 and C2, so that

if ui = 0, di belongs to C1
if ui = 1, di belongs to C2

We denote by P the set of all possible vectors and call it *objects population.*

Now let R be the quadruple (a,b,c,d) representing the coefficients of two linear regression functions fr1 and fr2:

fr1 = ax+b and fr2 = cx+d

Note that the quadruple R can be also represented as a binary vector, by changing coefficient representation into binary numbers. We denote by Q the set of vectors R, and call it as *function population.*

Using the above definitions we can now write the algorithm for 2 clusters and two-dimensional space of data:

```
CLUSTER(D): populate P and Q with random data
 REPEAT
   FOR every vector from P as Ui
      create two data sets C1 and C2 containing
      objects from D grouped by Ui elements

      compute regression functions: f1 for objects
      from C1 and f2 for objects from C2

      compute indetermination coefficients fi1 and fi2
      for f1 and f2 respectively

      let max(fi1, fi2) be the fit function for Ui
   END;
   using the fit functions perform genetic operations on P

   for the best individual from P compute regression
   functions f1 and f2

   create individual R using coefficients from f1 and f2

   insert R into Q

   FOR every vector from Q as Ri
         FOR every element from D as di
             Let dist1 be the Euclidean distance
             from di to fr1 line

             Let dist2 be the Euclidean distance
             from di to fr2

             if dist1 > dist2  insert di into C2
             else insert di into C1
```

```
        END;
    compute the regression functions f1 for the
    objects from C1 and  f2 for the objects from C2

    estimate indetermination coefficients fi1 and fi2
    for f1 and f2

    let max(fi1, fi2) be the fit function for Ri
  END;
  using the fit functions perform the genetic
  operations on Q

  create individual Ux using the C1 and C2 distributions
  for the best individual from Q

  insert Ux into P

UNTIL indetermination coefficients are satisfactory;
```

This algorithm contains effectively two competing populations. One of them, represented by the set P contains individuals that evolve distribution of data set objects between clusters, while the second one - represented by the set Q - contains individuals evolving the regression functions. The best individuals are transferred (after conversion) between these two populations. The experiments show that the Q population allows for quick but rough estimation of clusters, while P population fine-tunes the solution.

This algorithm has been implemented in an experimental system and used for clustering small sets of data (200 data objects maximum). Some examples of the results are presented in Figure 3 and Figure 4.

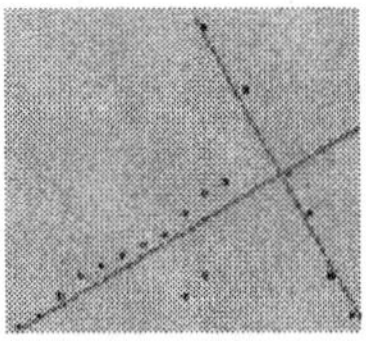

**Fig. 3.** Maximum indetermination coeff. = 0.08

## 4 Scaling-up the problem into multiple dimensions

For the practical use of this algorithm, one should be able to cope with objects characterized by more than two attributes. In such a multidimensional space it is much harder to discern linear trends. The multiple regression function

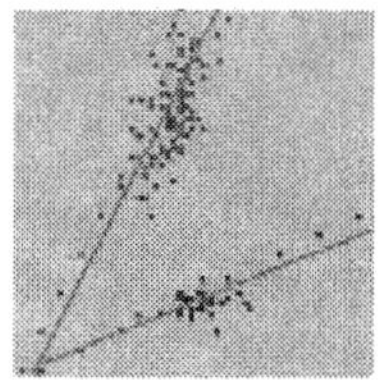

**Fig. 4.** Maximum indetermination coeff. = 0.35

has the form of a hyper-plane, thus is more difficult to imagine and visualize. That is why a multidimensional version is expected to reveal lots of interesting knowledge from numerical databases.

In the multiple regression a dependent variable is a vector:

$$y = \begin{bmatrix} y_1 \\ y_2 \\ \dots \\ y_n \end{bmatrix}$$

Independent variable $X$ is a matrix:

$$X = \begin{bmatrix} x_1 1 & x_1 2 & \dots & x_{1,k+1} \\ x_2 1 & x_2 2 & \dots & x_{2,k+1} \\ \dots & \dots & \dots & \dots \\ x_n 1 & x_n 2 & \dots & x_{n,k+1} \end{bmatrix}$$

$\beta$ is a vector of $k$ multiple regression coefficients, $\varepsilon$ is a vector of $n$ random addends. In this case the linear regression function has the form:

$$y = X\beta + \varepsilon \tag{7}$$

and the estimator of vector $\beta$ is

$$b = (x^T X)^{-1} X^T y \tag{8}$$

The linear indetermination coefficient has the form:

$$\phi = \sqrt{\frac{y^T y - b^T X^T y}{y^T y - \frac{1}{n}(\mathbf{1}^T y)^2}} \tag{9}$$

Scaling the algorithm may be a difficult task, because with the numbers $k$ and $n$ growing, the calculations on the above matrices, especially matrix inversion, are polynomialy hard. The only way seems to be the use of the regression approximation algorithm [2].

There are plenty of possible applications of the clustering algorithms with multiple regression, not to mention such examples like banking analyses, demographics or engineering. In the next chapter we describe an application, which actually originated the presented idea of clustering. The application is concerned with modeling the traffic in cellular telephone network.

## 5 Applications for cellular network planning

The idea of using regression in clustering has been inspired by the data mining project performed by a team at Warsaw University of Technology for one of the Polish cellular telecom operators [6]. One of the problems encountered during the implementation of the project was prediction of the traffic for GSM cells.

The network expansion is one of the most important activities for a young cellular telecom provider. It creates a big demand for optimal prediction of the traffic. The operator would like to estimate the number of calls that would be generated over a certain time span on the area where the expansion is planned and new base station are proposed. Such information is crucial for the optimal design of the station equipment - there must be enough transceivers to ensure that every subscriber in the GSM cell created by this station is able to place or receive a call. On the other hand, there should not be too much unused radio channels, because this would mean unnecessary costs.

As a starting point, for our analysis we have extracted geographical information1 about the existing GSM cells, together with measured traffic values averaged over certain period. In the company's GIS database a classification schema was used for the terrain types. It was one of the characteristics of the existing cells. The classification was a result of a priori intuition, rather than any statistical or data mining experiments. Roughly the classification contained the following classes.

{Fields, Forests, Water, (Rocks, Seashores, Swamps), (Roads, Concrete, Parks), Suburbs, Urban, Dense urban, Industrial}

Using data from GIS, as the first step we have applied multiple regression analysis to estimate traffic value for each cell. As expected, the quality of prediction was quite poor, for the same reasons that were illustrated in Example 1. Therefore we have decided to cluster cells using an extended variant of the algorithm sketched in this paper. The resulting clusters not only allowed us to improve prediction accuracy (now the result reaches 85% of accuracy with less than 10 clusters), but also helped to find out better classification schema for the cells for subsequent experiments. More details about the experiment may be found in [7].

## 6 Conclusion

The method described in this paper should not be treated as an universal clustering methodology. Partitioning of the data set, achieved by using the algorithm turns out to be useful in special situations, mostly when classical regression analysis gives unsatisfactory results, in spite of the belief that there should be strong correlation between data set elements.

The presented clustering method is probably most useful for mining in numerical data from purely technical applications. It is indeed still a largely unexplored area of automatic knowledge discovery, where our insight about collected data, as well as visualization and manual analysis capabilities are limited. This kind of data mining applications are very different from that experienced in classical, i.e. related to marketing or customer care, data mining [8].

The algorithm presented here is in its first stage of development. First of all it should be extended to include other than linear regression function fitting. Finding a method for automatic selection of the number of clusters would also be very desirable. Improvements have to be done to genetic population representation and fit function, as the currently used Max function is probably not the optimal solution. Finally the genetic operations used in the experimental implementation can be improved.

In [7] another clustering method in the context of linear regression has been proposed. It was an extension to K-means clustering. One of the next steps in our research will also be an evaluation of the two methods and finding out the application areas for them.

**Acknowledgements**: We would like to thank all members of the Data Mining team at Warsaw University of Technology, especially Professor Mieczysşaw Muraszkiewicz, for help given during the preparation of this paper.

## References

1. Duran, B.S, Odell, P.L (1974) Cluster Analysis - A Survey. Lecture Notes in Economics and Mathematical Systems, Vol. 100
2. Statsoft Inc.: (2000): Electronic Statistics Textbook. Tulsa, http://www.statsoft.com/textbook/stathome.html
3. Netter, J., Wasserman, W., Whitmore, G.A., (1993) Applied Statistics. Allyn and Bacon, pages 531-649
4. Back T., (1996) Evolutionary Algorithms in Theory and Practice. Oxford University Press
5. Michalewicz, Z.,(1996) Genetic Alghorithms + Data Structures = Evolution Programs. Springer Verlag
6. W. Daszczuk, P. Gawrysiak, Gerszberg, T., Kryszkiewicz, M., MielJcicki, J., Muraszkiewicz, M., Okoniewski, M., Rybiñski, H., Traczyk, T., Walczak, Z., (2000) Data Mining for Technical Operation of Telecommunications Companies: a Case Study. 4th World Multiconference on Systemics, Cybernetics and Informatics (SCI'2000)
7. Gawrysiak, P., Okoniewski, M., (2000) Applying data mining methods for cellular radio network planning. Intelligent Information Systems Conference 2000
8. Berry, M.J.A., Linoff, G., (1997) Data Mining Techniques: For Marketing, Sales, and Customer Support. John Wiley & Sons

# Taxonomy Building: Cases or Attributes ?

Mieczyslaw A. Klopotek

[1] Institute of Computer Science, Polish Academy of Sciences, Warsaw, Poland
[2] Institute of Computer Science, University of Podlasie, Siedlce, Poland

**Abstract.** This paper analyses properties of conceptual hierarchy obtained via incremental concept formation method called "flexible prediction" in order to determine what kind of "relevance" of participating attributes may be requested for meaningful conceptual hierarchy. The impact of selection of simple and combined attributes, of scaling and of distribution of individual attributes and of correlation strengths among them is investigated.
Paradoxically, both: attributes weakly and strongly related with other attributes have deteriorating impact onto the overall classification. Proper construction of derived attributes as well as selection of scaling of individual attributes strongly influences the obtained concept hierarchy. Attribute density of distribution seems to influence the classification weakly
It seems also, that concept hierarchies (taxonomies) reflect a compromise between the data and our interests in some objective truth about the data.
To obtain classifications more suitable for one's purposes, concept hierarchy of attributes rather than of objects should be looked for. A proposal of bayesian network based clustering is proposed.
Keywords: incremental concept formation; relevance of attributes; statistical and probabilistic aspects;

## 1 Introduction

Most knowledge discovery methods strive to obtain a kind of explicit (by dividing the set of observed objects into sets) or implicit (by deriving a dependence function between attributes of objects) "clustering" of objects based on a kind of "similarity" of them. There exist numerous statistical clustering methods (single linkage, k-means, ...) as well as ones elaborated within artificial intelligence community (conceptual clustering, incremental concept formation, ... and many others). Many seem to share one common feature: complaints about impact of "irrelevant" attributes which worsen the satisfaction with the resulting clustering.

This paper tries to shed some light into the question what that "irrelevance" may mean. To make the presentation of our position more clear, we concentrate of the method of incremental concept formation proposed by Fisher and colleges, called "flexible prediction". In section 2 we recall basic concepts of this method. In section 3, recalling our own results, we demonstrate that "relevance" means cheapness in achieving ones goals. In section 4 we demonstrate the impact of scaling of an attribute onto its "relevance". In sections 5,6 we show the impact of uniform probability distribution on classification process. Section 7 shows that pairs of strongly interrelated variables can dominate the overall classification. Section 8 summarizes our investigation and presents a proposal of modification of the approach to clustering tasks.

## 2 Purpose and Method of "Flexible Prediction" Paradigm

Fisher and colleges [2–8] proposed a new type of clustering called "flexible prediction"., which has been implemented in their COBWEB system (currently extended in ECOBWEB). The goal of clustering via "flexible prediction" is to obtain such a hierarchy of concepts that the probability of prediction of sub-class membership from the value of a single parameter is maximized together with the probability of prediction of the value of the attribute from sub-class membership. The optimization criterion was: maximize the function [4]:

$$eval = M^{-1}\left(\sum_{C_i} p(C_i) \sum_{A_j \in \mathtt{D}} \sum_{V_{jk}} p(A_j = V_{jk}|C_i)^2 - \sum_{A_j \in \mathtt{D}} \sum_{V_{jk}} p(A_j = V_{jk})^2\right) \tag{1}$$

with:

| | |
|---|---|
| D | - set of discrete attributes |
| $p(C_i)$ | - probability that an object belongs to Sub-category $C_i$ |
| $p(A_j = V_{jk})$ | - probability that the discrete parameter $A_j$ takes the value $V_{jk}$. |
| $p(A_j = V_{jk}\|C_i)$ | - respective conditional probability within the sub-category $C_i$ |
| M | - number of sub-categories. |

The concept hierarchy is developed incrementally, with each new object in a sequence being classified on the top level into one of the existing classes or a separate one is created for it depending on which operation will maximize the above expression. The same is repeated on sublevels of the hierarchy.

Applicability for diagnosis of plant diseases was claimed [5].

Gennari et al. [8] extended this methodology to continuous attributes claiming success both for artificial and natural domain examples ("forming diagnostically useful categories"). The optimization criterion for concept hierarchy was [8]:

$$eval = M^{-1}\left(\sum_{C_i} p(C_i) \sum_{A_j \in \mathtt{K}} 1/\sigma_{A_j C_i} - \sum_{A_j \in \mathtt{K}} 1/\sigma_{A_j}\right) \tag{2}$$

with:

| | |
|---|---|
| K | - set of continuous attributes |
| $\sigma_{A_j}$ | - standard deviation continuous parameter $A_j$ |
| $\sigma_{A_j C_i}$ | - respective standard deviation within the sub-category $C_i$ |
| M | - number of sub-categories. |

Gennari et al. [8] derived their formula - up to a constant factor depending on probability distribution considered - from Fisher's one eqn(1) by substituting unconditional and conditional probabilities may be substituted by the respective probability density functions and summing with integration.

## 3 All Relevant versus Some Relevant

Developers of "flexible prediction" paradigm noticed that irrelevant attributes negatively influence the quality of the obtained hierarchy. One shall however ask what does it mean that the attribute is irrelevant.

In a study, reported in [9] we assumed that a set of binary attributes $A_1,...,A_n$ (n less than 10) be relevant for a diagnostic task (previously studied using statistical methods). We made the naive assumption that if two attributes $A_i$, $A_j$ are relevant, then their logical conjunction $A_i \wedge A_j$, disjuction $A_i \vee A_j$ and negation $\neg A_j$ should also be relevant. In this way we built all the anywhere distinct boolean functions of the relevant attributes. Starting with the set of "relevant" attributes we tried to construct the classification hierarchy of objects. It turned out that the optimization criterion eqn.(1) drove each object into a separate case unless two objects were characterized by exactly the same values of given attributes: any two objects proved to be equally similar to one another. The proof that this tendency is an intrinsic property of the flexible prediction algorithm is given in [9].

Clearly, our set of derived attributes contained such absurd functions as always true and always false ones, but even if one drops them, the situation does not improve in any way. The lesson from that study is that in order to obtain a concept hierarchy we need first to ponder some attributes from the space of primary and derived relevant attributes. One may do it on the grounds of e.g. importance for our target task (more weight for more important ones) and/or on costs of measurement of a given attribute (more weight for "cheaper" attributes). But doing so we pre-specify the concept hierarchy we will derive from our data. And if we would like to get a different concept hierarchy, a different pondering of the same set of attributes for the very same set of data will do. We need only to outline our concept hierarchy in terms of class membership of clustered objects, and then appropiately ponder the (derived) attributes describing each class (assigning significantly larger weights to higher hierarchy levels). Hence we gain real knowledge from the data only in that case where we do attribute pondering prior to seeing the data.
By the way, this is exactly what statisticians always insist on: define statistical tests you want to perform before you start collecting the data.

# 4 Attributes Equally Pondered and the Effect of Rescaling

Usually we have no other choice but to decide which attributes are the basis of the clustering to be performed now. Within this set of attributes it is natural to assume the same pondering (weighting). We will consider both optimization criterion (1) and (2) to evaluate them from this point of view.

It seems that in formula (2) authors pretended to obtain only a formal and visual similarity with (1). To obtain scale-free property, however, the shape of the formula for continuous attributes should be a little bit different.

$$eval' = \overline{K}^{-1} \sum_{C_i} p(C_i) \sum_{A_j \in K} \frac{\sigma_{A_j}}{\sigma_{A_j C_i}} - 1 \tag{3}$$

This formula assures the same result for any linear transformation (i.e.scale) of attributes which were taken into account.

However, the need of "scale-freedom" effect is not bound to continuous attributes only.

The scaling effect for discrete attributes will be demonstrated by the following example: Let us consider the attribute A taking 6 different values $v_1, v_2, v_3, v_4, v_5, v_6$. Then its contribution to the evaluation function (eqn.(1)) is:

$$eval_A = \sum_{C_i} p(C_i) \sum_{k=1}^{6} p(A = v_k|C_i)^2 - \sum_{k=1}^{6} p(A = v_k)^2 \tag{4}$$

Let us "rescale" this attribute as to obtain an attribute B taking values $w_1, w_2, w_3$ as follows: B= $w_1$ iff A= $v_1$ or A= $v_6$, B= $w_2$ iff A= $v_2$ or A= $v_5$, B= $w_3$ iff A= $v_3$ or A= $v_4$. Then B contributes:

$$eval_B = \sum_{C_i} p(C_i) \sum_{k=1}^{3} p(B = w_k|C_i)^2 - \sum_{k=1}^{3} p(B = w_k)^2 \tag{5}$$

$$= \sum_{C_i} p(C_i) \sum_{k=1}^{3} p(A = v_k or A = v_{7-k}|C_i)^2 - \sum_{k=1}^{3} p(A = v_k or A = v_{7-k})^2$$

Squaring out gives us (taking into account that probability of disjoint events equals sum of probabilities of the events):

$$\begin{aligned} eval_B = eval_A + \textstyle\sum_{C_i} p(C_i) \sum_{k=1}^{3} 2p(A = v_k|C_i)p(A = v_{7-k}|C_i) \\ - \textstyle\sum_{k=1}^{3} 2p(A = v_k)p(A = v_{7-k}) \end{aligned} \tag{6}$$

Since $p(A = v_k|C_i)$ for each k=1,2,...,6 can be treated as a function having as its domain the set of subcategories $\{C_i\}$, one can consider the following random variable:

$$Y_k == p(A = v_k|C_I) = y_k(I)$$

I is the indicator random variable. One can check that expectation of $Y_k$

$$E(Y_k) = p(A = v_k), \qquad k = 1, 2, ..., 6$$

It follows from (6) therefore that

$$eval_A = eval_b - 2\sum_{k=1}^{3} cov(y_k(I), y_{7-k}(I)) \tag{7}$$

Let us consider now the reverse rescaling procedure: we start with the attribute B and afterwards we are trying to split its 3 values into 6. The intuition suggests us that if way of splitting does not take into account any information about membership of the record to certain subcategory $C_i$ then no change should result in the evaluation function.

We model "non-informative splitting" in the following way.

First we randomly generate the record according to probabilities of subcategories (i.e. $\{p(C_i)\}$). Realization of the random variable I is given, therefore at this stage. From other point of view a subcategory is chosen first.

One can observe that evaluation function for discrete attributes does not depend on any one-to-one transformation of values of attributes. It follows therefore that "non-informative splitting" can have only the numeric effect if the probability

$$p(B = w_k|C_i)$$

is split in a random way in two parts.

If the splitting is performed in the second stage of random generation procedure we always would have a negative correlation between the components

$$p(A = v_k|C_i) + p(A = v_{7-k}|C_i)$$

of $p(B = w_k|C_i)$.

It follows then from (7) that evaluation function for the attribute with more values is higher than for that with fewer values. All 3 co variances are negative.

Such result is difficult to take as rational. The attribute A add no classification information when comparing with B.

## 5 Unbounded Splitting of a Class for Uniformly Distributed Continuous Attributes

In this section we will consider somewhat ideal clustering situation in the case of continuous attributes.

Assume that each attribute $A_j$ takes values in the interval of the length $\Delta_j$. The behaviour of attributes is very positive and clear from the point of view of distinguishing subcategories $C_i$. This behaviour is formalized in the following way.

Each attribute for the whole population has the uniform distribution within its interval. For the subcategories attributes take values only within intervals of the lengths which corresponds to probability of the subcategory. It means that attribute $A_j$ for subcategory $C_i$ has values within the interval of length:

$$\Delta_j \cdot P(C_i)$$

For given attribute open subintervals which represent M subcategories are assumed to be disjoint. The value of attribute gives therefore the sure classification of the object (record) which corresponds to this value.

To conclude the description of the above ideal situation one can notice that distribution for subcategory (i.e., conditional distribution for records within $C_i$) must be uniform either.

The elementary calculations lead to the following simple expression of evaluation function (2) and (3):

$$eval_{in(2)} = \frac{(M-1)2\sqrt{3}}{M} \sum_{A_j \in K} \frac{1}{\Delta_j} \tag{8}$$

$$eval_{in(3)} = M - 1 \tag{9}$$

The second result for the idealized clustering situation seems to be more rational than for the first one. The proposed evaluation function depends neither on the domains of attributes nor on their number. Actually the entire clustering information is included in one attribute. All attributes are copies of each other from this point of view.

Of course the lengths $\Delta_j$ have nothing to do with precision of clustering. The precision is higher, however, for the attribute which classifies 3 subcategories than for attribute classifying 2 clusters. So it seems rational that the form (9) has stronger relationship with M than (8).

## 6 Shift of Mass Between Classes of Different Density

Let us check one more aspect of attribute behavior. Let us approximate the overall attribute distribution with pieces of uniform density (e.g. a histogram). Let us examine the optimization tendency of the splitting criterion. Let us consider the following experiment:
Let us take two "neighboring" classes $C_1, C_2$: two uniformly distributed neighboring intervals (densities $D_1$ and $D_2$ respectively) with lengths b and a. The contribution of these intervals to the evaluation is:
$p(C_1) = D_1 * b, p(C_2) = D_2 * a, \sigma_{AC_1} = (2\sqrt{3})^{-1}b, \sigma_{AC_2} = (2\sqrt{3})^{-1}a$, hence:

$$M^{-1}\left((p(C_1)/\sigma_{AC_1} + p(C_2)/\sigma_{AC_2}) - 1/\sigma_A\right) =$$

$$M^{-1}\left(\left(D_1 * b/((2\sqrt{3})^{-1}b) + D_2 * a/((2\sqrt{3})^{-1}a)\right) - 1/\sigma_A\right) = \tag{10}$$

$$M^{-1}\left(\left(D_1 * 2\sqrt{3} + D_2 * 2\sqrt{3}\right) - 1/\sigma_A\right)$$

This actually means the following: the contribution of a attribute depends on the densities of intervals and not on their widths. We want next to optimize the criterion by shifting the boundary between the intervals increasing the class $C_1$ at the expense of the class $C_2$ so that $C_2$ consists only of an interval with width a-x and density $D_2$, and $C_1$ consists of an interval with length $b$ and density $D_1$ and an interval $x$ with density $D_2$. It is obvious that the contribution of $C_2$ to the evaluation function will remain the same so we need only to consider the class $C_1$. We will try to find out what value shall be taken by $x$.

For consideration of standard deviation within class $C_1$ we need to rescale the densities $D_1, D_2$ of subintervals b and x to $d_1 2, d_2$ so that $d_1 b + d_2 x = 1$. Variance of $C_1$ then equals to:

$$\sigma^2_{AC_1} = \int_{-b}^{0} d_1 y^2 dy + \int_{0}^{x} d_2 y^2 dy - \left(\int_{-b}^{0} d_1 y dy + \int_{0}^{x} d_2 y dy -\right)^2 =$$

$$= d_1 b^3/3 + d_2 x^3/3 - (-d_1 b^2/2 + d_2 x^2/2)^2 =$$

$$= d_1 \frac{b^3}{3} + d_2 \frac{x^3}{3} - d_1^2 \frac{b^4}{4} - d_2^2 \frac{x^4}{4} + 2 d_1 d_2 \frac{b^2 x^2}{4}$$

We introduce the coefficient $q$ such that $d_2 = q d_1$, then $d_1(b + qx) = 1$, Just $d_1 = \frac{1}{b+qx}$, $d_2 = \frac{q}{b+qx}$. With this substitution we get:

$$\sigma^2_{AC_1} == \frac{1}{b+qx}\frac{b^3}{3} + \frac{q}{b+qx}\frac{x^3}{3} - \frac{1}{(b+qx)^2}\frac{b^4}{4} - \frac{q^2}{(b+qx)^2}\frac{x^4}{4} + 2\frac{q}{(b+qx)^2}\frac{b^2x^2}{4}$$

Probability of class $C_1$ is now $p_{C_1} = D_1 * b + D_2 * x$ with $D_2/D_1 = d_2/d_1 = q$, hence

$$p_{C_1}/\sigma_{AC_1} = \frac{D_1}{\sqrt{\frac{1}{(b+qx)^3}\frac{b^3}{3} + \frac{q}{(b+qx)^3}\frac{x^3}{3} - \frac{1}{(b+qx)^2}\frac{b^4}{4} - \frac{q^2}{(b+qx)^4}\frac{x^4}{4} + 2\frac{q}{(b+qx)^4}\frac{b^2x^2}{4}}} \tag{11}$$

To maximize the quotient, the denominator, hence the squared denominator must be minimized. The derivative $d(squareddenominator)/dx = q * (1 - q) * (b + qx)^{-5} b^2 x(b + x)$. will be negative (hence steadily falling with increase of x) iff q exceeds 1 which means $d_1 < d_2$ , which means that lower density intervals will swallow higher density ones. We see that mutual prediction tends to isolate extremely narrow modes from a multimodal distribution. We have here again a lesson that discretization of the predicted attribute is essential.

## 7 Overfitting a Continuous Attribute

Let us consider again the discrete mutual prediction function of [5] for a selected attribute A and the classifying variable C:

$$\sum_x \sum_y p(A=y) \cdot \cdot (A=y|C=x) * p(C=x|A=y) = \sum_x \sum_y \frac{p(A=y \wedge C=x)^2}{p(C=x)}$$

Let us generalize it to a continuous "classification" variable C and continuous attribute A connected by a bivariate normal distribution:

$$\int_{-\infty}^{\infty} \int_{-\infty}^{\infty} \frac{\left(\frac{1}{2\Pi\sqrt{1-R^2}\sigma_x\sigma_y} \exp\left(\frac{1}{2(1-R^2)}\left((\frac{x-\mu_x}{\sigma_x})^2 - 2R(\frac{x-\mu_{A_j}}{\sigma_x})(\frac{y-\mu_y}{\sigma_y}) + (\frac{y-\mu_y}{\sigma_y})^2\right)\right)\right)^2}{\frac{1}{\sqrt{2\Pi}\sigma_x} \exp\left(\frac{1}{2}(\frac{x-\mu_x}{\sigma_x})^2\right)}$$

$$dxdy = \left(2\sigma_y\sqrt{\Pi}\sqrt{1-2R^2}\right)^{-1} \qquad (12)$$

The resulting formula points at the following:

- Dependence on attribute scale $\sigma$ - the larger the range of attribute values, the smaller attribute variance the higher its importance
- Dependence on correlation: the stronger the correlation (closer to 0.7!!!!) the higher the attribute importance.

REMARK: for correlations over 0.7 - nonsense values. 0.7*0.7=0.49. - if C gets closer to A (higher correlation) then the term concerning A in Fisher's evaluation function will absolutely dominate the whole expression, hence overfitting towards one of the attributes is guaranteed.

We shall conclude from this case study in "continuous classification" that strongly interrelated attributes can dominate the classification hierarchy so that they will disable it to predict values of other attributes of interest. Therefore when designing an evaluation function for a set of relevant attributes, if we want to have a balanced mutual prediction capability, correlation between the classification and each attribute of interest should negatively influence the weight of that attribute in the classification evaluation function.

## 8 In Search for Reasonable Alternatives

In this paper the flexible prediction (FP) paradigm for knowledge discovery from a set of cases has been studied. It has been demonstrated that:

- the optimization criterion of FP drives each object into a separate case unless two objects were characterized by exactly the same values of given attributes: any two objects proved to be equally similar to one another, if we take primary relevant attributes and all their derived attributes,

- for uniformly distributed continuous attributes the optimization function behaves in a not optimal way
- mutual prediction paradigm of COBWEB evaluation function tends to isolate extremely narrow modes from a multimodal distribution for continuous attributes
- the importance of an attribute in the optimization depends on its scale in an unwanted way
- the importance of an attribute in the optimization depends on its correlation with the classification criterion: the stronger the correlation the higher the attribute importance.

As attributes as such cannot be considered as objectively given, the derived concept hierarchy does not reflect any state of real world, but is rather a combination threreof and of our personal beliefs, with beliefs being in position of outweighing the real world evidence. Threfore it is better to consider a hierarchy of attributes that will be clustered by the real world cases.

We would like to propose below such a characterization based on bayesian networks.

Bayesian networks are a representation of joint probability distribution. Hence they describe global relationships among all attributes involved. Many methods, including Chow/Liu algorithm [1], enforce connection between attributes even poorly related to one another. "Concept hierarchy" of attributes may be a chance to visualize these relationships in a more systematic way.

The Chow/Liu algorithm works in the following way: it selects a pair X,Y of attributes with the largest distance DEP(X,Y) ($DEP(X,Y) = \sum_{x,y} P(x,y) \cdot \log \frac{P(x,y)}{P(x) \cdot P(y)}$) and treats this pair as a "seed tree" for the subsequent incremental construction of a tree. In the incremental part nodes still not included are added to the existent tree based on maximalization of the DEP(X,Y) criterion where X is in the tree, and Y not.

It is easily verified that such a policy causes some nodes to be connected to nodes that are objectiovely not the closes ones, if the intrinsic probability distribution does not stem from a tree-like distribution.

An attribute hierarchy may be created to avoid this problem. Consider the following procedure: At a node of hierarchy first select a pair X,Y of attributes with the largest distance DEP(X,Y). Insert them into the first subnode. Then find select a pair X,Y of attributes with the largest distance DEP(X,Y) such that X is still not in any subnode (Y maybe or maybe not, if the maximum number of subnodes is reached, Y must be from one of the subnodes). If X,Y both do not belong to any subnode, create a new subnode for X,Y. Otherwise insert X into the subnode of Y. If all attributes fall into the same subnode of the hierarchy, terminate growing the hiewrarchy from the node. Otherwise proceed the same way with the subnodes.

Consider for example the bayesian network in Fig.1 created by the Chow/Liu algorithm. If we assume the limitation of at most 2 subnodes, then a hierarchy of attributes will be grown in two steps as indicated in Fig.2 and Fig.3.

We can easily verify the following properties:

**The measure is extendable to continuous attributes**

We can apply the following procedure: We discretize the continuous attribute first e.g. into two subintervals, calculate DEP(X,Y), then reinterate the process subdividing the intervals into two parts until the value converges or the number of elements in the interval falls below a lower bound. If we assume that the joint distribution in X,Y is normal with correlation coefficient R, then we can estimate the limit value for DEP(X,Y) as

$$\int_{-\infty}^{\infty}\int_{-\infty}^{\infty} dxdy\frac{1}{2\Pi\sqrt{1-R^2}\sigma_x\sigma_y}e^{\left(\frac{1}{2(1-R^2)}\left((\frac{x-\mu_x}{\sigma_x})^2-2R(\frac{x-\mu_{A_j}}{\sigma_x})(\frac{y-\mu_y}{\sigma_y})+(\frac{y-\mu_y}{\sigma_y})^2\right)\right)}$$

$$log\frac{dxdy\frac{1}{2\Pi\sqrt{1-R^2}\sigma_x\sigma_y}e^{\left(\frac{1}{2(1-R^2)}\left((\frac{x-\mu_x}{\sigma_x})^2-2R(\frac{x-\mu_{A_j}}{\sigma_x})(\frac{y-\mu_y}{\sigma_y})+(\frac{y-\mu_y}{\sigma_y})^2\right)\right)}}{dx\frac{1}{\sqrt{2\Pi}\sigma_x}\exp\left(\frac{1}{2}(\frac{x-\mu_x}{\sigma_x})^2\right)dy\frac{1}{\sqrt{2\Pi}\sigma_y}\exp\left(\frac{1}{2}(\frac{y-\mu_y}{\sigma_y})^2\right)}dxdy =$$

$$= \int_{-\infty}^{\infty}\int_{-\infty}^{\infty} dxdy\frac{1}{2\Pi\sqrt{1-R^2}\sigma_x\sigma_y}$$

$$e^{\left(\frac{1}{2(1-R^2)}\left((\frac{x-\mu_x}{\sigma_x})^2-2R(\frac{x-\mu_{A_j}}{\sigma_x})(\frac{y-\mu_y}{\sigma_y})+(\frac{y-\mu_y}{\sigma_y})^2\right)\right)}$$

$$\left(log(\frac{1}{\sqrt{1-R^2}})\right.$$

$$+\left(\frac{1}{2(1-R^2)}\left((\frac{x-\mu_x}{\sigma_x})^2-2R(\frac{x-\mu_{A_j}}{\sigma_x})(\frac{y-\mu_y}{\sigma_y})+(\frac{y-\mu_y}{\sigma_y})^2\right)\right)$$

$$\left.-\left(\frac{1}{2}(\frac{x-\mu_x}{\sigma_x})^2\right)-\left(\frac{1}{2}(\frac{y-\mu_y}{\sigma_y})^2\right)\right) =$$

$$= log(\frac{1}{\sqrt{1-R^2}}) \tag{13}$$

We see immediately that **the measure is scale insensitive** from the above formula for continuous attributes. For discrete ones one may think that attributes X and X' are identical except that the value $x_1$ of the attribute X is split into two values $x_1'$ $x_1$" of X' randomly with proportions p:(1-p). Now:

$$DEP(X',Y) = P(x_1',y)\cdot\log\frac{P(x_1',y)}{P(x_1')\cdot P(y)} + P(x_1",y)\cdot\log\frac{P(x_1",y)}{P(x_1")\cdot P(y)} +$$

$$+\sum_{other\ x,y} P(x,y)\cdot\log\frac{P(x,y)}{P(x)\cdot P(y)} =$$

$$= p\cdot P(x_1,y)\cdot\log\frac{p\cdot P(x_1,y)}{p\cdot P(x_1)\cdot P(y)} + (1-p)\cdot P(x_1",y)\cdot\log\frac{(1-p)\cdot P(x_1,y)}{(1-p)\cdot P(x_1)\cdot P(y)} +$$

$$+\sum_{other\ x,y} P(x,y)\cdot\log\frac{P(x,y)}{P(x)\cdot P(y)} =$$

$$= P(x_1, y) \cdot \log \frac{P(x_1, y)}{P(x_1) \cdot P(y)} + \sum_{other\ x,y} P(x, y) \cdot \log \frac{P(x, y)}{P(x) \cdot P(y)} = DEP(X, Y)$$

That is, adding random noice does not change on average the distance DEP(X,Y). It is straightforward that **the measure can be applied to combination of discrete and continuous attributes.**

Analogous procedures may be elaborated for other classical bayesian network learning algorithms.

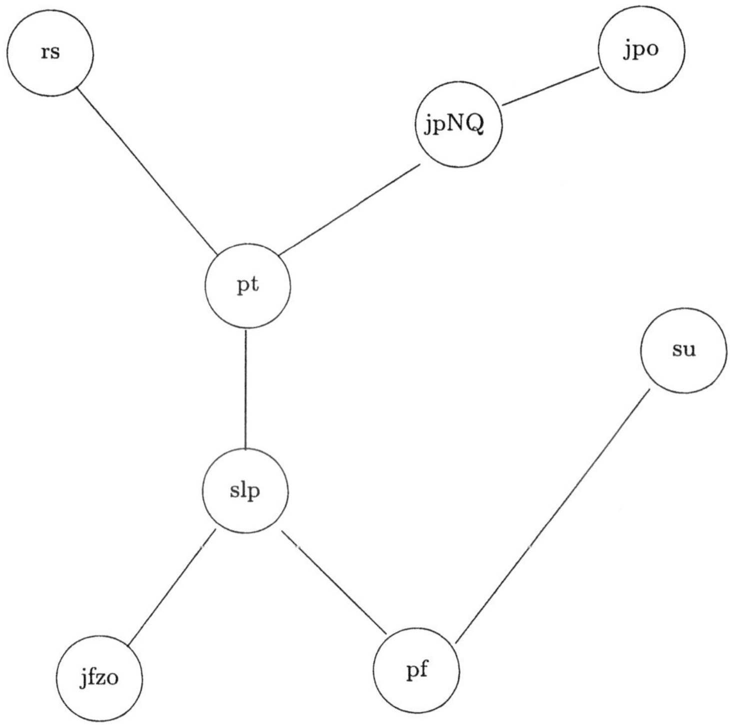


**Fig. 1.** The original Chow/Liu

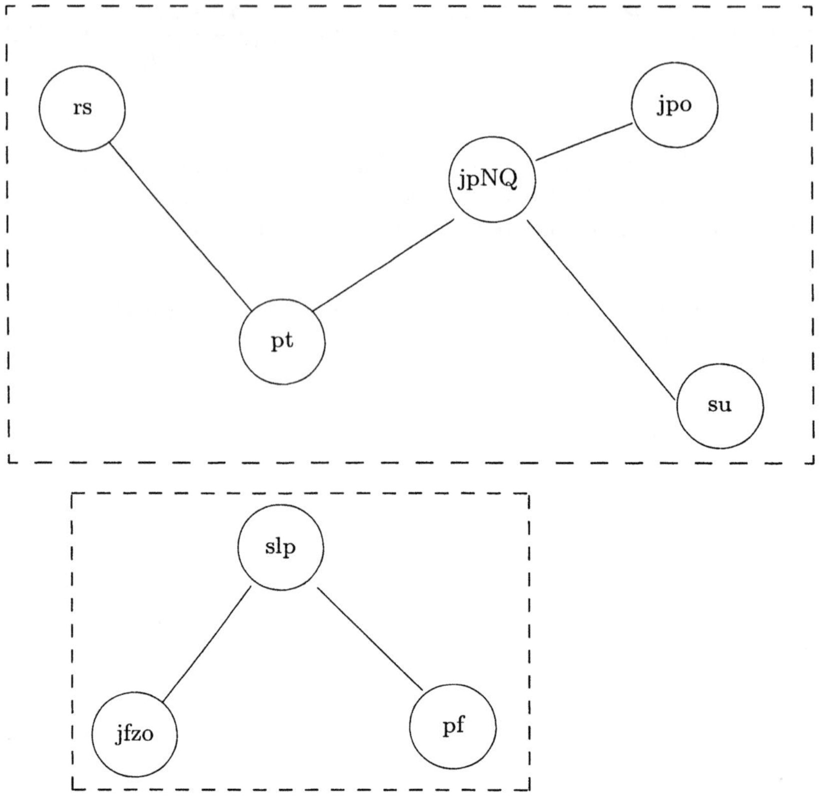


**Fig. 2.** The hierarchy growing with subnode limitation =2, step 1

It becomes immediately obvious that

- Objects are not separated as each node of the hierarchy is always based on the entire database. Also attributes will not be isolated as at least two will be kept in a single node.
- Whatever set of derived attributes is taken, a given pair of attributes will fall into structurally similar subparts of the tree. Added or missing attributes can drive them more apart or more close but remain in the same area of the tree when a homomorpohism is applied.
- Though bayesian networks do not handle in general continuous attributes (e.g. Chow/Liu [1]), some do (e.g. TETRAD [12]), and it is possible to make clustring also over these continuous variables.

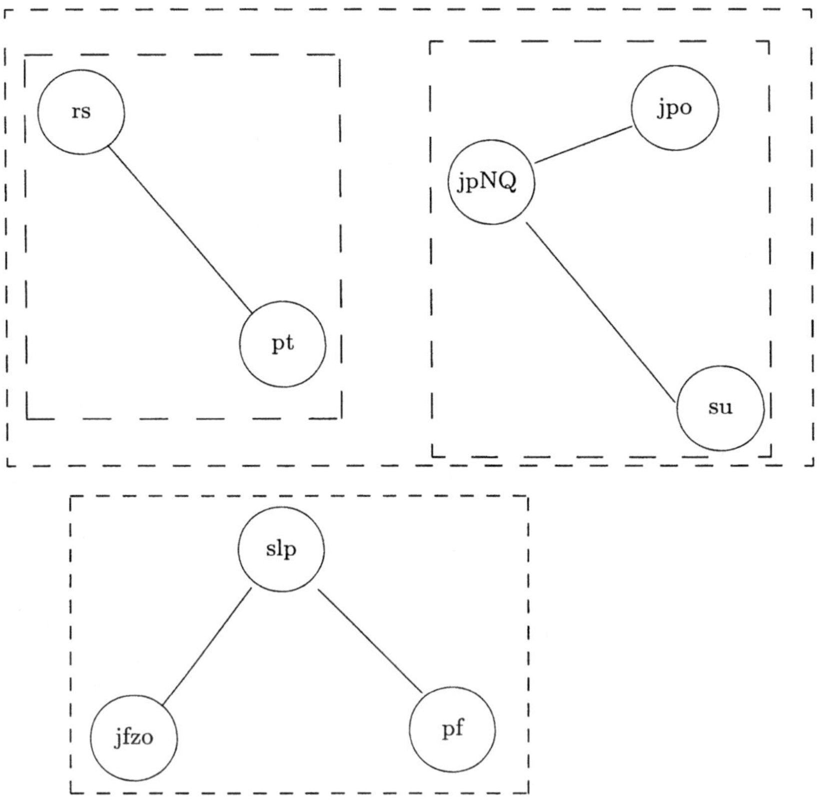


**Fig. 3.** The hierarchy growing with subnode limitation =2, step 2

- Mutual prediction paradigm, present in Chow/Liu, may be easily substituted with prediction by a larger number of attributes if they are relevant, taking other Bayesian learning algorithms.
- The Chow/Liu distance criterion is not sensitive to scale (random split of values does not increase the DEP(X,Y) measure).
- Attributes strongly correlated to each other and not to the other ones are isolated and do not disturb the relationships among the remaining ones.

## References

1. C.K.Chow, C.N.Liu: Approximating discrete probability distributions with dependence trees, *IEEE Transactions on Information Theory*, Vol. IT-14, No.3, (1968), 462-467

2. Fisher D., Langley P.: Approaches to conceptual clustering, Proc. 9th IJCAI, Los Angeles, 1985, pp. 691-697
3. Fisher D.: Knowledge acquisition via incremental conceptual clustering, Machine Learning 2,2,1987, pp. 139-172
4. Fisher D.H.: Conceptual clustering. learning from examples and inference, Proc. 4th International Workshop on Machine Learning, Irvine, Morgan Kaufman, 1987, pp. 38-49
5. Fisher D.H.: Noise-tolerant conceptual clustering, Proc. IJCAI'89 Vol. 2, pp. 825-830
6. Fisher, D., Hapanyengwi, G. "Database Management and Analysis Tools of Machine Learning." Journal of Intelligent Information Systems, 2, 1993, 5–38.
7. Fisher, D. . Iterative optimization and simplification of hierarchical clusterings. Journal of Artificial Intelligence Research, 4,1996, 147-178.
8. Gennari J.H., Langley P., Fisher D.: Models of incremental concept formation, Artificial Intelligence 40 (1989) 11-61
9. Kłopotek M.A.: On the Phenomenon of Flattening 'Flexible Prediction' Concept Hierarchy, in: Ph. Jorrand, J. Kelemen, Eds.: *Fundamentals of Artificial Intelligence Research*, International Workshop Smolenice Czech-Slovakia, 8-13 Sept. 1991, Lecture Notes in Artificial Intelligence 535 , Springer-Verlag, Berlin Heidelberg New York 1991, 99-111
10. Kłopotek M.A.: Dependence of evaluation function on correlation coefficient in the concept formation method "FLEXIBLE PREDICTION" (in Polish) in: P. Sienkiewicz, J. Tchórzewski Eds.: *Sztuczna Inteligencja i Cybernetyka Wiedzy (cybernetyka - inteligencja - rozwój)*, PTC, WSRP w Siedlcach. Siedlce-Warszawa 23-24.9.1991, pp. 37-42
11. M.A.Kłopotek, A.Matuszewski: On Irrelevance of Attributes in Flexible Prediction. Proc. 2nd Int. Conf. on New Techniques and Technologies for Statistics (NTTS'95), Bonn, 19-22 Nov., 1995, Publisher: GMD Sankt Augustin, pp 282-293.
12. P.Spirtes, C.Glymour, R.Scheines: *Causation, Prediction and Search*, Lecture Notes in Statistics 81, Springer-Verlag, 1993.

# Using Grade Correspondence Analysis to Merge Populations and Detect Latent Orders*)

**Wiesław Szczesny [1),2)] and Olaf Matyja [1)]**

[1)] Institute of Computer Science, Polish Academy of Sciences, Ordona 21, 01-237 Warsaw, Poland

[2)] Department of Econometry and Computer Science, Warsaw Agricultural University, Nowoursynowska 166, 02-787 Warsaw, Poland

*Abstract:*

*The grade correspondence analysis (GCA) has been used to solve classification problems with a response variable and a vector of nonnegative explanatory variables. Still it can be used in various other areas as well. In this paper, so called sorting GCA algorithm is applied first to a data matrix. This algorithm results in a set of row and column permutations, corresponding to local maxima of Spearman's* $\rho^*$. *Usually the results are slight variations of the main order that can be found in the data, but some reflect minor orders. Applying the GCA algorithm again to the table of GCA results provides an opportunity to find clusters of results and therefore various prime orders of the data. Another problem considered in this paper concerns the comparing and merging of populations of data collected from different sources. GCA methods allow us to detect the differences and associations among populations and therefore provide insight relative to their being merged into one table.*

*Key words:*

*classification, correspondence analysis, grade parameters, latent structure, response variable, stochastic dependence, visual intelligent information system.*

*) *Partially supported by the State Committee for Scientific Research under the research project # 8 T11F 013 17*

## 1. Latent orders in two populations treated separately

General information about grade correspondence analysis (GCA) can be found in [1], [3] and [5], while a wider overview of the correspondence analysis has been presented e.g. in [2].

In this section the technique of applying twice so called GCA sorting algorithm is presented. The method was first introduced in [4]. The following steps can be distinguished:

a) GCA is applied to the input table. The algorithm changes the order of the columns and rows. It starts from a random row and column order, then the rows and columns are sorted alternately until a local maximum of Spearman's $\rho^*$ is achieved. This procedure is repeated. Each of the results corresponds potentially to some latent ordering of data. As many of the results are identical or very similar, it's important to recognize some higher-level trends.

b) To achieve this goal, a similarity table between column permutations is calculated (a permutation of columns determines the permutation of rows as well, since it can be achieved by simple sorting of the grade regression). The table provides initial information regarding the main clustering of the results.

c) Finally, the GCA sorting algorithm is used again, but on the similarity table instead of the input data. The GCA asserts similarity between adjacent rows or columns. Looking at the sorted table we can determine the main latent orders by observation, or – more precisely – determine them by any clustering method (including GCA-based).

The process will be applied, in turn, to data matrices from two populations, say A and B. The two sets of object (over 300 cases in each) are disjoint, while variables (columns) are exactly the same, and all are non-negative.

The data come from a survey of different formulas for the production of concrete, and were investigated in the research project mentioned above. They were taken from two different sources, and therefore we cannot assume that both populations can be merged without previous analysis.

The data will not be discussed, as it has no influence on the method. It's sufficient to comment that one of the variables is a response variable (#7) and the others are explanatory ones. In this particular case we decided to set a restriction upon the GCA algorithm to place the response variable always in the first position (leftmost) and moreover we set much more weight to this variable during the normalization. The GCA algorithm asserts the maximum influence of the leftmost variable to the order of rows.

Starting from 500 different pairs of random permutations of rows and columns, the GCA algorithm achieved 10 local maxima in the first population and 6 in the second. The overview of the column positions in each maximum has been shown in the Tables 1 and 2.

Table 1. Values and frequencies of the local maxima of ρ* and permutations of variables for population A.

| local maximum | ρ* | frequency | permutation of variables | | | | | | |
|---|---|---|---|---|---|---|---|---|---|
| A1 | 0.187288 | 51 | 7 | 4 | 5 | 6 | 1 | 2 | 3 |
| A2 | 0.186678 | 58 | 7 | 4 | 6 | 5 | 1 | 2 | 3 |
| A3 | 0.186553 | 77 | 7 | 4 | 5 | 1 | 6 | 2 | 3 |
| A4 | 0.179479 | 16 | 7 | 6 | 5 | 4 | 1 | 2 | 3 |
| A5 | 0.178099 | 9 | 7 | 5 | 6 | 1 | 4 | 2 | 3 |
| A6 | 0.177614 | 8 | 7 | 6 | 5 | 1 | 4 | 2 | 3 |
| A7 | 0.176939 | 72 | 7 | 5 | 6 | 1 | 2 | 4 | 3 |
| A8 | 0.17659 | 41 | 7 | 6 | 5 | 1 | 2 | 4 | 3 |
| A9 | 0.175252 | 139 | 7 | 4 | 3 | 5 | 6 | 1 | 2 |
| A10 | 0.174668 | 29 | 7 | 4 | 3 | 6 | 5 | 1 | 2 |

Table 2. Values and frequencies of the local maxima of ρ* and permutations of variables for population B.

| local maximum | ρ* | frequency | permutation of variables | | | | | | |
|---|---|---|---|---|---|---|---|---|---|
| B1 | 0.204192 | 368 | 7 | 6 | 1 | 2 | 5 | 3 | 4 |
| B2 | 0.148761 | 19 | 7 | 3 | 4 | 6 | 1 | 5 | 2 |
| B3 | 0.148654 | 28 | 7 | 3 | 4 | 1 | 6 | 5 | 2 |
| B4 | 0.148586 | 13 | 7 | 3 | 4 | 6 | 1 | 2 | 5 |
| B5 | 0.148317 | 7 | 7 | 3 | 4 | 1 | 6 | 2 | 5 |
| B6 | 0.147452 | 65 | 7 | 4 | 3 | 1 | 6 | 5 | 2 |

Positions of rows for a local maximum can be derived from the column permutations and therefore are not presented in the tables. Columns entitled "ρ*" and "frequency" in the table give information about the strength of a local maximum, and of number of starts for which the GCA algorithm finished in this particular maximum.

In order to explain these tables, we will focus on the population B, as this happens to be much more regular than A. Looking at the table we notice that the first, the most frequent result (B1) differs from the rest. Maxima B2-B6 are just slight variations of the same order. The most popular among these maxima – B6 – achieves a ρ*, which is much smaller than in case of B1. Those two orders can be considered as reflections of two different latent structures.

In population A, the conclusions are not so obvious. While not having sufficient intuition about possible latent orders, we can still determine them using the GCA algorithm a second time. As mentioned before, this algorithm is based on the changing the order of the rows and columns to achieve a maximum value of ρ*. Yet in this particular case, the permutations of columns in Tables 1 and 2 are essential and should not be changed. To solve this problem we proceed as in [4]: we calculate a table of similarity between any two rows of Table 1 and run GCA sorting against this output. The graphical over-representation maps of results are shown on the Fig. 1.

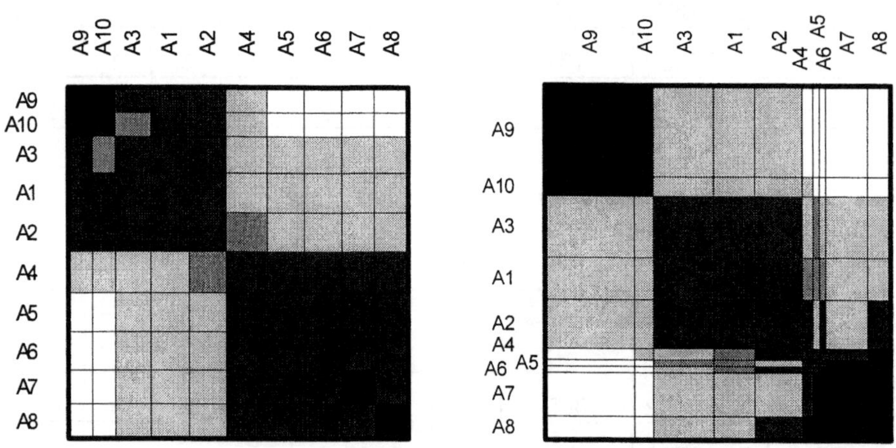


Fig. 1 Over-representation maps of the GCA similarity table for the population A. The left map is drawn with no regard to the frequencies, on the right, each row and column has a width multiplied by a frequency of the respective maximum.

Regarding Fig. 1, we notice two or three clusters of ρ* maxima (and therefore latent orders). The upper and middle cluster on the right map reflect the first cluster on the left map.

Then we use the same operations for Table 2 and obtain Fig. 2.

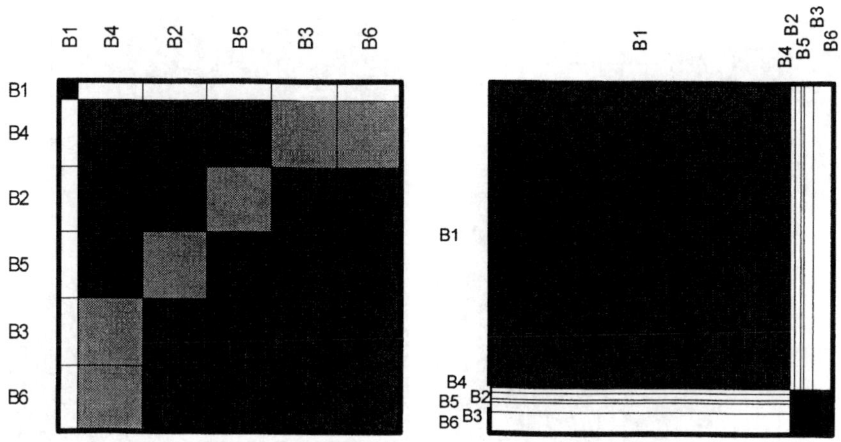


Fig. 2 Over-representation maps of the GCA similarity table for the population B. The both maps are drawn as in the Fig. 1, i.e. the left one with no regard to the frequencies, the right one with widths multiplied by frequencies of the maxima.

As we expected looking at the Table 2, there are definitely only two latent orders. One, very regular, consisting of the maximum B1, which is very frequently reached in the GCA procedure. The second latent structure, built from all other maxima, is less regular (5 variations), and is much less frequent in GCA results.

## 2. Merging populations

Now, having insight regarding the latent orders in both populations, the structures in the sum of the populations can be considered. We join objects from the both populations and name the result set C. The merged table is not included in the paper, as the local maxima of set C are included into the Table 3.

We apply the procedure (steps a, b, and c at the beginning of Section 1) to the merged data. At this time we achieve much more local maxima (21), which reflects less regularity of the merged set of data, as seen in Fig. 3.

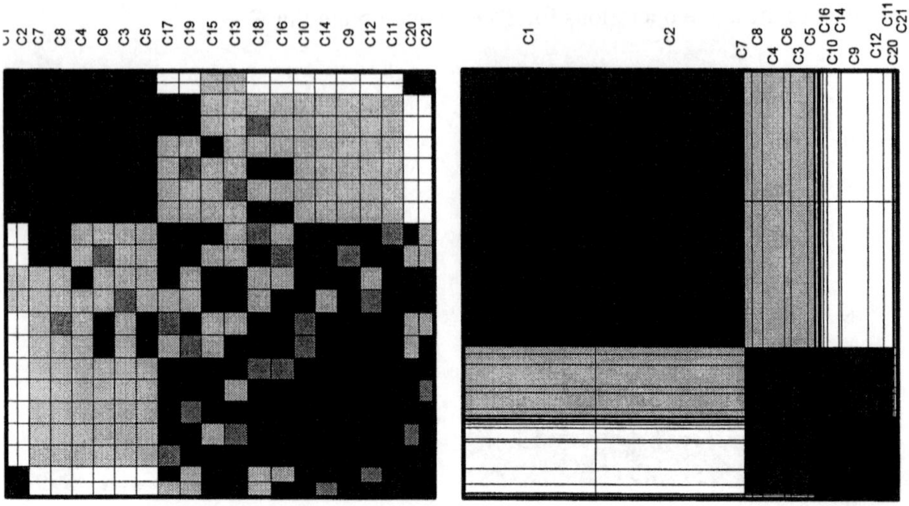


Fig. 3 Over-representation maps of the GCA similarity table for merged populations (which constitute new population C) without (left) and with (right) frequencies taken into account.

The maps on the Fig. 3 are not so clear as those for populations A and B taken separately, yet still two main clusters are visible (especially in the right map).

Now let us join permutations from populations A, B and C, and perform only the steps b and c of the algorithm. The result is shown in Table 3.

In this table the rows are sorted not by ρ*, but according to the order taken from the similarity table after the running of the GCA algorithm. The resulting plot of ρ* for local maxima in this order is given in Fig. 4. There seem to be two peaks, one in the first half between A7 and C2 and the other in the second half around C10, each suggesting the existence of the strong latent order. These peaks refer to local maxima B1 and A9 with large frequencies in Table 3.

We notice five permutations from populations A and B that appear in the population C as well. This validates in some way those permutations as latent orders of data. Four of them come from population A, the fifth from population B. The pairs of adjacent identical permutations are marked gray in Table 3. All permutations from the middle cluster of the population A (A1, A2, and A3) are thus validated by some results on the merged populations – they belong to the five remarked pairs.

Table 3. Local maxima for the populations A, B and C matched together.

| Local maximum | ρ* | frequency | Permutation of variables | | | | | | |
|---|---|---|---|---|---|---|---|---|---|
| A8 | 0.17659 | 41 | 7 | 6 | 5 | 1 | 2 | 4 | 3 |
| C1 | 0.187821 | 135 | 7 | 6 | 5 | 1 | 2 | 4 | 3 |
| A7 | 0.176939 | 72 | 7 | 5 | 6 | 1 | 2 | 4 | 3 |
| B1 | 0.204192 | 368 | 7 | 6 | 1 | 2 | 5 | 3 | 4 |
| C2 | 0.187603 | 148 | 7 | 6 | 1 | 5 | 2 | 4 | 3 |
| A5 | 0.178099 | 9 | 7 | 5 | 6 | 1 | 4 | 2 | 3 |
| A6 | 0.177614 | 8 | 7 | 6 | 5 | 1 | 4 | 2 | 3 |
| A4 | 0.179479 | 16 | 7 | 6 | 5 | 4 | 1 | 2 | 3 |
| C7 | 0.170909 | 8 | 7 | 4 | 5 | 6 | 1 | 2 | 3 |
| A1 | 0.187288 | 51 | 7 | 4 | 5 | 6 | 1 | 2 | 3 |
| C4 | 0.171506 | 22 | 7 | 4 | 6 | 5 | 1 | 2 | 3 |
| A2 | 0.186678 | 58 | 7 | 4 | 6 | 5 | 1 | 2 | 3 |
| C8 | 0.170847 | 13 | 7 | 4 | 5 | 1 | 6 | 2 | 3 |
| A3 | 0.186553 | 77 | 7 | 4 | 5 | 1 | 6 | 2 | 3 |
| C3 | 0.171588 | 17 | 7 | 4 | 6 | 1 | 5 | 2 | 3 |
| C6 | 0.171076 | 8 | 7 | 4 | 1 | 5 | 6 | 2 | 3 |
| C5 | 0.171236 | 8 | 7 | 4 | 1 | 6 | 5 | 2 | 3 |
| C17 | 0.158521 | 2 | 7 | 4 | 5 | 3 | 6 | 1 | 2 |
| C15 | 0.160336 | 2 | 7 | 4 | 6 | 3 | 5 | 1 | 2 |
| C19 | 0.158339 | 3 | 7 | 4 | 5 | 3 | 1 | 6 | 2 |
| C20 | 0.146531 | 2 | 7 | 3 | 6 | 5 | 1 | 4 | 2 |
| C13 | 0.160549 | 1 | 7 | 4 | 6 | 3 | 1 | 5 | 2 |
| C21 | 0.146506 | 5 | 7 | 3 | 6 | 1 | 5 | 4 | 2 |
| C18 | 0.158453 | 5 | 7 | 4 | 1 | 3 | 5 | 6 | 2 |
| C16 | 0.158867 | 6 | 7 | 4 | 1 | 3 | 6 | 5 | 2 |
| A9 | 0.175252 | 139 | 7 | 4 | 3 | 5 | 6 | 1 | 2 |
| C10 | 0.161495 | 18 | 7 | 4 | 3 | 6 | 5 | 1 | 2 |
| A10 | 0.174668 | 29 | 7 | 4 | 3 | 6 | 5 | 1 | 2 |
| C14 | 0.160398 | 6 | 7 | 4 | 3 | 5 | 1 | 6 | 2 |
| C9 | 0.161809 | 44 | 7 | 4 | 3 | 6 | 1 | 5 | 2 |
| C12 | 0.160627 | 30 | 7 | 4 | 3 | 1 | 5 | 6 | 2 |
| B6 | 0.147452 | 65 | 7 | 4 | 3 | 1 | 6 | 5 | 2 |
| C11 | 0.161173 | 17 | 7 | 4 | 3 | 1 | 6 | 5 | 2 |
| B2 | 0.148761 | 19 | 7 | 3 | 4 | 6 | 1 | 5 | 2 |
| B3 | 0.148654 | 28 | 7 | 3 | 4 | 1 | 6 | 5 | 2 |
| B4 | 0.148586 | 13 | 7 | 3 | 4 | 6 | 1 | 2 | 5 |
| B5 | 0.148317 | 7 | 7 | 3 | 4 | 1 | 6 | 2 | 5 |

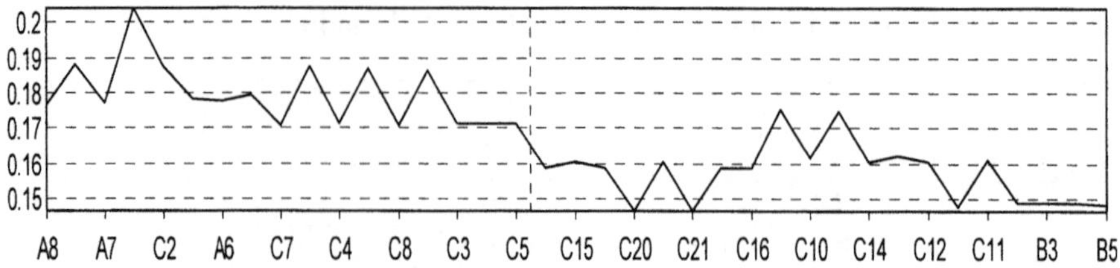


Fig. 4 Chart of ρ* for permutations in Table 3 with marked two distinct clusters.

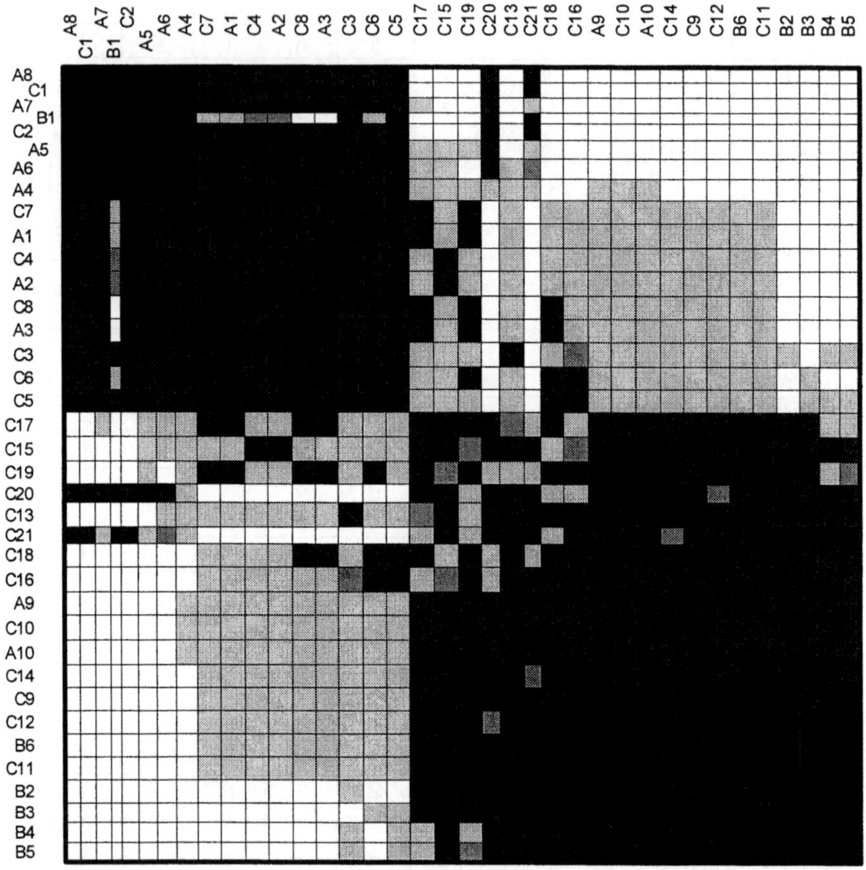


Fig. 5 The over-representation map for the similarity matrix of local maxima (with no regard to frequencies) for populations A, B and C.

The over-representation map of the similarity matrix for the maxima as given in Table 3 are presented in Fig. 5. The two big clusters (say L - left and R - right) appear as two big dark squares on this figure. We also recognize these two clusters on the plot of ρ* column in Fig. 4.

This division in two such clusters seems to be most accurately, yet other clusters also can be distinguished. Especially the first eight permutations form an interesting cluster. The cluster (say E) is shown in Fig. 5 as a small black square at the upper-left corner. It is better distinguished as a big black square (upper-left too) in Fig. 6. These permutations correspond to the cases in which the response variable (#7) is very close to variable #6, with variable #4 on further positions, and variable #3 staying at the opposite side. In all other permutations (except two small outliers – C20 and C21), variable #4 is either adjacent to #7 or at the next position, while variable #3 is changing its place gradually from the position most distant to the position next to #7.

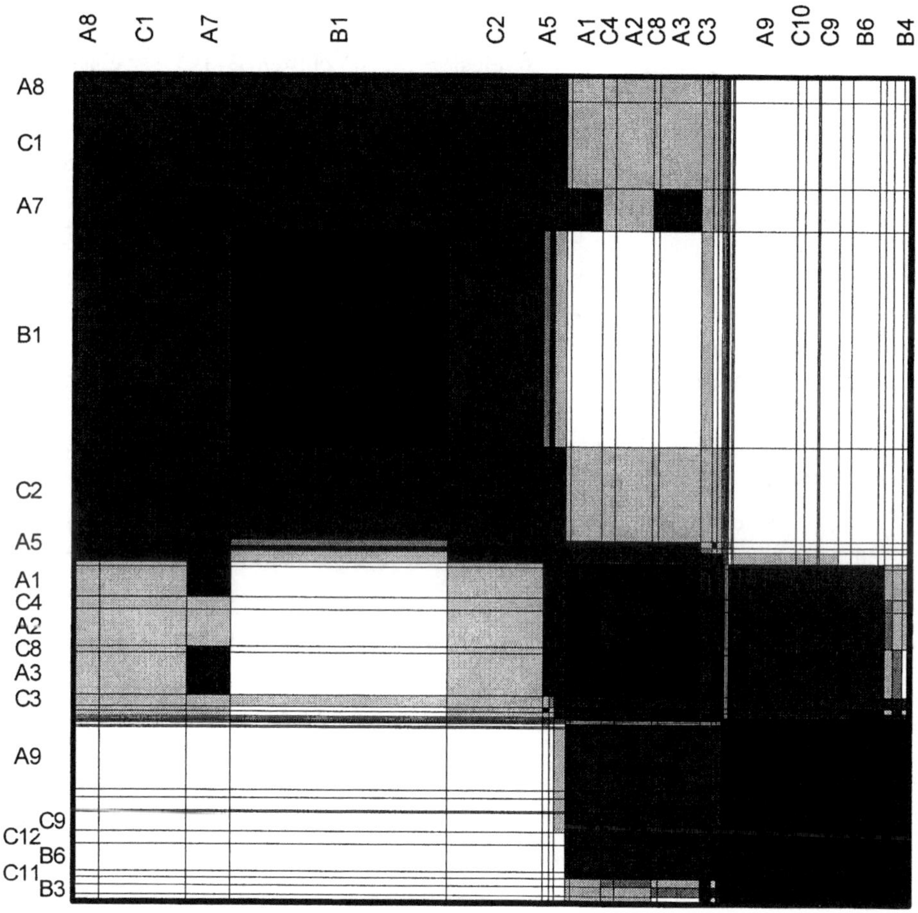


Fig. 6 The over-representation map for the similarity matrix of the local maxima (with regard to frequencies) for populations A, B and C.

## 3. Final remarks

In the population A, there were two or three clusters, in the population B two clusters corresponding to possible latent orders. The latent orders L, R and E found in Table 3 match clusters from populations A, B and C very well, as shown in Table 4:

Table 4. Comparison of clusters of populations A, B and C ordered according to Table 3.

<table>
<tr><th colspan="2" rowspan="2">Clusters in Table 3</th><th colspan="2">Population A partitioned into</th><th rowspan="2">Population B</th><th rowspan="2">Population C</th></tr>
<tr><th>2 clusters</th><th>3 clusters</th></tr>
<tr><td rowspan="2">L</td><td>E</td><td rowspan="2">2nd cluster</td><td>3rd cluster</td><td>1st cluster (B1)</td><td rowspan="2">1st cluster</td></tr>
<tr><td></td><td>2nd cluster</td><td></td></tr>
<tr><td rowspan="3">R</td><td rowspan="3"></td><td></td><td></td><td></td><td rowspan="2">2nd cluster</td></tr>
<tr><td>1st cluster</td><td>1st cluster</td><td></td></tr>
<tr><td></td><td></td><td>2nd cluster (rest)</td><td></td></tr>
</table>

If the populations A and B were incomparable, in the merged population the latent orders would vanish, or in the opposite way – all five orders would persist. The populations appeared yet to be well matching one to another.

## 4. References


1. Ciok A., Kowalczyk T., Pleszczyńska T.: Algorithms of grade correspondence-cluster analysis, The Collected Papers on Theoretical and Applied Computer Science, 1995, 7, 5-22

2. van der Heijden P. G. M., Correspondence Analysis of Longitudinal Categorical Data, DSWO Press, Leiden, 1987.

3. Matyja O., Szczesny W.: Visualization in prediction based on grade correspondence analysis, In Klopotek M.A., Michalewicz M., Wierzchoń S.T. (Eds), Intelligent Information Systems, Proceedings of the IIS'2000 Symposium, Bystra, Poland 12-16 June, 2000, Physica-Verlag, 2000, 289-301.

4. Szczesny W.: Grade correspondence analysis applied to questionnaire data. The analysis of level of skill, degree of disability, and employment status of disabled computer specialists in Poland. Submitted.

5. Szczesny W.: Detecting rows and columns of contingency table, which outlie from a total positivity pattern. Control and Cybernetics, 2000, vol. 29, no. 4. (to appear)

# Mining the Preference Relations and Preference Graphs

Jan M. Żytkow[1,2](+) & Daniel Arredondo[1]

[1]Computer Science Department, UNC Charlotte, Charlotte, N.C. 28223
and [2]Institute of Computer Science, Polish Academy of Sciences
zytkow@uncc.edu

**Abstract.** When knowledge mining starts from contingency tables, many types of knowledge become apparent that would otherwise went unnoticed. In this paper we start from contingency tables for pairs of attributes whose domains are ordered. The domain of each attribute can be interpreted as a preference list. We present a common 2-d pattern that can be collectively called preference relation. Preference relation tells that one of the choices is accepted to a higher degree over another. On one end of the spectrum, a weak preference borders equivalence relation between choices. On the other, a very strong preference is similar to subset relation. We present several tests that can distinguish various forms of preference relation knowledge and also subset and equivalence. Our experience in data mining with the application of the 49er system shows that the exploration of many databases frequently leads to large numbers of preference-type regularities. Large numbers of preference-type regularities can be combined into concise, useful forms of preference graphs. We compare preference graphs to taxonomies and inclusion graphs. We illustrate the presented algorithms by applications on the International Social Survey Program (ISSP) databases.

## 1 From contingency tables to other forms of knowledge

Elsewhere (Zytkow & Zembowicz, 1996) we argue that contingency tables are the basic form of 2-D regularities while other forms of knowledge can be treated as their special cases. For instance, a relation is a subset of the Cartesian product of the values of several attributes. A contingency table, in addition to that, provides for each cell $(v_1, v_2)$ in the Cartesian product the count of all events in the data with the combination of attribute values $v_1$ and $v_2$. Relations are special cases, with the count of zero in some cells, above zero in all other cells, but without information about the relative frequency of events. The following partial order (figure 1) with contingency tables on the left shows other patterns as special cases:

Contingency tables are easy to generate and investigate. They express statistical regularities, distinguishing statistically probable combinations of events from those improbable (Fienberg, 1980; Gokhale & Kullback, 1978). Some contingency tables show special regularities. In this paper we focus on regularities that we call preference relations. Many relations in that category are typically discovered in biological databases, and in responses to various

```
                                    multi-function --> function
                                   /                           \
contingency table --> relation ---> preference ----------->equivalence
                                   \           \               /
                                    -----------> subset ------>
```

**Fig. 1.** Many special regularities can be detected in contingency tables

questionnaires. When a number of preference relations are detected in contingency tables, they may be combined into preference graphs. Preference graphs are similar to subset graphs (zytkow & Zembowicz, 1997).

### 1.1 US survey on the role of government: our souce of examples

The database used in our examples comes from the International Social Survey Program (ISSP) databases collected over the period of 15 years. As a part of the survey program, 1985 survey focused on the role of government in Australia, West Germany, Great Britain, United States, Austria and Italy. Each survey includes 141 attributes, mostly multiple choice questions. In our examples we use the results of the survey conducted in the United States, which includes 677 records. Each record of 141 values is a response of a single respondent. We will call that database US-GOVT-1985.

An application of 49er (Zembowicz & Zytkow, 1993) to those data generated thousands of regularities in the form of contingency tables. A significant number of those regularities belong to the category which we call preference regularities. They are the main focus of this paper.

### 1.2 Preference regularities inferred from contingency tables

Let us start from an example. Consider the following responses to several questions of the form "Should X be allowed?":

```
1        DEFINITELY ALLOWED
2        PROBABLY ALLOWED
3        PROBABLY NOT ALLOWED
4        DEFINITELY NOT ALLOWED
```

Notice that the lower is the value, the more allowed (preferred is the option).

Consider two attributes, that can be substituted for X: "NATIONAL-ANTI-GOVERNMENT-STRIKE" and "PROTEST-PUBLICATIONS." The following contingency table derived from US-GOVT-85 shows very strongly that in the view of respondents protest publications are much more allowed (preferred) than national anti-government strike:

The attribute "protest publications allowed" is preferred by the respondents collectively, according to this table over "national anti-government

Table 1. a contingency table that shows preference for protest publications over national anti-government strike in responses to US-govt-1985 questionnaire.

Attribute:
NATIONL-ANTI-GOVT-STRIKE

| NATIONL-ANTI-GOVT-STRIKE | | | | |
|---|---|---|---|---|
| 4 | 115 | 98 | 63 | 80 |
| 3 | 45 | 34 | 30 | 8 |
| 2 | 40 | 18 | 4 | 1 |
| 1 | 49 | 4 | 3 | 1 |
| | 1 | 2 | 3 | 4 |

Attribute: PROTEST-PUBLICATIONS

Probability of random fluctuation Q = 1.40E-13
Cramer's V = 0.20

strike allowed". For an individual respondent represented by record $x$, attribute A2 is preferred (more allowed) than A1 when A2(x) ¡ A1(x). A2 is preferred, because its value is more allowed than the value of A1. We have to pay attention to the order of preference for each attribute and reverse it to ensure the uniform treatment of "¡" as preferred".

If all respondents preferred "protest publications allowed" over "national anti-government strike allowed", the only positive entries in Table 1 would be above the diagonal. But since there are many entries on the diagonal, many respondents equally agree or disagree with both forms of protest. All entries under the diagonal mean the reverse preference by 21 individual respondents. In the world of human preferences full agreement is rare if existent at all. Table 1 summarizes all individual choices and shows the overall strong preference for "protest publications allowed."

The numbers in Table 1 grow in the direction from one count in the cell (1,4) to 115 counts in (4,1). That means that the highest difference is preferred by the highest proportion of respondents. But preferences may be not as strong. Table 2 reveals a similar pattern, but preference for protest publications is now weaker. The number of respondents who allow protest publications over racist public meetings (the area above the diagonal) is 232 while 104 respondents show the other preference.

Table 3 illustrates one more step in the direction of limited preference. It is clear that public protest meetings are collectively preferred over protest demonstrations: the number of counts above the diagonal is 180, compared to 56 counts below the diagonal. But the majority of counts are distributed on the diagonal and directly above the diagonal (488), compared to 409 in Table 2.

Table 2.

Attribute:
RACIST-PUBLIC-MEETINGS

| | | | | |
|---|---|---|---|---|
| 4 | 37 | 38 | 43 | 48 |
| 3 | 16 | 35 | 23 | 20 |
| 2 | 63 | 60 | 31 | 14 |
| 1 | 137 | 25 | 7 | 7 |
| | 1 | 2 | 3 | 4 |

Attribute: PROTEST-PUBLICATIONS

Probability of random fluctuation Q = 3.62E-29
Cramer's V = 0.27

Table 3.

Attribute:
PROTEST-DEMONSTRATIONS

| | | | | |
|---|---|---|---|---|
| 4 | 10 | 23 | 13 | 41 |
| 3 | 22 | 42 | 42 | 6 |
| 2 | 70 | 80 | 18 | 7 |
| 1 | 200 | 19 | 4 | 2 |
| | 1 | 2 | 3 | 4 |

Attribute: PUBLIC-PROTEST-MEETINGS

Probability of random fluctuation Q = 3.60E-76
Cramer's V = 0.41

Hundreds of preference regularities may occur in one survey database. They may be found in squared contingency tables of different size, such as 3*3, 5*5. But they may also occur in non-square tables, for instance 4*5. Before we discuss the meaning of the border case of 2*2 tables, let us briefly consider a 3*3 table for two questions on whether the publication of economic plans and defense plans should be allowed:

1 NEWSPAPER ALLOWED
2 CAN'T CHOOSE
3 GOVERNMENT PREVENT

Table 4.

Attribute:
MEDIA-PUBL-ECONOM-PLANS

| | | | |
|---|---|---|---|
| 3 | 7 | 12 | 208 |
| 2 | 6 | 33 | 29 |
| 1 | 83 | 39 | 236 |
| | 1 | 2 | 3 |

Attribute: MEDIA-PUBL-DEFENSE-PLANS

Probability of random fluctuation Q = 8.57E-26
Cramer's V = 0.27

It is clear that more respondents prefer publication of economic plans over defense plans. We will now consider similar relations in 2*2 tables, which will allow us to apply a set-theoretic and logic interpretation that can be extended to larger tables.

### 1.3 Subset and equivalence regularities in 2*2 tables

Consider two types of tables, depicted in Figure 2, for Boolean attributes A1 and A2. Non-zero numbers of occurrences of particular value combinations are indicated by n1, n2, and n3. Zeros in the cells indicate that the corresponding combinations of values do not occur in data from which the table has been generated. The upper table in Figure 2, for instance, shows that 0 objects are both A1 and non-A2 (labeled ¬A2 in the table), while n2 objects are neither A1 nor A2. From the zero values we can infer inductively, with the significance that increases as we consider more data, that these value combinations do not occur in the population represented by data.

| | | |
|---|---|---|
| A1 | 0 | n1 |
| ¬A1 | n2 | 0 |
| | ¬A2 | A2 |

The regularity expressed in this table is equivalence:
For all x, ( A1(x) if and only if A2(x) )
2 classes can be defined: (1) A1 and A2, (2) non-A1 and non-A2

| | | |
|---|---|---|
| A1 | 0 | n1 |
| ¬A1 | n2 | n3 |
| | ¬A2 | A2 |

The regularity expressed in this table is implication:
For all x, ( if A1(x) then A2(x) ) or equivalently:
For all x, ( if non-A2(x) then non-A1(x) )

**Fig. 2.** Contingency table that leads to concepts of empirical contents.

The lower table in Figure 2 leads to weaker conclusions. Only the values A1 and non-A2 carry predictive contents: objects which are A1, are also A2. Equivalently, objects which are non-A2, are non-A1. In terms of preference regularities, A1 is preferred over A2. The implication can be read: "If A2 is permitted then A1 is also permitted."

As another boundary case of preference regularity we consider logical equivalence depicted in the upper table. We will analyze it in detail in the next section, but we will replace zeros that occur in Figure 2 by small values that are far more widespread and can be viewed as approximate equivalence.

### 1.4 Approximate equivalence

Preference can continuously change into weak equivalence, shown in Table 4 or into a stronger equivalence, shown in Table 5. Different degrees of equivalence are border cases for the preference regularities. Later on when we define preference graphs, equivalence will be very useful in defining levels in the graph.

Table 5.

```
Attribute:
RACIST-PUBLIC-MEETINGS
------+------+------+------+------+
    4 |   13 |   20 |   17 |  115 |
------+------+------+------+------+
    3 |    6 |   27 |   30 |   34 |
------+------+------+------+------+
    2 |   29 |   86 |   21 |   36 |
------+------+------+------+------+
    1 |  135 |   25 |    4 |   20 |
------+------+------+------+------+
      |    1 |    2 |    3 |    4 |
           Attribute: REVOLUT-PUBLIC-MEETINGS (#9)

 Probability of random fluctuation Q = 1.83E-71
                             Cramer's V = 0.39
```

In real databases, rarely we see regularities without exceptions. Instead of cells with zero counts, we can expect cells with numbers small compared to those in other cells. We want to tolerate limited exceptions. Rather than directly compare the numbers in different cells to determine whether a table approximates equivalence, we use Cramer's $V$, set at a threshold close to 1.0. The Cramer's $V$ coefficient is based on $\chi^2$, which measures the distance between tables of actual and expected counts. For a given $M_{row} \times M_{col}$ contingency table

$$V = \sqrt{\frac{\chi^2}{N \min(M_{row} - 1, M_{col} - 1)}},$$

Table 6.

Attribute:
RACIST-PUBLISH-BOOKS

| | | | | |
|---|---|---|---|---|
| 4 | 4 | 15 | 15 | 124 |
| 3 | 7 | 19 | 54 | 14 |
| 2 | 26 | 113 | 21 | 25 |
| 1 | 143 | 23 | 6 | 8 |
| | 1 | 2 | 3 | 4 |

Attribute: RACIST-PUBLIC-MEETINGS (#12)

Probability of random fluctuation Q = 4.33E-131
Cramer's V = 0.52

where $N$ is the number of records. Cramer's $V$ measures the predictive power of a regularity. The strongest, unique predictions are possible when for each value of one attribute there is exactly one corresponding value of the other attribute. For ideal correlation, $\chi^2$ is equal to $N \min(M_{row} - 1, M_{col} - 1)$, so Cramer's $V = 1$. On the other extreme, when the actual distribution is equal to expected, then $\chi^2 = 0$ and $V = 0$.

Our examples demonstrate higher values of $V$ for approximate equivalence (0.52 in Table 6; 0.39 in Table 5; 0.41 in Table 3; while only 0.27 in Table 2 and 0.20 in Table 1).

# 2 From preference tables to preference networks

We will now describe a way to detect and combine many preference relations.

## 2.1 Testing for preference

The inclusion relation between the scopes of two Boolean attributes may be determined from the "triangular", 4-cell contingency tables. For example, the following table represents inclusion of attribute $A$ in $B$, $A \subset B$,

| | | |
|---|---|---|
| $A$ | a | 0 |
| $\neg A$ | b | d |
| | $B$ | $\neg B$ |

$a$, $b$, $d$ indicate non-zero counts of records, $c = 0$. This table could be also interpreted as implication of property $B$ from property $A$, that is by $A \Rightarrow B$.

Four inclusion cases are possible for $2 \times 2$ contingency tables, depending on which cell has zero counts. To allow some small level of noise and error, we admit some exceptions. For example, instead of $c = 0$ we require $max(c/(a+c), c/(d+c)) < \delta$, where $\delta$ is the tolerance (typically 10%).

Similarly to equivalence, subset relation is not limited to Boolean attributes and can be inferred from large contingency tables. For instance, if a table includes 0 counts for the combination of values $d_3$ and $e_7$ of attributes $D$ and $E$, then $D = d_3 \subset \neg E = e_7$. If $D$ and $E$ have many values, there is little practical value in such subset relations because they cover only very limited cases and possess little empirical content.

### 2.2 Preference network

A significant number of 2-D regularities in a database can represent inclusions (Moraczewski et. al, 1995). Inclusions can be conveniently combined into an inclusion graph, in which vertices represent attributes while directed edges stand for inclusion between extensions of attributes.

Constructing the inclusion graph 49er stores equivalent attributes on the same node to reduce the subset edges. For example, if $A \subset B$ and $B \equiv C$, then $A \subset C$ is removed. Transitivity of the inclusion also permits reduction of the graph: if $A \subset B$ and $B \subset C$, then the inclusion $A \subset C$ is removed. These steps reduce the number of nodes and edges in the inclusion graph while preserving its predictive content.

To divide the typically large inclusion graphs into meaningful pieces, 49er uses the maximum subsets, which are not subsets of any other node in the inclusion graph. For each maximum node $M$, it extracts the subgraph $G_M$ of all subsets of $M$. Graphs $G_M$ typically have strong domain-specific interpretation, representing, for instance, all species which inhabit various selective parts of the environment settled by the species $M$. After removing all edges shared with any other subgraph $G_{M'}$, the remaining subgraph $G^*_M$ has the interpretation of all species which are more selective than $M$ but not more selected than any other species, except those under $M$. Each $G^*_M$ graph can be interpreted in domain-specific terms. The following algorithm describes inclusion graph formation and analysis.

**<u>Algorithm:</u> Build Inclusion Graph and extract subgraphs $G^*_M$**

given the list of significant contingency tables
  Select inclusions from contingency tables
  Build inclusion graph
  Remove redundant edges
  **for** each maximum node $M$
    $G_M \leftarrow$ graph of all subsets of $M$
    $G^*_M \leftarrow G_M$ after removing edges shared with any other graph $G_{M'}$

### 2.3 Survey database exploration

Consider application of 49er on the survey on the role of government, conducted in the United States. It consists of 141 numerical attributes (answers to multiple choice questions) and 677 records (respondents). The search in the space of 2-D attribute combinations without slices evaluated $0.5 \times 1181 * 1180 \approx 7 \times 10^5$ hypotheses. Although many interesting regularities are usually found in data subsets, the number of attributes in this database prohibits data slicing. Allowing only a partition into two slices per attribute leads to $0.5 \times 1180 \times 1179 \times 2 \times 1181 \approx 1.6 \times 10^9$ hypotheses to be tested. 49er would take some 2 years to complete this task. In 10 hour search without slices 49er discovered 16577 statistically significant contingency tables. 49er determined that 594 tables capture equivalences of attributes, and applied the taxonomy formation method described in the previous section. The merging of hierarchy units resulted in interesting discoveries. One grid element included 29 species which turned out to be not established permanently in the flora; it showed that they occur in the vicinity of a mill. Another 9-attribute class, occupying just two grid elements, contained species fugitive from gardens. Several 6-attribute classes have been also detected. Since these and all other merged hierarchy units were extremely unbalanced, and hierarchy formation did not lead to any node reduction, the resultant multi-level hierarchy has not been interesting.

6364 contingency tables passed the test for approximate subset. After merging equivalent nodes and removing redundant edges, this number was reduced to 2475. 2358 contingency tables express "positive" inclusions (that is, $A \subset B$) while the remaining 117 represent exclusions of ranges of the corresponding plant taxa $A$ and $B$ ($A \subset \neg B$ or $\neg A \subset B$). These are not used in the inclusion graph. The algorithm described earlier in this chapter formed 302 subgraphs $G^*_M$, each corresponding to one maximum element $M$. The species in each $G^*_M$ are characteristic to a specific environment. The further away from $M$, the narrower is the ecological amplitude of the species. For instance, in a subgraph of species preferring moist areas, the root corresponds to a common meadow plant *Ranunculus acris*, growing on wet soils, that is missing only in the downtown and several dryer areas, while one of the lowest descendents is *Calla palustris*, growing only in peat-bogs, very wet, natural habitats (Moraczewski et. al, 1995).

The following figure 3 depicts a small part of one of the connected preference graphs:

# 3 Summary

We have presented an algorithm for conceptual hierarchy formation from knowledge in the form of contingency tables. We used the soybean database as an example. It turned out that four diseases hidden in the soybean data coincide with the four leaves in taxonomies generated by our algorithm. In contrast to fixed rules which define concepts in many machine learning systems, our approach offers the choice among definitional descriptors in selecting a recognition procedure. Depending on the observable concepts available

```
         public
         protest
         meetings
          ^   ^
         /     \
        /       \
       /         \
  protest        protest
demonstrations   publications
       ^          /     \
       |         /       \
       |        /         \
       racist               \
       meeting               \
          ^                   \
          |                    \
          |                     \
       racist                    \
       teach                national
       children             anti-
                            government
                            strike
```

**Fig. 3.** A part of one of the connected preference graphs

in a given situation, alternative definitional descriptors can be used, so that missing values do not pose a problem in our approach in contrast to many machine learning systems.

We also have shown that many subset relations can be combined into subset graph, which is useful in making inferences and interpreting knowledge about many subsets.

## References


1. Fienberg, S.E. 1980. *The analysis of cross-classified categorical data*, MIT Press.
2. Fisher, D.H. 1987. Knowledge Acquisition Via Incremental Conceptual Clustering, *Machine Learning* 2: 139-172.
3. Gokhale, D.V. & Kullback, S. 1978. *The Information in Contingency Tables*, New York: M.Dekker.
4. Klösgen, W. (1992). Patterns for Knowledge Discovery in Databases in: ed *Proceedings of the ML-92 Workshop on Machine Discovery (MD-92)*, Aberdeen, UK. July 4, p.1-10.
5. Moraczewski, I., Zembowicz, R. & Żytkow, J.M. 1995. Geobotanical Database Exploration. In Working Notes of the AAAI Spring Symposium. Forthcoming.

6. Sudnik-Wojcikowska, B. 1987. *The flora of Warsaw and its changes in 19th and 20th Centuries* (in Polish), Warsaw: Warsaw University Publ.
7. Troxel, M., Swarm, K., Zembowicz, R. & Żytkow, J.M. 1994. Concept Hierarchies: a Restricted Form of Knowledge Derived from Regularities. In: Proc. of Methodologies for Intelligent Systems, ed. M. Zemankova & Z. Ras, Springer-Verlag.
8. Żytkow, J., & Zembowicz, R., (1993) Database Exploration in Search of Regularities, *Journal of Intelligent Information Systems*, 2, p.39-81.

# Multi-Dimensional Gaussian and Cauchy Mutations

Andrzej Obuchowicz

Technical University of Zielona Góra, Institute of Control and Computation Engineering, ul. Podgórna 50, 65–246 Zielona Góra, Poland

**Abstract.** The aim of this work is to focus the attention of researchers concerned with evolutionary algorithms on the fact that the most probable location of the mutated points in multi-dimensional Gaussian and Cauchy mutations is not in a close neighborhood of the origin, but at a certain distance from it. In the case of the Gaussian mutation this distance is proportional to the norm of the standard deviation vector and increases with the landscape dimension. This may cause a decrease in the sensitivity of the evolutionary algorithm to narrow peaks when the landscape dimension increases. Moreover, it is proved that the multi-dimensional Cauchy mutation is not isotropic and the directions parallel to the axes of the reference frame are preferred. The effectiveness of the evolutionary algorithm using the Cauchy mutation strongly depends on the choice of the reference frame. New Gaussian-like and Cauchy-like mutations are proposed in order to overcome the considered difficulties.

## 1 Introduction

Most applications of the evolutionary algorithms which make use of the floating-point representation of population individuals apply the Gaussian mutation as a mutation operator [4]. A new individual $\boldsymbol{x}$ is obtained by adding a normally-distributed random value to each entry of a selected parent $\boldsymbol{y}$:

$$x_i = y_i + N(0, \sigma_i), \quad i = 1, \dots, n. \tag{1}$$

Such a mutation operator is applied in several well-known "standard" algorithms, e.g. Evolutionary Strategies [5], Evolutionary Programming [2], GENOCOP [4], and some weakly known Evolutionary Search with Soft Selection [3].

The multi-dimensional Gaussian mutation owes its popularity to the fact that it describes the natural behaviors, among other things the following:

- the vector of standard deviations $\boldsymbol{\sigma} = [\sigma_i | i = 1, \dots, n]$ (1) controls the "mutation radius" $R_\sigma = ||\boldsymbol{\sigma}||$, which can be interpreted as an estimate of the mean distance between the base $\boldsymbol{y}$ and mutated $\boldsymbol{x}$ points;
- the probability that a point $\boldsymbol{x}$ is obtained from a point $\boldsymbol{y}$ decreases as the distance between these points, $||\boldsymbol{x} - \boldsymbol{y}||$, increases.

The above two characteristics are unquestionable. But one has to be very careful when trying to generalize the following properties of the one-dimensional Gaussian mutation:

- the mutation radius $R_\sigma \approx \sigma$ if $\sigma_1 = c \cdots = \sigma_n = \sigma$ (*variance–dimensional problem*);
- the probability that $||\boldsymbol{x} - \boldsymbol{y}|| \in [r, r + dr]$ decreases as long as $r$ increases (*surrounding problem*).

In this work we prove that the above is false in the context of the multi-dimensional Gaussian mutation.

In recent years ([6,7]) the Cauchy mutation has been successfully applied to various global optimization problems. In this case, the normally-distributed random variable $N(0, \sigma_i)$ (1) is substituted by a random variable generated with one-dimensional Cauchy distribution. Although the shape of the Cauchy density function resembles a Gaussian bell, it approaches abscissas very slowly, increasing the probability of escaping from local optima. It is not possible to define a mutation radius of the Cauchy mutation because of an infinite value of the variance and hence the *variance-dimensional problem* does not exist in this context, but the *surrounding problem* still calls for a solution.

Application of multi-dimensional Cauchy mutation in an evolutionary algorithm generates another serious problem. If each entry of a selected parent is mutated by adding a random variable generated with one-dimensional Cauchy distribution, then the resulting offspring may be treated as a random vector with a multi-dimensional Cauchy distribution which is not isotropic. Since the directions parallel to the axes of the reference frame are preferred, the effectiveness of the evolutionary algorithm based on the Cauchy mutation strongly depends on the choice of that frame (*symmetry problem*).

The aim of this work is to present the essence of the above-mentioned problems with multi-dimensional Gaussian and Cauchy mutations and consequences of their applications in evolutionary algorithms. New Gaussian-like and Cauchy-like mutations which overcome these problems are proposed.

## 2 Gaussian mutation

A mutation function which describes the transformation of an element $\boldsymbol{y}$ into $\boldsymbol{x}$ in accordance with the Gaussian mutation (1) has the form

$$g_G(\boldsymbol{x} - \boldsymbol{y}) = \prod_{i=1}^{n} \frac{1}{\sqrt{2\pi}\sigma_i} \exp\left( - \frac{(x_i - y_i)^2}{2\sigma_i^2} \right). \tag{2}$$

For simplicity, throughout the paper we assume that $\sigma_1 = \cdots = \sigma_n = \sigma$ and therefore

$$g_G(\boldsymbol{x} - \boldsymbol{y}) = \left( \frac{1}{\sqrt{2\pi}\sigma} \right)^n \exp\left( - \frac{||\boldsymbol{x} - \boldsymbol{y}||^2}{2\sigma^2} \right). \tag{3}$$

The probability that the point obtained after mutation will be located in the volume $([x_i, x_i + dx_i]^n | i = 1, \ldots, n)$ is given by

$$dP_G = g_G(\boldsymbol{x} - \boldsymbol{y})d\omega, \tag{4}$$

where $d\omega = dx_1 dx_2 \ldots dx_n$.

## 2.1 Variance-dimensional problem

The first problem with the multi-dimensional Gaussian mutation stems from the fact that, in case $\sigma_1 = \cdots = \sigma_n = \sigma$, the mutation radius reduces to

$$R_\sigma = ||\boldsymbol{\sigma}|| = \sigma\sqrt{n} \tag{5}$$

and, consequently, it increases with the dimension $n$ of the adaptation landscape. The mutation radius influences the algorithm sensitivity with respect to narrow peaks. If the mutation radius is large enough in comparison with the width of a peak, then the evolution may make no account of this peak and terminate on a lower and wider one. This fact involves a decrease in the algorithm sensitivity to narrow peaks when the landscape dimension increases. A simple solution to this problem is to replace the standard deviation $\sigma$ with the term $\sigma/\sqrt{n}$, i.e., we get

$$x_i = y_i + N(0, \sigma/\sqrt{n}), \quad i = 1, \ldots, n \tag{6}$$

and

$$dP_{nG} = g_{nG}(\boldsymbol{x} - \boldsymbol{y})d\omega = \left(\frac{1}{\sigma}\sqrt{\frac{n}{2\pi}}\right)^n \exp\left(-\frac{n||\boldsymbol{x} - \boldsymbol{y}||^2}{2\sigma^2}\right)d\omega. \tag{7}$$

This type of mutation makes the mutation radius independent of the landscape dimension. Accordingly, the mutation radius is equal to the initially declared value of $\sigma$. This feature enables us to compare the performance of the algorithm in landscapes of different dimensions. Unfortunately, the delineated method does not solve the next problem.

## 2.2 Surrounding problem

The second problem is related to the probability of locating the mutated point $\boldsymbol{x}$ in the nearest surrounding of the base point $\boldsymbol{y}$. Let us consider the relationship between the probability $dP_G$ and the distance between the base and mutated points $||\boldsymbol{x} - \boldsymbol{y}||$. For that purpose, an $n$-spherical reference frame with the origin at the base point $\boldsymbol{y}$ will be introduced. The corresponding transformation equations have the forms (for $\boldsymbol{z} = \boldsymbol{x} - \boldsymbol{y}$):

$$\begin{aligned} z_1 &= r\cos(\alpha_1), \\ z_2 &= r\sin(\alpha_1)\cos(\alpha_2), \\ z_3 &= r\sin(\alpha_1)\sin(\alpha_2)\cos(\alpha_3), \\ &\vdots \\ z_n &= r\sin(\alpha_1)\sin(\alpha_2)\ldots\sin(\alpha_{n-1}), \end{aligned} \tag{8}$$

where $r \in \mathbb{R}_+ \cup \{0\}$, $\alpha_{n-1} \in [0, 2\pi)$ and $(\alpha_i \in [0,\pi) | i = 1, \ldots, n-2)$.

Using (8) in (4) the probability $dP_G$ can be obtained from

$$dP_G = \left(\frac{1}{\sqrt{2\pi}\sigma}\right)^n \exp\left(-\frac{r^2}{2\sigma^2}\right) r^{n-1}\sin^{n-2}(\alpha_1)\sin^{n-3}(\alpha_2)\ldots\sin(\alpha_{n-2})d\omega', \tag{9}$$

where $d\omega' = dr d\alpha_1 d\alpha_2 \ldots d\alpha_{n-1}$. Due to the nonnegative values of the radius and the sine function in the interval $[0,\pi)$, the magnitude operator of the transformation Jacobian may be omitted. Equation (9) can thus be rewritten in the form

$$dP_G = \left(\frac{1}{\sqrt{2\pi}\sigma}\right)^n \exp\left(-\frac{r^2}{2\sigma^2}\right) r^{n-1} dr d\Omega = g_G(r) dr d\Omega, \tag{10}$$

where $d\Omega = \prod_{i=1}^{n-1}\left(\sin^{n-(i+1)}(\alpha_i)d\alpha_i\right)$ is the infinitesimal $n$-dimensional solid angle. It is very interesting that for a small $r$ the value of the probability $dP_G$ is low. The most probable distance $r_0$ is non-zero but

$$r_0(n) = \arg\max g_G(r) = \sigma\sqrt{n-1} \tag{11}$$

and $r_0(n) \to \infty$ as $n \to \infty$. If the Gaussian mutation with the standard deviation $\sigma/\sqrt{n}$ (6) is used, then the most probable distance is

$$r_0(n) = \sigma\sqrt{(n-1)/n} \tag{12}$$

and $r_0(n) \to \sigma$ as $n \to \infty$.

In order to confirm the above theoretical results, a simulation experiment has been carried out for $10^6$ points generated in accordance with (1) and (6) for $n = 2, 3, 4, 5$, $\sigma = 1$ for each one-dimensional mutation and the base point $\boldsymbol{y} = 0$. The histograms of the distances between the base and the points mutated according to (1) (Fig. 1(a)) show that the probability of location a point in the close neighborhood of the base point is low and decreases with $n$. The maxima of histograms are obtained at $r_0(n) = \sigma\sqrt{n-1}$. In the case of the mutation (6) (Fig. 1(b)) the effect of the *surrounding problem* is limited to the circle with radius $\sigma$. The resulting histograms fully confirm the foregoing theoretical considerations.

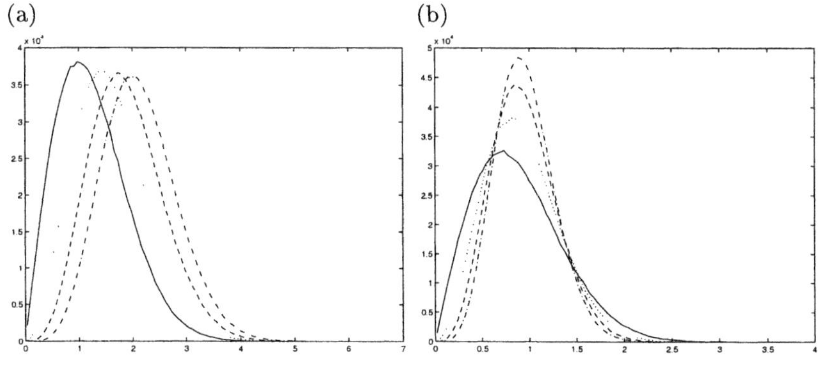


**Fig. 1.** Histograms of the distances between the base and $10^6$ points mutated according to (1) (a) and (6) (b); $n = 2$ — solid line, $n = 3$ — dotted line, $n = 4$ — dashed line, $n = 5$ — dash-dot line, other characteristics in the text.

The observed effect of the multi-dimensional Gaussian mutation is produced by the following fact: The volume of the subspace $d\omega'$ (9) depends on the radius $r$, i.e., $dV = dSdr \sim r^{n-1}dr$, where $dS$ is the area of the $n$-dimensional spherical sector. The probability that for the mutated point we have $\boldsymbol{x} \in d\omega'$ is proportional to the probability density $g_G(r)$ in this subspace and to the $dV$.

## 3 Cauchy mutation

A new individual $\boldsymbol{x}$ is obtained by adding a random value to each entry of the selected parent $\boldsymbol{y}$, i.e.,

$$x_i = y_i + C(0, \tau_i), \quad i = 1, \ldots, n. \tag{13}$$

where $C(u, \tau)$ is a random value obtained according to the one–dimensional Cauchy mutation with the density function defined by

$$g(x) = \frac{1}{\pi} \frac{\tau}{\tau^2 + (x - u)^2}, \tag{14}$$

$\tau > 0$ being a scale parameter [1,7]. The shape of $g(x)$ is centered at $u$ and resembles that of a Gaussian density function, but it approaches the axes so slowly that the variance is infinite and the expectation fails to exist. A comparison between one-dimensional Cauchy and Gaussian density functions is presented in Fig. 2. The mutation function describing the transformation of $\boldsymbol{y}$ into $\boldsymbol{x}$ in accordance with the multi-dimensional Cauchy mutation has the form

$$g_C(\boldsymbol{x} - \boldsymbol{y}) = \pi^{-n} \prod_{i=1}^{n} \frac{\tau}{\tau^2 + (x_i - y_i)^2}, \tag{15}$$

where, for simplicity, $\tau = \tau_1 = \tau_2 = \cdots = \tau_n$, cf. (13).

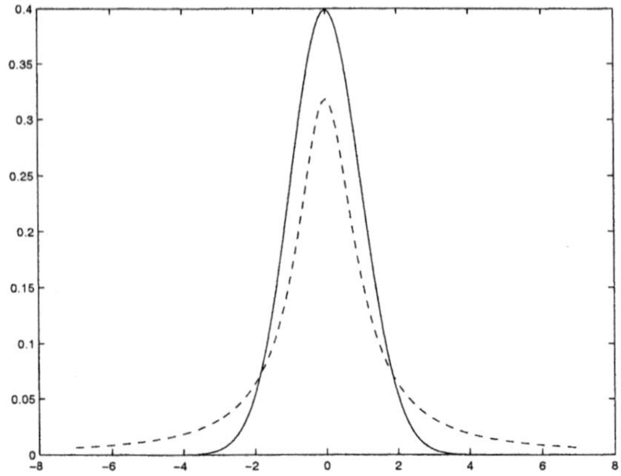


**Fig. 2.** Gaussian (solid line) and Cauchy (dashed line) probability density functions ($\sigma = 1$, $\tau = 1$ and $u = 0$).

### 3.1 Symmetry problem

The two-dimensional Cauchy density function is presented in Fig. 3(a). Unlike the Gaussian mutation, the Cauchy density function is not isotropic. Figure 3(b) presents the sections of the four-dimensional Cauchy density function for different spatial directions of abscissas (the direction $[k_1, k_2, k_3, k_4]$ represents a line $\{[\lambda k_1, \lambda k_2, \lambda k_3, \lambda k_4] \mid \lambda \in \mathbb{R}\}$). It is easy to see that the rate of convergence of the density function shape strongly depends on the chosen direction.

Since the directions parallel to the axes of the reference frame are preferred by the multi-dimensional Cauchy mutation, the effectiveness of the evolutionary algorithm which uses this mutation strongly depends on the choice of that frame.

### 3.2 Surrounding problem

The origins of the surrounding problem for the Cauchy mutation are the same as for the Gaussian mutation. The probability that the distance between the mutated point $\boldsymbol{x}$ and the parent $\boldsymbol{y}$, $r = \|\boldsymbol{x} - \boldsymbol{y}\|$, is determined by both the density function $g_C$ of (15) and the volume of the subspace $d\omega'$ in (9). The interpretation of the analytical form of this probability (rewritten in the $n$-spherical reference frame) is not so clear as in the case of the Gaussian mutation, because the radius and angles are not independent random

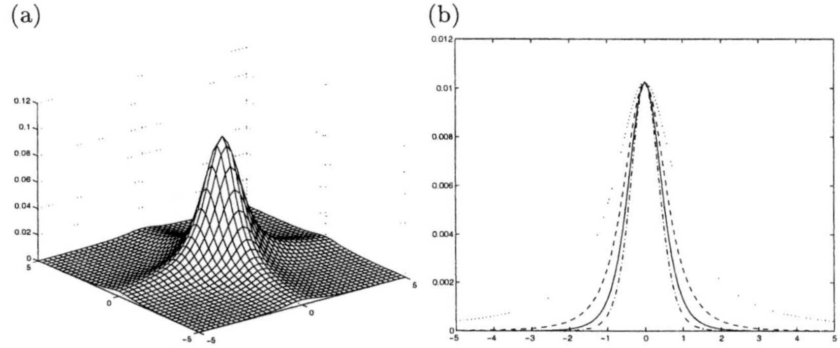

**Fig. 3.** Two–dimensional Cauchy density function (a). Four one–dimensional sections of the four–dimensional Cauchy density function (b), along the directions [1,0,0,0] (dotted line), [1,1,0,0] (dashed line), [1,1,1,0] (solid line) and [1,1,1,1] (dash-dot line). We have $\tau = 1$ and $u = 0$ for both the figures.

variables:

$$dP_C = \pi^{-n} \prod_{i=1}^{n} \left( \frac{\tau}{\tau^2 + z_i^2} \right) r^{n-1} \sin^{n-2}(\alpha_1) \sin^{n-3}(\alpha_2) \ldots \sin(\alpha_{n-2}) d\omega', \tag{16}$$

$(z_i \mid i = 1, \ldots, n)$ being defined by (8).

The surrounding problem is clearly illustrated in Fig. 4, where the histograms of the distances between the base and $10^6$ points mutated in accordance with (13) are drawn for $n = 2 \div 5$, $\tau = 1$. The peak of the maximum probability decreases and broadens, and the histogram becomes flatter as $n$ increases. On the one hand, macro-mutations are more probable for high landscape dimensions than for low ones. On the other hand, the probability of generating an offspring near a parent point decreases as the dimension $n$ increases.

## 4 Proposed mutations

The analysis performed in the previous sections shows that in general the common conviction regarding the distribution of the distance $\|\boldsymbol{x} - \boldsymbol{y}\|$ in the multi-dimensional Gaussian and Cauchy mutations is not justified. In this section, we propose new Gaussian-like and Cauchy-like mutations which overcome the *variance-dimension, surrounding* and *symmetry* problems.

The mutated point can be calculated as follows:

$$\boldsymbol{x} = \boldsymbol{y} + \boldsymbol{Z}, \tag{17}$$

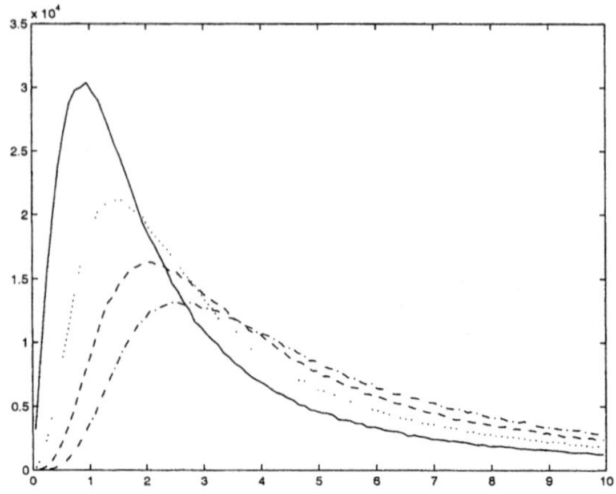


**Fig. 4.** Histograms of the distances between the base and $10^6$ points mutated in accordance with the Cauchy mutation; $n = 2$ — solid line, $n = 3$ — dotted line, $n = 4$ — dashed line, $n = 5$ — dash-dot line, other characteristics in the text.

where the vector $\boldsymbol{Z}$ is obtained from the formulas

$$\begin{aligned} Z_1 &= r\cos(\alpha_1), \\ Z_2 &= r\sin(\alpha_1)\cos(\alpha_2), \\ Z_3 &= r\sin(\alpha_1)\sin(\alpha_2)\cos(\alpha_3), \\ &\vdots \\ Z_{n-1} &= r\sin(\alpha_1)\ldots\sin(\alpha_{n-2})\cos(\alpha_{n-1}), \\ Z_n &= r\sin(\alpha_1)\ldots\sin(\alpha_{n-2})\sin(\alpha_{n-1}). \end{aligned} \tag{18}$$

Here $\alpha_{n-1}$ is a uniformly-distributed random angle ($\alpha_{n-1} = U[0, 2\pi]$) and the other angles ($\alpha_{n-k-1} \in [0, \pi) \mid k = 1, \ldots, n-2$) are randomly chosen with the probability density functions

$$f(\alpha_{n-k-1}) = K_k \sin^k(\alpha_{n-k-1}), \tag{19}$$

where $k = 1, \ldots, n-2$ and

$$K_k = \begin{cases} \frac{1}{2}\frac{3\cdot 5\cdot\ldots\cdot(2l+1)}{2\cdot 4\cdot\ldots\cdot 2l}, & \text{for } k = 2l+1, \\ \frac{1}{\pi}\frac{2\cdot 4\cdot\ldots\cdot 2l}{3\cdot 5\cdot\ldots\cdot(2l-1)}, & \text{for } k = 2l. \end{cases}$$

In other words, the direction of the vector $\boldsymbol{Z}$ is randomly chosen with a uniform distribution.

In order to obtain a new Gaussian-like or a new Cauchy-like mutation, the norm $r = ||\boldsymbol{Z}||$ can be chosen as

$$r = |N(0, \sigma)| \tag{20}$$

or

$$r = |C(0, \tau)|, \tag{21}$$

respectively.

The probability $dP_{NO}$ corresponding to the new Gaussian-like mutation can be calculated from the following formulas:

$$dP_{NO} = \frac{K}{\sqrt{2\pi}\sigma} \exp\left( -\frac{r^2}{2\sigma^2} \right) \sin^{n-2}(\alpha_1) \sin^{n-3}(\alpha_2) \ldots \sin(\alpha_{n-2}) d\omega', \tag{22}$$

and for the new Cauchy-like mutation we have

$$dP_{CO} = \frac{K}{\pi} \frac{\tau}{\tau^2 + r^2} \sin^{n-2}(\alpha_1) \sin^{n-3}(\alpha_2) \ldots \sin(\alpha_{n-2}) d\omega', \tag{23}$$

where $d\omega' = dr d\alpha_1 d\alpha_2 \ldots d\alpha_{n-1}$ and

$$K = \prod_{k=1}^{n-2} K_k = \begin{cases} \left(\frac{n-2}{2}\right)! \pi^{-\frac{n-2}{2}}, & \text{if } n \text{ is even,} \\ \frac{(n-1)!}{\left(\frac{n-1}{2}\right)!} 2^{-n} \pi^{-\frac{n-1}{2}}, & \text{if } n \text{ is odd.} \end{cases}$$

Figure 5 shows the histograms of the distances $||\boldsymbol{x} - \boldsymbol{y}||$ for $10^6$ points generated in accordance with both proposed mutations and dimensions $n = 2, 7$. The probability of point location decreases with $r$ and is independent of the landscape dimension. The same histograms can be obtained for any $n$.

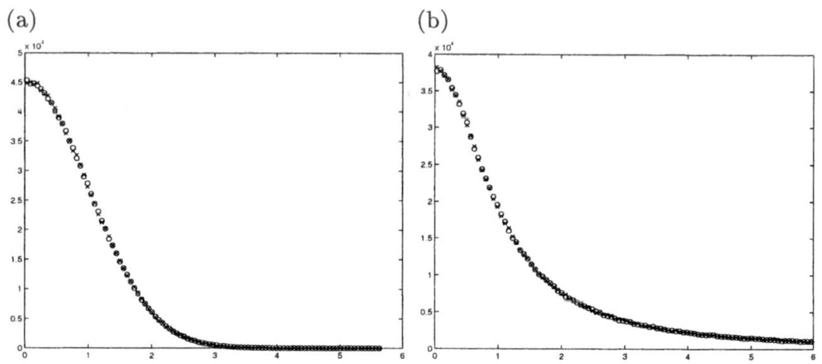


**Fig. 5.** Histograms of the distances between the base and $10^6$ mutated points generated in accordance with the Gaussian-like mutation (a) and the Cauchy-like mutation (b); $n = 2$ — crosses, $n = 7$ — circles, $\sigma = 1$ and $\tau = 1$.

## 5 Conclusions

The multi-dimensional Gaussian mutation is the most popular mutation technique in the evolutionary algorithms based on the floating-point representation of individuals. Unfortunately, there exists a common conviction that the most probable location of the offspring is the nearest neighborhood of the parent individual. This is correct, however, only for the one-dimensional mutation, but in the case of an $n$-dimensional one the most probable location moves from the center of mutation to the "ring" of the radius proportional to the norm of the standard deviation vector (the surrounding problem), which increases with the landscape dimension if the standard deviation of each entry is fitted (the variance-dimensional problem).

In recent years the multi-dimensional Cauchy mutation has attracted much attention. The evolutionary algorithms which use the Cauchy mutations seem more effective in comparison with the algorithms based on the Gaussian mutation in the majority of global optimization problems. But the multi-dimensional Cauchy density function obtained as the product of $n$ independent one-dimensional Cauchy density functions is not isotropic (the symmetry problem). The convergence of the density function to zero is different for different directions in the $n$–dimensional real space.

Two new mutations (Gaussian-like and Cauchy-like) have been proposed to overcome the above-mentioned problems and to guarantee the attraction of the base individual neighborhood and the isotropic density function of mutation. It would be interesting to analyze the influence of the proposed mutation on exploitation and exploration performances of an evolutionary algorithm. This problem determines our future research.

## References

1. Bäck, T., Fogel, D.B., and Michalewicz, Z., (Eds.) Handbook of Evolutionary Computation. Institute of Physics Publishing and Oxford University Press, NY, 1997.
2. Fogel, L.J., Owens, A.J., and Walsh, M.J., Artificial Intelligence through Simulated Evolution. Wiley, NY, 1966.
3. Galar, R., Handicapped individua in evolutionary processes. Biological Cybernetics, Vol. 51, 1985, pp.1–9.
4. Michalewicz, Z., Genetic Algorithms + Data Structures = Evolution Programs. Springer-Verlag, Berlin Heidelberg, 1996.
5. Rechenberg, I., Cybernetic solution path of an experimental problem. Roy. Aircr. Establ., libr. Transl. 1122, Farnborough, Hants., UK, 1965.
6. Yao, X., and Liu, Y., Fast evolutionary programming. Evolutionary Programming V: Proc. 5th Annual Conference on Evolutionary Programming, L.J. Fogel, P.J. Angeline, and T. Bäck, Eds. Cambridge, MIT Press, MA, 1996, pp. 419–429.
7. Yao, X., and Liu, Y., Evolutionary programming made faster. IEEE Trans. on Evolutionary Computation, Vol. 3, No. 2, 1999, pp. 82–102.

# Statistical Genetic Algorithms

**Andrzej Ossowski**[1], **Anna Święcicka**[2]

[1)] *Institute of Fundamental Technological Research,* PAS

ul. Świętokrzyska 21, 00-049 Warszawa, Poland

aossow@ippt.gov.pl

[2)] *Department of Computer Science,* Białystok University of Technology

ul. Wiejska 45A, 15-351 Białystok, Poland

amzs@ii.pb.bialystok.pl

**Abstract.** *The problem of optimisation of complex systems with statistical fitness function has been considered. Examples of processes with statistical fitness functions in science, technology and medicine have been given. Statistical genetic algorithms for solving such optimisation problems have been proposed.*

***Keywords:*** *probability space, fitness function, genetic algorithm, optimisation,*

## 1. Introduction

Genetic algorithms, in the classical sense, are iterative optimisation procedures that apply genetic operations *mutation*, *crossover* and *selection* to produce subsequent populations of solutions of a given problem [1]. An essential element of any genetic algorithm (*GA*) is a *fitness function* $f$ as an optimised quality index. It is usually assumed that the fitness function can be determined for any individual (solution) what is necessary to perform genetic operations and particularly crossover and selection.

In this work we consider certain complex optimisation problems applicable in practice for which a fitness function is not given directly in the form of an exact formula but rather can be determined by experiments performed over a real system. In such problems the fitness function is a statistic that refers to a class of real objects being over random and unpredictable external conditions. Therefore, attributes of any object determines only its potential quality(fitness) so that it is not sufficient to observe one or two selected objects in order to characterise the fitness of the whole class. For example, by accident an elder and well antelope can be killed by a leopard while a young ill one can escape. The fitness of a class of objects is thus a statistical property in its nature and is not determined directly by objects attributes. We propose the so-called *statistical genetic algorithms* (*SGA*) to solve such optimisation problems.

## 2. Classes of objects as probability spaces

It is a typical situation in practice to study classes of objects that can be treated as probability spaces. If we describe a class of objects by a space $(X, \mu)$ where $\mu$ is a probability measure on a bounded region $X \subset R^n$, then any real object belonging to that class can be represented by a single point $\mathbf{x} \in X$ uniquely identified with a finite collection of real coordinates/attributes $(x_1,...,x_n) \in R^n$ ([2,3]). It is clear that all real objects belonging to any class $(X, \mu)$ are always represented by a finite or at most countable subset of the continuous space $X$ The measure $\mu$ determines the space distribution of real objects in this sense that the measure $\mu(U)$ of any measurable set $U \subset X$ is equal to the probability that a real object randomly chosen from the class is represented by a point belonging to $U$. In particular $\mu(X) = 1$. Therefore it is possible that there are many real objects with the same attributes.

Let us assume that we have a family of classes represented by probability spaces $X_C = \{X(\mathbf{c}) = (X_\mathbf{c}, \mu_\mathbf{c}) : \mathbf{c} \in C\}$ parametrised by a finite number of attributes $\mathbf{c} = (c_1,...,c_m) \in C \subset R^m$, where $C$ is a compact region.. We assume for simplicity that all spaces $X_\mathbf{c}$ are contained in a bounded region $X \subset R^n$. Given a fitness function $f : X_C \longrightarrow R$ (i.e. a concept on the space $X_C$), the problem of optimisation (e.g. maximisation) of $f$ with respect to $\mathbf{c} \in C$ can be formulated. Unfortunately the fitness function describing classes of objects rarely is given as a direct formula but should be estimated from experiments performed on a class of objects. This is because the probability measure $\mu_\mathbf{c}$ describing the class usually is not known a priori.

We assume that there is a quality function $q: X \rightarrow R$ and the fitness of any class $X(\mathbf{c})$ is determined by the qualities $q(\mathbf{x})$ of all objects $\mathbf{x} \in X_\mathbf{c}$. If the probability distribution on $X(\mathbf{c})$ is not given, it has to be estimated from experiments. This task is practically feasible, if it is sufficient to study a finite number of objects belonging to $X_\mathbf{c}$ in order to obtain an estimate of the fitness of the whole class $X(\mathbf{c})$ i.e. if the fitness function is statistically computable.

<u>Definition 1</u>: The fitness function $f: X_C \longrightarrow R$ is *statistically computable* if for any $\mathbf{c} \in C$ there is a sequence of statistical functions $s_{\mathbf{c},m} : X^m(\mathbf{c}) \longrightarrow R$ such that

$$s_{\mathbf{c},m}(\mathbf{x}^1,\dots,\mathbf{x}^m) \longrightarrow f(X(\mathbf{c})) \tag{1}$$

as $m \longrightarrow +\infty$ for any random collection of points $\mathbf{x}^1,\dots,\mathbf{x}^m \in X$. The statistical computability means that the fitness function of the class $X(\mathbf{c})$ can be estimated with any accuracy from the knowledge of attributes of a finite number of objects belonging to $X(\mathbf{c})$.

<u>Definition 2</u>: The family of statistical functions $\{s_{\mathbf{c},m} : X_\mathbf{c} \rightarrow R,\ \mathbf{c} \in C,\ m=1,2,..\}$ is said to be *coherent* if $|\, s_{\mathbf{c}1,m}(\mathbf{x}^1,\dots,\mathbf{x}^m) - s_{\mathbf{c},2,m}(\mathbf{x}^1,\dots,\mathbf{x}^m)\,| \longrightarrow 0$ as $m \longrightarrow \infty$ for any $\mathbf{c}_1, \mathbf{c}_2 \in C$ such that $\mathbf{x}^1,\dots,\mathbf{x}^m \in X(\mathbf{c}_1) \cap X(\mathbf{c}_2)$. (see also [2,3])

The coherence guarantees that the fitness of all classes $X(\mathbf{c})$ has the same asymptotic statistical sense. In the particular case any family of statistics $s_m : X^m \longrightarrow R$, $m=1,2,\dots$ global on the space $X$ determines a coherent set of statistics $\{\, s_{\mathbf{c},m} : \mathbf{c} \in C$ and $m=1,2,\dots\}$ on $X_C$ such that $s_{\mathbf{c},m} = s_m|_{X(\mathbf{c})}$.

<u>Definition 3</u>: The fitness function $f: X_C \longrightarrow R$ is *regular* if it is statistically computable and admits a coherent family of statistical functions on $X_C$.

It is clear that the optimisation in a given class $X_C$ is practically feasible only for regular fitness functions. This is an essential limit for our possibilities of recognition and/or optimisation of complex systems (classes of objects). However, we can hypotesise that all fitness functions that are natural concepts on spaces representing classes of real objects should be regular [2,3]. In particular, any self-optimising process in the real world should evolve according to a regular fitness function. Therefore we assume in further considerations regularity of all fitness functions.

## 3. Statistical genetic algorithms

Let us consider a family of classes $X_C = \{X(\mathbf{c}) = (X_\mathbf{c}, \mu_\mathbf{c}): \mathbf{c} \in C\}$. If a fitness function $f: X_C \longrightarrow R$ is given as a function of $\mathbf{c}$, then a genetic algorithm ($GA[f]$) can be used to solve the problem of maximisation of $f$ with an assumed accuracy. To do that an appropriate problem discretisation is applied. Since the region $C$ is compact in $R^m$ there is a finite subset $B \subset C$ for every $\varepsilon > 0$ such that the Euclidean distance $d(\mathbf{c}, B) \leq \varepsilon$ for any $\mathbf{c} \in C$. We can uniquely represent any point $\mathbf{b} \in B$ by a finite binary chromosom and perform genetic iterations in order to obtain solutions of the approximate optimisation problem in $X_B = \{X(\mathbf{b}) = (X_\mathbf{b}, \mu_\mathbf{b}): \mathbf{b} \in B\}$ with the accuracy $\varepsilon$.

In practice, however, the fitness of a given class of objects usually is not known directly because it is determined by the averaged fitness of all objects belonging to the class. Thus we can perform standard genetic operations (mutations and crossover) in the space of chromosoms $B$ but cannot deduce the fitness of a given chromosom $\mathbf{b} \in B$ without information on the corresponding class $X(\mathbf{b})$. Conversely, we can estimate the fitness of any class $X(\mathbf{b})$ but cannot perform mutation and crossover without operating with chromosoms $\mathbf{b}$. That is why in optimisation in the space $X_B$ we have to deal in fact with a statistical genetic algorithm ($SGA[f]$) transforming simultaneously populations of parametrised classes $X(\mathbf{b}^{(k)})=[X(\mathbf{b}^1),..., X(\mathbf{b}^k)]$ and populations of binary chromosoms $\mathbf{b}^{(k)}= [\mathbf{b}^1,...,\mathbf{b}^k]$.

A genetic iteration in the $SGA[f]$ should be performed in the following order. First, for the initial population of classes $X(\mathbf{b}^{(k)})=[X(\mathbf{b}^1),..., X(\mathbf{b}^k)]$ the corresponding fitness $f^1,..., f^k$ are estimated by using appropriate statistics. Then, applying classical genetic operations (mutation and crossover) to the corresponding population of chromosoms $\mathbf{b}^{(k)} =[\mathbf{b}^1,...,\mathbf{b}^k]$ one can easily define generalised genetic operations in the space $X_B$ as follows

$$X^*(\mathbf{b})) = X(\mathbf{b}^*)\ ,\ X(\mathbf{b}^i)\otimes X(\mathbf{b}^j) = X(\mathbf{b}^i\otimes \mathbf{b}^j), \tag{2}$$

where the symbols " * ", " ⊗ " denote mutation and crossover operation, respectively.

The above relations determine a natural homomorphism between the "algebra" of binary chromosoms $B$ and the algebra of parametrised classes of objects $X_B$ . If we denote by $M[f]$ the crossover and mutation operations performed on binary chromosoms and by $S[f]$ the selection operation performed on classes of objects, then the statistical genetic algorithm $SGA[f]$ can be described by the following symbolic formula

$$SGA[f](X(\mathbf{b}^{(m)})) = S[f]((X(M[f](\mathbf{b}^{(m)}))) = X(GA[f](\mathbf{b}^{(m)})). \tag{3}$$

It is important to note here that the described statistical genetic operations are performed without the knowledge of the exact values of the fitness function. However, in the classical case, genetic calculations based on crossover, mutation and selection operations usually are random i.e. are not uniquely determined by the fitness of individuals in the actual population. This enables to achieve *ergodicity* of a given algorithm and avoid its *premature convergence*. Therefore, it is possible to perform proportional selection in *SGA*s by using statistical estimates $s_{\mathbf{c},\,m}(\mathbf{x}^1,\ldots,\mathbf{x}^m)$ instead of exact values of the fitness function $f$. This is justified by the fact that the conditional probability

$$\mathrm{P}(\,s_{\mathbf{c}1,\,m}(\mathbf{x}^1,\ldots,\mathbf{x}^m) > s_{\mathbf{c}2,\,m}(\mathbf{y}^1,\ldots,\mathbf{y}^m) \mid f(X(\mathbf{c}_1\,) \leq f(X(\mathbf{c}_2\,)), \tag{4}$$

by the assumed convergence (1), tends to zero for large $m$.

## 4. Recursive estimations of regular fitness functions

The problem of classification of regular fitness functions on a given space $X_C$ may be difficult. More easily is to determine such coherent collections of statistics $S_{\mathbf{c},\,m}$ , $m$ =1,2,... that are convergent as $m \longrightarrow \infty$. If numerical calculations suggest such a convergence, then the existence of a regular fitness function on $X_C$ determined by the collection of statistics can be expected.

Since computational effort in statistical genetic calculations is determined by the complexity of the statistical fitness function estimated particularly convenient in calculations are the so-called recursive statistics.

Definition 4: A collection of statistics $S^1{}_m$, ..., $S^k{}_m$, $m$ =1,2,... is said to be *recursive* if for every $m$ the following recurrent formulae are valid

$$S^j{}_{m+1} = F^j\,(S^1{}_m, ..., S^k{}_m, \mathbf{x}^{m+1}, m)\,,\; j = 1,...,k, \tag{5}$$

where $F^1,...,F^k$ are real functions $R^{k+1} \times N \longrightarrow R$.. In particular a statistics $S_m$ is recursive if $S_{m+1} = F(S_m, \mathbf{x}^{m+1}, m)$.

This means that the values of recursive statistics in the next iteration can be determined as functions of the statistics in the actual iteration. Therefore, recursive statistics can be relatively easy calculated for large cumulative populations of real objects.

In practice, usually a quality function $q : X \longrightarrow R$ of objects is given and the fitness function of a class of objects can be estimated by statistics of the form $S_{\mathbf{c},\,m}(q(\mathbf{x}^1),...,q(\mathbf{x}^m))$. The most useful and natural fitness functions are *average quality* and *dispersion* of quality of objects belonging to a class $X(\mathbf{c})$. The statistical computability of such fitness functions is guaranteed by the fundamental limit theorems of mathematical statistics. The classical statistics

$$e_{\mathbf{c},m} = \frac{1}{m}\sum_{i=1}^{m} q(\mathbf{x}^i)\,, \quad \sigma_{\mathbf{c},m} = \sqrt{\frac{1}{m}\sum_{i=1}^{m}\left\|q(\mathbf{x}^i) - e_m\right\|^2} \tag{6}$$

for $\mathbf{x}^1,...,\mathbf{x}^m \in X_C$ can be used in practical calculations.

Similarly, statistical moments of higher orders and the median of the probability distribution on $X(\mathbf{c})$ can be considered as regular fitness functions. Practical interpretations and significance of the such classical statistical fitness functions are obvious.

It is important for practical applications the following

Proposition: The average quality $e_{\mathbf{c},m}$ is a recursive statistics. The average and dispersion form a pair of recursive statistics.

*Proof*: To prove the above statements it is sufficient to observe that the statistics $e_{\mathbf{c},m}$ , $\sigma_{\mathbf{c},m}$ satisfy the following recursive equations

$$e_{\mathbf{c},m+1} = (m\, e_{\mathbf{c},m} + q(\mathbf{x}^{m+1}))/(m+1), \tag{7}$$

$$\sigma_{\mathbf{c},m+1} = \sqrt{\frac{1}{m+1}\left[m\sigma_{\mathbf{c},m}^2 + \frac{m}{m+1}\left(q(\mathbf{x}^{m+1}) - e_{\mathbf{c},m}\right)^2\right]}. \tag{8}$$

that can be derived directly from definitions (6). □

There is also another important fitness function of on the space $X_{\mathrm{C}}$, namely

$$Q(X(\mathbf{c})) = \max_{\mathbf{x}\in X_{\mathrm{C}}} [q(\mathbf{x})]. \tag{9}$$

Such a function, independent on the probability distribution on $X(\mathbf{c})$ is useful in cases when the fitness of a class of objects is determined by a critical object belonging to that class. This is the case for example in stability investigations. Statistical computability of (9) is ensured for a wide class of quality functions $q(\mathbf{x})$. The following simple statistics

$$Q_{\mathrm{c},\,m}(\mathbf{x}^1,\ldots,\mathbf{x}^m) = \max\,[q(\mathbf{x}^1),\ldots,\, q(\mathbf{x}^m)] \tag{10}$$

can be applied to its estimation. It is obvious that

$$Q_{\mathrm{c},\,m+1}(\mathbf{x}^1,\ldots,\mathbf{x}^{m+1}) = \max\,[Q_{\mathrm{c},\,m}(\mathbf{x}^1,\ldots,\mathbf{x}^m),\, q(\mathbf{x}^{m+1})] \tag{11}$$

what means that the fitness function (9) is also recursive.

It is important in statistical genetic algorithms that exact values of the fitness function are not necessary for calculations. Since the condition of proportional selection (4) is probabilistic in its nature non-exact fitness estimates can be applied instead at the beginning.

However, from iteration to iterations the available estimates are more and more exact so that a given statistical genetic algorithm tends to behave as a classical one.

## 5. Processes with statistical fitness functions

In science, technology and medicine we very often deal with processes that transform classes of objects and probability distributions. We provide in this section a theoretical description of such processes as well as general concepts of process optimisation based on the introduced formalism.

Let us assume that we have two classes $(X, \mu)$, $(Y, \nu)$ of objects represented uniquely by a finite collection of coordinates/attributes $\mathbf{x} = (x^1,\ldots,x^k) \in X \subset R^k$, $\mathbf{y} = (y^1,\ldots,y^l) \in Y \subset R^l$, respectively. By a process we mean here a map $P$ which transforms any input $\mathbf{x} \in X$ onto an output $\mathbf{y} = P(\mathbf{x}) \in Y$ (as is shown in Fig.1.), where $X$, $Y$ is the space of all possible inputs and outputs, respectively. In practice the map $P$ is realised by a real system. The map $P$ describes a process in this sense that the system starts many times to transform given inputs onto certain outputs. Thus, any pair $(\mathbf{x}, \mathbf{y}=P(\mathbf{x}))$ can be interpreted as a realisation of the process.

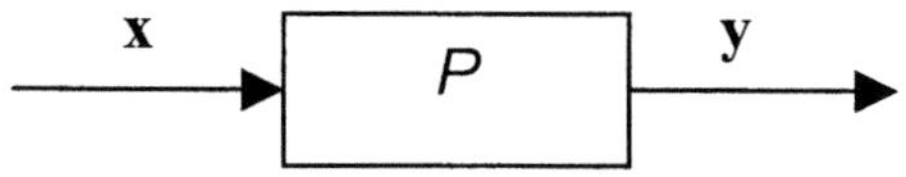


Fig.1. The block scheme of a process

If there is on the input space $X$ a probability measure $\mu$ determining the distribution of real input objects, then a non-uniform distribution of the output objects appears on the space $Y$ in general. Hence a probability measure $\nu=P(\mu)$ is induced on $Y$ by the process under consideration. Therefore, to describe the process $P$ it is sufficient to provide the associated class of objects

$$Z = (X\times Y, \mu\times P(\mu)), \tag{12}$$

where $\mu\times\nu$ denoted the standard product of probability measures.

Real processes usually are dependent on certain parameters **c**. In the case of such a process $P = P[\mathbf{c}]$ the problem of parametric optimisation of the process with respect to an appropriate quality index (*fitness function*) can be formulated. It is clear that this is equivalent to the optimisation in the parametrised family of classes $Z(\mathbf{c})=(X\times Y,\ \mu\times P[\mathbf{c}](\mu))$ of process realisations as objects. Thus a statistical genetic algorithm described in the previous sections can be applied to solve that problem.

We usually want to find optimal, constant values of the parameters **c** that maximise the process effectiveness. It is usually known a quality function $q: X\text{x}Y \longrightarrow R.$ of any realisation $(\mathbf{x}, \mathbf{y}=P(\mathbf{x}))$ of the process. The process fitness is dependent on the attributes of all input and output objects, in general i.e. it is a statistical quality function e.g.

$$E(P) = \langle q(\mathbf{x}, P(\mathbf{x}))\rangle_X \ , \tag{13}$$

where $\langle\ \rangle_X$ denotes the average over $\mathbf{x} \in X$ with respect to the measure $\mu$. We assume that the fitness $E(P)$ is statistically computable i.e. it can be estimated on the basis of finite samples of process realisations $(\mathbf{x}^i, \mathbf{y}^i = P(\mathbf{x})),\ i = 1,\ldots,N.$

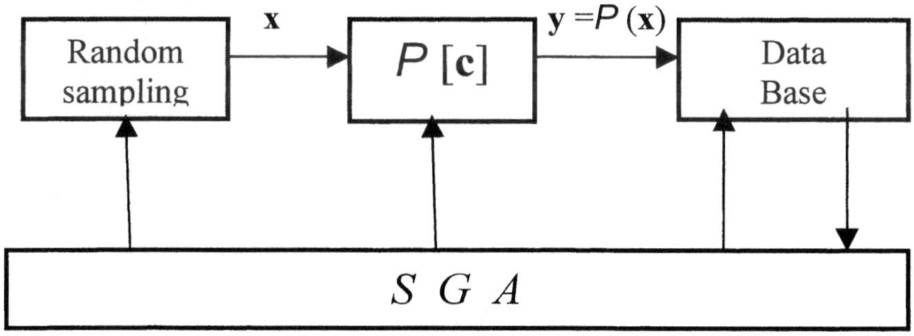


Fig.2. The block scheme of the generalised genetic optimisation

The block scheme of the statistical genetic optimisation of the process parameters is show in Fig.2. The process with the actual values of parameters **c** is tested by random sampling. A finite number of samples $(\mathbf{x},\ \mathbf{y} = P[\mathbf{c}](\mathbf{x}))$ is recorded in the system database. Then a statistical estimate of the fitness function (quality) of the process is computed. The above procedures is repeated for a population of different process parameters **c**. After these preparations the statistical genetic algorithm *SGA* performs genetic operations (crossover and mutations) with binary representations of the process parameters **c** and the sampling is performed for new generated chromosoms and fitness of the new classes is estimated. Finally, the algorithm performs proportional selection in order to generate the next population.

## 6. Perspectives of application in science, technology and medicine

We show in this section that the introduced ideas are closely related to very concrete practical situations. To do that we discuss some general optimisation problems considered in science, technology and medicine, namely the problem of parametric optimisation of technological and therapeutic processes as well as dynamical systems.

This is a common situation in science to optimise parameters **c** of a complex real dynamical system $S(\mathbf{x}, \mathbf{c})$, where **x** is a finite vector of state. If no physical/numerical model of the system is available, the only successful method of system optimisation can be based on the observation (in a finite time periond $T$) of system trajectories starting from various initial conditions $(\mathbf{x}_0, t_0)$. Each trajectory can be treated as an object. A number of measured trajectories can be evaluated with respect to a quality index expressing certain interesting dynamical properties of the system (e.g. a rate of convergence to the stationary state of the system). Then the fitness of the system (a stability index) is estimated e.g. by using (10). The space $X(\mathbf{c})$ of all possible trajectories of the system as the space of objects is usually uncountable. Hence, since the number of measured trajectories is always finite, such an approach is justified under the silent assumption of regularity (statistical computability) of a dynamical property as a fitness function of the system. If the trajectories measured are generated e.g. in response to random pulses of external excitations of the system, then a natural probability measure on the space $X(\mathbf{c})$ is induced. Thus we have a parametrised family of probability spaces and it is possible to apply to system optimisation an appropriate statistical genetic algorithm.

In the case of a simple discrete technological process $P$ there is a class of initial pieces/parts $(X, \mu)$ independent on the process. Any part $\mathbf{x} \in X$ is characterised by certain attributes $(x_1,...,x_k) \in R^k$ e.g. dimensions and/or material characteristics. The measure $\mu$ determines space distribution of subsequent parts introduced into the technological process $P$. In the result of technological operations a given part $\mathbf{x}$ is transformed onto an output part $\mathbf{y} = P(\mathbf{x})$ usually characterised by another set of attributes $(y_1,...,y_l) \in R^l$. In general, a technological process is random and non-unique i.e. initial parts with the same attributes can be transformed onto different final parts and/or different initial parts can be transformed onto final parts of the same attributes. Therefore, the probabilistic space of final parts (output products) $(Y, \nu)$ can also be distinguished, where the measure $\nu = P(\mu)$ determines the space distribution of final products of the process $P$. Since any technological process is usually dependent on certain process parameters $\mathbf{c}$ the problem of parametric optimisation of a process $P[\mathbf{c}]$ can be formulated. In technology, the process quality $E(P)$ is determined by the average quality of the final parts. It may be also important to achieve in the process a suitable repetability. Then a dispersion like statistic should be taken as the process fitness.

A similar situation is in the case of therapeutic processes $T$ which are discrete in principle. The class $(X, \mu)$ of "initial" patients suffering from a given disease can be introduced. This class will never be known exactly because in any instant only a finite number of patients can be registered as initial patients. Thus the space $X$ determines the range of possible patient attributes $(x_1,...,x_k)$ while the measure $\mu$ - the probability distribution of the subsequent registered cases. In the result of the therapy applied to initial patients certain distribution of the output patients is obtained. Thus, a probability space $(Y, \nu)$ of the cured patients can also be introduced, where the measure $\nu = T(\mu)$ determines the achieved output distribution of patient attributes. An average or median therapeutic effect is usually used as the fitness of the therapeutic process or another coherent collection of statistics specific for a given disease. The efficiency and risk of the therapeutic process can be optimised with respect to essential parameters (e.g. drugs doses) by using a suitable *SGA*.

## 7. Conclusion

The described ideas and conceptions can be applied to parametric optimisation of a wide class of processes and technological / therapeutic processes in particular. Preparation of a standard universal software for statistical genetic computations is the aim of the future work of the authors.

## Acknowledgements

The authors are grateful to professor J. Żytkow for informative talks and inspiration.

## References

[1] MICHALEWICZ Z.: Genetic Algorithms + Data Structures = Evolution Programs, Springer-Verlag. Berlin, 1996.

[2] ŻYTKOW J.: Discovery of Concept Expansion, in Intelligent Information Systems VIII, Ustroń 99

[3] OSSOWSKI A., ŻYTKOW J.: Geometric approach to a coherrent set of operational definitions, in Intelligent Information Systems, Bystra 2000.

[4] OSSOWSKI A.: Geometria Baz Danych, in IV Konferencja Naukowa nt. Sztuczna Inteligencja SzI-15'2000, Siedlce-Warszawa, 2000.

# Cellular Automata Approach to Scheduling Problem in Case of Modifications of a Program Graph

**Anna Święcicka[1], Franciszek Seredyński[2] and Mariusz Jażdżyk[3]**

[1] Department of Computer Science, Białystok University of Technology
Wiejska 45A, 15-351 Białystok, Poland, e-mail: amzs@ii.pb.bialystok.pl

[2] Polish-Japanese Institute of Information Technologies
Koszykowa 86, 02-008 Warsaw, Poland
and
Institute of Computer Science, Polish Academy of Sciences
Ordona 21, 01-237 Warsaw, Poland
e-mail: sered@ipipan.waw.pl

[3] Warsaw University of Technology
Nowowiejska 15/19, 00-665 Warsaw, Poland

***Abstract***: *In this paper we propose using cellular automata (CAs) to perform distributed scheduling tasks of a parallel program in the two processor system. We consider a program graph as a CA with elementary cells interacting locally according to a certain rule which must be found. Effective rules for a CA are discovered by a genetic algorithm (GA). With these rules, CA-based scheduler is able to find allocations which minimize the total execution time of the program in the two processor system. We show efficiency of discovered rules in case of modifications of a program graph. These modifications include changing the values of the weights of some randomly chosen tasks or (and) edges of a program graph. We also show that discovered rules may be used to find optimal or suboptimal solutions of other program graphs constructed on the base of a given program graph.*

*Keywords: cellular automata, genetic algorithms, scheduling problem*

## 1. Introduction

The problem of scheduling tasks of a parallel program in a parallel architecture remains a challenge for practitioners and researchers in the area of parallel computing. The problem is known to be NP-complete in its general form. Therefore effective solutions of the problem are proposed in the form of heuristics based on different mathematical platforms. To this stream of research belong scheduling algorithms based on applying techniques derived from nature. We follow this line of research and propose in the paper to use CAs to create distributed scheduling algorithm.

CAs are discrete dynamical systems made up of a large number of components. It is an interesting feature of these systems that although these components only interact locally, complex global behaviour can emerge. This is very similar to the behaviour of many systems in the real world, so CAs are often used to model such systems. In this paper we show that CAs can be effectively used to solve complex problem - scheduling tasks of a parallel program in the two processor system.

Our approach to a scheduling problem differs from those described in the literature. Although, as we mentioned, there have been many approaches to the scheduling domain, almost all algortihms have concentrated on producing a single schedule that is as close to optimal as possible. These optimal schedules are often very sensitive to slight perturbations in conditions, which in the real world may occur. On the other hand, our CA-based scheduling algorithm is resistant to such changes in conditions.

The remainder of the paper is organized as follows. The next section discusses accepted models of a parallel program and a parallel system in the context of a scheduling problem. Section 3 provides a background on CAs. Section 4 contains a description of a proposed CA-based scheduling algorithm with genetic algorithm-based engine for discovering scheduling rules. Results of experimental study of the scheduler are presented in Section 5. In particular, on the example of a program graph called *g18* we show efficiency of discovered rules in case of modifications of a program graph. These modifications include changing the values of the weights of some randomly chosen tasks or (and) edges of a program graph. We also show that discovered rules may be used to find optimal or suboptimal solutions of other program graphs, constructed on the base of a given program graph. Last section contains conclusions.

## 2. Scheduling problem

A multiprocessor system is represented by an undirected unweighted graph $G_s = (V_s, E_s)$, called a *system graph.* $V_s$ is the set of $N_s$ nodes of the system graph representing processors with their local memories of a parallel computer of MIMD architecture. $E_s$ is the set of edges representing bidirectional channels between processors and defines a topology of the multiprocessor system. Figure 1a shows an example of a system graph representing a multiprocessor system consisting of two processors *P0* and *P1*. This topology will be used in all experiments presented in this paper. It is assumed that all processors have the same computational power and a communication via the links does not consume any processor time.

A parallel program (see Figure 1b) is represented by a weighted directed acyclic graph $G_p = (V_p, E_p)$, called a *precedence task graph* or a *program graph*. $V_p$ is the set of $N_p$ nodes of the graph representing elementary tasks, which are indivisible computational units. Weights $b_k$ of the nodes (marked on nodes) describe the processing time needed to execute a given task on any processor of a multiprocessor system. There exists a precedence constraint relation between the tasks *k* and *l* in the program graph if the result produced by task *k* has to be send to task *l*. $E_p$ is the set of edges of the precedence task graph describing the communication time between the tasks. Weights $a_{kl}$ of the edges (marked on edges) describe a communication time between pairs of tasks *k* and *l*, when they are located in neighbour processors. If the tasks *k* and *l* are located in the same processor than the communication time between them is equal to 0.

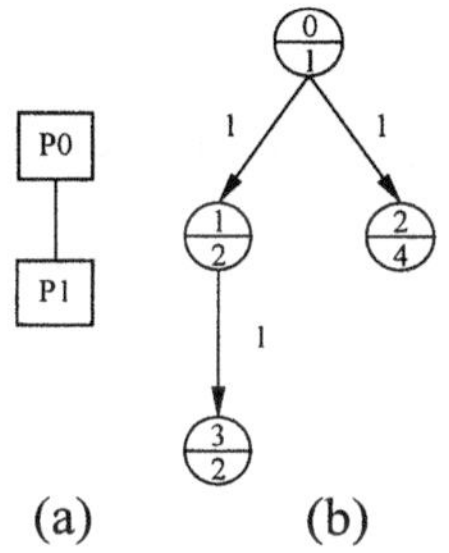


Fig. 1: Examples of a system graph (a) and a precedence task graph (b)

The purpose of *scheduling* is to distribute the tasks among the processors in such a way that the precedence constraints are preserved and the response time *T* (the total execution time) is minimized. A found optimal schedule is usually represented by a Gantt chart (see Figure 2) showing allocation of tasks to processors and times when a given task starts and finishes execution.

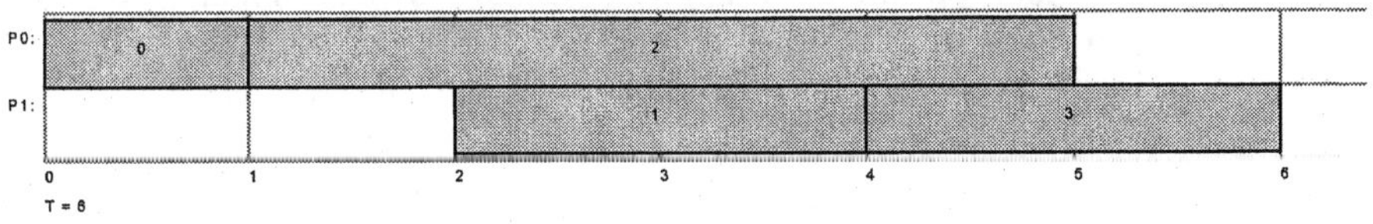


Fig. 2: Optimal schedule represented by a Gantt chart for a problem from Fig. 1

The response time *T* for a given precedence task graph depends on an allocation of tasks in multiprocessor topology and some scheduling policy applied in individual processors. While allocations of tasks are changed by the algorithm, a scheduling policy remains constant. It defines an order of processing tasks, ready to run in a given processor. We will assume that a scheduling policy is the same for all processors of the system. The scheduling problem is known to be NP-complete in its general form, even in the case of only two processors.

## 3. Cellular automata

CAs [3,7] are dynamical systems in which space and time are discrete. The cellular array is $n$-dimensional, where $n$ = 1, 2, 3 is used in practice. In this paper we shall concentrate on one–dimensional CAs.

A one-dimensional CA consists of a spatial lattice of $N$ cells, each of which, at time $t$, can be in one of $k$ states. In this paper we assume that each cell is a Boolean variable: $a_i^t \in \{0,1\}$ ($i$=0,1,...$N$-1). The collection of all local states is called the *configuration*. A CA has a single fixed rule, which is used to update each cell. The rule maps from the states in a neighbourhood of a cell to a single state, which is the update value for that cell. In a one-dimensional CA, the neighbourhood of a cell includes the cell itself and some *radius r* of neighbours on either side of the cell.

The equations of motion for a CA are often expressed in the form of a *rule table*: a look-up table listing each of the neighbourhood patterns, and the state to which the central cell in that neighbourhood is mapped. For example, Table 1 presents one possible rule table for a one-dimensional, binary-state CA with radius $r$=1. Each possible neighbourhood $\eta$ is given, along with the "output bit" $a$ to which the central cell is updated.

Table 1: An example of a rule table for a one-dimensional, binary state CA with $r$=1

| $\eta$ | 000 | 001 | 010 | 011 | 100 | 101 | 110 | 111 |
|---|---|---|---|---|---|---|---|---|
| $a$ | 0 | 1 | 1 | 1 | 0 | 1 | 1 | 0 |

The CA starts out with some initial configuration (IC) of cell states. To run the CA, the look-up table is applied, usually synchronously, to each neighbourhood in the current lattice configuration, respecting the choice of boundary conditions, to produce the configuration at the next time step.

## 4. Cellular automata-based scheduler

To design a scheduling algorithm with use of CA we assume that a nonlinear structure of a program graph is approximated by a one-dimensional CA of size $N_p$ [4]. It means that with each task of a program graph an elementary cell is associated. Figure 3 shows a possible CA corresponding to the program graph from Figure 1b. It shows that a cell corresponding to a task with a given order number (number outside table) is in some binary state (number inside table).

| | | | 0 | 1 | 2 | 3 | | | |
|---|---|---|---|---|---|---|---|---|---|
| 0 | 0 | 0 | 0 | 1 | 0 | 1 | 0 | 0 | 0 |

Fig. 3: The CA corresponding to the program graph from Fig. 1b

In our experiments the CA has $r$=3, with null boundary conditions: we assume that "absent cells" are always in state 0 (these absent cells are marked with dashed lines on Figure 3). Since we consider the two processor system, our automaton is a binary one. The state 0 or 1 of a cell means that a corresponding task is allocated either in the processor *P0* or *P1*, respectively. Each configuration corresponds to the allocation of tasks in the system graph. To calculate the value of *T* for the given allocation of tasks, we used the scheduling policy of the type: "a task with the highest dynamic level first" [4]. Another assumption is that the CA works sequentially, that means that at given moment of time only one cell updates its state. An order of updating states by cells is defined by their order number corresponding to tasks in a program graph.

CA corresponding to our program graph evolves according to its rule. Initial states of CA correspond to an initial allocation of tasks in the two processor system. Changing states of CA results in changing an allocation of tasks in the system. It results in changing the response time *T*. We want to know if exists a rule for CA providing for any initial allocation of tasks converging CA to an allocation which minimizes *T*.

There are two phases of our algorithm: a phase of learning rules and a phase of normal operating. The purpose of the learning phase is discovery effective rules for scheduling. Searching effective rules is conducted with use of a GA [1,2,6,4]. The GA begins with a population of *P* randomly generated CA rules, each encoded as a string of the rule table output bits in lexicographic order of neighbourhood patterns. The length of the rule is calculated as $k^{2r+1}$. A rule's fitness is estimated by: (i) randomly choosing *I* initial configurations, which correspond to initial allocations of a program graph into a system graph; (ii) running the rule on each initial configuration for *M* time steps; (iii) measuring the response time *T* for each final allocation. A fitness value for the rule is the average value of *T*. The GA works as follows. A new set of ICs of size *I* is generated. A fitness value is calculated for each rule in the population. A number *E* of the best rules ("elite") is copied without modification to the next generation. The remaining *P-E* rules for the next generation are formed by crossover between randomly chosen pairs of elite rules. The parent rules are chosen from the elite with replacement. The offspring from each crossover are each mutated with probability $p_m$. This process is continued a predefined number *G* of generations and when is completed discovered rules are stored.

In the phase of normal operating, when a program graph is initially randomly allocated, CA is initiated and equipped with a rule taken from the set of discovered rules. We expect in this phase that for any initial allocation of tasks of a given program graph, CA will be able to find allocation of tasks, providing the minimal or near minimal value of $T$.

## 5. Results of experiments

A number of experiments with program graphs available in the literature has been conducted [4,5]. The goal of experiments described in this paper is to examine if discovered rules can be used to find schedules for other program graphs. We will focus our attention on one program graph refered as *g18*. This graph is shown on Figure 4. Computational costs of tasks are shown in the figure. Communication costs are all the same and equal 1. The optimal response time $T$ for this program graph in the two processor system is equal 46.

Experiment #1: CA-based scheduler for *g18*: learning rules and normal operating

As we mentioned earlier, a neighbourhood of a cell with radius $r$=3 was used, what resulted in 128-bit long CA rule. The parameter values we used were the following. For each CA in the population, $I$=50 and $M$=50. We set $P$=100, $E$=50 and $G$=100. We used a two-points crossover and a bit-flip mutation with $p_m$=0.03.

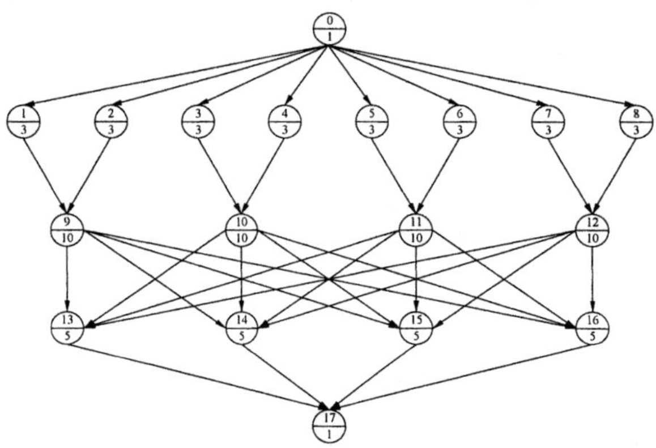

Fig. 4: Program graph *g18*

One typical run of the GA is shown on Figure 5. On this figure one can see three different plots of the average of $T$: the minimal (*min*), the average of the elite (*av el*) and the average of the population (*av pop*), changing during evolutionary process. The GA needs not more than 12 generations to discover a CA rule providing the average value of $T$ equal 46 (optimal value).

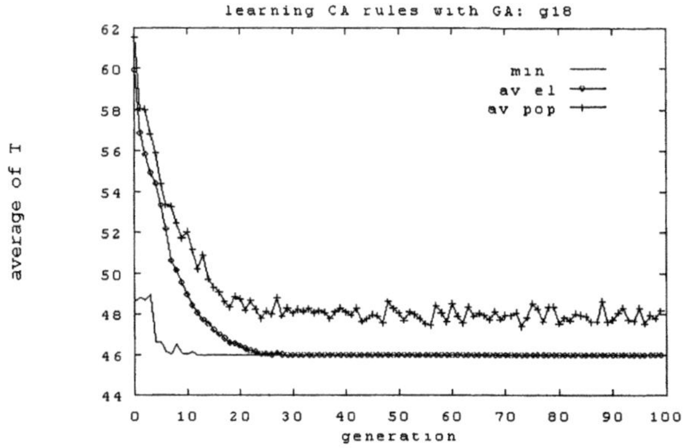


Fig. 5: CA-based scheduler for the *g18*: learning mode

Figure 6 shows a run of the CA-based scheduler with the best found rule after 100 generations, starting from randomly generated initial configuration. Left part of the figure presents a space-time diagram of the CA consisting of 18 cells and the right part shows graphically a value of *T* corresponding to the allocation found in a given step. One can see that after the step 0, cells of the CA are in some states corresponding to the allocation of tasks (white cell – a corresponding task is allocated in *P0*, black cell – a task is allocated in *P1*) and the value of *T* corresponding to this allocation is greater than 50. Then the CA starts to change its states what results in changing values of *T*. One can see that the CA needs about 15 time steps to converge to tasks' allocation corresponding to the minimal value of *T*.

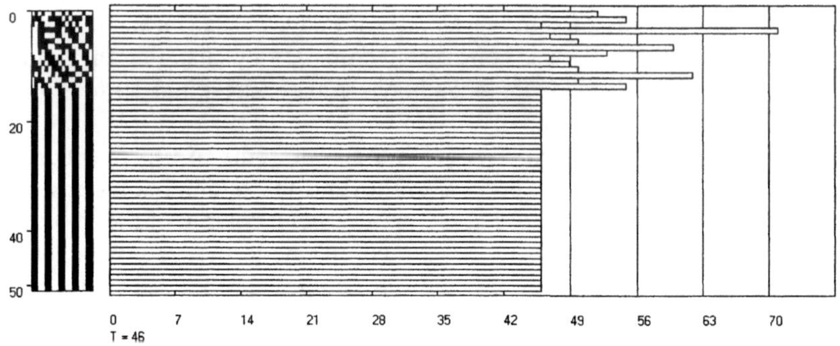


Fig. 6: Space-time diagram of CA-based scheduler with the best found rule

After run of the GA its population contains rules suitable for CA-based scheduling. Quality of these rules we can find out in the normal operating mode. We generate some number of test problems and use them to test each of found rule. Figure 7 shows results of the test conducted with 1000 random initial allocations of the *g18*. For each found rule the average value of *T* found by a CA in the test problem is shown. One can see that over 60 rules are able to find an optimal scheduling for each representative of the test.

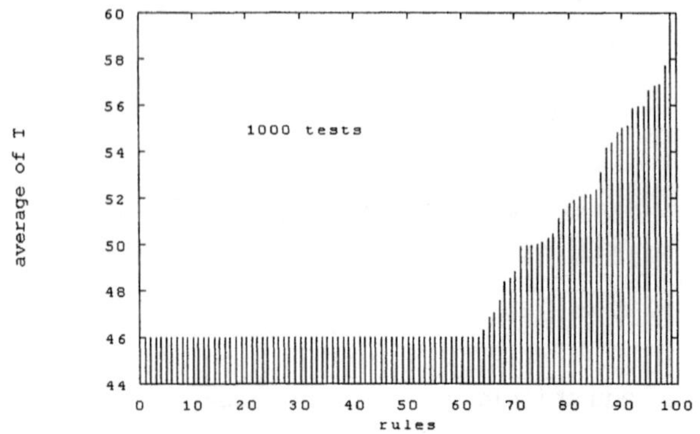


Fig. 7: Normal operating mode for *g18*: the average value of *T*

Experiment #2: modifications of the program graph *g18*

In the previous experiment the GA was able to discover CA rules to solve a given instance of the scheduling problem. The question which arises is whether discovered rules are sensitive to some modifications of our program graph. To find it out, discovered rules were used in operating mode to find solutions of some other program graphs. These graphs were constructed from the *g18* by introducing some random modifications to it. These modifications included changing the values of the weights of some randomly chosen tasks or (and) edges. This way we obtained 30 new program graphs. The ways in which these graphs were constructed are given in Table 2. In this table in the brackets there are given the new values of the weights of some tasks or (and) edges. That means that e.g. the program graph called *g18_22* was constructed from *g18* by changing the values of the weights of: the task 15 to 8, the edge between the tasks 3 and 10 to 3 and the edge between the tasks 9 and 13 to 3.

Then we used a standard GA (with a chromosome of a given individual coding an allocation of tasks to processors) to find the optimal solutions of our new program graphs. The results are given in the second column of the Table 3.

As we mentioned earlier, discovered rules for the *g18* were used in operating mode to find solutions for the new program graph. We used five the best rules from the final population of the GA and tested them on 1000 random initial allocations of our new program graphs. All the parameter values (e.g. the number of time steps *M*, the scheduling policy) remained the same. The best average response time *T* (from five runs of the scheduler in the normal operating mode) for each program graph is given in the third column of the Table 3. One can see that in an over half of the cases the best discovered rules were able to find an optimal scheduling for each representative of the test. In the remaining cases obtained solutions are close to the optimal results. These solutions are obtained without a process of discovering rules and without using GA to find optimal schedules.

Table 2: New program graphs constructed from the *g18*

| Program graph | Changing the values of the weights of | |
|---|---|---|
| | the tasks | the edges |
| *g18_1* | 7 (4) | - |
| *g18_2* | 10 (3) | - |
| *g18_3* | 15 (4) | - |
| *g18_4* | 8 (1), 14 (6) | - |
| *g18_5* | 6 (2), 9 (2) | - |
| *g18_6* | 7 (5), 14 (6) | - |
| *g18_7* | 7 (1), 17 (2), 4 (4) | - |
| *g18_8* | 10 (3), 14 (1), 1 (2) | - |
| *g18_9* | 8 (4), 11 (18), 15 (6) | - |
| *g18_10* | - | 9 → 14 (4) |
| *g18_11* | - | 15 → 17 (2) |
| *g18_12* | - | 2 → 9 (2) |
| *g18_13* | - | 8 → 12 (3), 10 → 14 (4) |
| *g18_14* | - | 11 → 16 (5), 12 → 16 (5) |
| *g18_15* | - | 16 → 17 (2), 2 → 9 (2) |
| *g18_16* | - | 7 → 12 (3), 9 → 14 (3), 10 → 14 (4) |
| *g18_17* | - | 11 → 16 (5), 12 → 16 (5), 16 → 17 (2) |
| *g18_18* | - | 9 → 16 (4), 11 → 15 (4), 12 → 15 (5) |
| *g18_19* | 15 (2) | 0 → 4 (2) |
| *g18_20* | 17 (3) | 0 → 7 (2) |
| *g18_21* | 0 (2) | 1 → 9 (3) |
| *g18_22* | 15 (8) | 3 → 10 (3), 9 → 13 (3) |
| *g18_23* | 16 (8) | 5 → 11 (3), 9 → 16 (3) |
| *g18_24* | 17 (2) | 7 → 12 (4), 9 → 15 (5) |
| *g18_25* | 9 (9), 10 (8) | 10 → 16 (4) |
| *g18_26* | 13 (4), 14 (7) | 11 → 14 (2) |
| *g18_27* | 15 (7), 17 (2) | 11 → 16 (4) |
| *g18_28* | 4 (5), 7 (5) | 12 → 15 (5), 0 → 1 (5) |
| *g18_29* | 5 (4), 9 (14) | 15 → 17 (4), 0 → 3 (3) |
| *g18_30* | 8 (4), 6 (4) | 13 → 17 (5), 0 → 5 (4) |

Table 3: The best response time *T* received for program graphs

| Program graph | Standard GA (*T*) | CA-based scheduling algorithm (*T*) |
|---|---|---|
| *g18_1* | 47 | 47.0 |
| *g18_2* | 43 | 49.0 |
| *g18_3* | 46 | 46.0 |
| *g18_4* | 46 | 46.89 |

| *g18_5* | 42 | 47.82 |
|---|---|---|
| *g18_6* | 48 | 48.91 |
| *g18_7* | 47 | 47.89 |
| *g18_8* | 41 | 48.0 |
| *g18_9* | 51 | 54.0 |
| *g18_10* | 46 | 46.0 |
| *g18_11* | 46 | 46.0 |
| *g18_12* | 46 | 46.0 |
| *g18_13* | 46 | 46.0 |
| *g18_14* | 46 | 46.0 |
| *g18_15* | 46 | 46.0 |
| *g18_16* | 46 | 46.0 |
| *g18_17* | 46 | 46.0 |
| *g18_18* | 46 | 46.0 |
| *g18_19* | 45 | 46.0 |
| *g18_20* | 48 | 48.0 |
| *g18_21* | 47 | 47.0 |
| *g18_22* | 48 | 49.0 |
| *g18_23* | 48 | 49.0 |
| *g18_24* | 47 | 47.0 |
| *g18_25* | 45 | 45.0 |
| *g18_26* | 47 | 48.0 |
| *g18_27* | 48 | 49.0 |
| *g18_28* | 48 | 48.0 |
| *g18_29* | 49 | 50.65 |
| *g18_30* | 47 | 47.0 |

Experiment #3: program graphs constructed on the base of the *g18*

In this experiment we used discovered rules to find solutions of other program graphs constructed on the base of the *g18*. A program graph called *g36* was constructed through the linking the *g18* to its final task. The weight of the linking edge was set to 0. A program graph called *g54* was constructed through the linking the *g18* to the final task of the *g36* and setting the weight of the linking edge to 0. In a similar way other program graphs (*g72*, *g90* and *g108*) were constructed.

Then we used five the best rules for the program graph *g18* and tested them on 1000 random initial allocations of our new program graphs. All the parameter values remained the same except the number of time steps *M*. The values of *M* used in experiment were the following. For the program graph *g36* *M* was set to 150, for *g54* – to 200, for *g72* – to 300, for *g90* – to 350 and for *g108* – to 450, respectively. We set new values of *M* ($\approx 4 * N_p$) because the more cells a CA has the more time steps may be necessary to converge to a stable allocation. The way of calculating *M* is some heuristic based on many observations of behaviour of CAs. The best average response time *T* (from five runs of the scheduler in the normal operating mode) for each program graph is given in the third column of the Table 4. Obtained results are compared with these received by means of a standard GA .

Table 4: The best response time *T* received for program graphs

| Program graph | Standard GA (*T*) | CA-based scheduling algorithm (*T*) |
|---|---|---|
| *g36* | 92 | 93.0 |
| *g54* | 138 | 138.0 |
| *g72* | 184 | 185.0 |
| *g90* | 230 | 230.0 |
| *g108* | 276 | 277.0 |

One can see that the best rules obtained for the program graph *g18* can successfully find an optimal or near optimal scheduling for each representative of the test.

## 6. Conclusions

We have presented in the paper the CA-based scheduling algorithm. The goal of experiments was to examine if discovered rules can be used to find optimal schedules for other program graphs, without the learning phase. The results of conducted experiments are very promising. They show that the GA is able to discover CA rules suitable to solve the scheduling problem not only for a given instance of the problem. What is interesting, our CA-based scheduling algorithm is resistant to modifications of a given program graph. This algorithm discovers not a single schedule but rather "a scheduling function", which successfully transforms any initial allocation to the optimal or near optimal one. The preliminary results also show that discovered rules may be used to find optimal or suboptimal solutions of other, not known in advance instances of the problem. The future work will include systematic study of behaviour of the CA-based scheduling algorithm for other known problem instances and answering the question whether solutions found for these instances can be used as subsolutions in the process of quick discovery of solutions for new generated problem instances.

**Acknowledgments**

The first author gratefully acknowledges support from Białystok University of Technology (grant W/II/5/99).

# References


[1] R. Das, M. Mitchell, J.P. Crutchfield, *A Genetic Algorithm Discovers Particle-Based Computation in Cellular Automata*, in Y. Davidor, H.-P. Schwefel, R. Männer (eds.), Parallel Problem Solving from Nature – PPSN III, LNCS 866, Springer, 1994, pp. 344-353.

[2] F. Seredyński, *Discovery with Genetic Algorithm Scheduling Strategies for Cellular Automata*, in Parallel Problem Solving from Nature – PPSN V, LNCS 1498, A. E. Eiben, T. Back, M. Schoenauer and H.-P. Schwefel (eds.), Springer, 1998, pp. 643-65.

[3] M. Sipper, *Evolution of Parallel Cellular Machines*, LNCS 1194, Springer, 1997.

[4] A. Święcicka, F. Seredyński, *Evolving Cellular Automata Structures to Solve Multiprocessor Scheduling Problem*, Intelligent Information Systems IX, Proceedings of the Workshop held in Bystra, Poland, June 12-16, 2000, pp.115-119.

[5] A. Święcicka, F. Seredyński, *Cellular Automata Approach to Scheduling Problem*, PARELEC 2000 - International Conference on Parallel Computing in Electrical Engineering, Trois-Rivieres, Quebec, Canada, August 27-30, 2000, pp. 29-33.

[6] A. Święcicka, F. Seredyński, K. Łuszczyk, *Cellular Automata-Based Multiprocessor Scheduling*, PARELEC `98 - International Conference on Parallel Computing in Electrical Engineering, Białystok, September 2-5, 1998, pp. 264-268.

[7] S. Wolfram, *Universality and complexity in cellular automata*, Physica D, 10, 1984, pp. 1-35.

# Multimodal Optimization with Artificial Immune Systems

**Sławomir T. Wierzchoń**

Institute of Computer Science, Polish Academy of Sciences, Warsaw, Poland

Dept. of Computer Science, Białystok Univ. of Technology, Białystok, Poland

e-mail: stw@ipipan.waw.pl

***Abstract***: *A simple and easy to implement algorithm for multimodal function optimization is proposed. It is based on clonal selection and programmed cell death mechanisms taken from natural immune system. Empirical results confirming its usability are presented, and review of other related approaches is given.*

*Keywords: Artificial Immune Systems, Multimodal Optimization, Clonal Selection, Affinity Maturation*

## 1. Introduction

Stochastic iterative search techniques proved to be a useful tool in solving hard optimization problems. Their popularity follows from at least three features, ([3], pp. 1-8): they are easy to implement, they are very general (in a sense there is no special requirements on the kinds of optimization problem), and lastly, they proved to be satisfactory in finding good, fast solutions to a wide spectrum of hard problems. These techniques can be divided into two main categories: local search and population-based search or evolutionary algorithms (EAs for brevity). While techniques from the first category maintain a single "current best solution", population-based techniques maintain a population of tentative solutions that are modified in a way resembling natural evolution. That is, good candidates have greater chance to be entered into next population (by means of so-called *selection*), their best features will be propagated through future populations (by so-called *crossover*), and lastly, slight experimentation is done over these candidates (by *mutation*).

An attractive feature of an EA is its exploitative aspect: According to Holland's Schema Theorem, [9], the algorithm assigns exponentially increasing number of trials to the observed best parts of the search space, what results in a convergence to a single point, being a searched optimum. However, this convergence is not always advantageous. As stated by Gaspar and Collard in [8], in fact it contradicts basic principle of natural evolution, where a great diversity of different species is observed. In other words, classical EAs cannot maintain sufficient population diversity, i.e., EAs behave poorly when solving multimodal optimization problems.

A "classical" technique allowing explore new areas of the search space without destroying good candidates already acquired is that of sharing and restricted mating proposed in 1987 by Goldberg and Richardson (consult [9] for details). An optimum, or simply a peak in a search space, is treated as resource that a sub-population, or species can exploit. The individuals near the peak, treated as species, have to share the resource of that peak. Perceived fitness, i.e. the EA's perception of the objective function, depends on the number of candidates located near the peak: the more the candidates the lower the fitness is, as the resource becomes overused, what reduces selective pressure in that area of search space. Apart of perceived fitness the similarity metric is used to restrict crossover to most similar candidates only. This idea makes two assumptions, however: (a) the number of peaks is known in advance, and (b) the peaks are uniformly distributed throughout the search space. In comparison with "traditional" evolutionary algorithm the time complexity of this algorithm is increased by $O(n^2)$, where $n$ is the population size. This additional time is needed to perform the fitness sharing calculations. Another serious problem with real implementation is that of niche radius: if both the assumptions are fulfilled, a simple recipe can be used to estimate the radius. However, there are functions where these assumptions are not satisfied.

Beasley et al., [1], introduced a sequential niche technique. It can be treated as a simple extension to existing unimodal techniques as it involves multiple runs of an EA (or other search technique), each finding one maximum. Again, a vital assumption is that the number of interesting optima is known in advance, and that these optima are spread approximately uniformly throughout the search space. A number of problems with this algorithm was reported in [1]: inaccuracy, incompleteness, extra runs, and - again - the problem with niche radius.

To avoid the problems with the assumptions (a) and (b), and to make the implementation less expensive, Spears, [16], replaced the distance metric by labels attached to each individual. Each label consists of $t$ tag bits what allows distinguish $2^t$ sub-populations. To attain fitness sharing, the perceived fitness is obtained by dividing the row fitness of each individual by the size of its sub-population. Such an idea appears to be useful in finding the high peaks in the search space. To find lower peaks, additional mechanism restricting mating further had to be used.

Recently, a new biologically inspired technique, so-called *artificial immune systems* (AIS), have been proposed to solving multimodal function optimization problems. The learning/adaptive mechanisms used by the natural immune system allows continuous generation of new species of so-called antibodies responsible for detection and destruction of foreign molecules, called antigens or pathogens. Current estimates show that although the human genome contains about $10^5$ genes, it is able to produce antibodies repertoire that can recognize at least $10^{16}$ pathogens. The enormous diversity of the antibodies developed by the immune system is the key to its pattern recognition capabilities (consult [14] for brief review of natural immune systems from a mathematical perspective).

Using this idea we propose a novel, simple and efficient, algorithm for solving multimodal optimization problems. Contrary to popular binary AIS, where pathogens and antibodies are represented as binary strings, this algorithm uses more natural, real-valued representation. This way the wide range of parameter values encountered in numerical optimization task can be exploited efficiently.

The paper is organized as follows. Section 2 provides a brief overview of the main mechanisms used by the immune system. Current approaches to the multimodal function optimization are reviewed in Section 3. In Section 4 new algorithm is presented and numerical results are given. Section 5 concludes the paper.

## 2. Basic facts from immunology

The basic building blocks of the immune system are white blood cells, or lymphocytes. There are two major classes of lymphocytes: B-lymphocytes, or B-cells, produced in the *bone marrow* in the course of so-called clonal selection (described later), and T-lymphocytes, or T-cells, processed in the *thymus*. Roughly speaking B-lymphocytes are related to humoral immunity: they secrete antibodies. Among the B-cells are „memory cells". They live relatively long and "remembering" foreign proteins they constantly restimulate the immune response of the organism. On the other hand, T-lymphocytes are concerned with cellular immunity: they function by interacting with other cells. T-lymphocytes divide into CD4 lymphocytes or helper T-cells, and CD8 lymphocytes, called cytoxic or killer T-cells, that eliminate intracellular pathogens. Generally, helper T-cells activate B-cells promoting their growth and differentiation into an antibody-secreting state. Activated B-cells cut protein antigens into smaller parts (peptides) and present them to killer T-cells. These last cells are responsible for killing virally infected cells and cells that appear abnormal. In the sequel we will focus on B-cells only.

A lymphocyte has about $10^5$ receptors, which are of the same structure. In the case of B-cells, the receptor is an immunoglobulin (antibody) molecule embedded in the membrane of the cell. These receptors are constructed from inherited gene segments (libraries) and they come into being in the process of random recombination of segments from different libraries. The process relies upon random selection of a genetic component from each of the libraries. There are many possible combinations of the available components, so the immune system can generate a large number of antibodies even though the libraries contain a limited amount of genetic information. Additionally the libraries evolve in time.

*Clonal selection* is another mechanism guaranteeing large diversity of the receptors. When a cell is activated by binding to pathogens, it secretes a soluble form of its receptors and, simultaneously, it clones itself. Clones are not perfect, but they are subjected to somatic mutation (characterized by high mutation rate) that result with children having slightly different receptors than the parent. These new B-cells can also bind to pathogens and if they have a high affinity (i.e. "similarity") to the pathogens they in turn will be activated and cloned. The rate of cloning a cell is proportional to its "fitness" to the problem: fittest cells replicate the most. The somatic mutation guarantees sufficient variation of the set of clones, while selection is provided by competition for pathogens. This mechanism was employed by Hunt and Cooke, [12], to create a learning system, and by Bersini and Varela, [2] in solving optimization problems.

Further diversity of the B-cells repertoire is maintained by the replacement of poorly behaving cells. They are simply killed and new, randomly generated, cells are introduced. Approximately five percent of the B-cells is replaced every day by new lymphocytes generated in the bone marrow.

Clonal selection (operating on individuals), stochastic gene selection (operating on genes that determine the specificity of antibodies) and programmed death of cells are the main mechanisms providing an exponential number of combinations. Potentially the NIS can produce $10^{15}$ different receptors, although an estimated number of receptors present in a body at any given time varies between $10^8$ - $10^{12}$.

The main goal of the immune system is to protect an organism against pathogens. Abstract treatment of this goal leads to the notion of Artificial Immune System, or AIS. Here, a problem with unknown solution can be treated as a pathogen, while the solution to this problem as an antibody. Recently edited volume [5] reviews ideas and applications of AIS while Perelson and Weisbuch [14] give an exhaustive overview of basic facts concerning immunology and analytical methods used in the field.

# 3. Current works on immune optimization

Perhaps the first work investigating potential application of the immune metaphor in solving numerical optimization problems was the paper by Bersini and Varela, [1], who proposed immune recruitment mechanism (IRM). It appeal to the programmed death of cells called here meta-dynamics of the immune system and relying upon continuous generation of new species, i.e. new points in the search subspace delimited by the *n* best points. This algorithm was tested on umimodal problems however.

In 1993 Forrest et. al., [6], and Smith et. al, [15], have shown that an immune system model combined with a genetic algorithm can be used to evolve a set of antibodies that recognize a range of diverse pathogens. In both works the authors focused on a binary immune system where pathogens and antigens were represented as binary string of fixed length. Constructing their algorithm the authors referred to the following properties of the immune systems:

- pathogens are typically encountered sequentially,
- an immune system responds with only a subset of its lymphocytes - those that come in contact with pathogen (to mimic this a sample of size $\sigma$ was chosen randomly without replacement each time a new pathogen has been entered),
- there is competition for antigens so that the cells that bind with the highest affinity (measured here by the Hamming distance) grow the fastest, and
- antibodies are improved by somatic mutation.

Careful analysis of the algorithm behavior has shown its two interesting features. First, the algorithm was able to maintain diverse sub-populations within a given population of individuals. The existence of such sub-populations was insensible on the similarity (measured by the Hamming distance) among pathogens. For small sample size, $\sigma$, generalist antibodies were evolved that match all pathogens through the identification of common schemata, and for high $\sigma$ specialist antibodies could be produced each of which matches a different pathogen. Second important property was that, the process of such sub-populations formation was similar to the fitness sharing. However the fitness sharing in this new algorithm is *implicit* in the sense that the algorithm determines the number of peaks dynamically without regard on the number of peak and the distance between peaks.

Hajela and Lee, [10], used this last property to design a number of algorithms devoted to solving structural optimization problems and multi-criteria decision problems. All these approaches are adaptations of the diversity algorithm described above.

Hightower [13] extended further the diversity algorithm proposing stochastic gene expression algorithm (SGEA). In their approach a population consists not of entire antibodies but of gene libraries mentioned earlier. The fitness of a library is computed as the fitness of randomly generated antibodies what leads to the population with partially expressed fitness. More precisely, the phenotype of an individual (i.e. expressed antibody strings) does not completely represent its genotype (the total collection of gene segments in the library). Hence, best parts of the search space discovered in one cycle are rather different from best parts identified in the next cycle as random segment selection allows the segments to be temporarily hidden from selection stage of the genetic algorithm. An interesting feature of the SGEA is that the antibodies evolve such as to maximize the average Hamming distance to the other antibodies in the library. SGEA was used in function optimization problem, the Holland's Royal Road (or HRR) function, and its superior performance over an EA using complete gene expression has been observed. Two other experiments using variants of HRR functions confirmed the former observation. Again, the algorithm admits an implicit fitness sharing allocating antibody genes to multiple pathogens. Hart and Ross, [11], used SGEA to produce robust schedules for a dynamic job-shop scheduling problem in which jobs arrive continually, and the environment is subject to change due to practical reasons. In this approach pathogen represents a set of changes that can occur forcing changes in a schedule while antibody represents a schedule.

The problem of multimodal function optimization was addressed explicitly by Fukuda et. al. in [7]. Their algorithm refers to basic mechanism discussed earlier and consists of six steps. The first step is the recognition of antigen, i.e. the identification of the optimization problem. Next, memory cells are used to produce antibodies that were effective in the past. The affinity of the antibodies to the newly entered pathogens is computed. "Good" solutions are saved as memory cells for the next iterations while the surplus of solution candidates is eliminated what corresponds to storing locally optimal solutions. Next, good antibodies proliferate proportionally to their affinity value, while proliferation of an antibody with extremely high concentration is suppressed what corresponds to maintaining the diversity of searching directions. Finally, in place of suppressed antibodies new lymphocytes are produced by using genetic operations of mutation and crossover. Depending on the problem complexity these steps are repeated 200-2000 times. The algorithm uses a number of control parameters, and highly elaborated information-theoretic measures to quantify affinity values, proliferation and suppression factors.

De Castro and von Zuben proposed in [4] much simpler algorithm employing the clonal selection metaphor. Again, it consists of six steps and starts with generating a set of candidate solutions. In the second step a number of best (with respect to an affinity measure) candidates is selected. These candidates are reproduced with the rate proportional to their goodness. Next, each copy is subjected hypermutation with the rate inversely proportional to its goodness. Most fitted mutants are used to compose the memory set. Finally, a number of poorly behaving antibodies (perhaps these with lower fitness) is replaced by randomly generated individuals. In comparison with previous algorithm it is much simpler: the number of control parameters is highly reduced, and an affinity measure is the only measure employed. The efficiency of the algorithm was tested on three problems: a binary characters recognition problem, a multimodal optimization task, and an instance of the Traveling Salesmen Problem with 30 cities.

All the algorithms mentioned up to this moment used binary representation of antibodies (candidate solutions) and were designed for static optimization problems.

Gaspar and Collard, [8], proposed another algorithm devoted to time dependent problems. Their implementation distinguishes four stages. The algorithm starts with an initial random population of antigens. Then evaluation phase starts; it relies upon computing so-called exogenic activation (i.e. antibody affinity to a given pathogen) and endogenic activation (i.e. antibody similarity to other antibodies from the current repertoire). The third stage is clonal selection performed differently on endo- and exo-activated antibodies. The last stage, called recruitment phase, reselects simply antibodies to next iteration. The experiments reported in [] show that the system is able to discover new optima, and what is more important, it is able to react over time. Its convergence is never complete what guarantees its readiness to discover new optima.

# 4. A new algorithm

The algorithm presented below integrates implicitly many of the mechanisms just described. It is designed to identify as many as possible local optima of a function of $n$ variables over the set $X \subseteq \mathbf{R}^n$, where $X$ is a Cartesian product of the intervals $[x_{i,min}, x_{i,max}]$, $i = 1,\ldots,n$. It uses explicit representation of candidate solutions, i.e., real-valued representation.

The basic component of the implementation is a memory set, denoted $M$, i.e. a set of candidate solutions, or points in $\mathbf{R}^n$, initiated randomly. The clonal selection and suppression of ineffective candidates are used to evolve the candidates during subsequent iterations. A simple heuristic governs the evolution: a candidate $m \in M$ is replaced by a mutated clone, $c$, if $c$ being similar to $m$ is better than $m$.

The algorithm consists of five steps:

1. *Initialization.* Choose randomly $|M|$ candidates and place them in the memory set $M$. The size $|M|$ is fixed in all the iterations.
2. *Cloning and mutation.* Each candidate $m \in M$ produces fixed number, $|c|$ of mutated clones, that are stored in a set $C$ of size is $|C| = |M|\cdot|c|$.
3. *Selection.* For each candidate $m \in M$ find a clone $c^m$ most similar to $m$. If $c^m$ is better that $m$, replace $m$ by $c^m$.
4. *Suppression.* For each candidate $m \in M$ find another candidate $m^*$ most similar to $m$. Leave the better candidate in $M$ and replace the worse candidate by new randomly generated candidate.
5. Repeat steps 2-4 until termination condition is met.

Here a mutated clone $c = (y_1,\ldots,y_n)$ of a candidate $m = (x_1,\ldots,x_n)$ is generated according to the rule $y_i = x_i + \Delta_i$·`rand[0,1)`, $i = 1,\ldots,n$, where `rand[0,1)` represents a uniformly distributed random variable that ranges from zero to one, and $\Delta_i = x_{i,min} - x_i$ or $\Delta_i = x_{i,max} - x_i$ (the decision which value $\Delta_i$ to choose is made randomly). This way each $y_i$ is correctly located within a corresponding domain $[x_{i,min}, x_{i,max}]$.

To study the algorithm properties a number of experiments have been performed. First of all the algorithm has been tested on one- and two-dimensional multimodal functions. These were:

- The (one-dimensionall) functions F1-F4 used by Beasley in [1].
- Modified Himmelblau's function, also used in [1]:
  $F5(x,y) = 200 - (x^2 + y - 11)^2 - (x + y^2 - 7)^2$, $x,y \in [-5,5]$
- Function used in [4]: $F6(x,y) = x\cdot\sin(4\pi x) - y\cdot\sin(4\pi y + \pi) + 1$, $x,y \in [-1,2]$
- Modified six-hump camel back function:
  $F7(x,y) = -(4 - 2{,}1x^2 + x^4/3)x^2 - xy - 4(1 + y^2)y^2$, $x \in [-3,3]$, $y \in [-2,2]$

In each case the algorithm was able to recover all the solutions in $X$ corresponding to the peaks of the tested function, see figures 1-3, representing most interesting cases. In all these experiments it was assumed that the algorithm succeeds if the maximal Euclidean distance between a real and identified peak does not exceeds a threshold value $d$ ($d = 0.05$ in our case). Note that the sequential niche algorithm was able to locate peaks of the F5 function in the mean distance $d = 0.2$ from real peaks.

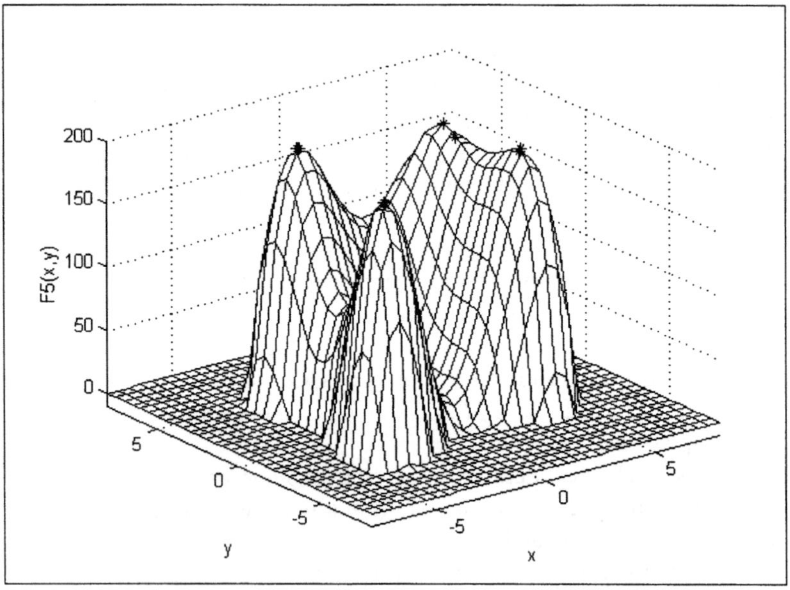


Figure 1. Function F5. Memory size $|M| = 10$. Results after 46 iterations.

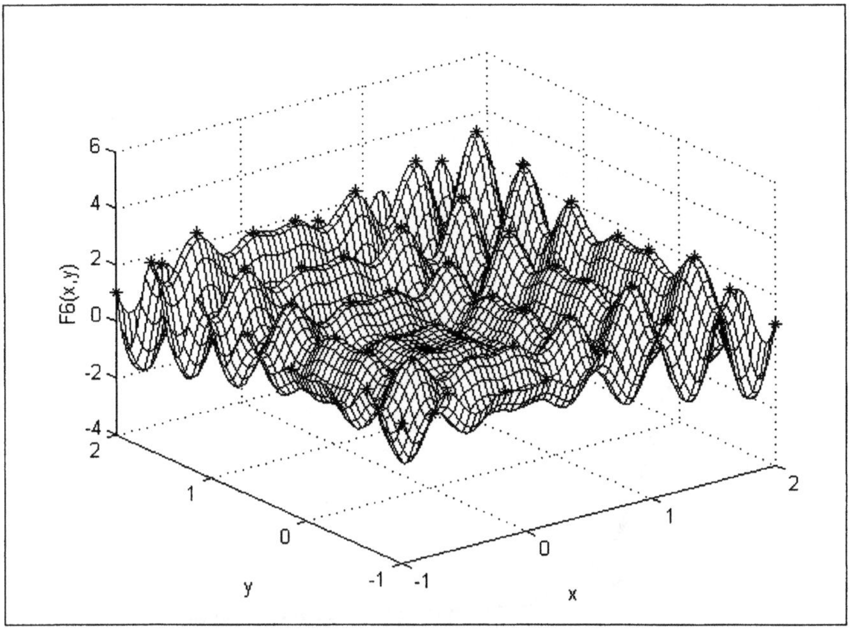


Figure 2. Function F6. Memory size $|M| = 50$. Results after 200 iterations.

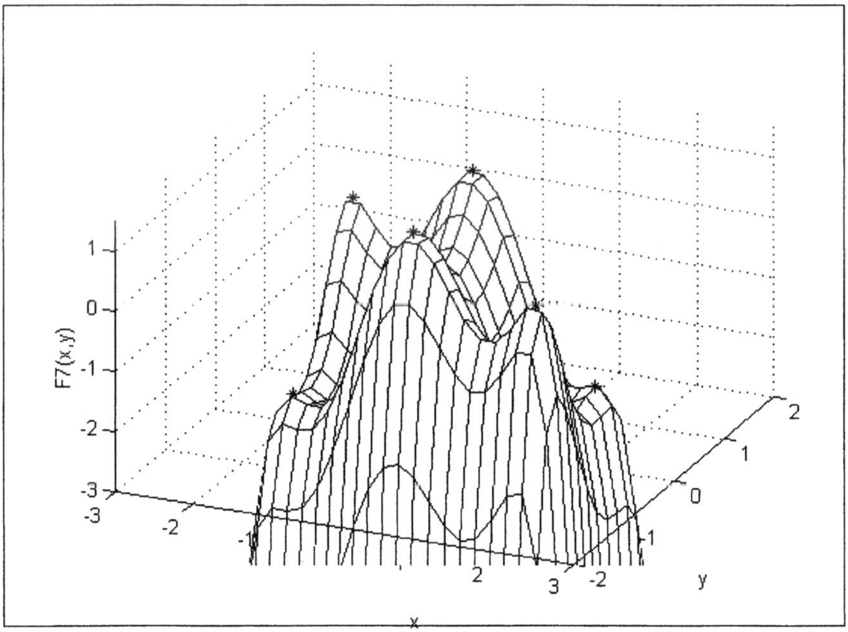


Figure 3. Function F7. Memory size $|M| = 10$. Results after 50 iterations.

Second, the convergence of the algorithm was examined. Particularly, we were interested how many runs (in average), i.e. repetitions of the steps 2-4 of the algorithm is needed to identify all peaks of a given function. Certainly this number depends on $|M|$ and $|c|$, hence we denote it as $\langle n(|M|,|c|)\rangle$. Surprisingly, $\langle n(|M|,|c|)\rangle$ considered as a function of $|M|$ approaches a limit value without regarding the value of $|c|$, see Figure 4.

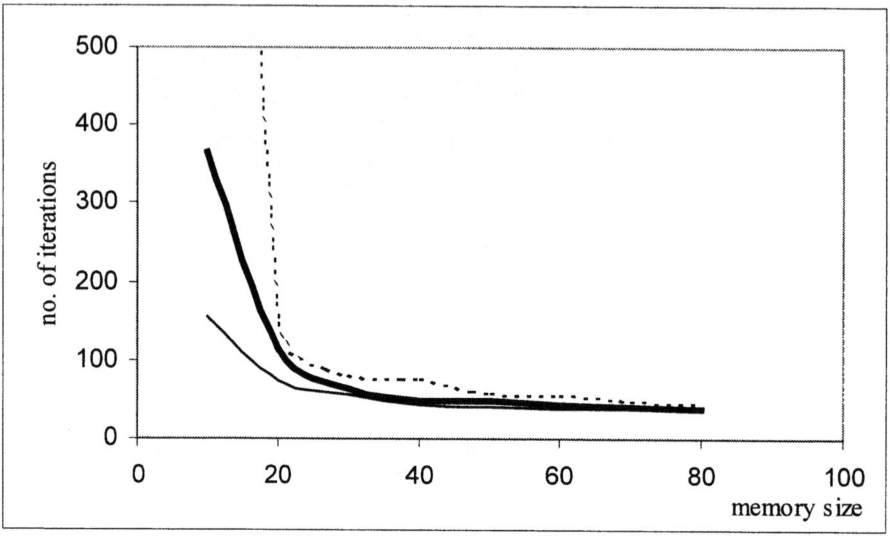


Figure 4. The convergence of mumber of iterations as a function of memory size. Dashed line corresponds to $|c| = 5$, thick line to $|c| = 10$, and thin line to $|c| = 20$.

The number of function evaluations, considered as a function of memory size, admits a global minimum, see Figure 5. This minimum is located near the value of $|M|$ over which the number of iterations decreases insignificantly.

To explain these properties, note that the step 4 prevents overusing resources located in a single peak. In our experiments with $|M| = 30$, at most 8 candidates were located at all the peaks (within the radius $d$) at the same time. Thus the remaining candidates were engaged in searching for other possibly existing peaks. This behavior resembles a process observed in the immune system and called affinity maturation. It is a Darwinian process of variation and selection. When a B-cell recognizes a pathogen, it does two things: (a) It secretes a soluble form of its receptors, called antibodies, which bind to pathogens and inactivate them, and (b) The B-cell clones itself with high mutation rate. In effect, memory cells present, on average, higher affinity than those of the early stages of system functioning. Figure 6 illustrates how the quality of our artificial system improves in time. The algorithm behaves very stable: once a peak has been identified it never lost. With very small memory sizes, say $|M| = 2$, the algorithm works as a global optimizer, i.e. it visits randomly peaks until the highest peak is found.

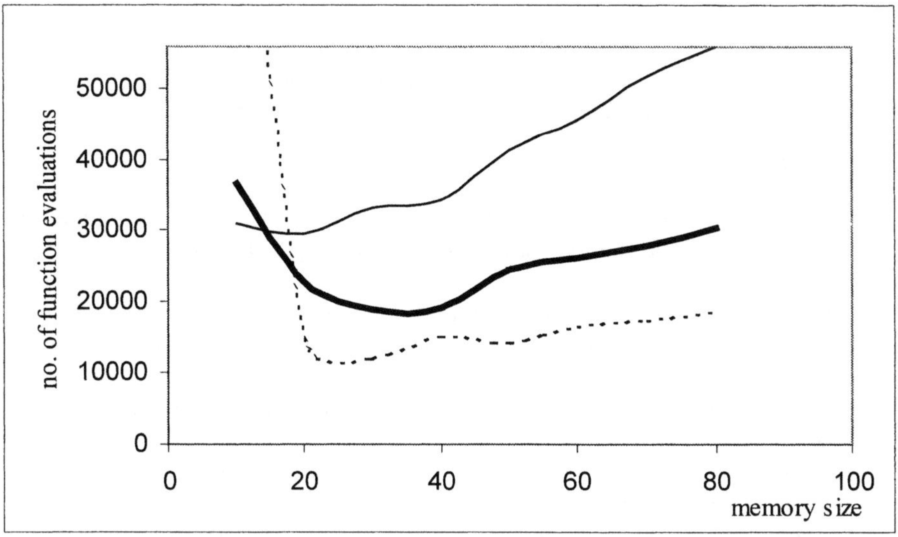


Figure 5. The number of function evaluations as a function of memory size. Dashed line corresponds to $|c| = 5$, thick line to $|c| = 10$, and thin line to $|c| = 20$.

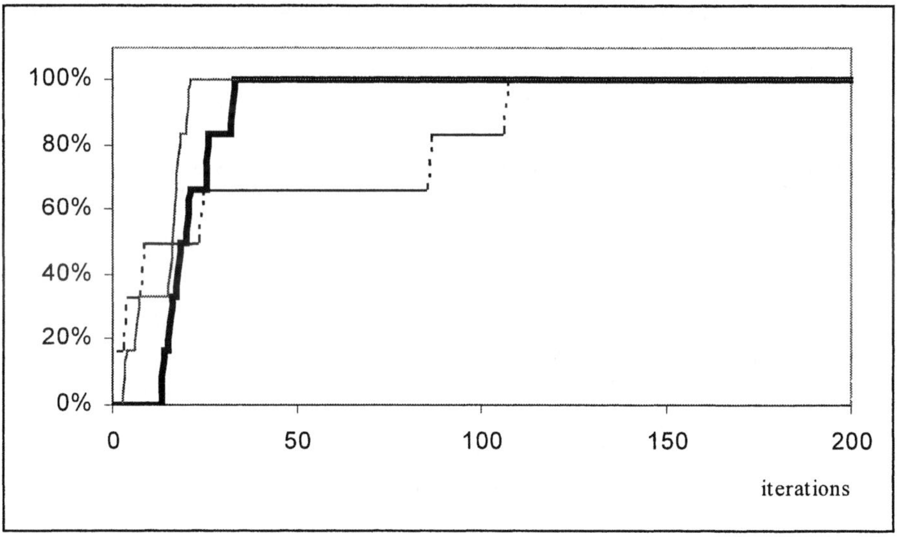


Figure 6. Fraction of identified peaks, for $|M| = 30$. Dashed line corresponds to $|c| = 5$, thick line to $|c| = 10$, and thin line to $|c| = 20$.

# 5. Conclusions

A new algorithm for multimodal function optimization inspired by the immune metaphor has been described. Current results show that the main immune mechanisms of clonal selection and cell suppression can be successfully applied to engineering problems. Using relatively small population of candidate solutions we are able to solve complicated function optimization problems. Reducing the size of the memory set, the algorithm performs global optimization tasks as well.

## References

1. Beasley, D., Bull, D.R., Martin, R.R. A sequential niche technique for multimodal function optimization. *Evolutionary Computation* **1**: 101-125, 1993
2. Bersini, H., Varela, F.J. Hints for adaptive problem solving gleaned from immune networks. In Proc. of the first workshop on Parallel Problem Solving from Nature, LNCS 496, pp. 343-354, Springer-Verlag 1990
3. Corne, D., Dorigo, M., Glover, F. (eds.). *New Ideas in Optimization.* McGraw-Hill: 1999.
4. de Castro, L.N., von Zuben, F.J. The clonal selection algorithm with engineering applications. *GECCO'00.*
5. Dasgupta, D. (ed.) *Artificial Immune Systems and Their Applications.* Springer-Verlag 1999
6. Forrest, S, Javornik, B., Smith, R.E., Perelson, A.S. Using genetic algorithms to explore pattern recognition in the immune system. *Evolutionary Computation,* **1**:191-211, 1993
7. Fukuda, T., Mori, K., Tsukiyama, M. Parallel search for multi-modal function optimization with diversity and learning of immune algorithm. In: [5], pp. 210-220
8. Gaspar, A., Collard, Ph. From Gas to artificial immune systems: Improving adaptation in time dependent optimization. In: Proc. of the 1999 Congress on Evolutionary Computation, pp. 1859-1866
9. Goldberg, D.E. *Genetic Algorithms in Search, Optimization and Machine Learning.* Addison-Wesley: 1989
10. Hajela, P., Lee, J. Constrained genetic search via schema adaptation. An immune network solution. *Structural Optimization* **12**: 11-15, 1996
11. Hart, E., Ross, P. The evolution and analysis of a potential antibody library for use in job-shop scheduling. In [5], pp. 185-202
12. Hunt, J.E., Cooke, D.E. Learning using an artificial immune system. *J. of network and Computer Applications,* **19**: 189-212, 1996
13. Hightower, R. *Computational aspect of antibody gene families.* Ph.D. Thesis, University of New Mexico, 1996
14. Perelson, A.S., Weisbuch, G. Immunology for physicists. *Reviews of Modern Physics,* 69:1219-1265, 1977
15. Smith, R.E., Forrest, S., Perelson A.S., Searching for diverse, cooperative populations with genetic algorithms. *Evolutionary Compuation.,* **1**:127-149, 1993.
16. Spears, W.M. Simple population schemes. In: Proc. of the 1994 Evolutionary Programming Conference, World Scientific: 1994, pp. 296-307

# Bayesian Network Mining System

**Mieczysław A. Kłopotek[1,2], Sławomir T. Wierzchoń[1], Maciej Michalewicz[1], Marek Bednarczyk[1], Wiesław Pawłowski, [1] Andrzej Wąsowski[2]**

[1]Institute of Computer Science, Polish Academy of Sciences, Warsaw, Poland

[2]Faculty of Mathematics and Information Science, Warsaw University of Technology

***Abstract:*** *The paper provides an exhaustive description of a new system serving learning, viewing and reasoning with Bayesian networks.*

*Keywords: Bayesian networks, Learning, Reasoning, Computer Implementation*

## 1. Introduction

Bayesian networks [9], also called belief networks or Bayesian belief networks, encode properties of probability distributions using directed acyclic graphs (dag). Their usage is spread among many disciplines such as Artificial Intelligence, Decision Analysis, Economics, Genetics, Philosophy, and Statistics. Bayesian networks are popular due to existence of numerous efficient methods of quantitative reasoning with probabilities if the joint probability distribution has an underlying dag structure. Reasoning about conditional and marginal independence of variables in a qualitative manner is also possible. Also a number of methods for reconstruction of Bayesian networks from data have been elaborated [2,3,7,8,9,11,12,13,15]. They are of considerable interest because the most compact Bayesian belief networks are assumed to encode causal relationships among variables.

A Bayesian network is a dag, nodes of which are labeled with variables and conditional probability tables of the node variable given its parents in the graph.

The joint probability distribution is then expressed by the formula:

$$P(x_1,\ldots\ldots\ldots,x_n)= \Pi_{i=1\ldots n} P(x_i \,|\pi(x_i))$$

where $\pi(x_i)$ is the set of parents of the variable (node) $x_i$.

E.g. in Fig.1 we have:

$$P(a,b,c,d,e,f) = P(a)\,P(b|a)\,P(c|a)\,P(d|b,c)\,P(e|b,c)\,P(f|e)$$

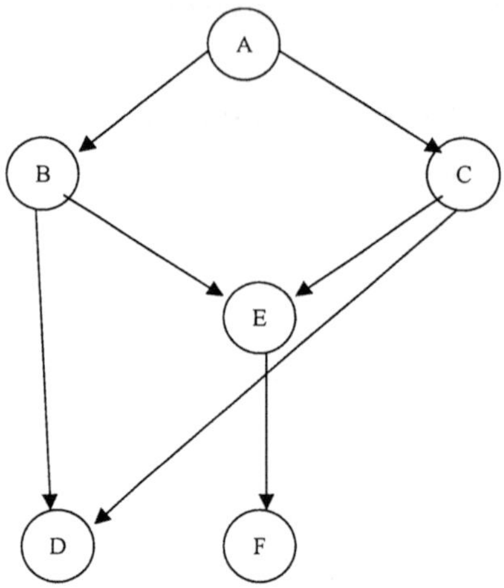


Fig.1. A Bayesian network

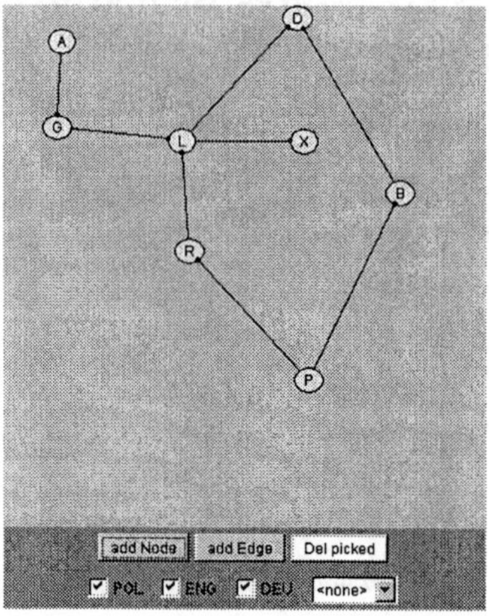


Fig.2. Another Bayesian network - as represented in the system (BATMAN viewer)

On the one hand, Bayesian networks allow for efficient reasoning, and on the other they contain information on conditional independences among variables. Geiger, Verma and Pearl [4] demonstrated that the so-called d-separation property in a dag implies conditional statistical independence, and missing d-separation (except for a set of networks with zero measure, that means highly improbable ones) implies missing conditional independence. Beside this, if edges of a network reflect causal relationships among variables, then the network is minimal. This last property suggests that the Bayesian network can be reconstructed if at least part of conditional independence properties is known.

Detailed methods of discovery of Bayesian networks from data based on this suggestion have been elaborated in the past. Among them are the algorithms by Chow and Liu [2], by Pearl [9], by Spirtes, Glymour and Scheines [12]: SGS, PC, PC+, CI and FCI, by Cooper and Herskovitz [3]: K2 and many other.

Reasoning in Bayesian networks allows for prediction of conditional probability of some hypotheses given a set of observations. Methods of reasoning have been elaborated by Pearl [9], Shafer and Shenoy [10], Wierzchoń [14], and other.

In our research we have developed Bayesian network software to create a foundation for studying various algorithms of Bayesian network learning and reasoning. It is a service software that a user does not need to install anything but he or she needs only to prepare input data in appropriate format on his/her local computer and to use a WWW browser. The software currently allows for

- learning Bayesian networks from data
- viewing and hand editing of Bayesian networks
- transforming Bayesian networks to internal structures called Markov trees
- reasoning with Markov trees.

To take full advantage of the functionality, a user needs to use a Netscape browser, java and java-script enabled.

## 2. Data Formats Used

The system maintains files (when they are generated) with extensions:

- .net - for Bayesian networks
- .mt - for Markov trees
- .res - for results of reasoning

Beside this, the system uses the .dbf file format for input data. In this section we briefly present details concerning input data formatting, and remarks on how Bayesian networks are represented.

### 2.1. User Data (.dbf)

Data for Bayesian network learning should be stored in a dBase III or dBASE IV file in numeric fields of width equal 2. Each attribute can take up to 100 different values numbered from 0 to 99. They must be written in columns of CHAR type of width 2. All cells in the table must be filled-in. Column names are used as node names of resulting Bayesian network.

For Bayesian networks learning we assume thus discrete data. The .dbf file [17] with user's data should be stored on his or her local computer. All the other files are stored on the service computer (e.g. the beata.ipipan.waw.pl machine).

The .dbf format is used by database systems like dBASE III, dBASE III+, dbaseIV, foxBASE, foxPro, CodeBase, Clipper (all registered trademarks). Most data processing programs can import and/or export dBASE III/IV files. For compatibility, however, we insist that field names of length exactly 10 are used.

## 2.2. Files with Bayesian Network (.net)

Bayesian networks are represented in BENIOFSKI format, which is a slight modification of BNIF format. Detailed description of BENIOFSKI format is available at the [16]. Here only short introduction to the format is presented. The name of output file consists of 8-digit accessibility code generated by the system and ".net" extension, e.g. 12345678.net. The name of the network contains the name of output dBase file. Nodes names are the same as the names of corresponding attributes in dBase file.

Files generated by the RENEG systems (described later) are compatible with the requirements of BATMAN application.

# 3. Learning Bayesian Networks

## 3.1. Bayesian Network Learner RENEG

The system RENEG performs a remote generation of Bayesian networks from data. It accepts dBASE databases sent via WWW. A database has to have discrete attributes (numerical ones) with a low number of possible values. The system allows choosing a learning algorithm and generates a Bayesian network representing dependencies among the attributes of the submitted sample.

The system RENEG allows also to visualize the network and to reason with it.

The learner implements nine different algorithms for generation of Bayesian networks from data. The user may pass the local access path to his data file, give the parameters needed for the selected algorithm and then wait for a reply. Depending on problem size and algorithm the computation time ranges from seconds to hours for the answer.

At present, implemented are the algorithms of Chow/Liu, of Pearl, K2 of Cooper et al., SGS of Spirtes/Glymour/Scheines, their PC, their PC*, their FCI and a Framework algorithm.

## 3.2. Learning Methods

### Chow-Liu Algorithm, Pearl's Algorithm

The algorithm proposed by Chow and Liu [2] is one of the earlier learning algorithms. It correctly reproduces tree-like structures only. However it can be a useful tool for finding convenient approximations of complex graphical (multiply connected) structures.

The algorithm is based on a simple idea, namely a maximal spanning tree of a complete graph is searched. Here each node of the graph corresponds to a single database attribute. To weight the graph edges Kullback-Leibler's distance is used.

The output of the Chow-Liu algorithm is an undirected tree. To translate it into proper Bayesian network the edges of the tree are arbitrarily directed. It means a user chooses only one node as a root and the program orients its edges properly.

Pearl [9] proposed an extension of the algorithm that was implemented in RENEG system as Pearl's algorithm. Again the Kullback-Leibler's distance is used to orient some arrows and consistent orientation of the remaining edges. As a result a polytree structure is obtained. The user should define numerical approximation of zero, since the algorithm compares Kulback-Leibler's distance to zero.

### SGS Algorithm

SGS algorithm, [11], learns one's own activity for simple d-separation tests. Variable d-separation in Bayesian networks is equivalent to conditional variable independence. So, the algorithm intensely executes expensive independence and conditional independence tests on delivered file. From this regard SGS is the slowest algorithm implemented.

It starts from rough generation of the network structure, and next orientation of some edges is carried out. In original version partially oriented structure is returned representing the class of all potential Bayesian nets. The present implementation uses the pog-to-dag[1] algorithm, consult [7] for details, to obtain one completely structure of a Bayesian network from class turned by the SGS. The algorithm will demand provision of significance level for test of independence $\chi^2$. The lower the significance level the more attributes are recognized as independent and the fewer edge will be contained in the resultant net.

### Algorithms PC and PC*

The PC and PC* algorithms [12] are modifications of the algorithm SGS. The modification relies upon limiting the expensive d-separation tests by reducing the set of candidate nodes that could d-separate a given pair of variables. The PC algorithm investigates only neighbors of the pair, and PC* - only neighbors on undirected paths between the pair of nodes. As a result both algorithms are much faster than their prototypes keeping similar efficiency.

---

[1] pog is a shorthand of "partially ordered graph".

Both the algorithms start from the identification of the structure of the network, thereafter the orientation of some edges is determined. Hence the original version of the algorithm returns a partially oriented structure, representing a whole class of Bayesian networks. The current implementation uses thereafter the pog-to-dag algorithm to obtain a single completely oriented structure of Bayesian network belonging to the class returned by PC. Both algorithms share common tuning parameters:

- Significance level for independence test $\chi^2$. The lower the significance level the more attributes are considered independent and the less edges will be present in the resulting network.
- Pair selection strategy for d-separation tests. This test is carried out for all attribute pairs in the sample. Complexity for each pair depends on the number of edges eliminated in previous tests. Therefore additional strategies (PC-2 and PC-3) were introduced selecting for the test first those edges, which have the highest rejection probability. The PC-1 strategy uses the lexical ordering of pairs that is without any additional heuristics.

### K2 Algorithm

K2, [3], is a greedy algorithm that searches the space of candidate solutions and constructs iteratively a network. At each step K2 adds one directed edge. This is that edge that improves total fitness of the network to the sample distribution. The functioning stops when no further improvement is possible. The algorithm uses fitness function proposed by Cooper and Herskovits.

Although K2 is fast and easy to implement, its disadvantage is that we must enter "cognitive" order of variables, i.e. we must define which variable is a possible parent for a subset of variables. Since in real-life situations such a requirement is hard to satisfy, a possible remedy is to start algorithm with as much as possible cognitive orders and choosing the most appropriate solution. However, RENEG system does not return fitness value.

The algorithm requires one more input parameter (apart of the cognitive order), namely the maximal number of parents for each node. Choosing smaller number of parents reduces computation time in case of large networks.

### FCI and FCI* Algorithms

The FCI [12] is the only algorithm used in the RENEG that searches for hidden variables. Thus the assumption that the sample attributes form self-contained and consistent set is not necessary. The algorithm is based on the idea used in formulating the PC algorithm, but some modifications and extensions are added here (e.g. searching for exclusive paths).

The algorithm operates on partly directed graphs. The original version returns a structure representing the whole class of compatible Bayesian networks. This implementation applies algorithms pog-to-dag and edge reversal, to obtain a completely oriented Bayesian network from the class identified by FCI.

FCI* algorithm differs from FCI like PC* differs from PC, i.e. the main difference concerns the size of d-separating files tested in the first stage of both algorithms. Input parameters in both cases are identical. The user must decide on:

- Confirmation level for the $\chi^2$ test. The lower the level, the more attributes are treated as independent. This implies that the resulting network will be sparser.
- How to choose pairs to d-separation test? This test is performed for all pairs of nodes in a graph. Time complexity for each pair hardly depends on how many edges have been eliminated in previous tests. Thus, two additional strategies, PC-1 and PC-2, have been proposed. They choose edges characterized by highest removal probability. PC-1 strategy tests the pairs in the lexicographic order, i.e. without any additional heuristics.

Results are presented in the format BENIOFSKI. Further, the file is appended with a list of variables having hidden parents.

**Framework Algorithm**

The framework algorithm [7] is a heuristic which can be placed somewhere between the K2 [3] and BENEDICT [1] algorithms. It searches the space of potential solutions and constructs resulting network depending on current situation.

In comparison with K2 the solution is extended by one, directed or undirected edge, which improves fitness of the solution. This way the framework algorithm avoids premature edge orientation, what is a disadvantage of other existing algorithms. The algorithm stops when further fitness improvement is impossible.

The algorithm needs one input parameter: numerical approximation of zero. This is the value defining minimal admissible improvement in fitness that does not result in stopping computations.

## 3.3. Using the Learner

**Submission of generation of a Bayesian network**

In the window shown below a user can give indispensable information to order calculations. First, he or she should give his/her name and e-mail. After the end of calculations the system will send the user information and URL with indication on reception of results.

Further, the name of input file containing the sample to analyze must be given. The button Browse helps to find the file on user's local disc. The file will be sent on server system RENEG and given as entry of learning algorithm. The sample has to match requirements of the given algorithm and to be in suitable format (dBase III/IV).

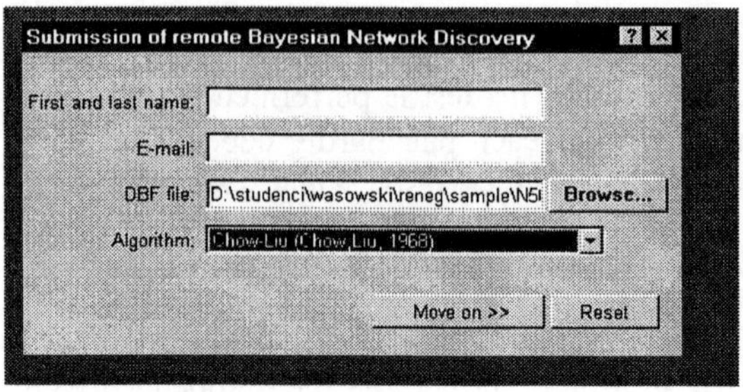


Fig.3. Initiating calculations

The last information requested is the name of the learning algorithm. The user can choose one of the algorithms already described.

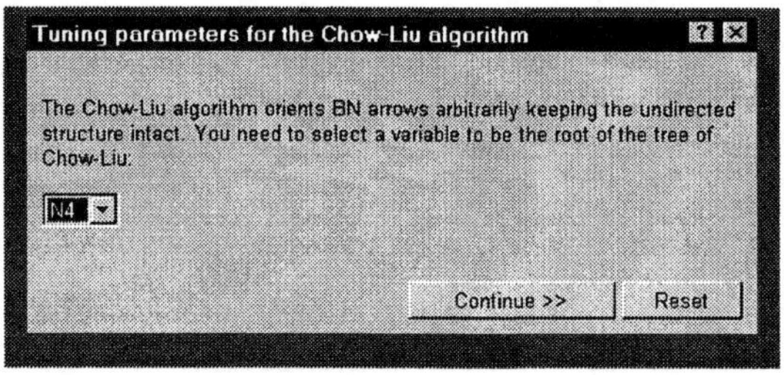


Fig.4. Choosing algorithm specific parameters

After choosing the algorithm the user has to click the button Continue >> and he or she should wait for further question on the parameters for selected algorithm. Before appearing of the following window some time may elapse, because the file indicated by the user has to be uploaded on server and initially interpreted. If the test set is large and Internet heavily burdened this can last even more than several of minutes.

After defining input parameters (or accepting their default values) the system returns information that the task has been accepted and starts computations.

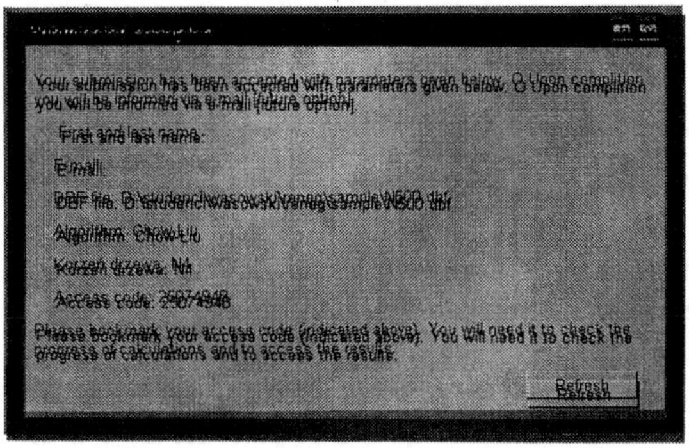


Fig.5. Job acceptance screen

**Progress control**

User who knows one's own code of access (provided by the system after beginning of calculations, and also sent with electronic post in information about end of calculations), can control state of calculations by means of WWW Browser. It will suffice, having chosen from menu main position Calculation progress monitoring, to enter first and family name and the access code (access id) and to click the button OK. First and family name must be spelled exactly the same way as during submitting the calculations.

The window Calculation progress is very similar to the window submission accepted and contains all information about user's submission: user's name, e-mail, file name, chosen algorithm and its parameters. The moment of starting the calculations and access identifier are also visible. The first line contains the status. ( e.g. "Learning in progress" or "Computation terminated"). The information on completion of calculations is at the same time a hyperlink to the resultant file. The results can be saved then locally.

In case an e-mail sender is installed, the monitoring of calculation progress may be achieved conveniently be waiting for an e-mail. If in the window generation submission user has given e-mail address, then the system may e-mail him a message confirming the completion of calculations. The message contains an URL address where the results can be collected. As the message contains also the access id, there is no need to save it anywhere else. The Cut&Paste method can be used to check the generation parameters of the RENEG system or to view the results using BATMAN. .

**Checking user's task state.**

Window *Accepted task* contains full information about user's task, i.e. user name and e-mail, data-file name, the algorithm chosen and its parameters. Further, starting time its displayed as well as so-called accessibility code.

The code allows to verify status of user's task and it allows to read final results by using the command checking task state from the main menu. When a data sample is relatively small, what implies short time of computations, it sufficies to choose in a while after starting computations the button *Refresh*. This command displays automatically information on how advanced the computations are without inserting the accessibility code. This code is necessary when a user asks for information during new session (e.g. after new connection to Internet by dial-up provider).

Results are presented in the format BENIOFSKI. A user can save on hard dish the file with Bayesian network, or he can open the file using graphical browser BATMAN. To choose this last option the accessibility code is necessary.

A useful way to check task state is making use of e-mail. To attain this one should enter e-mail address in the window ***generation submission***. The system sends a message when the Bayesian network will be identified. The message contains URL address to download the results as well as the accessibility code.

# 4. Bayesian Network Viewer/Editor Batman

BATMAN-editor is a tool designed for visual creating, editing and performing other operations on Bayesian networks over the Internet.

BATMAN-editor has the form of a Java$^{TM}$ applet that can loaded into a HTML browser page. The networks can be stored and retrieved locally (for HotJava browsers only). Authorized users can also use and extend the library of networks already constructed, maintained at a remote site.

BATMAN-editor allows performing visual creation of the Bayesian network: by inserting nodes (representing events) and edges (representing their direct causal relationships), updating them and by inserting the necessary descriptions of strength of relationships in terms of conditional probability tables. Upon request consistency checks can be carried out: checking for acyclicity of the network, consistency of conditional probability assignments etc.

The BATMAN editor allows for multilingual annotation of the network (currently three languages: German, Polish and English) including labeling of nodes (names for statistical variables associated with events and discrete variable values). The user can switch between the languages when viewing the network and conditional probability values.

The BATMAN editor can also be used as a visualization tool for Bayesian networks created by others or by some automatic tool (e.g. by a Bayesian network learning algorithm, as in this system). In this case the user has the possibility to modify the graphical image of the Bayesian network (location of the nodes on the graphical screen).

# 5. Bayesian Network Transformer

It takes the Bayesian network and transforms it into a Markov tree that is more suitable for reasoning. Actually two types of transformation are implemented: by simulated annealing and an hypernode factorization algorithm.

The Bayesian network is not very suitable for efficient reasoning. Therefore, if one intends to reason with the Bayesian network that have just been generated, one need to start the transformation to Markov tree. There exist various technologies how the transformation to Markov tree may be carried out. We implement here only the hypergraph method and the simulated annealing method. The user can choose one of them.

# 6. Markov Tree Reasoner

Reasoner is a tool for forward and backward reasoning exploiting knowledge representation in terms of Bayesian networks transformed to Markov-trees. The resoner can also be used for explanation of the results anf for query analysis, and for decision analysis.

## 6.1. Reasoner

To start the reasoner, the operation of transformation of a Bayesian network to a Markov tree. Must have been carried (only once after each modification of the Bayesian network)

Now the user may want to know "What is the most probable value of X given that event Y=y took place" with X and Y being the variables (fields or attributes in original database, and x,y their possible values). After entering the access code he sees the list of variables from his problem with possibility to set some of them. E.g. he may set variable Y to value y. Below this list there are three selection fields where one can choose the target variable. E.g. X on one of the lists.

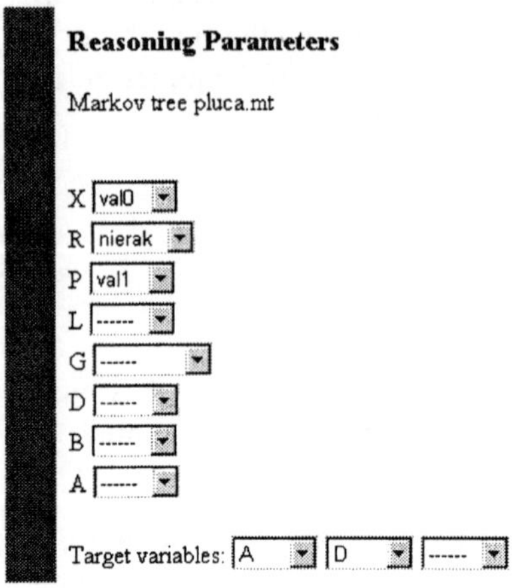


Fig.6. Initiating reasoning

If everything was O.K., a confirming window, otherwise an error message will appear. Upon success one has to go to the option "Results - view results of reasoning with Markov Tree"

## 6.2. Get Reasoner Results

The user has to remember his Access ID as long as he uses the generated net, also when accessing the results of reasoning. The results are in form of a list of variables selected as tagets of reasoning along with their most probable values (probability is also indicated).

# 7. Experimental study.

Using the program, an experimental study of performance of individuial algorithms has been carried out. As an example, the Fig.7 summarizes our findings on dependence of execution time on sample sizes, with time represented on logarithmic scale. It shows that the execution time of all the algorithms grows exponentially with time. However, the SGS and the Framework algorithm perform particularly poor and results couldn't be calculated in reasonable time for sample sizes above 1500.

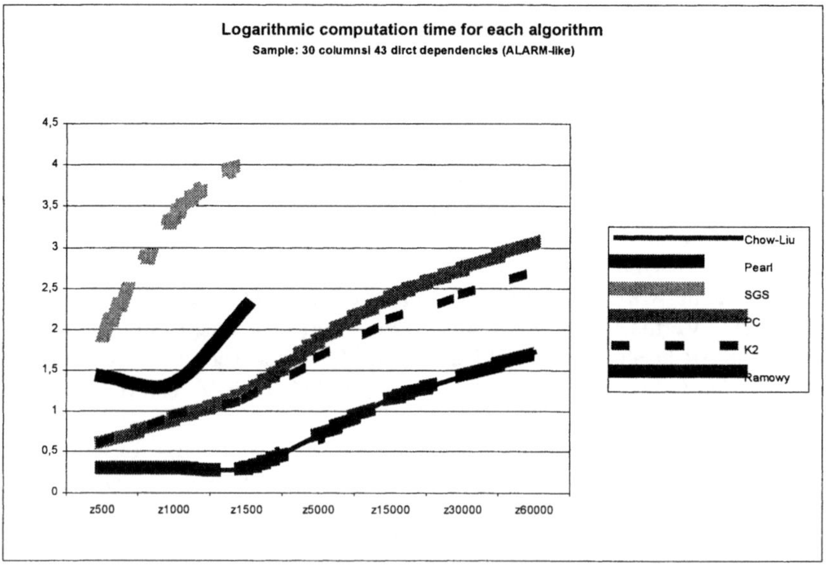


Fig.7. Comparative study of algorithm performance. Execution time dependence (vertical axis) in logarithmic scale on sample size (horizontal axis).

# 8. Summary

An integrated system for representing deep knowledge in the form of graphical structures, and reasoning within such a graphical representation has been described. The system can be used as an educational/experimentation tool for students, or as a professional tool for manipulating with knowledge available from remote knowledge bases.

Though both individual learning algorithm implementations are for Bayesian networks as well as visualization tools for them [11-13,18-21], we are not aware of any system combining learning, reasoning and visualization in a single framework with remote access for the whole service. As several algorithms are implemented and the implementation opens possibility of integrating further algorithms, we hope that an intense comparative study of capabilities of individual algorithms will be made possible.

## References


1. S. Acid, L.M. de Campos: An algorithm for finding minimum d-separating sets in belief networks, forthcoming, 1996.
2. Chow C.K., Liu C.N. Approximating discrete probability distributions with depndence trees. IEEE Trans. on Information Theory 14(3), 1968, 462-467.
3. G.F.Cooper, E.Herskovits: A Bayesian method for the induction of probabilistic networks from data. *Machine Learning* 9 (1992), 309-347
4. D.Geiger, T.Verma, J. Pearl: d-Separation: From theorems to algorithms. In: M.Henrion, R.D.Shachter, L.N.Kamal, J.F.Lemmer (eds): *Uncertainty in Artificial Intelligence* 5, Elsevier Science Publishers B.V. (North-Holland), 1990, 139-148
5. M.A.Kłopotek: Partial Dependency Separation - a new concept for expressing dependence/independence relations in causal networks. *Demonstratio Mathematica.* Vol XXXII No 1,1999, pp. 207-226.
6. M.A.Kłopotek: Methods of Identification and Interpretations of Belief Distributions in the Dempster-Shafer Theory (in Polish), IPI PAN Publisher, Warsaw 1998, ISBN 83-900820-8-x.
7. M.A. Kłopotek, S.T. Wierzchoń: Partial D-Separation for Discovery of Bayesian Networks from Data. R. Trappl, ed.:Cybernetics and Systems. Proc. EMCSR'2000, 25-28.4.2000, Vienna, Austrian Society for Cybernetics, Vol. 2, pp. 707-712.
8. W. Lam and F. Bacchus: Learning Bayesian Belief Networks: An Approach based on the MDL Principle, *Computational Intelligence*, vol. 10, pp. 269-293, 1994.
9. J. Pearl: *Probabilistic Reasoning in Intelligent Systems: Networks of Plausible Inference*, Morgan Kaufmann, San Mateo CA, 1988
10. G. Shafer, P.P. Shenoy, R. Logan: Propagating belief functions in qualitative Markov Trees. *Intn. J. of Approximate Reasoning*, 1(1987)349-400
11. P. Spirtes, C. Glymour, R. Scheines: Causality from probability. In: G. McKee ed.: *Evolving knowledge in natural and artificial intelligence,* London: Pitman, 1990, 181-199
12. P. Spirtes, C. Glymour, R. Scheines: *Causation, Prediction and Search*, Lecture Notes in Statistics 81, Springer-Verlag, 1993.
13. T. Urban, T. Kaempke: Recovering dependency graph in uncertain data. M. Mohammadian, ed: Computational Intelligence for Modelling, Control and

Automation. Evolutionary Computing & Fuzzy Logic for Intelligent Control, Knowledge Acquisition & Information Retrieval. Concurrent Systems Engineering Series Vol. 55. IOS Press Amsterdam, Berlin, Oxford 1999, pp. 476-481.

14. S.T. Wierzchoń, Knowledge Representation and Manipulation within Dempster-Shafer Framework (in Polish), IPI PAN Publisher, Warsaw 1996, ISBN 83-900820-5-5, 215 pp.
15. Y. Xiang, S.K.M. Wong and N. Cercone: A'Microscopic' study of minimum entropy search in learning decomposable Markov networks. *Machine Learning*, Vol. 26, No.1, 65-92, 1997.
16. Proposal of a Bayesian Network InterOperability Format Standard for Knowledge Interchange (BENIOFSKI) http://www.ipipan.waw.pl/~klopotek/crit2/index.html
17. dBASE III,IV,5 DBF file format: http://www.apptools.com/dbase/faq/qformt.htm
18. JavaBayes. URL: http://www.cs.cmu.edu/People/javabayes/index.html, its Bayesian network formats BIF version 0.15BIF version 0.1 XMLBIF ver. 0.3 http://www.cs.cmu.edu/~javabayes/Home/node7.html#SECTION00710000000000000000
19. Microsoft Belief Network Tools for Bayesian Inference, URL: http://www.research.microsoft.com/research/dtg/msbn/, its XML Belief Network File Format: http://www.research.microsoft.com/dtas/bnformat/
20. MCL++ Library of Machine Learning functions: http://www.sgi.com/Technology/mlc/
21. Information about Hugin : URL: http://www.hugin.dk/

# Intelligent Techniques in Stock Analysis

Halina Kwaśnicka, Marcin Ciosmak

Department of Computer Science, Wrocław University of Technology
Wyb. Wyspiańskiego 27, 50-370 Wrocław, Poland
kwasnicka@ci.pwr.wroc.pl

**Abstract.** The paper presents computer system, named **S**tock **M**arket **E**lectronic **E**xpert (**SMEE**), for Stock Market Analysis. It is developed as friendly, useful and credible computer program giving advises concerning investment policy on Stock Market. Fundamental and technical analysis are made automatically, and – on the base of obtained partial results – system produces evaluation of companies' attractiveness as well as comments and suggestions for users in text format. The system uses some filter stated by the user in the program. **SMEE** was tested using real data from the Warsaw Stock Exchange. Obtained results reveal high accuracy.

*Keywords*: *Stock market analysis, fuzzy expert system, neural network*

## Introduction

Computers are useful for such tasks as analyzing and prediction of Stock Exchange, computer programs can play the role of expert or advisor for investors. Different Stock Exchange can be analyzed using similar techniques, because all of them work under near the same law. The popular techniques for Stock analysis are *Fundamental Analysis* and *Technical Analysis*.

Very popular techniques from the field of Artificial Intelligence, used for financial analysis are *Artificial Neural Networks* (Mitchell 1997, Żurada, Barski, Jędruch 1996). But recently, others intelligent techniques, as expert systems and genetic algorithms, are developed to improve the judgement of traders, to derive automated trading strategies or to optimize portfolio management. Some examples of such attempts one can find in (Deboeck 1994).

In the presented project we tray to develop computer program useful for each trader, in fact for every one of us, who would like to invest on Stock. We focus on Warsaw Stock Exchange and developed system is verified using the data from this Stock. The general aim of our project can be defined as:

> To introduce a bit of intelligence into a computer program, enough to make it capable to analyze Stock Market data and sharing obtained results with users.

More detailed goal is:

> Evaluation of attractiveness of particular company (stock) in the **WSE** (**W**arsaw **S**tock **E**xchange).

Realization of above goal requires, that developed computer program ought to:

- use standard techniques of fundamental analysis,
- use standard techniques of technical analysis,
- use selected (appropriate) intelligent techniques for patterns matching,
- analyze obtained partial results in the intelligent way,
- present all required result in the friendly way,
- allow for adding new users and companies, and bringing up to date all market quotations from the text files,
- manage database keeping data from the two groups: companies and users.

The paper is structured as follow. The first part after introduction contains general description of the system. In the next section we describe techniques which we use in particular modules – fuzzy expert systems and artificial neural networks. The results given by the system using real data from the Warsaw Stock Exchange are presented and discussed in the fourth section. Short summary ends the paper.

## Stock Market Electronic Expert – an overview

Developed computer program **SMEE** (**S**tock **M**arket **E**lectronic **E**xpert) improves and makes more efficient classic techniques of stock analysis. Intelligent techniques are used for prediction of changes in the market quotations. The general schema of the **SMEE** system is shown in **Fig.** 1. The *Central Unit* of the system (box 15) plays the role of control mechanism. It communicates with users by the *User Interface* (box 14). Communication between the system and users is possible only via *User Interface* and *Central Unit*. *Central Unit* controls all modules in the system.

*Fundamental Analysis*, in general, makes forecast on the base of macroeconomic data. It uses basic financial status of companies and macroeconomic data such as exports, imports, money supply, interest rates, foreign exchange rates, inflationary rates, etc. (Deboeck 1994).

In **SMEE**, modules collected in box named *Fundamental Analysis Tools* consist of the four Fuzzy Expert Systems – for four groups of indices.

*1. Capital market indices*

- Price/Earning ratio (P/E) – it suggests stocks that can be bought because their long run price increasing is high:

$$P/E = \frac{market\ price\ of\ one\ share}{gain\ on\ one\ share}, \tag{1}$$

where:

$$gain\ on\ one\ share = \frac{net\ profit}{number\ of\ issued\ stock}. \tag{2}$$

- Cover Ratio index (CovR) – it tells about inclination of company to pay dividend:

$$CovR = \frac{divident\ on\ one\ share}{gain\ on\ one\ share}. \tag{3}$$

- Price/Book Value index (P/BV) – it informs about the relative market to book value of the company:

$$P/BV = \frac{(market\ price\ of\ one\ share) \cdot (amount\ of\ issued\ stock)}{book\ value\ of\ company}. \tag{4}$$

- Dividend Yield index (D/Y) – ratio of dividend, it allows to compare efficiency of investment in the Stock Market with others (e.g., bank) investment:

$$D/Y = \frac{dividend\ on\ one\ share}{price\ of\ one\ share}. \tag{5}$$

2. *Indices of effectiveness*

- Financial Effectiveness index (FE) – it tells about amount of somebody else's capital (e.g., credit) used by the company:

$$FE = \frac{assets}{company\ capital}. \tag{6}$$

- Return on Assets index (ROA) – rates of assets efficiency:

$$ROA = \frac{net\ profit}{assets}. \tag{7}$$

- Return On Equity index (ROE) – rate of profit from the company capital, known as index of capital efficiency:

$$ROE = \frac{net\ profit}{company\ capital}. \tag{8}$$

- Net Profit Margin index (NPM) – known also as index of trade efficiency:

$$NPM = \frac{net\ profit}{net\ trade} \tag{9}$$

3. *Indices of rotation*

- Assets Turnover index (AT):

$$AT = \frac{net\ trade}{assets}. \tag{10}$$

- Inventory Turnover index (IT):

$$IT = \frac{trade}{reserves}. \tag{11}$$

- Payments (Obligations) Turnover index (PT):

$$PT = \frac{net\ trade}{obligations}. \quad (12)$$

*4. Indices of liquidity*

- Current Ratio (CR) – it defines ability of company to meet obligations in time:

$$CR = \frac{circulating\ capital}{current\ obligations}. \quad (13)$$

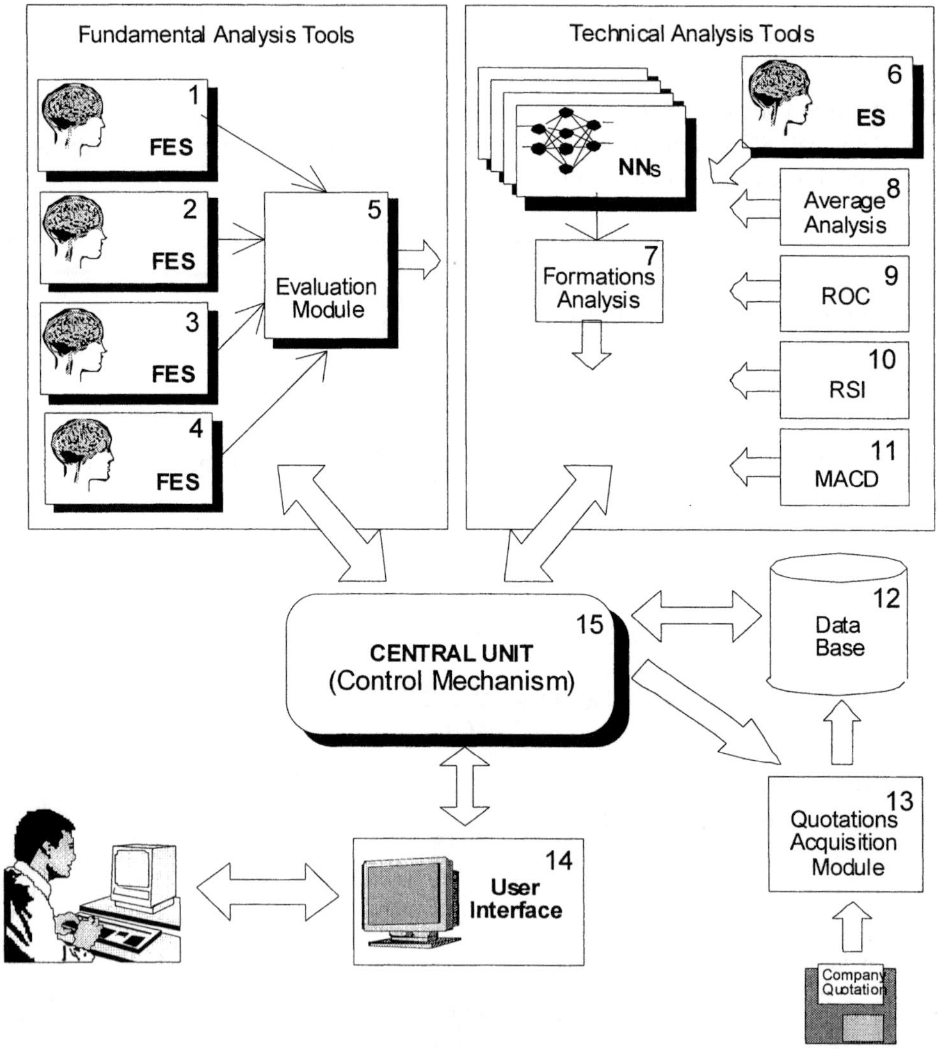


**Fig. 1.** The general scheme of the Stock Market Electronic Expert

- Quick Ratio (QR) – also called Acid Test, it is more restrictive than the former one:

$$QR = \frac{(circulating\ capital) - reserves}{current\ obligations}. \tag{14}$$

Evaluation module (box 5) produces joint attractiveness of the company as means weighted attractiveness given by the particular *fuzzy expert systems* (boxes 1, 2, 3, and 4) on the base of each from the four groups indices analysis.

*Technical Analysis*, in general, makes prediction by exploiting implications hidden in past trading activities, by analyzing patterns and trends shown in price and volume charts. It assumes that history will repeat itself and correlation between price and volume reveals market behavior (Deboeck 1994).

In **SMEE**, box named *Technical Analysis Tools* consists of the one *Expert System*, one module for matching and interpreting formations in graphs of stock prices – it uses four artificial neural networks, and four simple modules – each of them provides indices of technical analysis: moving averages prices analysis, ROC, RSI, and MACD indices.

Expert System – box 6 in **Fig.** 1, uses *point & figure* graphs for reasoning. Simple rules allow system to find trading signals (sell or buy) and to evaluate strength of trend on the base of point & figure graphs analysis.

Formation Analysis – box 7 in **Fig.** 1, uses four artificial neural networks (NNs) as tools for pattern recognition. NNs are used as searchers of significant formations on the graphs of price and graphs of volume. Formations can be treated as trading signals, but it should be considered together with others indices.

Moving average is used for analysis of trends (box 8). Resistance and support lines are characteristic trends used during technical analysis. If we can draw both lines (resistance and support) and they are parallel, we obtain trend canal. Breaking of trend lines indicates possible changes of stock price.

Boxes numbered 9, 10, 11, and 12 are modules for interpreting violence indices – ROC, RSI, and MACD:

- ROC – index of changes, it is based violence index. It represents a velocity of price changes:

$$\forall_{n \in N},\ ROC_t(n) = \frac{quotation(n)}{quotation(n-1)} \cdot 100, \tag{15}$$

where: $t$ – number of sessions from which ROC is calculated,
$n$ – number of Stock session,
$N$ – set of sessions, the period in which we want to calculate ROC,
$quoation(n)$ – price of one share during $n^{th}$ session.

- RSI – index of relative strength, a kind of measure of share strength:

$$\forall_{n \in N},\ RSI_t(n) = 100 - \frac{100}{1 + \frac{RCZ_t(n)}{ZCZ_t(n)}}, \tag{16}$$

where: $t$ – number of sessions from which RSI is calculated,

$n$ – number of Stock session,
$N$ – set of sessions, the period in which we want to calculate RSI,
$RCZ_t(n)$ – average change of price "up" between $(n\text{-}t)^{th}$ and $n^{th}$ sessions,
$ZCZ_t(n)$ – average change of price "down" between $(n\text{-}t)^{th}$ and $n^{th}$ sessions.

If between $(n\text{-}t)^{th}$ and $n^{th}$ sessions decreasing of price is absent, the $ZCZ_t(n)=0$, and RSI cannot be calculated. It is assumed that, in such cases, RSI=100 (Czekała 1998).

- MACD – Moving Averages Convergence Divergence – index of convergence and divergence of moving averages. Two exponential moving averages are used for MACD calculation: MACD is a result of subtraction of shorter moving average from the longer one.

## Stock Market Electronic Expert – implemented algorithms

The three kind of intelligent techniques are embodied into the **SMEE**. Four used Fuzzy Expert Systems are similar, they differ mainly in knowledge embodied. They are parts of fundamental analysis. One Expert System analyses point & figure graphs. It contains a set of simple rules. As tools for pattern recognition we apply Artificial Neural Networks. Their task is to recognize defined patterns on the price graphs and volume graphs. The length (a number of sessions) of patterns is not stated, NNs have to search different length patterns.

### Fundamental Analysis Modules

In this section we shortly describe all modules used in fundamental analysis. All of them are fuzzy expert systems, they produce partial results – attractiveness of company. *Evaluation Module* (box 5, **Fig.** 1) produces final result of fundamental analysis.

**Fuzzy Expert System (FES)**

Expert System (**ES**) is a computer program capable to replace human expert in usually narrows domain. To fulfil the above task, **ES** has to have embodied appropriate knowledge and inference skills (Mitchell 1997, Mulawka 1996). The core of **ES** is *Inference Engine*. It uses *Knowledge Base* to infer new *facts* on the base of known *true* facts. Usually domain knowledge is represented in the form of inference rules: if $p_1 \wedge p_2 \wedge \ldots \wedge p_n$ then $q_r$. **ES** must be able to *explain* produced conclusions. A module for knowledge acquisition is also a part of typical **ES**. Communication **ES** $\leftrightarrow$ user occurs by friendly *Interface*.

A number of methods were developed to cover uncertain and/or incomplete knowledge. One of such techniques is *Fuzzy Logic* (Mitchell 1997). In fuzzy logic, the same fact can belong to a number of sets with given *membership* values. Membership function can have any shape, but triangular and trapezoid ones are very popular, they are simple and give satisfactory results (**Fig.** 2). The fuzzy inference is shown in **Fig.** 3.

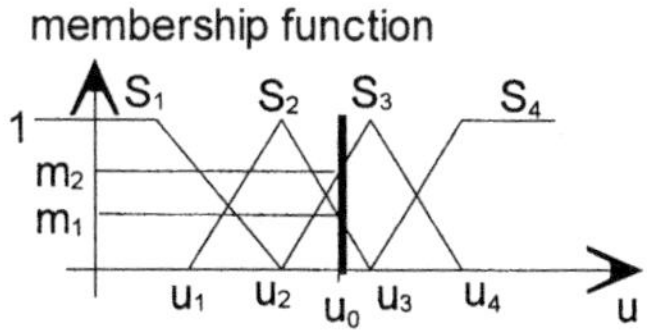


**Fig. 2.** Fuzzy sets (an example)

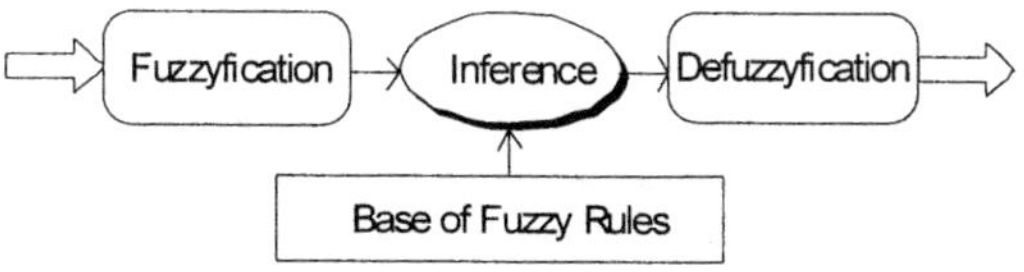


**Fig. 3.** Idea of fuzzy inference

Fuzzyfication process is made on the base of fuzzy sets defined for the input variable: in **Fig.** 2 we can see that crisp value $u_0$ belongs to the set $S_2$ with membership function equal to $m_1$, and to the set $S_3$ with membership $m_2$. Defuzzyfication process is the calculation of crisp value of output variable. We do it using *Center of Gravity* method (Ciosmak 2000).

**FES for capital market indices interpretation**

*Fuzzy Expert System* (box 1, **Fig.** 1) estimates attractiveness of given stock (company) on the base of Price/Earning ratio (P/E) and Price/Book Value index (P/BV). For P/E we assume two fuzzy sets: low, high (L,H); for P/BV – three sets: *law*, *medium*, *high* (L, M, H). Output variable, Attractiveness (A) has three triangular sets: *law*, *medium*, *high* (LA, MA, HA). Knowledge base contains rules shown in Table 1. The system concludes attractiveness of company in a form of number from the range [0,10]. The second step is calculation of indices CR and D/Y. On the base of their values, system produce suggestions for the user in a text format, e.g.:

**Table 1.** Set of fuzzy rules on the base of P/E and P/BV

| P/E\P/BV | L | M | H |
|---|---|---|---|
| L | MA | HA | MA |
| H | LA | MA | LA |

1. if *attractiveness* < *treshold_attractiveness* then *do not invest*
2. if *attractiveness* ≥ *treshold_attractiveness* and *CR* ≥ *sCR* and *D/Y* ≥ *sD/Y* then *invest for dividend*
3. if *attractiveness* ≥ *treshold_attractiveness* and *CR* ≥ *sCR* and *D/Y* < *sD/Y* then *do not invest because effectiveness of dividend is very low* (*you should find others investment*)
4. if *attractiveness* ≥ *treshold_attractiveness* and (*CR* ≥ *sCR* or *CR does not exist*) then *invest because the increase of stock price is possible* (*investment policy of company*)

**FES for indices of effectiveness interpretation**

Fuzzy Expert System (box 2, **Fig.** 1) estimates attractiveness of given stock (company) in five steps. The first step is made on the base of Financial Effectiveness index (FE) in the context of market average (mFE) and branch average (bFE). For both indices (mFE and bFE), three fuzzy sets are defined (L, M, H). System inferences about company attractiveness: *very law*, *low*, *good*, *high*, *very high* (vLA, LA, GA, HA, vHA). Set of rules is given in Table 2. Attractiveness is calculated and scaled to the range [0,10]. In the second step system estimates attractiveness of company using Return on Assets index (ROA) in the context of market average (mROA) and branch average (bROA). For both input variables we use two fuzzy sets (L, H), for output variable – attractiveness, we define three sets (LA, MA, HA). Simple rules are shown in Table 3. Third and fourth steps are similar to the second one, but system uses Return On Equity (ROE) and Net Profit Margin

**Table 2.** Set of fuzzy rules on the base of bFE and mFE

| bFE\mFE | L | M | H |
|---|---|---|---|
| L | vLA | LA | LA |
| M | GA | GA | GA |
| H | HA | HA | vHA |

**Table 3.** Set of fuzzy rules on the base of bROA and mROA

| bROA\mROA | L | H |
|---|---|---|
| L | LA | MA |
| H | MA | HA |

(NPM) indices respectively. The fifth step is simple calculation of average attractiveness obtained in the former four steps.

**FES for indices of rotation interpretation** and **FES for indices of liquidity interpretation**

These fuzzy expert systems (boxes 3 and 4, **Fig.** 1) work in similar way as previous one. The last system estimates attractiveness on the base of Current Ratio (CR) and Quick Ratio (QR) indices, but the former one uses Assets Turnover (AT) and Inventory Turnover (IT) indices. Both systems calculate output attractiveness as average value. They all generate text commentary for the user.

Box 5 in **Fig.** 1 – Evaluation Module, calculates final attractiveness on the base of Fundamental Analysis using outputs of four fuzzy expert systems:

$$A = \sum_{i=1}^{4} a_i \cdot w_i \, , \tag{17}$$

where: $A$ – final attractiveness,

$a_i$ – output of $i$th analyzer (boxes 1, 2, 3, 4, **Fig.** 1)

$w_i$ – weight for $i$th analyzer: $w_i$ = 0.4, 0.2, 0.2, 0.2 for $i$=1, 2, 3, 4 respectively.

Analysis of indices is significant part of fundamental analysis. The above described system is able to evaluate financial condition of company and to generate short text description for the user. Final assessment given by the system allows user for easy and complete comparison of companies. Such system can be useful, but together with technical analysis should give more credible results.

## Technical Analysis Modules

The part of **SMEE** responsible for technical analysis consists of one simple expert system – his task is to interpret *point & figures* graphs. Analysis of price graphs is made using four different neural networks. The other modules calculate and interpret some indices useful in Stock Market analysis.

**Expert system for point & figure analysis**

System (box 6, **Fig.** 1) receives preprocessed *point & figure* chart, and we expect that it find characteristic formations on this figure. We distinguish 12 formations. All formations are defined as set of simple rule, considering internal representation of figures. Figures are represented in the form useful for computer processing. The system automatically evaluates figures from the point of view of trade signals and strengths of found trends. The wider description of this task and used set of rules one can find in (Ciosmak 2000).

**Artificial Neural Network (NN) as pattern recognition tool**

Price formations are significant part of technical analysis. We use four feedforward neural networks: two of them work with graphs of price changes, two – with graphs of volume changes. One network is trained to recognize patterns directly on the real prices and one is trained on the base of increments in successively quotations. The same situation is with volume changes graph: one NN works on the volume changes, the second on the increments. Networks searching formations on the price graphs were trained for 7 formations, networks searched formations on the volume graphs were trained for 5 formations. Parameters of used networks are defined in table 4. The NNs were developed after a number of experiments with the task of pattern recognition. Emergent problems were analyzed and taken into account during developing process. A number of tests with real data from the Warsaw Stock Exchange (**WSE**) confirm correctness of NNs modules.

**Table 4.** Parameters of used neural networks in technical analysis

| Parameter | NN 1 | NN 2 | NN 3 | NN 4 |
|---|---|---|---|---|
| Number of input neurons | 20 | 20 | 20 | 20 |
| Number of hidden neurons | 13 | 12 | 11 | 9 |
| Number of output neurons | 7 | 7 | 5 | 5 |
| Learning rate ($\eta$) | 0.4 | 0.4 | 0.2 | 0.4 |
| Momentum ($\alpha$) | 0.9 | 0.9 | 0.9 | 0.9 |
| Error (Ep) | 0.005 | 0.0005 | 0.05 | 0.005 |
| Times of learning [epoch] | ≈2500 | ≈1500 | ≈15000 | ≈1000 |

**Central Unit** (**CU**) manages tasks of all analyzers and it communicates with users. **CU** is focused on:

- calling analyzers for user demand,
- supplying analyzers with needed data from the system database,
- receiving and interpretation of results produced by analyzers,
- generation of companies evaluation,
- generation of suggestions – each user establish filters (program options), the strength of suggestion is generated on the base of all company evaluations existing in the system, it ranges from 1 (the least attractive) to 10 (the most attractive).

**SMEE** is easy for users, therefore adding data concerning new quotations is simple, it can be done by reading text file, gathering for example from the home page of **WSE**.

## Stock Market Electronic Expert – experiments with real data

Computer program has to be installed under Microsoft Windows 95/98/2000/NT. All windows and parameter description are in Polish. Portfolio and history of transactions of each user are stored in database. Exemplary windows are shown in **Fig.** 4, 5, 6, 7.

Fig. 6. SMEE - main menu

Developed system should support user financial decision. A number of experiments have been made for **SMEE** verification. Full description of experiments is in (Ciosmak 2000), here we present only excerpts from them.

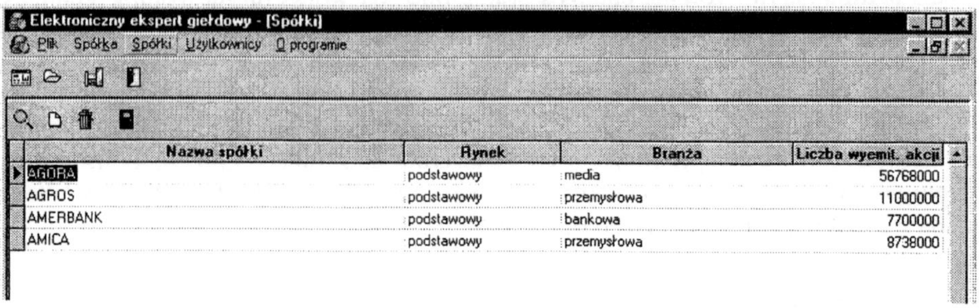


**Fig. 4.** SMEE – companies window

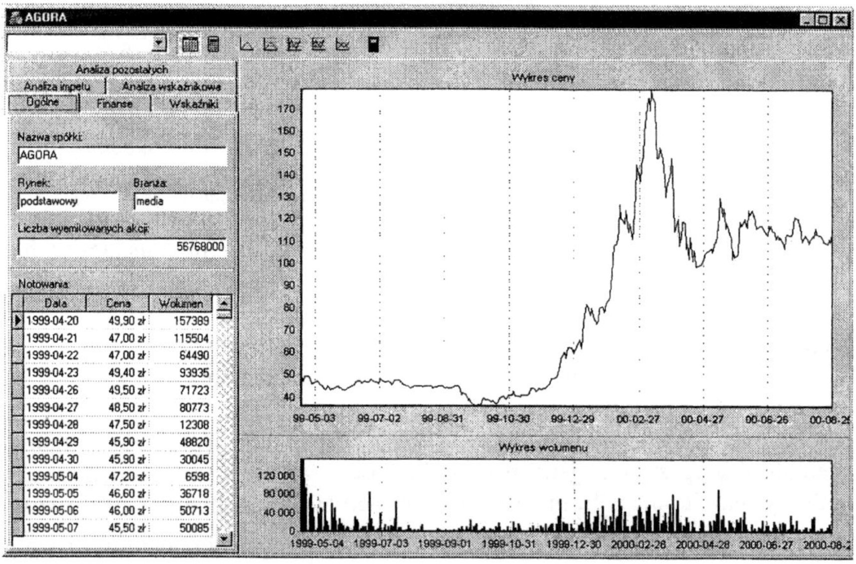


**Fig. 5.** SMEE – examples of company window

**Experiment 1.** Test of credibility of market price forecast using standard parameters.

For this experiment we have randomly selected 30 companies. Considered quotations begin on 20 October 1999. For each company, following financial data are used by the system: a number of issued shares; assets; company capital; net trade (year); net profit (year); dividend on share; book value.

Standard system parameters are no restrictive, therefore we should assume soft criteria of forecast accuracy, namely:

- forecast of *increase* is accurate if during the period not less then two months, the market price reaches 120% of initial value (dated on 29.10.1999),
- forecast of *decrease* is accurate if during the period no less then two months, the market price decreases up to 90% of initial value (dated on 29.10.1999), and – during the same period, it increases no higher then 110% initial price (dated on 29.10.1999).

We accept result as *forecast of increase* only if signal *to bay* is produced with strength attribute greater or equal to 7, and as *forecast of decrease* only if signal *to sell* is produced with strength attribute greater or equal to 7. The results are collected in Table 5. The sign '+' means that forecast is adequate, but '–' that obtained forecast does not fulfill stated criteria.

Accuracy rate is equal to 78% what seems to be satisfactory. It is worth to mention that the system does not produce suggestion which gives user great financial loss. Majority of suggestions concerning baying seems to bring profit.

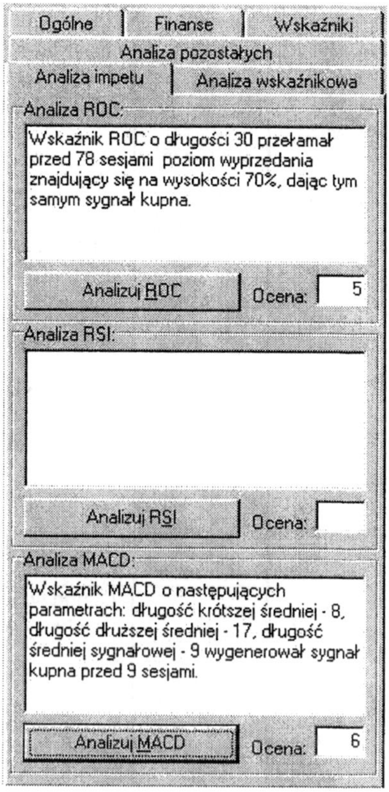


**Fig. 7.** SMEE – violence analysis

**Experiment 2.** Test of credibility of market price forecast using standard parameters, but the beginning of the analysis period comes when we observe the end of boom.

We take into account the period in which we observe the end of boom (31 March 2000). Here, the accuracy rate is equal to 60% (Table 6). But only two forecasts are 'quite' wrong (for BIG and Amica, two lasts rows in Table 6), what means that they suggest price increasing, but real price decreased. For the other companies for which forecast is marked as wrong, forecasted changes of market price are in proper direction but they are too slow to fulfill assumed criteria. In this experiment, predictions of prices decreasing dominate, Warsaw Stock Exchange entered the phase of slump. Somebody investing according to forecasts given by the system could not expect high profits, but potential losses are also not very high.

**Table 5.** Summary results obtained in experiment 1

| Company | Sugestion (forecast) | Real changes of market prices | Forecast accuracy |
|---|---|---|---|
| Dębica | to bay (increase) | First 20 days: decrease up to 92%, next increase up to 125% (to 03.01.2000) | + |
| Mennica | to bay (increase) | Market price increase up to 144% (to 22.12.99), next – up to 197% (17.03.2000) | + |
| KGHM | to bay (increase) | Increase of price up to 113% (27.12.99), next to 149% (25.02.2000), forecast does not fulfill initial conditions. | – |
| Amica | to bay (increase) | 27.12.99 price=136%, without significant decrease, in next months it increases up to 205% (29.03.2000). | + |
| Kable | to bay (increase) | 18.11.99 market price decreases below 90% | – |
| Best | to bay (increase) | To the end of 99, price increases up 126%. | + |
| Indykpol | to bay (increase) | Increase up to 135% to the end of 99. | + |
| Delia | to bay (increase) | No significant increases or decreases | – |
| Softbank | to bay (increase) | During two months increase to 124%, next months – huge increase – to 291% (the end of March 2000). | + |
| Irena | to bay (increase) | Increase up to 137% (27.12.99) | + |
| Prokom | to bay (increase) | Increase up to 143% (the end of 1999), next higher increase (353%) | + |
| Cersanit | to bay (increase) | Increase up to 126% (27.12.99.), next to 243% (07.04.2000) | + |
| Bre | to bay (increase) | Increase up to 120% before the end of 99. | + |
| BIG | to bay (increase) | Increase up to 160%, next – to 238% | + |
| Bytom | to sell (decrease) | Not significant (but more then 110%) increase. Forecast does not fulfill criteria. | – |
| Elektrim | to sell (decrease) | During few days (to 08.11.99), decrease up to 70% | + |
| Bakoma | to sell (decrease) | Decrease up to 89% (18.11.99) | + |
| Agros | to sell (decrease) | Market price quickly decreases up to 88% | + |

In other experiments some analyzers are excluded. Using two analyzers, **SMEE** was able to give forecasts with accuracy rate equal to 72%, but in 3 cases forecasts are quite wrong (5 companies do not fulfill forecast criteria). The analysis of moving averages plays the big role in this experiment (it is used together with *point & figures* analyzer).

**Table 6.** Summary results obtained in experiment 2

| Company | Sugestion (forecast) | Real changes of market prices | Forecast accuracy |
|---|---|---|---|
| Indykpol | to sell (decrease) | Market price decrease, but during 2 months, price is still greater then 90% of initial value. | – |
| Kable | to sell (decrease) | Market price decrease up to 75% (to 25.04.2000). | + |
| Softbank | to sell (decrease) | Market price decrease up to 63% (to 09.05.2000). | + |
| Jelfa | to sell (decrease) | Market price decrease up to 88% (to 26.05.2000). | + |
| Agora | to sell (decrease) | Market price decrease up to 86% (to 29.04.2000). | + |
| Elelektrim | to sell (decrease) | Market price decrease up to 78% (to 24.05.2000). | + |
| Pekao | to sell (decrease) | Market price decrease up to 88% (to 17.04.2000). | + |
| Prokom | to sell (decrease) | Market price decrease up to 75% (to 09.05.2000). | + |
| Rafako | to sell (decrease) | Market price decrease up to 79% (to 29.05.2000). | + |
| Warta | to sell (decrease) | Market price decrease up to 73% (to 26.05.2000). | + |
| Handlowy | to bay (increase) | Increase up to the middle of July, but too slow, so forecast is not accurate. | – |
| Cersanit | to bay (increase) | Increase, but only to 107% (07.04.2000.), next – decrease. | – |
| Bytom | to bay (increase) | Increase up to 107% (24.04.2000), too slow. | – |
| BIG | to bay (increase) | Wrong forecast, market price decrease up to 69% during 20 days. | – |
| Amica | to bay (increase) | Wrong forecast, market price decrease up to 69% (during days). | – |

## Summary

The developed system seems to work acceptable. Experiments show that obtained forecasts have about 70% accuracy – this result can be seen as satisfying for such difficult task. Majorities of the "wrong" forecasts are obtained only because changes on the Stock Exchange are too slow, taking into account defined criteria, but the directions of changes are adequate. It is very significant feature of the system, because 'quite wrong' forecast can cause big financial loss for potential users. In all experiments, only 14% forecasts are quite wrong, that means, they bring potential investors losses.

The system has big possibilities to analyze and to present obtained results, however the user interface can be extended.

The program is ready for use by potential investors, but the authors have not invested in the Stock Exchange and do not take responsibility for profits and losses of potential users.

**References**

Baborski A., Efektywne zarządzanie a sztuczna inteligencja (Artificial Intelligence and Effective Management), Akademia Ekonomiczna im. O. Langego, Wrocław 1994.

Baryłko B., *Giełda krok po kroku: poradnik inwestora giełdowego* (*Stock Market Step by Step: Handbook of Stock Investor*), Poltext, Warszawa 1994.

Bień W., *Rynek papierów wartościowych* (*Stock Market*), Stowarzyszenie Księgowych w Polsce, Warszawa 1992.

Ciosmak M., *Techniki sztucznej inteligencji w analizie giełdy* (*Artificial Intelligent Techniques in Stock Market Analysis*), Master Thesis, Wrocław University of Technology, Wrocław, 2000.

Czekała M., *Rynek kapitałowy. Analiza fundamentalna i techniczna* (*Fundamental and Technical Analysis if Stock Market*), Akademia Ekonomiczna im. O. Langego, Wrocław, 1998.

Deboeck G.J. (Ed.), *Trading on the Edge. Neural, Genetic, and Fuzzy Systems for Chaotic Finansal Markets*, John Willey & Sons, Inc., 1994.

Dorsey T.J., *Wykresy punktowo-symboliczne* (*Point & Figure Graphs*), Dom Wydawniczy ABC, Warszawa 1998.

Hertz J., Krogh A., Palmer R., *Wstęp do teorii obliczeń neuronowych* (*Introduction to the Theory of Neural Computation*), WNT, Warszawa 1995.

Komar Z., *Sztuka spekulacji* (*The Art of Speculation*), PRET S.A., Warszawa 1993.

Lechowicz A., Mączka W., *Poradnik inwestora giełdowego*, (*Handbook of Stock Investor*) BEST, Kraków 1994.

Mitchell T.M., *Machine Learning*, The McGraw-Hill Companies, Inc., 1997.

Mulak M., Rąpała J., *Analiza akcji na wykresach point & figure* (*Analyze of stock on the base of point & figure graphs*), Wrocław 1997.

Mulawka J., *Systemy ekspertowe* (*Expert Systems*). WNT, Warszawa 1996.

Murphy J.J., *Analiza Techniczna* (*Technical Analysis*), WIG-Press, Warszawa 1995

Pring M., *Podstawy analizy technicznej* (*Background of Technical Analysis*), WIG-Press, Warszawa 1998.

Ritchie J.C., *Analiza fundamentalna* (*Fundamental Analysis*), WIG-Press, Warszawa 1997.

Sopoćko A., *Giełda papierów wartościowych* (*Stock Market*), PWE, Warszawa 1991.

Tadeusiewicz R., *Sieci neuronowe* (*Neural Networks*), Akademicka Oficyna Wydawnicza, Warszawa 1993.

Żurada J., Barski M., Jędruch W., *Sztuczne sieci neuronowe* (*Artificial Neural Networks*), PWN, Warszawa 1996.

Home page of WGPW, URL: http://www.gpw.com.pl/.

# Models of Multiple Response Independence

Andrzej Matuszewski*, Krzysztof Trojanowski**
Institute of Computer Science, Polish Academy of Sciences, Warsaw, Poland
(amat@ipipan.waw.pl)*, (trojanow@ipipan.waw.pl)**

## Abstract

We consider the problem of how to measure a "correlation" (or interdependence) between two survey-questionnaire questions. In the real-life questionnaires it is usual to offer several options-answers for most of the questions. Some (or many) questions give the possibility to choose more than one answer. There are very few statistical methods that enable inferences for the questions with multiple answers. We consider two statistics of the chi-square type that serve to confirm a dependence of two questions. As a theoretical basis a notion of "independence" between two multiple questions should be introduced. We propose two definitions (or actually types of definitions): "random" and "generalized Poisson" independences. A simulation study was performed, which is based on those notions. The study confirms applicability of the chi-square statistics, which are similar to the classical ones.

Keywords: Questionnaire data, discrete statistical analysis, correlation, chi-square statistics, contingency tables, Monte Carlo simulation, data mining, Poisson distribution.

## 1 Introduction

In the last years we have been considering a possibility to incorporate into the statistical methodology (and further, to the statistical software) a new capability. These are the references: (Matuszewski 1996, 1999, 2000, with Bali, 1998)

There are very many databases that contain results of the survey questioning of different populations of human responders. It seems that the existing methodology and software do not assume (in a sufficient way - for some recent general results see: (Agresti, 1999 and 2000), (Decady and Thomas, 2000), ( Loughin and Scherer, 1998)) the fact that a person questioned can choose more than one answer among those that are offered.

The problem of how to analyze such "multiple-response" data has many deep aspects. All of them are connected with discrete statistics. To establish a firm investigation in this area, some theoretical background (basically Agresti and Andersen works) is necessary. Lloyd (1999) has recently written a relevant monograph in this field.

There are three basic aspects of the research on multiresponse that make the research effort more concrete. These aspects define general restrictions any researcher should take into account. Then the research would be relevant for the data mining.

1. The framework must be established, which links a specific investigation with a possible application setting within the questionnaire based data analysis. E.g. responder is limited to give at most 3 (say) answers from the set of 6 (say) alternatives. As a consequence all results that will (hopefully) appear, are applicable from one hand. It should be taken into account that data-analysts (questionnaire data has been intensively analyzed for many years) can use at least one "classical" method for that application setting. The specific new algorithm must be compared (in a final stage) with the classical ones, therefore.
2. Since all frameworks are at the beginning stage, all research problems are (or has an important aspect) connected with the measurement of an appropriate "correlation" for the pair of questions.
3. Even at this stage one should consider existing commercial and non-commercial software (normally quite sophisticated) that can solve specific problems.

This paper can be treated as a sort of introduction to the multiresponse area. We show some results either.

## 2 Basic notions

Assume that two multiresponse survey questions: **A** and **B** have respectively $A$ and $B$ possible choices as answers. These questions are presented to $I$ responders. It means that a person $i$ ( $i \leq I$ ) can choose any number ($\leq A$) of answers for the question **A** and also any number ($\leq B$) of answers for the other question.

There exist two approaches for measuring "correlation" between: **A** and **B.** We will explain them for the case: $A$ and $B$ both equal 3. Since this case is sufficient to present all relevant aspects of our setting, we will continue the 3x3 case throughout.

First general approach can be called "vote-collecting" because the numbers of votes for proposed (in the questionnaire) answers is most relevant.

In this paper we deal with other approach to the assessment of correlation (or interdependence) between **A** and **B**, which will be called: selective coincidence. This approach has two basic features.

1. Responders that did not choose anything or did choose everything to at least one of two questions, are not taken into account for the assessment

of correlation between these questions. Of course those responders can be taken into account for another pair of questions.

2. Unique choices of answers have higher weights than double choices, since the former are "more selective". The formalization of this statement is the following.

Instead of (classical) two-way contingency table we consider its generalization that takes into account a "natural" division of each responder's count. If a given responder chose: 2 (in general: $c$) answers to question **A** and: 2 (in general: $d$) answers to question **B,** then this fact is represented in 4 (in general in: $cd$) cells of the contingency table. Of course it means that one person has 4 (in general in: $cd$) cell-contributions to the "correlation measure" that we are interested in.

The new proposal is oriented for a sort of a "democratic system" i.e. to make all responders' contribution to correlation **equal.** As a consequence we propose to make weights equal to ¼ (in general to: $1/cd$) for all contributions of one responder.

## 3 Two simulation models

We define here the models that will serve us as an analytical basis for the Monte Carlo experiments described in the following sections.

The general motivation for these models can be described this way. We want to use the test statistic that is as close as possible to the traditional chi-square oriented for the two-way contingency table. We will attempt to check the distribution of this statistic under the distribution of answers (for a group of responders), which pretends to be a model of independence between **A** and **B**. To focus on that independence we will assume (in this paper) a uniform distribution of answers for each question separately.

First model called: the random has the following aim. Within this model one can simulate a sample of responders, who give the answers (to **A** and **B**) completely at random. The model has a minimal number of parameters that can be considered: $I$ - defined above, and $M$ – a number of samples of responders to be generated.

For a (simulated) responder the following generation of his answers to questions: **A** and **B** is performed.

First, the numbers of answers to both questions is randomly chosen. As it was commented above, only numbers 1 and 2 make sense. The pair of independent guesses (with equal probability) from the set: {1,2} is generated, therefore.

Secondly the appropriate number of choices of answers from the set {1,2,3} for **A** and **B** questions is generated also at random i.e. with the same probability (equal to 1/3) without repetitions.

For one sample of $I$ responders, a Monte Carlo simulation algorithm produces the following weighted frequencies:

$w_{ab}(c,d)$ = weighted number of responders who have chosen $c$ answers to **A** question, $d$ answers to **B** question and among the pairs of answers they have given there is a pair $a,b$.

The $w$ frequencies fulfill the following equations that involve the "classical", easy-to-understand frequencies. These equations take into account weights introduced in the preceding section.

$w_{ab}(1,1) = n_{ab}$

$m_{ab} = w_{ab}(1,1) + 2\cdot ( w_{ab}(1,2) + w_{ab}(2,1)) + 4\cdot w_{ab}(2,2)$

$n_{ab}$ – is a number of responders, who have chosen answers: $a$ and $b$ for the questions: **A** and **B** respectively, assuming that they must choose exactly one answer for both questions (it is an element of the classical contingency table)

$m_{ab}$ – is a general number of "votes" for the pair of answers: $a$ and $b$, excluding persons that do not fulfill the selective coincidence principle

The second model: the generalized Poisson has a different "philosophy". Instead of generation of "responders", as above, the model performs a direct Monte Carlo generation of entries $w_{ab}(c,d)$ of four 3x3 tables ($c,d$ = 1,2). The Poisson distribution seems to be most appropriate for this sake - some arguments in favor will be presented in the next section. In section 6 a specific generalization of Poisson distribution will be proposed, which allows generation of non-integer $w_{ab}(c,d)$ entries. In this experiment we will assume that all entries (i.e. variables with generalized Poisson distributions) are independent.

The democratic principle that equals contributions of all responders in the correlation measurement is not the only aim that can be reached. The other is the simplicity of the procedure of this measurement. A two-dimensional procedure, based on combinations of answers to **A** and **B** only, should be available.

# 4 Arguments for applicability of chi-square statistic

One can introduce the generalized two-way contingency table with elements:

$$W_{ab} = w_{ab}(1,1) + w_{ab}(1,2) + w_{ab}(2,1) + w_{ab}(2,2) \qquad (1)$$

Do exist arguments that enable using in practice of data analysis the classical chi-square statistics based on the table [ $W_{ab}$ ]? This question can be reformulated as follows.

One can treat $w_{ab}(c,d)$ as a three-way contingency table with the third dimension summed up as in the equation (1). In this setting first dimension is connected with $a$ and the second with $b$. Are there theorems that offer interpretation of marginal two-way chi-square statistic (for $a$ and $b$), which test the independence? We have to check if our models of independence fulfill the assumptions of those theorems. Assume that some specific assumptions are violated. Those violations (detected) will cause specific differences that occur in Monte Carlo experiments.

We make that check for the generalized Poisson model first. As a starting point we take a Poisson as one of the three classical distributional models considered as a basis of the so-called loglinear analysis. This analysis is applicable (in its most usual setting) to the (classical) multi-way contingency tables and introduces a specific hierarchy of those tables.

Loglinear analysis was introduced in the sixties (of this century) and was finally described in the monograph by Bishop, Fienberg and Holland (1975). More readable descriptions that can serve as bases of the university courses, can be found e.g. in the books of Fienberg (1978) and Andersen (1990). There exists an extensive software that performs loglinear analysis. Great majority of the standard statistical computer packages (including STATISTICA and SPSS) can perform this analysis.

The most important and very convincing property of the loglinear analysis is the following. Loglinear equations contain parameters that can be constructively estimated. Also meaningful statistical hypotheses can be formulated for those parameters. These hypotheses are checked through chi-square statistics. It is definitely very elegant that both: estimations and hypotheses tests have the same form for three basic types of statistical distributions that can be considered for the loglinear equations. One of those distributions is the Poisson. Each cell of the contingency table has the independent Poisson distribution with a "loglinearly" defined parameter.

To reduce one dimension of three-way contingency table a specific independence condition should be proved. In our setting the 3x3 matrix distributions of $w_{ab}(c,d)$, corresponding to 4 possible pairs of $(c,d)$, should be identical and independent. Changes in definitions of the generalized Poisson distribution that will be proposed during the Monte Carlo experiment, are the only causes of violation of loglinear restrictions, therefore.

There exists another source of motivation oriented for the Poisson distribution. Thall (1992) introduced a new type of methodology that can be applied to our contingency tables. He considered three-way contingency tables with independent-Poisson-distributed entries. He found that also for other parameters (than loglinear) the chi-square statistic, for marginal two-way contingency table, is optimal for testing the independence between **A** and **B.**

In the random model there is fulfilled only one important condition, of those required by the loglinear analysis. The expectations of four: 3x3 tables $w_{ab}(c,d)$, for $(c,d)$ that changes, are equal. It will be confirmed in the next section. One can not say that a distribution of each of those tables does not depend on changing $(c,d)$, however. The dependence is different than that appeared in the generalized Poisson, where it accounts basically in differences in the expectations.

To find out a most important feature of the random model let us consider the $w_{ab}(2,1)$ table. The table summarizes information of those among $I$ responders who have chosen 2 answers to the question **A** and 1 answer to **B**. Since two values (equal to 1/2) of a given responder enter to the same column of $w_{ab}(2,1)$ table, the components of the same column become positively correlated. For example if a responder has chosen the third alternative for **B** question (i.e. his $b$=3), his both cell contributions enter the same third column of $w_{ab}(2,1)$ table.

Such dependency is definitely not allowed neither in loglinear nor in Thall formalizations for the contingency tables. It is still stronger for the $w_{ab}(2,2)$ table, where both row and column dependencies enter.

## 5 Cell behavior

We present the behavior of elementary (new-type) contingency tables i.e. matrices $w_{ab}(c,d)$ with last arguments within the (1,2)x(1,2) set. To have a first look of that behavior we will present: mean, standard deviation and coefficient of skewness of $w_{ab}(c,d)$ for the random model.

It is clear that all $w_{ab}(c,d)$ entries for a given $(c,d)$, behave in the same way for all: $a,b\leq 3$. We will concentrate on the same cell (say $(a,b)$ = (1,1)), therefore.

All the simulations below are made for $M$ = 5000, while $I$ (number of responders) changes. For each type of cell, two simulations were performed to assess the exactness of estimation.

| *I* = 10 | | |
|---|---|---|
| Mean | St.Dev. | Skew. |
| *(c,d)* = (1,1) | | |
| 0.276400 | 0.515806 | 1.748218 |
| 0.263600 | 0.502161 | 1.878825 |
| *(c,d)* = (1,2) | | |
| 0.268500 | 0.356347 | 1.245385 |
| 0.273100 | 0.358039 | 1.226628 |
| *(c,d)* = (2,1) | | |
| 0.274300 | 0.351759 | 1.133519 |
| 0.275500 | 0.360105 | 1.247599 |
| *(c,d)* = (2,2) | | |
| 0.275900 | 0.245288 | 0.742130 |
| 0.278600 | 0.251435 | 0.803109 |

| $I$ = 30 | | |
|---|---|---|
| Mean | St.Dev. | Skew. |
| $(c,d)$ = (1,1) | | |
| 0.843800 | 0.898645 | 0.995931 |
| 0.823800 | 0.894043 | 1.039017 |
| $(c,d)$ = (1,2) | | |
| 0.842500 | 0.632395 | 0.737251 |
| 0.852300 | 0.647703 | 0.780200 |
| $(c,d)$ = (2,1) | | |
| 0.834300 | 0.636297 | 0.699080 |
| 0.829400 | 0.623276 | 0.680208 |
| $(c,d)$ = (2,2) | | |
| 0.823900 | 0.431626 | 0.439630 |
| 0.828600 | 0.430330 | 0.411913 |

| $I$ = 80 | | |
|---|---|---|
| Mean | St.Dev. | Skew. |
| $(c,d)$ = (1,1) | | |
| 2.214800 | 1.453920 | 0.612144 |
| 2.235200 | 1.458049 | 0.623823 |
| $(c,d)$ = (1,2) | | |
| 2.239200 | 1.048667 | 0.386894 |
| 2.197400 | 1.025302 | 0.423658 |
| $(c,d)$ = (2,1) | | |
| 2.205400 | 1.010156 | 0.404772 |
| 2.233200 | 1.038765 | 0.414794 |
| $(c,d)$ = (2,2) | | |
| 2.221100 | 0.697110 | 0.247602 |
| 2.221500 | 0.709939 | 0.257135 |

The behavior of the above estimations of basic statistical parameters is not surprising. To understand them properly one must take into account the famous central limit theorem. We will use only the intuitive meaning of that theorem.

With the growing numbers of components distribution of counts becomes more normal (skewness coefficients are closer and closer to zero) or symmetric. Also standard deviations are relatively (comparing with means) smaller and smaller. It should also be taken into account that with $c+d$ growing the number of components of the count also grows for fixed $I$.

# 6 Behavior of chi-square type statistics

In the literature and within the computer software production, two formulas of (two-way) chi-square statistic are most popular: Pearsonian and the loglikelihood ones. By the formula (1) we use sums of 4 weighted frequencies: $w_{ab}(c,d)$ as input data for these formulas. These statistics are optimal as tests of independence and assuming independence (between **A** and **B**) they have asymptotic chi-square distribution with 4 degrees of freedom.

Both our models of independence oriented for generation of answers to multiresponse questions fulfill perfectly independence (between **A** and **B**) conditions. Some other assumptions are not fulfilled for the random model, which is first in the Monte Carlo experiment.

| Mean | St. Dev. | Skew. |
|---|---|---|
| $I$ = 10<br>Pearsonian | | |
| 1.947534 | 1.175454 | 1.080573 |
| 1.917655 | 1.188311 | 1.167752 |
| Loglikelihood | | |
| 2.332488 | 1.395289 | 0.972912 |
| 2.296377 | 1.412006 | 1.066441 |
| $I$ = 30<br>Pearsonian | | |
| 1.956219 | 1.351340 | 1.323347 |
| 1.927374 | 1.320184 | 1.290275 |
| Loglikelihood | | |
| 2.084239 | 1.516118 | 1.436543 |
| 2.049482 | 1.480882 | 1.417548 |
| $I$= 80<br>Pearsonian | | |
| 1.898487 | 1.299672 | 1.279339 |
| 1.891571 | 1.312510 | 1.368562 |
| Loglikelihood | | |
| 1.927777 | 1.341625 | 1.369248 |
| 1.920133 | 1.349488 | 1.415698 |

As a first comment it should be pointed out that tables with at least one $W_{ab}$ = 0 can not be taken into account for the loglikehood chi-square statistic for arithmetic reasons. This resulted in increasing averages of that statistic while comparing with the Pearsonian one, especially for smaller $I$.

It should be stressed that both chi-square statistics "should" tend to the distribution, which has the expectation equal to 4 (and positive skewness).

The random model definitely fulfills the independence hypothesis, but statistics tend to the smaller value: roughly 2. This unexpected convergence requires some additional comments.

It is clear that the only reason that made all 9 components of the chi-square statistic formula smaller (than the classical ones) is the behavior of non-integer parts of those 9 contingency table entries. To confirm this obvious statement a simulation were performed with weights, corresponding to multiple choices, equal to zero. Averages for the chi-square statistics were close to 4.

One reason that can diminish the differences between observed and expected frequencies was already mentioned in the previous section: "more normal" distribution of the non-integer $w_{ab}(c,d)$ . Another reason (linkage in row and columns for one responder) was commented in section 4.

Now we will consider our second formalization of independence. The forthcoming Monte Carlo simulation will also be focused on the possibility that chi-square statistic converges in average to the smaller value than its expectation i.e. value 4.

The Poisson distribution as a second most important statistical distribution (after the normal distribution mentioned above) has a very extensive literature. We can make reference to the Haight (1967) and Ord (1972) monographs e.g.. They cited various generalizations of that distribution, which were employed either for theoretical or very practical purposes.

For our purposes restricted to this presentation only, we will use the relation described below.

We will apply, for simulation procedure, the following (most usual) definition of the cumulative distribution function *CDF*.

$$\mathrm{CDF}(X(\alpha),x) = \mathrm{Prob}\,(X(\alpha) \leq x)$$

where:

$X(\alpha)$ – is the name of random variable that depends on a parameter $\alpha$,

$x$ – is formally any possible real number, but actually only values taken by $X(\alpha)$ are relevant.

There exists (e.g. Haight, 1967) the following equality fulfilled for the Poisson distribution. It links this distribution with another one (of the gamma type), which is defined for all positive real numbers.

$$CDF(\mathrm{Poisson}(\alpha),x) = 1 - CDF(\mathrm{Gamma}(1+x),2\alpha) \qquad (2)$$

This formula, which in the classical form is valid only for the integer $x$ values, allows us definition of a Poisson distribution generalized to the values with decimals: .25, .5, .75 that we need.

We will present some "practical" features of our Poisson model of independence between two multiresponse variables, first.

In the simulations, which are described below we use the parameter $\alpha$ of all Poisson distributions equal to 1. It is a "realistic" value. Recall that the sample size of 30 (responders) for the random model resulted in cell entries with observed frequencies equal to 0.83 (see section 5). We should add, however, that formula (2) results in slight diminishing of expectation for $w_{ab}(1,2)$, $w_{ab}(2,1)$ and $w_{ab}(2,2)$. The expectation of two former cells is equal to 0.814, while the latter (which corresponds to responders with two answers to both: **A** and **B**) is equal to 0.729. The final expectation of all sums $W_{ab}$ is therefore slightly higher than 3.3 in this setting.

It should be pointed out that within the Poisson independence model there is no need to impose the weights for $w_{ab}(1,2)$, $w_{ab}(2,1)$ and $w_{ab}(2,2)$. This model is constructed (from the beginning) to account a necessary division for these cells. In the random model these cells has simply higher probability of occurrence – that's why they are weighted.

Nevertheless we make some additional weighting for generalized Poisson model, which will be interpreted afterwards.

Below the simulation results are shown. The main aim of the table is an estimation of the expectation of chi-square statistics. Each entry is an average of several calculations based on 4000 or 5000 repetitions each. The accuracy of the estimations (with the mean square error as criterion) is less than 0.05.

| Additional weights to the Poisson variables | | | Estimation of the mean of chi-square statistic | |
|---|---|---|---|---|
| Integer-valued | 0.5-valued | 0.25-valued | Pearsonian | Loglikelihood |
| 1 | 1 | 1 | 4.08 | 4.46 |
| 1 | 0.8 | 0.6 | 3.43 | 3.74 |
| 1 | 0.65 | 0.4 | 3.14 | 3.42 |
| 1 | 0.5 | 0.25 | 2.87 | 3.13 |
| 1 | 0.3 | 0.15 | 2.80 | 3.06 |
| 1 | 0.1 | 0.1 | 3.13 | 3.40 |
| 1 | 0 | 0 | 3.97 | 4.74 |

We concentrate now on the first row of the results to establish the most important findings.

This simulation is motivated by the model of Thall from one hand and the random model from the other. The parameter $\alpha$ of all Poisson distributions is the same. Two assumptions of the Thall model are not fulfilled, however.

$w_{ab}(1,2)$, $w_{ab}(2,1)$ and $w_{ab}(2,2)$ have not equal expectations and also smaller than 1 as they "should" have.

The distributions are not exactly of the Poisson type.

The fact that chi-square statistics do not diminish their values, as they did for the random model, supports our earlier observation on the importance of dependencies (of row and columns) that arise while simulating the data of a given responder.

Random model takes into account these dependencies, while the Thall model does not.

Now we will comment the other rows of the above table with the simulation results. The non-integer components were multiplied by the values smaller than 1 before summing in (1).

The last row corresponds to the loglinear model and obviously for this case chi-square statistic tends in average to its expectation equal to 4. There are no non-integer components in this model.

Even a very small contribution of non-integer responders, diminish the value of chi-square statistic as can be seen from other rows of the table.

## 7 A conclusion

A possibility of multiple responses for questionnaire survey-questions, motivates an introduction of contingency tables with non-integer entries. Such tables can be treated as a form of basic information on the structure of interdependency between two multiresponse questions. Classical chi-square statistics can be applied to those tables and this is our constructive proposal.

We identified two reasons for diminishing values of chi-square statistics for two-way contingency tables. More important reason is connected with the row and/or column dependencies that arise for multiresponse contingency tables. Two types of further research efforts seem to have, therefore, an importance for the inference methodology in multiresponse.

1. Establishing forms of limiting distributions for chi-square statistics.
2. Considering the specific forms of row and columns dependence while establishing bootstrap estimation of p-value of chi-square (or other) statistic.

Another reason for diminishing statistic (under the independence between **A** and **B**) is a small contribution of non-integer part within the sum that corresponds to the answers pairs: *a*, *b*.

Diminishing test statistic makes the test (in this case: of independence between **A** and **B**) conservative. It can be applied for valid inferences anyway.

Further research should take into account some results on dependency within the general chi-square statistic context. Those results are included in: (Brier, 1980), (Rao and Scott, 1984).

## Literature

Agresti A. "Categorical Data Analysis", Wiley, 1990.

Agresti A. Random effects modeling of multiple binary responses using the multivariate binomial logit-normal distribution, Biometrics (2000)

Agresti A. "An Introduction to Categorical Data Analysis", New York: J. Wiley 1996.

Agresti A., Liu L-M, "Modelling a categorical variable allowing arbitrary many category choices", Biometrics 55, 936-943, 1999.

Andersen E. B., „The statistical analysis of categorical data", Springer Verlag, 1990.

Brier S. S., "Analysis of contingency tables under cluster sampling", Biometrika, 67, pp. 591-596, 1980.

Decady Y.J., Thomas D.R., "A simple test of association for contingency tables with multiple column responses", Biometrics 56, pp.893-896, 2000.

Fienberg S. E., „The analysis of cross-clssified categorical data", MIT Press, 1978.

Haight F. A., "Handbook of the Poisson distribution", J. Wiley, 1967.

Lloyd Ch. J., "Statistical analysis of categorical data", J. Wiley, 1999.

Loughin T., Scherer P. N., Testing association in contingency with multiple column responses, Biometrics 54, 630-637, 1998.

Matuszewski A., „Consecuencias estadisticas de analisis de tres variables dentro de formalismo de Dempster-Shafer", Memorias del XIII Foro Nacional de Estadistica, Culiacan (Mexico), 1996.

Matuszewski A., „Characterization of dependendence between two multivalued variables through the Rasch model - application to construction data-mining algorithms for survey data", Intelligent Information Systems VII, Proceedings of the Workshop held in Malbork, pp. 128-131, 1998.

Matuszewski A., "Rasch model and correlation for discrete variables", Proceedings of Intelligent Information Systems VIII, Ustroń, pp. 322- 326, 1999.

Matuszewski A., "Chi-square type statistics for correlation assessment of two multiresponse survey questions", Proceedings of "Intelligent Information Systems IX", Bystra, pp.83-89, 2000.

Matuszewski A., Bali G., „Un modelo de interdependencia entre respuestas multiples aplicado a la natacion de alto rendimiento", Memorias del XIII Foro Nacional de Estadistica, Monterrey N.L., pp. 103-108, 1998.

Ord J. K., "Families of frequency distributions", Ch. Griffin, London, 1972

Rao J. N. K., Scott A.J., "On chi-squared tests for multi-way tables with cell proportions estimated from survey data", Annals of Statistics 12, 46-60, 1984.

Thall P. F., "Score tests in the two-way layout of counts", Commun. Statist. – Theory Meth., 21, pp. 3017-3036, 1992.

# The Role of Support and Confidence in Collaborative Query Answering

Zbigniew W. Ras

UNC-Charlotte, Dept. of Computer Science, Charlotte, NC 28223, USA
Polish Academy of Sciences, Inst. of Comp. Science, Warsaw, Poland
e-mail: ras@uncc.edu or ras@wars.ipipan.waw.pl

**Abstract:** In this paper we show how support and confidence of agent requests for definitions of attribute values (rules) can be used by a distributed society of collaborating agents to improve query answering. Query answering system linked with each agent is different from solving queries by a conventional distributed database or cooperative database in the sense that it discovers rules, if needed, and uses them to resolve foreign attributes in a query. Each agent is seen either as a knowledge system coupled with a query-answering engine (see [8,9,10]) or an extended relational DB (usually incomplete) coupled with a query answering engine. The quality of a query answering system of an agent is dependent on definitions (knowledge) he receives from other agents. If definitions of foreign attributes to an agent are more precise, then the new query replacing the original query may give more precise answer. Both support and confidence of agents requests for definitions (rules) can be computed and used to decide which agents should be contacted first to answer queries or if needed asked for additional help.

**Keywords**: knowledge system, distributed agents, knowledge discovery, support and confidence of a rule.

## Introduction

Agents can communicate in two different ways. First are agents who share a common internal representation language, based on attribute values, so they can communicate without any external language at all. Then come agents that make no assumptions about each other's internal language, but they share a communication language that is a subset of another language. In this paper, we study only one form of communication in which any two agents share a common internal representation sublanguage based on attributes which domains overlap but semantical meanings of overlapping attributes usually differ. One of the actions available to such an agent is to learn new attributes from the language of another agent by requesting his definitions to be provided in terms of a common internal representation sublanguage for both of these agents. A dual purpose of communication is also to enlarge vocabularies of all agents so the communication between them will be easier, more efficient and often not needed to resolve user queries. Both syntax and semantics of internal representation languages of agents are constantly changing. The ultimate goal of this dynamic process is to reach a consensus among agents on a consistency level but not on a semantical level (their interpretation domains will always be different because objects represented by their database tuples are usually different). Another goal of a communication is to establish a trust and build societies of agents specialized in certain areas so they can handle user queries more efficiently and without requesting help of other agents.

## 1. Distributed Autonomous Agents.

In this section we introduce the notion of a support, total support, confidence and total confidence of a rule in a society of distributed autonomous agents. Also, we will discuss their role in making communication between agents more efficient and query answering more precise.

Let $A=\{a_1,a_2,a_3,...,a_m\}$ is a set of attributes and $DS=\{S_i : i \in\{1,2,\ldots,n\}\}$ is a society of distributed autonomous agents. Each agent $S_i$ is represented initially as a relational table $S_i(A_i)$. The set $\cup\{Dom(a): a \in A_i\}$ is seen as an alphabet of the internal representation language of agent $S_i$ based on $A_i \subseteq A$. The query answering system assigned to an agent is of the form of QAS or RQAS introduced in [8,9,10] and can be seen, in general, as an extended SQL.

For example, let us assume that $A=\{a_1,a_2,a_3,a_4,a_5,a_6,a_7\}$, $DS= \{S_1,S_2,S_3,S_4\}$ is a set of distributed autonomous agents where:
$S_1=S_1(\{a_1,a_2,a_3,a_4\})$, $S_2=S_2(\{a_1,a_4,a_5,a_6\})$, $S_3=S_3(\{a_1,a_2,a_4,a_6,a_7\})$ and, $S_4=S_4(\{a_2,a_3,a_4,a_7\})$.
Clearly, $Dom(a_1) \cup Dom(a_4)$ is the alphabet of the common internal representation language for agents $S_1$, $S_2$. Similarly, $Dom(a_1) \cup Dom(a_4) \cup Dom(a_6)$ is the alphabet of the common internal representation language for agents $S_2$, $S_3$. Terms and rules, defined below, show the structure of the internal representation language of any agent. If built from attributes, which partially do not belong to the alphabet of an agent, then they are called foreign to that agent. The meaning of terms and rules differs from agent to agent because relational tables representing them usually refer to different objects.

**Definition 1.**

1. If $a$ is an attribute in A and $v \in Dom(a)$, then $(a,v)$ is a term (property).
2. If $t$ and $(a,v)$ are terms then $t*(a,v)$ is a term.

**Definition 2.**

If $t_1$, $t_2$ are terms then $t_1 \rightarrow t_2$ is a rule.

**Notation.**
If $t = (a_1,v_1) * (a_2,v_2) * (a_5,v_5)$ , then $Att(t)=\{a_1,a_2,a_5\}$.

**Definition 3.**
Rule $t_1 \rightarrow t_2$ is called an association rule if $Att(t_1)$, $Att(t_2)$ are disjoint subsets of A.

Expression $Att(t_1) \rightarrow Att(t_2)$ is called an attribute association rule if $Att(t_1)$, $Att(t_2)$ are disjoint subsets of A.

**Notation.**
Let $\mathbf{N}_i(t)$ be a number of tuples in a relational table $S_i$ which have property t.

By a total support of a property t in a society of distributed agents $DS=\{S_i\}$ we mean $\mathbf{tsup}(t) = \Sigma\, \mathbf{N}_i(t)$.

By a support of a set of attributes B in a society of distributed agents $DS=\{S_i\}$ we mean $\mathbf{sup}(B)$ defined as the number of agents $S_i(A_i)$ such that $B \subseteq A_i$.

**Example 1**. Assume that $DS=\{S_1,S_2\}$ represents a society of distributed agents where:

Table $T_1$ of agent $S_1$:

| | a | b | c | d |
|---|---|---|---|---|
| X1 | a1 | b1 | c2 | d2 |
| x2 | a2 | b2 | c1 | d1 |
| x3 | a1 | b2 | c1 | d2 |
| x4 | a2 | b2 | c2 | d1 |
| x5 | a1 | b2 | c2 | d1 |

Table $T_2$ of agent $S_2$:

| | a | e | f | d |
|---|---|---|---|---|
| x3 | a1 | e2 | f1 | d2 |
| x4 | a2 | e2 | f2 | d1 |
| x6 | a1 | e2 | f1 | d2 |
| x7 | a2 | e1 | f2 | d1 |
| x8 | a2 | e1 | f1 | d1 |

Let $t = (a,a1)*(d,d2)$. Then: $\mathbf{N}_1(t) = 2$ , $\mathbf{N}_2(t) = 2$ , $\mathbf{tsup}(t) = 4$ , $\mathbf{sup}(Att(t))=2$.

Agent $S_1$ interprets the term t as {x1, x3} whereas agent $S_2$ as {x3, x6}.

**Definition 4.**
Support of an attribute association rule $B_1 \rightarrow B_2$ (denoted as **sup**($B_1 \rightarrow B_2$)) is defined as **sup**($B_1 \cup B_2$), which is a number of agents $S_i(A_i)$ satisfying the property $B_1 \cup B_2 \subseteq A_i$.

Total support of a rule $t_1 \rightarrow t_2$ (denoted as **tsup**($t_1 \rightarrow t_2$)) is defined as **tsup**($t_1 * t_2$), which is a number of tuples in all relational tables $S_i(A_i)$ having property $t_1 * t_2$.

Confidence of a rule $B_1 \rightarrow B_2$ (denoted as **conf**($B_1 \rightarrow B_2$)) is defined as **sup**($B_1 \rightarrow B_2$)/**sup**($B_1$).

Total confidence of a rule $t_1 \rightarrow t_2$ (denoted as **tconf**($t_1 \rightarrow t_2$)) is defined as **tsup**($t_1 \rightarrow t_2$)/**tsup**($t_1$).

**Example 2**. Assume that $DS=\{S_1,S_2\}$ is defined the same way as in the example above. Now, let us consider the rule $r = [(a,a_2)*(d,d_1) \rightarrow (b,b_2)]$. Then: **sup**(Att(r)) = 1 , **tsup**(r) = 2 , **conf**(Att(r)) = 1/2 , **tconf**(r) = 2/(2+3).

Assume now that **AR**(s,c) denotes the set of attribute association rules with support greater than s and confidence not less than c.

Similarly, we assume that **ARt**(s,c) denotes the set of all association rules with a total support greater than s and a total confidence not less than c.

Both sets **AR**(s,c) and **ARt**(s,c) can be generated from frequent sets (and frequent attribute sets) following the classical Agrawal's strategy. In the example above, {(a,a1),(d,d2)} is a frequent set for **ARt**(4,c) and {a,d} is a frequent attribute set for **AR**(2,c).

## 2. Quest for Definition

An agent $S_i$ can ask other agents for definitions of attributes and definitions of attribute values (foreign and local). Such definitions can be seen either as equations (extracted for instance by Zytkow's 49er) or as rules having decision parts being values of attributes to be learned and classification parts being terms of the internal representation language of the agent $S_i$. If value of a foreign attribute to agent $S_i$ constitutes the decision part of a rule, then such a rule can only be extracted from relational tables of other agents than $S_i$. Strategies for extracting such definitions in a distributed environment have been presented in other papers (see [8,9,10]).

**Example 3.** Assume that $DS=\{S_1,S_2,S_3,S_4\}$ is a group of four distributed autonomous agents where $S_1$, $S_2$ are defined the same way as in the Example 1 and $S_3$, $S_4$ are defined below:

Table $T_3$ of agent $S_3$:

| | a | b | d | f | g |
|---|---|---|---|---|---|
| x1 | a1 | b1 | d2 | f2 | g1 |
| x7 | a2 | b2 | d1 | f2 | g2 |
| x8 | a1 | b2 | d2 | f1 | g1 |

Table $T_4$ of agent $S_4$:

| | d | b | c | g |
|---|---|---|---|---|
| x2 | d1 | b2 | c1 | g2 |
| x8 | d2 | b2 | c2 | g1 |
| x9 | d1 | b1 | c1 | g2 |

Assume now that we ask agent $S_1$ to identify all tuples in his relational table satisfying the query $q=(a,a_1)*(f,f_1)$. Also, we may ask agent $S_1$ to contact minimum two other agents, if he is unable to handle our query alone. Clearly, the term $(f,f_1)$ in our query is not local for agent $S_1$. So, the request for definition $(f,f_1)$ in terms of attributes {a, b, c, d} has to be sent by $S_1$ to other agents in DS. The set {a,b,c,d,f} is not a frequent attribute set in **AR**(2,c) for DS. It can be easily checked that {a,d,f} is a maximal frequent attribute subset of {a,b,c,d,f} containing f. So, the actual query sent by agent $S_1$ to DS-$\{S_1\}$ will requests a definition of the value $(f,f_1)$ in terms of attributes a,d. Observe that the attribute association rule $\{a,d\}\rightarrow\{f\}$ has 100% confidence and the support 2 in DS-$\{S_1\}$. There are two association rules extracted from DS-$\{S_1\}$ which should be seen by agent $S_1$ as definitions of the foreign attribute f. They are given below:

$(a,a_2)(d,d_1) \rightarrow (f,f_2)$ with total confidence ¾ (in DS-$\{S_1\}$),
$(a,a_1)(d,d_2) \rightarrow (f,f_1)$ with total confidence ¾ (in DS-$\{S_1\}$).

The above two association rules, extracted by agents $S_2$, $S_3$ from their relational tables, are supported by the attribute association rule $\{a,d\}\rightarrow\{f\}$ with a confidence 100% so they can be rather safely used by the agent $S_1$ for processing foreign queries containing f.

The extended relational table assigned to agent $S_1$ is given below.

The new attribute f added to the table $T_1$ is called a foreign attribute because the values in column f are entirely dependent on values in relational tables of agents $S_2$ and $S_3$. If these tables are updated, column f may have to be updated too. Also, it has to be mentioned here that the new interpretation of attribute f adopted by agent $S_1$ is entirely based on the trust in relations among attributes a,d,f discovered by agents $S_2$ and $S_3$.

New table $T_1$ of agent $S_1$:

| | a | b | c | d | f |
|---|---|---|---|---|---|
| x1 | a1 | b1 | c2 | d2 | f1 |
| x2 | a2 | b2 | c1 | d1 | f2 |
| x3 | a1 | b2 | c1 | d2 | f1 |
| x4 | a2 | b2 | c2 | d1 | f2 |
| x5 | a1 | b2 | c2 | d1 | |

The process of learning foreign attributes gives a solid foundation to introduce the notion of a trust and build societies of agents specialized in certain areas.

**Bibliography**


[1] Bosc, P., Pivert, O., *Some approaches for relational databases flexible querying,* in **Journal of Intelligent Information Systems**, Kluwer Academic Publishers, Vol. 1, 1992, 355-382

[2] Chu, W.W., Chen, Q., Lee, R., *Cooperative query answering via type abstraction hierarchy,* in **Cooperating Knowledge-based Systems** (ed. S.M. Deen), North Holland, 1991, 271-292

[3] Cuppers, F., Demolombe, R., *Cooperative answering: a methodology to provide intelligent access to databases,* **in Proceedings 2nd International Conference on Expert Database Systems**, Virginia, USA, 1988

[4] Fayyad, U.M., Piatetsky-Shapiro, G., Smyth, Uthurusamy, R., *Advances in Knowledge Discovery and Data Mining*, AAAI Press/MIT Press, 1996

[5] Gaasterland, T., Godfrey, P., Minker, J., *An overview of cooperative answering,* **Journal of Intelligent Information Systems**, Kluwer Academic Publishers, Vol. 1, 1992, 123-158

[6] Grzymala-Busse, J., *Managing uncertainty in expert systems*, Kluwer Academic Publishers, 1991

[7] Pawlak, Z., *Rough sets and decision tables,* in **Proceedings of the Fifth Symposium on Computation Theory**, Springer Verlag, Lecture Notes in Computer Science, Vol. 208, 1985, 118-127

[8] Ras, Z., *Resolving queries through cooperation in multi-agent systems*, in **Rough Sets and Data Mining**, (Eds. T.Y. Lin, N. Cercone), Kluwer Academic Publishers, 1997, pp. 239-258

[9] Ras, Z., Joshi, S., *Query approximate answering system for an incomplete DKBS,* in **Fundamenta Informaticae Journal**, IOS Press, Vol. 30, No. 3/4, 1997, 313-324

[10] Ras, Z., *Collaboration control in distributed knowledge-based systems,* in **Information Sciences Journal**, Elsevier, Vol. 96, No. 3/4, 1997, pp. 193-205

# Criteria and Functions for Expert Information Representation Choice

Czesław Daniłowicz, Ngoc Thanh Nguyen

Wrocław University of Technology, Department of Information Systems
Wybrzeże S. Wyspiańskiego 27, 50-370 Wrocław, Poland
{danilowicz, thanh}@zsi.pwr.wroc.pl

**Abstract.** By expert information we mean the information given by a man-expert of a field of science and technology, or by some intelligent program (for example intelligent agents) in solving of some task. In this paper the problem of expert information representation choice is introduced and analyzed. The analysis was carried out on two levels of generality. On the first level, it was assumed that in the collection of possible solutions, a function expressing the distance between its elements is defined. Then, the conditions for the choice function which settles the representation of expert information, were established. It was pointed out that the best choice function is the one, that qualifies to the representation the objects with the lowest sum of the square distances from the objects representing expert information. On the second level, it was assumed that the structure of the object set is known. Six structures which describe expert information in the representation choice problem, are considered and analyzed. For these structures the computation complexity of choice problems is also investigated.

**Key words:** expert information, representation choice, distance function

## 1 Introduction

It happens sometimes that solving of a complex problem is entrusted to several experts (by an expert we understand a man-expert of a field of science and technology, or some intelligent program, for example an intelligent agent). If each of them does it separately then their solutions usually differ from each other [5], in other words, the experts are in conflict [21]. This phenomenon often has place independently from the kind of problems. Its reason consists of the autonomy feature of experts, the differences of their preferred methods, knowledge, belief and experience. If we have to deal with such a situation, we do not know what is the proper solution of the problem. We can, for example, take one of the solutions given by the experts and assume it to be the final solution, but it would be equivalent to rejecting the other solutions. An another approach to solving this task is relied on the choice of the proper solution not from the given by experts solutions, but from a larger set of solutions. Such set may be the set of all possible or admissible solutions of given problem. Thus the final solution may but do not have to belong to experts' solutions. In both cases, that is the choice of the final solution from given solutions and the choice from a larger set of solutions, the result should be recognized as rational if it respects the expert solutions.

In this paper the criteria and methods for rational choice of expert information representation are presented. It is assumed that expert information is represented by objects which belong to a universe. In practice the objects serving to representing expert information may have complex structures correspondingly to concrete applications. In this work the authors consider the structures often used in classification tasks. They consist of ordered partitions and coverings of finite sets and more general structures such as hierarchical partitions and coverings; weighted partitions and coverings. In the universes of mentioned structures the distance functions between objects are defined. These functions should mirror the differences (or similarities) between the objects. Next the criteria for representation choice functions are formulated. These criteria should guarantee the maximal consistency of chosen object to all the objects representing expert information. The authors proved that the best choice function is the one which minimizes the sum of squared distances between chosen object to the given.

The organization of this paper is the following: in section 2 a review of related works is presented. Section 3 presents the general representation choice problems, the criteria for choice and their analysis. Section 4 includes the definitions and properties of six structures of object sets. In section 5 the representation choices methods for particular structures and the possibilities for creating choice algorithms were considered. At last some conclusions are given in section 6.

## 2 Related works

The representation choice problem can be considered as one of consensus problems. Consensus theory has a root in choice theory. A choice from a finite set $A$ of alternatives is based on choice of some its subset. In the consensus-based researches, however, it is assumed that the chosen alternatives do not have to be included in the set presented for choice. On the beginning of this research the authors have dealt only with simple structures of the set $A$ (named *macrostructure)*, such as linear or partial order. Later with the development of computing techniques the structure of each alternative (named *microstructure*) have been also investigated. Most often the authors assume that all the alternatives have the same microstructure. On the basis of the microstructure one can determine a macrostructure of the set $A$. Among others, following microstructures have been investigated: linear orders [1], [15]; set partitions, $n$–trees [9]; semi-lattices [3]; time scenarios of events [19]. The following macrostructures have been considered: linear orders and distance (or similarity) functions. Consensus of the set $A$ is most often determined on the basis of its macrostructure by some optimality rules. If the macrostructure is a distance (or similarity) function then the Kemeny's median [1] is very often used to choose the consensus. According to Kemeny's rule the consensus should be nearest to the elements of the set $A$.

Consensus choice is often used to acquire a homogeneous profile for given heterogeneous situations. The aim of such processes is, for example, to achieve agreements in mobile systems [2], to restore the consistency of replicated data [8], to determine a common value for given processes in fault-tolerant distributed computing [4], [14], to specify a common scenario at presence of process failures in distributed computing [12], [22], to work out common goals with minimal cost of realization for agents in multiagent systems [23], or to unify the agents' knowledge profile about dynamic populations [10], [13], [17]. For solving conflicts in distributed systems some approaches are proposed in works [18], [20] in which the data conflicts are classified and postulates and choice functions for consensus are analyzed.

## 3 General representation determining problem and criteria for choice

The general representation determining problem is formulated as follows [7]: Let $U$ be a universe of objects, by $U_o$ we denote the set of all non-empty, finite subsets with repetitions of set $U$. Any set $A \in U_o$ is called a *profile* and any subset $B$ of set $U$ is called a *domain.* The choice of the representation of profile $A$ is relied on finding a subset of set $B$ which best represents the elements of set $A$. In this paper we assume that profile $A$ is a set of expert solutions, and domain $B$ should include their representation.

Thus a representation choice function should have the following signature:

$$R\colon U_o \times 2^U \to 2^U$$

where $R(A,B)=Z \subseteq B$.

We assume that the structure of set $U$ is known and is a function

$$\sigma: U \times U \to \Re,$$

which fulfils the following conditions: $\sigma(x,y) \geq 0$ and $\sigma(x,x)=0$ for all $x,y \in U$. Notice that these conditions are only part of metric conditions. As shown below, some interesting results of analysis are achieved on the basis of these assumptions. For many applications such weak conditions are useful for distance functions. Metric conditions are sometimes too strong for measuring the difference between real world objects [11].

The values of function $\sigma$ can be interpreted as the distances between elements of set $U$. Let $A \in U_o$, in this paper we use the following notations:

$$\sigma_n(x,A)=\sum_{a \in A}[\sigma(x,a)]^n \text{ for } n=1,2,\ldots;\ x \in U,$$

$$\sigma(x,A)=\sum_{a \in A}[\sigma(x,a)-(1/|A|)\sigma_1(x,A)]^2 \text{ for } x \in U.$$

The value $\sigma_n(x,A)$ can be interpreted as the difference degree of between element $x$ and profile $A$, while value $\sigma(x,A)$ expresses the difference between the distances from $x$ to the elements of profile $A$ or in other words, it illustrates the uniformity of these distances.

The subject of our investigations consists of the choice criteria which are the following functions:

1. Functions $R_n$ $(n=1,2,\ldots)$: $x \in R_n(A,B)$ iff $\sigma_n(x,A)=\min_{y \in B} \sigma_n(y,A)$,
2. Function $R_S$: $x \in R_S(A,B)$ iff $\sigma(x,A)=\min_{y \in B} \sigma(y,A)$,

These functions have the following properties:

**Theorem 1.** For given $A\in U_o$ and $B\subseteq U$ ($B$ is a finite set) there exists a natural number $m$ such that $R_n(A,B)= R_m(A,B)$ for all $n\geq m$.

From the above property it implies that if functions $R_n$ ($n$=1,2,...) are used to make the representation choice then from some value of $n$ the results will be the same.

**Theorem 2.** If $A\in U_o$, $B\subseteq U$ and $x\in R_2(A,B)$ then for each $y\in B$ one of the following dependencies should be held: $\sigma_1(x,A)<\sigma_1(y,A)$ or $\sigma(x,A)\leq\sigma(y,A)$.

Theorem 2 shows that the criterion $R_2$ is a very important criterion because the objects belonging to the representation determined by this criterion are the most similar to the elements of profile $A$, or their distances to elements of profile $A$ should be the most uniform. Thus to a certain degree function $R_2$ fulfils criteria $R_1$ and $R_S$ simultaneously.

Another approach to the problem is presented in work [16], in which the representation choice function is determined on the basis of axioms for choice.

# 4 The structures of expert information

## 4.1 Ordered partitions of sets

It is known that a partition of a set can be received when there is given a equivalence relation on it. The identification of equivalent objects is one of the most important tasks of classification methods. In practical applications the classes of a partition include the most similar objects. Usually classifying objects we can name the classes. The name of a class often represents a property which should be fulfilled by the objects belonging to this class. As the examples take a partition of books made on the basis of their knowledge domains, or patients by means of their X-ray films. Thus classes may be ordered by their names if they are known. The tool for this kind of partitions is called *ordered partition* and is defined as follows [6]:

**Definition 1.** $K$-class ordered partition of finite set $X=\{x_1,...,x_N\}$ is a sequence $P=(P_1,...,P_K)$, where $P_i\cap P_j=\emptyset$ for $i\neq j$ ($i,j=1,...,K$) and $\bigcup_{i=1}^{K} P_i = X$.

Notice that the order of classes can uniquely replace their symbolic names. A $K$- class ordered partition of set $X$ is not equivalent to a equivalence relation on $X$.

By $U_K(X)$ we denote the set of all $K$-class ordered partitions of set $X$.

## 4.2 Ordered coverings of sets

Representing expert information by means of ordered partitions we have assumed that an object has only one attribute. If we want to assign to an object more than one attribute then ordered partitions are not sufficient tool for this aim, for example, there may be a patient who is ill for more than one disease. In the task of book classification ordered partitions are proper tools if this task is relied on placing the books in different sections of the storeroom which are destined for different fields. If the aim of classification is to complete the subject catalogues then to the same book may correspond more than one catalogue card. This situation may have place if a book concerns more than one field. In this case one should use other structure, called *ordered covering* of sets.

**Definition 2.** By a $K$-class ordered covering of a finite set $X=\{x_1,...,x_N\}$ we call a sequence $C=(C_1,...,C_K)$, where $C_i \subseteq X$ for $i=1,...,K$.

Definition 2 implies that ordered coverings are more general structure than ordered partitions. The reason is that among the elements of sequence $C$ there may exist empty classes; some element of set $X$ may occur in more than one class, and some other element of set $X$ may not occur in any class of sequence $C$.

The set of all $K$- class ordered covering of set $X$ is denoted by $V_K(X)$.

## 4.3 Hierarchical ordered partitions and coverings

It is known that more general structures than partitions (corresponding to equivalence relations) are hierarchical classifications. Similarly, as the more general structures than ordered partitions and coverings we will define *hierarchical ordered partitions* and *coverings*. Such structures are useful in representation of multi-step process of classification. Notice that in ordered partitions and coverings the names of classes are identified by their indexes, however, in the case of hierarchical ordered partitions and coverings it is necessary to represent the classes and the relationships between classes occurring on all levels of the hierarchy. The proper tool for describing such situations should be a graph which is a directed tree.

Let $T$ be a directed tree, $r$ - its root, $W$ – set of nodes of $T$, which are not the root, and $L$ – set of leaves of $T$.

**Definition 3.** By a hierarchical ordered partition of finite set $X$, whose dendrogram is tree $T$, we call a function

$$P: W \cup \{r\} \to 2^X$$

which fulfils the following conditions:

a) $P(b) \subset P(a)$ if node $b$ is a sun of node $a$,

b) $P(b) \cap P(c) = \varnothing$ if nodes $b$ and $c$ are suns of $a$,

c) $\bigcup_{a \in L} P(a) = X$.

**Definition 4.** By a hierarchical ordered covering of finite set $X$, whose dendrogram is tree $T$, we call a function

$$C: W \cup \{r\} \to 2^X,$$

which fulfils the following conditions:

a) $C(r)=X$,

b) $C(b) \subset C(a)$ if node $b$ is a sun of node $a$.

The set of all hierarchical ordered partitions of finite set $X$ with dendrogram $T$ is denoted by $U_T(X)$, and the set of all hierarchical ordered coverings of finite set $X$ with dendrogram $T$ is denoted by $V_T(X)$.

### 4.4 Weighted partitions and coverings

Notice that an ordered partition of finite set $X$ is a sequence of its disjoint subsets, in which each element of $X$ occurs exactly one time. In such a partition the elements of $X$ represent the real world objects and the classes represent their attributes. We can change the interpretation, such that the attributes are represented by the objects from set $X$, and the real world objects are represented by classes. As stated above, ordered partitions properly describe the real world only if an object has exactly one attribute. If objects have more attributes then the adequate tool should be an ordered covering. Notice that in both cases the classification process must be totally unambiguous. It means that in the description of an object there must be unambiguous information by what attribute(s) it is characterized. Notice that it is not always possible, as the example, let us take predicting of football games. A man who fills in his coupon of pools must present unambiguous opinion, but predicting victory of given team A he is not always sure. He may, for example, value the victory of team A as 50%, draw as 30% and defeat as 20%. So if this person (as an expert) were asked for presenting his opinion about the chance of team A, he would not show the version which was written in the coupon, but the above ambiguous (fuzzy) opinion.

For this kind of information we define below weighted partitions and coverings of an objects set.

**Definition 5.** By $K$-class weighted partition of finite set $X$ we call a matrix $P=[p_{ij}]_{N\times K}$, where $p_{ij}\in[0,1]$ for $i=1,...,N$; $j=1,...,K$ and $\sum_{j=1}^{K} p_{ij}=1$ for $i=1,..,N$.

**Definition 6.** By $K$-class weighted covering of finite set $X$ we call a matrix $C=[c_{ij}]_{N\times K}$ where $c_{ij}\in[0,1]$ for $i=1,...,N$, $j=1,...,K$.

The sets of all $K$-class weighted partitions and coverings of set $X$ are denoted by $WU_K(X)$ and $WV_K(X)$ correspondingly.

## 5 Methods for determining of representations

### 5.1 Representation of ordered partitions

The structure of set $U_K(X)$ of $K$-class ordered partitions of set $X$ can be represented by distance function which is defined in the following way:

**Definition 7.** Let $P=(P_1,...P_k,...,P_l,...,P_K)\in U_K(X)$ and $x_n\in P_k$, by the move operation $R_n^l(P)$ of element $x_n$ to class $P_l$ we call the following operation

$$R_n^l(P)=(P_1,...,P_k\backslash\{x_n\},...,P_l\cup\{x_n\},...,P_K).$$

**Definition 8.** The distance $d(P,Q)$ between partitions $P,Q \in U_K(X)$ is the minimal number of element moves needed to transform partition $P$ into partition $Q$.

The way for choice of the representation of an ordered partitions' set, which fulfils criterion $R_1$ implies from the following theorem:

**Theorem 3.** If $A \in U_o$ where $U=U_K(X)$ and the structure of set $U$ is distance function $d$ then any element $x \in X$ in $R_1(A,U)$ should belong to the class with index $i$ if and only if it occurs the most of times in the $i$-th classes of partitions belonging to set $A$.

**Theorem 4.** The problem of determining the representation of ordered partitions on the basis of criterion $R_2$ is a NP-complete problem.

From above theorems it implies that the algorithm for representation choice if using criterion $R_1$ should have linear complexity, while for choice on the basis of criterion $R_2$ one should use heuristic or genetic algorithms. A heuristic algorithm was proposed in work [7].

## 5.2 Representation of ordered coverings

We define the distance function between ordered coverings of set $X$ by means of the following definitions:

**Definition 9.** Let $C=(C_1,...,C_l,...,C_K) \in V_K(X)$, we say that ordered covering $(C_1,...,C_l \setminus \{x\},...,C_K)$ arises as the result of elimination of element $x$ from class $C_l$ of ordered covering $C$, and covering $(C_1,...,C_l \cup \{x\},...,C_K)$ arises as the result of adding element $x$ to class $C_l$ of covering $C$.

**Definition 10.** By distance between ordered coverings $C,D \in V_K(X)$ we call the minimal number $\mu(C,D)$ of elimination and adding operations needed to transform covering $C$ into covering $D$.

Let $A$ be a profile from set $U_o$ (assume that $U= V_K(X)$), the way for determining the representation of given coverings from profile $A$ on the basis of criterion $R_1$ should be implied from the following theorem:

**Theorem 5.** Any element $x \in X$ in covering $R_1(A,U)$ should belong to the class with such index $k$, that $x$ occurs at least $M/2$ times in the $k$-th classes of coverings from profile $A$, where $M$ is the cardinality of set $A$.

**Theorem 6.** The problem of determining the representation of ordered coverings on the basis of criterion $R_2$ is a NP-complete problem.

## 5.3 Representation of hierarchical ordered partitions and coverings

The structure of set $U_T(X)$ of hierarchical ordered partitions of set $X$ is a distance function which is defined in the following way:

Let $P,P' \in U_T(X)$, we say that partition $P'$ arises from partition $P$ in the result of moving element $x$ from the leaf $a$ to the leaf $b$, if $x \in P(a)$ and $x \in P'(b)$, and the locations of the other elements are the same. For a moving operation of element $x$

from leaf $a$ to leaf $b$ a weight is determined as follows: By $Z$ we denote the set of the nodes of tree $T$, which are located on the shortest path from leaf $a$ to leaf $b$; the weight of moving $x$ from $a$ to $b$ is then equal to the sum of weights of the nodes from $Z$, where the weight of a non-root node is equal to $1/l$ for $l$ being the level of this node in tree $T$ and the weight is equal 0 for the root.

**Definition 11.** By distance $\gamma(P,Q)$ between hierarchical partitions $P,Q\in U_T(X)$ we call the minimal sum of weights of element moving operations which are needed to transform the partition $P$ into the partition $Q$.

In a similar way we can define the distance between hierarchical coverings.

Let now $A$ be a profile belonging to $U_o$ where $U=U_T(X)$. Let $\alpha(a,x)$ denotes the number of occurrences of element $x$ in the leaf $a$ of tree $T$ in partitions from $A$. By $r(b,c)$ we denote the sum of weights of the nodes which are located on the shortest path from leaf $b$ to leaf $c$ of tree $T$. Thus number $r(b,c)$ is equal to the weight of moving an element from leaf $b$ to leaf $c$. The way for determining the representation of hierarchical partitions and coverings on the basis of criterion $R_1$ should be implied from the following theorems:

**Theorem 7.** Any element $x\in X$ should be located in the leaf $a$ of tree $T$ in hierarchical partition $R_1(A,U_T(X))$, for which

$$\beta(a,x)=\min_{b\in L}\beta(b,x)$$

where

$$\beta(b,x)=\sum_{c\in L}r(b,x)\alpha(c,x).$$

**Theorem 8.** Let $A\in U_o$ where $U= V_T(X)$ and $M=|A|$, then any element $x\in U$ in hierarchical covering $R_1(A,U)$ should belong to such leaf $a$ of tree $T$ that the following dependency is held:

$$\alpha(a,x)\geq M/2.$$

**Theorem 9.** The problem of determining of the representation of hierarchical partitions (or coverings) on the basis of criterion $R_2$ is a NP-complete problem.

## 5.4 Representation of weighted ordered partitions and coverings

The distance function between weighted ordered partitions from $WU_K(X)$ should be defined in the similar way as the distance function between points in a $N\times K$–dimension space.

**Definition 12.** By the distance $\kappa(P,Q)$ where $P,Q\in WU_K(X)$ we call the following number

$$\kappa(P,Q)=\sqrt{\sum_{i=1}^{N}\sum_{j=1}^{K}\left(p_{ij}-q_{ij}\right)^2}\,.$$

In identical way we can define the distance function between weighted coverings from $WV_K(X)$. From the definition of distance function $\kappa$ one should notice that the choice of representation of weighted partitions and coverings according to function $R_1$ is a more complex problem than according to function $R_2$.

Let $U=WU_K(X)$ and $A\in U_o$. Set $A$ should have the following form:

$$A=\{P^{(i)} \mid i=1,\ldots,M\}$$

where $P^{(i)}$ is a matrix of dimension $N\times K$ representing a weighted partition of set $X$. The representation of profile $A$ chosen on the basis of criterion $R_2$ should be determined by means of the following theorem:

**Theorem 10.** Matrix $P^*$ belongs to $R_2(A,U)$ if and only if the following dependency is held

$$p^*_{ij} = (1/M)\sum_{P\in A} p_{ij}$$

for $i=1,\ldots,N$; $j=1,\ldots,K$.

A similar theorem may be formulated for the choice of the representation of weighted coverings on the basis of criterion $R_2$.

## 6 An example

In this section we present an example which should illustrate potential applications of above worked out methods in practice.

Let $X=\{x_1,\ldots,x_6\}$ be a finite set of IT students, which are classified by lecturers into the following groups: group of students talented in theoretical research, group of students talented in designing and group of students talented in programming. Each student, in an opinion of a lecturer, may belong to one or more classes as well as has not to belong to any class. Assume that there are three lecturers, whose opinions (in form of ordered coverings of set $X$), are presented as follows:

$O_1 = <\{x_2,x_3,x_4,x_5,x_6\},\{x_1,x_2,x_4,x_5,x_6\},\{x_1,x_2,x_3,x_4\}>$
$O_2 = <\{x_1,x_2,x_3\},\{x_1,x_2,x_4,x_5,x_6\},\{x_1,x_2,x_3,x_4\}>$
$O_3 = <\{x_1,x_2,x_3\},\{x_4,x_5,x_6\},\{x_1,x_2,x_3,x_4\}>$

Using representation choice functions $R_n$ ($n$=1,2,3) we have the following representations of above coverings:

- for $n$=1: $rep_1 = <\{x_1,x_2,x_3\},\{x_4,x_5,x_6\},\{x_1,x_2,x_3,x_4\}>$
- for $n$=2: $rep_2 = <\{x_2,x_3\},\{x_4,x_5,x_6\},\{x_1,x_2,x_3,x_4\}>$
- for $n$=3: $rep_3 = <\{x_2,x_3,x_4\},\{x_4,x_5,x_6\},\{x_1,x_2,x_3,x_4\}>$

The distances between the representations to the opinions are the following:

| | $O_1$ | $O_1$ | $O_1$ | $\sigma_1$ | $\sigma_2$ | $\sigma_3$ |
|---|---|---|---|---|---|---|
| $rep_1$ | 6 | 2 | 0 | 8 | 40 | 224 |
| $rep_2$ | 5 | 3 | 1 | 9 | 35 | 153 |
| $rep_3$ | 4 | 4 | 2 | 10 | 36 | 136 |

From the example it implies that for different values of $n$ the representations of given set are also different.

## 7 Conclusions

In this paper different structures of object sets, which describe expert information and the methods for representation choice are presented. For these structures and criteria for which the representation choice problems are not computationally complex, the authors present theorems implying immediately the algorithms. In the cases where representation determining is a NP-complete problem, it is necessary to create heuristic or genetic algorithms. For criterion $R_2$ two algorithms (one heuristic and one genetic) for determining the representation of binary sequences to which ordered partitions and coverings can be transformed, were worked out in [8].

## References


1. Arrow, K.J. (1963): *Social Choice and Individual Values*. Wiley New York.
2. Badache, N., Hurfin, M., Madeco, R. (1999): Solving the Consensus Problem in a Mobile Environment. In: *Proceedings of IEEE International Performance, Computing and Communications Conference*. IEEE Piscataway NJ, pp. 29-35.
3. Barthelemy, J.P., Janowitz, M.F. (1991): A Formal Theory of Consensus. *SIAM J. Discrete Math.* 4, 305-322.
4. Coulouris, G, Dollimore, J., Kindberg, T. (1996): *Distributed Systems, Concepts and Design*. Addison-Wesley.
5. Daniłowicz, C., Nguyen, N.T. (1987): Determining of the Problem Solutions Representations. In: Plander I. (ed.): *Artificial Intelligence and Information-Control Systems of Robots-87*. North-Holland, pp. 187-192.
6. Daniłowicz, C., Nguyen, N.T. (1988): Consensus-Based Partition in the Space of Ordered Partitions. *Pattern Recognition* 21, 269–273.
7. Daniłowicz C., Nguyen N.T. (1992): *Methods for choice of representation of ordered partitions and coverings*. Monographs, Wrocław University of Technology.
8. Daniłowicz, C., Nguyen, N.T. (2000): Consensus-Based Methods for Restoring Consistency of Replicated Data. In: Kłopotek, M., Michalewicz, M., Wierzchoń, S.T. (eds.): *Advances in Soft Computing, Proceedings of 9th International Conference on Information Intelligent Systems IIS'2000, Bystra Poland*. Physica-Verlag Heidenlberg New York, pp. 325-335.
9. Day, W.H.E. (1988): Consensus Methods as Tools for Data Analysis. In: Bock, H.H. (ed.): *Classification and Related Methods for Data Analysis*. North–Holland, pp. 312–324.
10. Ephrati, E., Rosenschein, J.S (1998): Deriving Consensus in Multiagent Systems. *Artificial Intelligence* 87, 21-74.
11. Fishburn, P.C. (1977): Condorset Social Choice Functions. *SIAM J. App. Math.* 33, 469–489.
12. Hurfin, M., Mostefaoui, A., Raynal, M. (1998): Consensus in Asynchronous Systems where Processes Can Crash and Recover. In: *Proceedings of Seventeenth IEEE Symposium on Reliable Distributed Systems*. IEEE Comput. Soc. Los Alamitos CA, pp. 280-286.
13. Katarzyniak, K, Nguyen, NT (2000): Using Consensus Methods to Determine Encapsulated Profiles of The World State Distributed in Multiagent Systems. In: *Proceedings of 14th Intennational Conference on System Engineering ICSE'2000*. Coventry, UK, pp. 300-304.
14. Lamport, L., Shostak, R., Pease, M. (1982): Byzantine Generals Problem. *ACM Trans. on Programming Languages and Systems* 4, 382-401.
15. Litvak, B.G. (1982): Expert Information: *Methods of Analysis and Gathering*. Radio i Sviaz, Moscow.
16. Nguyen, N.T. (1998): The Axiom Approach to the Experts Opinions Representation Choice Problem. In: Bubnicki, Z. (ed.): *Proceedings of the 13th International Conference on System Science*. Wrocław University of Technology, pp. 224–229.

17. Nguyen, N.T. (1999): A Computer-Based Multiagent System for Building and Updating Models of Dynamic Populations Located in Distributed Environments. In: Kącki E. (ed.): *Proceeding of 5th International Conference on Computer in Medicine.* Lódź University of Technology, 133-138.
18. Nguyen, N.T. (2000): Using consensus methods for determining the representation of expert information in distributed systems. *Lecture Notes on Artificial Intelligence* 1904, 11-20.
19. Nguyen, N.T. (2001): Representation choice methods as the tool for solving uncertainty in distributed temporal database systems with indeterminate valid time. To appear in: Proceedings of the 14th Int. Conf. on Industrial & Engineering Applications of AI & Expert Systems'2001, *Lecture Notes on Artificial Intelligence*, Springer –Verlag.
20. Nguyen, N.T. (2000): Using Consensus Methods for Solving Conflicts of Data in Distributed Systems. *Lecture Notes on Computer Science* 1963, 409-417
21. Pawlak, Z. (1998): An Inquiry into Anatomy of Conflicts. *Journal of Information Sciences* 108, 65-78.
22. Pease, M., Shorstak, R., and Lamport, L. (1980): Reaching Agreement in the Presence of Faults. *Journal of ACM* 27, 228-234.
23. Yan, K.Q., Wang, S.C., Chin, Y.H. (1999): Consensus under Unreliable Transmission. *Information Processing Letter* 69, 243-248.

# Intelligent Computing Systems with Actors – Parallel Dynamic Programming Algorithm of the Polygon Triangulation Problem

**Hua Hsueh and Boleslaw Mikolajczak**

Computer and Information Science Department, College of Engineering,
University of Massachusetts
Dartmouth, MA 02747, USA
bmikolajczak@umassd.edu

***Abstract.*** *In this paper parallel implementations of the Optimal Triangularization Problem are presented using Dynamic Programming Approach. Experimental results with respect to speedup as a function of the polygon size are given. Dynamic Programming implementation is compared with brute force approach from performance perspective. Actor-based parallel implementations are discussed.*

*Keywords: Parallel Dynamic Programming, Polygon Triangulation Problem, Computing Systems with Actors*

## 1. Introduction

Research on a methodology supporting a new generation of parallel/distributed computer systems is becoming increasingly important. This is due to the desire for building computer systems that can solve advanced problems on heterogeneous computing platforms. These computer systems are composed of many computational entities which cooperate/compete with each other upon solving problems.

As such, a model of computation is needed to exploit massive parallelism. A concurrent programming model, based on the notion of Actors, can be used as a foundation for these computer systems. Actors can be looked upon as active objects that execute concurrently and communicate with one another via message passing. The actor model provides an ability to allow an entity within one computer system to communicate with other entities within as well as outside its host computer system. An actor can send messages to some previously unknown actor even though they reside on different platforms. This property is essential to developing open systems.

There is a significant body of literature on the actor model. A book and several papers authored by Agha and a group at the University of Illinois at Urbana-Champaign (UIUC) extensively explored this model. Kafura from the University of Virginia, developed ACT++, a programming environment based on Actors. There is a group of researchers at Stanford University interested in seeing this model from a functional programming point of view. Recently, Actor Foundry (or more details, visit the web site http://osl.cs.uiuc.edu/foundry), a tool based on the actor model, was developed by the Open Systems Laboratory at UIUC.

The Actor model has an intimate bearing on objected-oriented modeling. The goal of this paper is to tap the actor model by solving the optimal polygon triangulation problem.

## 2. Object-Orientedness and Distributed Systems

Object-oriented paradigm is the mainstream in many aspects of the field of computer science. The most salient distinction that distinguishes the objected-oriented approach and the procedural one is that the former encapsulates both data and operations in one entity, whereas for the latter data and operations are separated and information flow or hierarchical information structures are being used. Software reuse is strengthened by object-orientation: inheritance and polymorphism. Maintenance of software benefits from embedding attributes and methods in one self-contained object. Inheritance is one of the prominent trademarks of the objected-oriented approach, due to which shared properties (data structures and procedures) within a category do not have to be repeated and can be passed on automatically from a parent class to its descents. Distributed computing, which involves multiple interconnected computers working through a network to attain a common goal, has considerably exacerbated the complexity of constructing computer systems. Object-oriented technique offers the flexibility to building progressively more complex computer systems and provides the environment where diverse software components can communicate across heterogeneous platforms.

## 3. Elements of Actor Systems

There are three features in the actor model: *actor, mail queue*, and *behavior.* Actors can be viewed as active objects that send messages to one another via mail queues. Each actor has a distinct mail queue address that can be used to identify itself from other actors. The communication among actors is asynchronous and messages are processed in a FIFO order. Actors, or computational agents, decode the messages received into three components:

(1) A finite set of messages which in the sequel will be sent to other actors
(2) A new behavior set determining the response to the subsequent messages

(3) A finite set of previously unknown actors.

A behavior set can be regarded as a set of public methods in the object-oriented programming. A message received by an actor can be processed only after it has managed to turn up the corresponding counterpart of the requested method in the behavior set. If it fails to do so, the message either can be discarded or be buffered until the behavior of the actor is modified so as to enable that method to become available. An actor's behavior can be dynamically changed upon receiving a message that specifies a substitute behavior set. Associated with each actor is also a set of acquaintances that can be learned of in three ways:

(1) From an argument passed in at the time of creation
(2) From messages received from other actors
(3) From the mail address returned by creating another actor by itself.

The unique mail queue address attached to each actor can be looked upon as an identification number distinguishing one actor from the others. This id number (mail queue address) can be passed around as part of a message to dynamically change the configuration of target actors, e.g., add one new element in the acquaintance set of the target actor. Knowing the mail queue address of another actor builds a point-to-point communication between two actors. Due to asynchronous communication, the order of the messages in the mail queue is not necessarily the same as that the messages are sent. One property of the actor model is that ultimate delivery of a sent message is guaranteed. In practice, this is a restriction imposed by the actual realization of the actor model in that the capacity of a mail queue based on hardware constraint cannot be infinite. Furthermore, the fulfillment of this promise also hinges on how an actor, upon processing messages, behaves according to some pre-specified rules regarding the actor's current state. The actor may treat a message normally, ignore it, or has it buffered.

The current internal state of an actor is reflected on its behavior set, which determines the actor's response to the message being processed. That is, whether an actor will come through in reaction to the request conveyed by a message is in large part rests upon the actor's current state at the time of processing. A message can also subsume a replacement behavior that will supersede the previous one and possibly change the internal state of the actor. Upon execution of a request specifying a replacement behavior, the actor uses a synchronization mechanism with a view to preserving state consistency. More specifically, the actor blocks processing of messages until its internal state has been updated completely, an avenue for avoiding race condition. The ramification of this change of behavior is that the next message is to be processed in accordance with the new internal state.

There are three basic operations performed by an actor:

(1) *New*: create a new actor. A new mail queue address will be returned by this operation and upon creation the new actor can take an initial behavior set and/or a set of initial acquaintances as input.

(2) *Send*: send a message. Messages are sent and received asynchronously by an actor. The recipient of a message is identified by its unique mail queue address.
(3) *Become*: change behavior. An actor's behavior can be modified as a result of responding to the most recent message that made such a request.

## 4. Optimal Polygon Triangulation

First we introduce several basic concepts: *convex polygon-* any line segment drawn between any two points on the boundary of a convex polygon is still contained in the interior or on the boundary of the polygon. *side-* a straight-line segment connecting two vertices on the boundary of a polygon. *chord-* a line segment drawn in the interior between any two nonadjacent vertices of a convex polygon. *Triangulation-* finding a set of chords that exhaustively subdivides a convex polygon into disjoint triangles. *Optimal triangulation* - a triangulation with the minimum sum of lengths of all line segments, including both sides and chords, formed in a triangulated convex polygon in the class of all possible triangulations.

If an n-sided convex polygon is to be triangulated, then there will be n-3 chords partitioning the polygon into n-2 non-overlapping triangles. We know that for any vertex of the polygon there are n-3 vertices nonadjacent to it (excluding itself and the two adjacent vertices from the total n vertices). To examine this let's first arbitrarily select one vertex from among the n vertices. If we draw lines between this vertex and any other nonadjacent vertex, we will have n-3 line segments, which form a set of chords of a particular triangulation. This set of chords in conjunction with the set of all sides constitutes a set of tightly coupled triangles. Any two adjacent triangles in the set coincide on one and only one chord. Then the number of triangles in a particular triangulation is (n-3)+1=n-2 because there are n-3 chords and this number is one less than the number of triangles.

Let us use a bottom-up method to rework the formula for the number of chords and the number of triangles in a triangulated polygon. To begin with, we consider an initial scenario: there is only one triangle with three vertices and three edges in a plane. We then add one vertex and one edge incident with the new vertex to the plane so as to connect the added vertex to some other vertex of the existing triangle with the new edge and shift the edge originally attached to the existing vertex just being connected to make that edge be connected to the added vertex. The graph ends up with a quadrangle. Notice that we are adding one vertex and one edge to increase the number of sides of the original polygon. We can continue this process to come by a polygon of any number of sides greater than three, If we "add back" the edge being shifted we will have a triangulated tetragon composed of two triangles, namely, a four-sided polygon with one chord. By shifting an existing edge, we are actually adding one triangle "implicitly" to the original polygon while still keeping the resultant graph a polygon, but with one more side. Put differently, a derived polygon has one more side and one can be triangulated into one triangle more than that of the polygon from which it originates. Now let us go back to the one-triangle scenario. Initially, the polygon encompasses 3 sides, and can be potentially triangulated into 1 (3-2) triangle and has 0 (3-3) chords. After adding one vertex and one edge, both the number of chords and number of triangles increase by 1. In other words, the number of chords as well as the number of triangles increases commensurately with the number of sides. Alternatively, we can regard the number of chords as a linear function of the number of sides of a polygon with the slope coefficient 1 and the intercept term –3. By the same token, the number of triangles can be viewed as a linear function of the number of sides of a polygon with slope coefficient 1 and the intercept term –2. That is, if we are to triangulate an n-sided polygon, the number of chords obtained will be n-3 and the number of triangles n-2.

The formula for the number of triangles can also be garnered by manipulating Euler's theorem on connected planar graphs: ***E**dges* – ***V**ertices* = ***R**egions –2*. To see the idea behind this theorem at work, let's revert to our initial one-triangle scenario: E=V=3, R=2 (the exterior region of the triangle is considered as a region in the theorem). On the left-hand side of the equation we have E-V = 3-3 =0, while on the right-hand side R-2 = 2-2 = 0. The values on the left-hand side and right-hand side are identical, so the theorem is applicable in the initial (one-triangle) situation. If we then add and connect one more vertex and one more edge to this graph the value on the left-hand side of the equation E-V=R-2 will stay the same because the added edge and vertex cancel out each other on the left-hand side. In addition, the value on the right-hand side remains unchanged as well for augmenting one vertex and one edge in the plane creates no extra region. If one more edge is drawn to bridge the newly added vertex with any other existing vertex on the graph to form a cycle then the number of edges is increased by one, so does the number of regions. This is tantamount to adding 1 on both sides of the equation. Thus the equation still holds as the same process (adding two edges and one vertex to the existing planar graph) goes on indefinitely.

Notice that this procedure is the "spitting image" of the foregoing modified bottom-up method (one additional triangle is generated after two edges and one vertex are added). With the grasp of the similarity, we are ready to go one step further to derive the formula for the number of triangles in a triangulated polygon. To begin with, we denote R, the number of regions in Euler's theorem, as the number of triangles in a triangulated polygon in light of the fact that a triangulated polygon is a connected planar graph. However, the outside region (i.e., the exterior area outside a polygon) is not a triangle, so we must subtract 1 from the right-hand side of the equation to exclude that area. The equation after rearranging (bring the constant term over to the other side and then switching the two sides) becomes R=E-V+1. We may use V in lieu of E-V realizing that they both contribute 1 to the value on the right-hand side when 1 additional region is created by adding 2 edges and 1 vertex (thus, E-V=2-1=1). Nonetheless, this substitution is good only when something is done to adapt the equation to accommodate the initial condition. Let's revisit the one-triangle scenario again. Originally we have E=V=3, hence E-V = 3–3 = 0. If we want to use V instead of E-V, then we have to subtract 3 from the right-hand side of the equation to make the values on both sides of the equation equal to 1. The resulting equation can therefore be written as R = V+1-3 = V-2. Since an n-sided polygon has n vertices, we just substitute n into the aforementioned equation for V and get R=n-2. R now represents the number of triangles in a triangulated n-sided polygon. This result is clearly in line with the formula presented at the outset of this section.

Given that the number of triangles into which an n-sided polygon can be triangulated is n-2, computing the number of chords is just a facile task. Knowing that any chord is shared by 2 triangles and that every triangle comprises 3 sides, we can figure out the number of chords by first subtracting the n sides, which can not count as chords, from the total number of sides for the n-2 triangles and then dividing the whole thing by two. Symbolically, $\frac{(n-2)*3-n}{2}=\frac{3n-6-n}{2}=\frac{2n-6}{2}=n\text{-}3$.

One may now raise the question that how we can be sure that the number of triangles that a polygon can be decomposed into is fixed regardless of how we may subdivide the polygon if we look at it from a top-down point of view. Well, we know that the total sum of the inside angles of a convex polygon with a fixed number of sides is invariant, namely, (n-2)*180°, no matter what kind of shape it assumes. If we could somehow triangulate an n-sided polygon into K, some number other than n-2, then the total sum of the inside angles of these triangles would be K*180°, a number definitely different from (n-2)*180°. This is a blatant contradiction of the property of invariance noted above. In passing, (n-2)*180° can be obtained in a way similar to the bottom-up approach with the additional aid of a circle and it also reveals the fact that the number of triangles is n-2.

Assume that the lengths a and b and the angle θ are known, so we can use the formula $c^2 = a^2+b^2-2ab(\cos\theta)$ from the law of cosines, which tells us that for a triangle any two sides and the angle between them uniquely determine the length of the third side, to compute the length c. Once c is known, $\cos\beta = \frac{a^2+c^2-b^2}{2ac}$ can be computed, again, by the law of cosines. Assume that angle α is also given, then the values of the sines and cosines of the two angles θ and α can readily be calculated. Furthermore, the values of sin(α-β) and cos(α-β) are immediately obtainable by the Subtraction Formulas. Now that the lengths c and d and the value of cos(α-β) are known now, we can continue in the same fashion to get the length e by the law of cosines. Let's restate this method in general. To obtain the lengths of all possible chords, we first randomly select one vertex of the polygon and compute the lengths of all chords emanating from it by following the procedure described above and repeat the same computation to all other vertices. Notice that each chord has the chance to be calculated twice. Because a line segment contains two endpoints, the edge can be incident from one vertex and to the other or the other way around. That is, the same line can be emitting from either one of the two endpoints. If the length of a chord is available from previous computations, we do not have to compute it twice.

One may wonder if we could exhaust all of the possible chords by taking the approach stated above. By "possible chords" we mean the union of the sets of chords for all of the possible triangulations, namely, the universe from which all the subsets of chords are derived. Although there are only n-3 chords for a particular triangulation of an n-sided polygon, different triangulations will have a different set of chords. Now let's investigate this suspicion. For an n-sided polygon, there are $\binom{n}{2}$ ways to connect any two of the n vertices with one line segment. However, to get the number of chords, we have to subtract n from this number for the n sides, which are not chords, are also included in the calculation of $\binom{n}{2}$. Therefore, the number of possible chords for an n-sided polygon is $\binom{n}{2}$ - n = $\frac{n(n-1)}{2*1}$ - n = $\frac{n^2-n-2n}{2} = \frac{n^2-3n}{2}$. If this number coincides with the number of cases we consider in computing the lengths of chords by the method mentioned above then we are all set. According to the method, for each vertex there will be n-3 chords projecting from it (excluding the two adjacent vertices and itself). After taking into account that each chord is encountered twice, we get the total number of possible chords is $\frac{n(n-3)}{2} = \frac{n^2-3n}{2}$, as it should be if the method is valid.

(4) Number of ways to triangulate a convex polygon:

(a) There are totally $\frac{1}{n-1}\binom{2(n-2)}{n-2}$ different ways to triangulate a convex polygon and it is known as the Catalan number. Before proceeding any further, an introduction to some related concepts seems in order.

There are two other problems that are isomorphic to the polygon triangulation problem: Rooted Ordered Binary Tree and Parenthesization of a Matrix-chain Product. The existence of these bijective transformations between the polygon triangulation problem and the above-mentioned two problems is conducive in the sense that we can solve the polygon triangulation problem without physically tackling it but rather merely through a positive transfer of some existing solution to a quite thoroughly studied problem.

## 5. Sequential Algorithms

In this section we will expand on two different algorithms for solving the optimal polygon triangulation problem: Brute Force and Dynamic Programming approach.

### 5. 1. Brute Force Approach

Brute force approach is usually considered impractical when we talk about algorithms, especially when the number of possible cases increases drastically along with the increasing input size. For example, if there is more than one optimal solution, we can juxtapose all of them and pick "the best". With regard to the optimal polygon triangulation problem, it is rarely the case where multiple optimal solutions exist.

The basic idea behind the brute force algorithm is to pare a polygon piece by piece. Suppose we have an n-sided polygon to deal with. The first step is to number each of the n vertices from 0 to n-1, preferably in the counterclockwise direction. Next we choose the line connecting vertex 0 and vertex n-1 as the base and produce a triangle by drawing lines between these two vertices and any other vertex so as to make the two lines drawn converge on the same vertex (the tip of the triangle). In this way we are trying to partition the polygon into three components: the medial triangle, the left sub-polygon, and the right sub-polygon. A sub-polygons may be null (of size zero) or a polygon with the number of sides more than or equal to 3. The total length (including sides as well as chords) of a particular triangulation can be obtained by summing up the total lengths of all these three parts. By definition, a null polygon has the total length equal to zero. If the sub-polygon is a triangle, then there is no need to further triangulate it; otherwise, it can be triangulated into more than one triangle and therefore we have to repeat the same subdivision procedure until the resulting sub-polygon become a triangle. The two chords, sides of the newly drawn triangle in the middle, are candidates for the bases of new triangles if the process needs to be continued. To exhaust all the cases, for each polygon, including the original one and the sub-polygons derived from it, we must go through the same procedure for every vertex between the two endpoints of the base.

### 5.2. Dynamic Programming Approach

The dynamic programming approach involves computing and saving the answers to all of the smaller problems for later use in solving a larger problem. This technique fits the polygon triangulation problem well in that a larger polygon is constructed by several smaller polygons. The idea underlying this approach is that an optimal solution to a smaller polygon is to be stored and shared amongst larger polygons with this smaller polygon as a component so as to avoid repeating the same calculation. Therefore, a table must be established so that we know exactly where to look up the values when we need them. One limitation of this approach is that only one optimal solution can be arrived at.

Let's now dissect the dynamic program algorithm for solving the optimal polygon triangulation problem. Prior to reaching an optimal solution to an n-sided polygon, we must solve the problems for polygons of any number of sides less than n. As in the brute force approach, we number the vertices counterclockwise from 0 to n-1. Also null polygons always have total length equal to zero. The perimeter of a triangle can easily be computed by adding up its three sides, given the edge table where the information about the lengths between any two vertices of the polygon is stored.

To gain an insight into how an optimal solution to a larger polygon is obtained, we first look at the fundamental data structure for this algorithm. The information kept in optimization table is organized in this way: the row index of the array represents the number of triangles a sub-polygon can be triangulated into and the column index represents the group number, defined as the least vertex number within all vertices of the sub-polygon. Accordingly, a group is just a set of consecutive numbers that collectively form a polygon with a certain number of sides. Having decided the data structure, we now elucidate how to populate the array. We use a (nested) triple FOR loop to achieve this aim: the first two FOR loops are used for traversing all of the positions in the two-dimensional array and the third one is for ferreting out the optimal solution to a particular sub-polygon. By manipulating the indices of the three FOR loops, we can get the total length of a particular triangulation at one fell swoop, provided that all previous results, that is, the optimal solutions to smaller polygons necessary for solving this larger one, are available. Assume the indices used to iterate the FOR loops are i, j, and k, respectively. Recall that the index i represents the number of triangles a sub-polygon can be triangulated into. So i ranges from 0 to n-2. When i=0 each of the n-1 elements in the first row is zero. When i=1, that is, a one-triangle situation, the perimeters of the triangles are readily computable by consulting the edge table. To fill up the remaining cells of the array, we proceed as this: the index i goes from 2 to n-2, j from 0 to n-2-i, and k from 1 to i. Note that when i increases, j decreases. Stated differently, as the number of sides of a sub-polygon, which determines how many triangles this sub-polygon can be triangulated into, increases, the number of groups that can be formed decreases. The index k is used as a cutting point to split a sub-polygon into two groups. From the brute force approach a polygon can be subdivided into three parts and the tip of the middle triangle serves as the key to generate the left and right sub-polygons. k can be regarded as the number of triangles in the left sub-polygon plus one (the middle triangle). At the extreme, that is, when the right sub-polygon is a null polygon, k is the number of triangles into which a polygon can be triangulated.

Apparently, the upper limit of k is i. When the left polygon is a null polygon, k is equal to 1 (the middle triangle). This justifies the range of k to be from 1 to i. Now we are in a position to construe how to compute the total length of a particular triangulation at one stroke by manipulating the indices i, j, and k. Given three vertices, we can easily obtain the perimeter of the triangle from the edge table. The numbers of the three vertices of the middle triangle can be identified by j, j+k, and j+i+1. Since j appears in all three of them, let us consider first the case when j is equal to 0. We know from before that k is the cutting point and i is the maximum cutting point. So we can deduce that the ending vertex is bound to be i+1. To take into account every group we just add j to each of the three numbers 0, k, and i+1. Getting the total length of the middle triangle is trivial, so the crux of the remaining problem is to acquire the total lengths of the left and right sub-polygons. From previous discussion, it is unequivocal that the number of triangles the left sub-polygon can be triangulated into is k-1, and i-k for the right sub-polygon. Thus, these two numbers can be looked upon as the row indices for the left and right sub-polygons, respectively. To reckon the column indices, once again, we consider only the case when the group number is 0 first. The clincher here is that the index k is the group number of the right sub-polygon. Since 0 is the group number for the left sub-polygon, to take every group into consideration, we as before add j to the two column indices and they end up with j and j+k, respectively. In sum, suppose the two-dimensional array is named "array" and Tri(a, b, c) represents the perimeter of the triangle formed by the three vertices labeled a, b, and c, the total length of a particular triangulation is: Tri(j, j+k, j+i+1) + array[k-1][j] + array[i-k][j+k]. To complete the solution, we need to search for the minimum value for each group. It requires only comparing the various total lengths for each value of k and singling out the minimum from among the computed values. Notice that after all jobs are done, the optimal solution to the n-sided polygon, not surprisingly, can be found in the position with row index n-2 and column index 0. It follows from the fact that the original polygon is the only sub-polygon that can be triangulated into n-2 triangles and the its least vertex number is 0.

### 5.3. Parallel Algorithms with Actors

#### 5.3.1. Brute Force Approach

The first actor is the edge table. Assume all edges have been computed by the method presented previously and are part of the knowledge of this actor. This actor returns the length between two points or the perimeter of a triangle. By taking the brute force approach, we can get the total lengths of all triangulations. We need actors that can operate independently and concurrently to fulfill task of different polygon triangulations. Initially, we create only one actor. If this actor ascertains that there is a possibility of a different triangulation, it will spawn new actor(s) to handle the new job without "putting itself out of the way" to take care of the detected potential triangulation. The newly created actors have the same ability as the their parent. During execution, they will not communicate with each other, but all of them at some points will have to consult the edge table via synchronous message passing in order to compute the total length of the triangulation. When the mission is accomplished, each actor sends the result to a centralized actor responsible for sorting out the optimal solution. The centralized actor maintains the up-to-date minimum total length. After all triangulation actors are finished, the optimal solution is displayed.

### 5.3.2. Dynamic Programming Approach

The actor keeping the edge length information introduced in the previous subsection can be reused in the dynamic programming approach. We need a two-dimensional array. Thus we need a startup actor to populate the array. Each cell of the array is occupied by an actor.

Aside from the null-polygon and one-triangle actors, all other actors must perform the task of seeking the optimal solution to the sub-polygon that each of them represents. All actors work concurrently, but solutions to smaller polygons must be ready before an actor needing the information can proceed for solving a larger problem. The actors treating larger polygons receive the necessary information via synchronous communication to ensure that they will not go on until all the data needed are computed.

## 5.4. Implementation

This chapter addresses implementation issues for solving the optimal polygon triangulation problem with the actor model. The actual Java code was part of the Hsueh's Master Thesis [1].

The class PTApp is first developed to implement the brute force algorithm and another separate class DPApp comes out later to deal with the dynamic programming algorithm. In the end these two classes are combined together for convenience. An instance of the class PTApp sets the scene for running the program. It instantiates the class EdgeReceptacle, which is the repertory used for storing the distances between any two points selected from among the n vertices of an n-sided polygon. A set of hypothetical data is hard-coded in the program ranging from 4 to 10 sides. If the number of sides is greater than 10, the length table are filled with zeros. This information of lengths is placed in a one-dimensional array to save space. Nevertheless, the array looking-up mechanism is hidden from the clients of the methods in this class. That is, a client can pass in two endpoints and expect to get the length between these two points. The conversion from an imaginary two-dimensional array to a realistic one-dimensional array is transparent to the clients. The additional work for computing the corresponding index of a one-dimensional array takes extra time than the time needed if a two-dimensional array were to be used instead. Denote n (the number of sides of a polygon) as the input size.

For the dynamic programming approach, which can take on relatively larger input size, the benefits from using a one-dimensional array stands out. The first instance of the class TriActor sets off the brute force algorithm. For our purpose is to list all the possibilities through parallelism, we make every effort to avoid interdependencies between any two processes. Each instance of TriActor represents a process and the information about the specific triangulation such as the number of chords and the constituent vertices of the chords is saved in its proprietary instance of the class TriComponent. TriComponent also retains a restarting point from where the triangulation process of the sub-polygon on the other side can proceed after the work on one side is done.

The role of a centralized entity is played by an instance of the class OptRegister. After concluding the task of triangulation, each TriActor sends the related information to OptRegister, which is responsible for coordinating the mutually independent TriActors in an attempt to find the optimal solution.

The dynamic programming algorithm is launched by an instance of the class DPApp. It initializes the two-dimensional array and sets the instances of the class DPActor in motion. DPActors perform concurrently in searching out the optimal solution to the particular sub-polygon by following the dynamic programming algorithm.

## 6. Empirical Results

An experimental result obtained by running the program on the SUN server (with four ULTRA-SPARC processors at 400 MHz each, and 512 MB of main memory) is shown graphically. Execution times are plotted against varying input size (numbers of sides of a polygon). The curve for the brute force algorithm

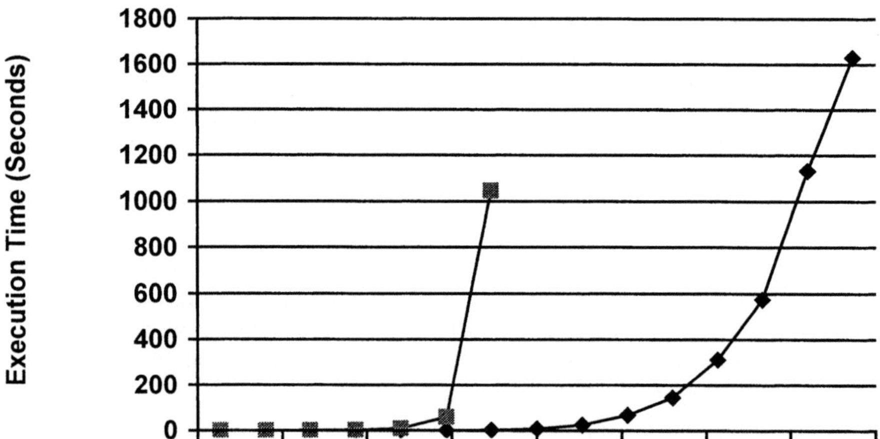


| | 4 | 6 | 8 | 10 | 20 | 25 | 35 | 45 |
|---|---|---|---|---|---|---|---|---|
| DP | 0,093 | 0,324 | 0,977 | 2,271 | 24,91 | 68,18 | 312,3 | 1133 |
| BF | 0,151 | 0,774 | 9,225 | 1046 | | | | |

**Number of Sides**

Fig. 1 Execution times plotted against varying input size algorithm

runs up much more sharply than does that for the dynamic programming algorithm. Empirical comparison between two algorithms is somewhat subtler than that derived from mathematical analysis. Let's take up the latter first. The dynamic programming algorithm is cubic, i.e., $O(n^3)$. By looking at the formula for the Catalan number, we can discern that the performance of the brute force algorithm is somewhere between a factorial and an exponential function. We can manifest this slant by further manipulating the formula for the Catalan number. This gives us a lower bound, i.e., $O(\frac{4^n}{n^2})$, for the Catalan number.

One may agree that both the mathematical analysis and the empirical result confirm the fact that the dynamic programming algorithm "one-ups" the brute force algorithm. The former has a smaller big O (from the mathematical analysis) and shorter execution time (from the empirical result). For the brute force algorithm, each possible triangulation requires an independent process. Thus the growing Catalan number of processes soon devours and gobbles up the available resources and makes collecting comparable data infeasible. The data for the dynamic programming algorithm, on the other hand, is still obtainable when the input size is 50. The curve for the dynamic programming algorithm is relatively smooth.

The execution time of running a program can not be exactly determined. For example, if cache or virtual memory is being used, then whether a page fault is about to occur in part determines the execution time. If a miss happens, it will conceivably take longer time to execute the program. This uncertainty causes the result of an experiment to be unpredictable even though the same program given the same input is executed. For a distributed system, the source of unpredictability is even wider. Such events as scheduling policies, context switches, I/O operations, and interrupts may occur in an unpredictable manner. Context switches can happen even in a multiprocessor system if there are more processes than there are physical processors. Message delays due to communication-link traffic and message-routing protocols have some probabilistic distribution. All these imply that execution time is no longer an exact function of input size.

We present in Fig. 2 the execution times for the sequential version as well as the concurrent version of the dynamic programming algorithm. The speedup is also graphed in Fig. 3.

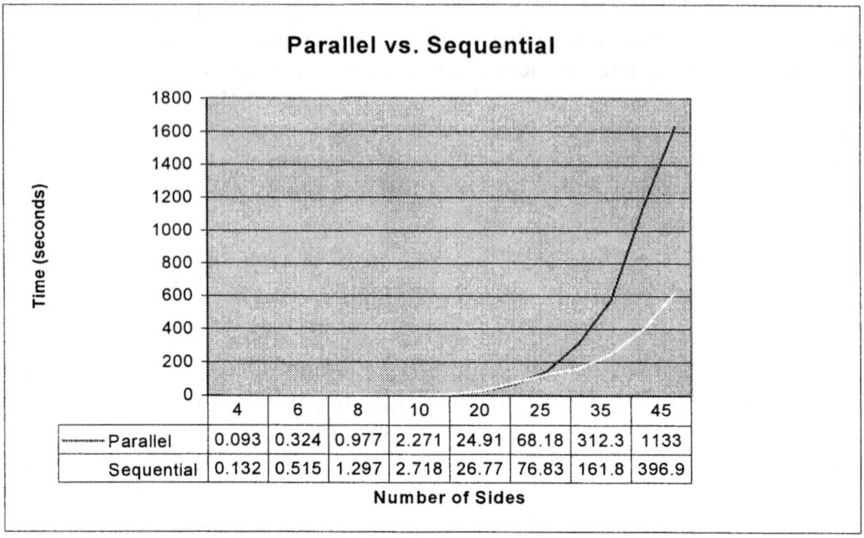


| | 4 | 6 | 8 | 10 | 20 | 25 | 35 | 45 |
|---|---|---|---|---|---|---|---|---|
| Parallel | 0.093 | 0.324 | 0.977 | 2.271 | 24.91 | 68.18 | 312.3 | 1133 |
| Sequential | 0.132 | 0.515 | 1.297 | 2.718 | 26.77 | 76.83 | 161.8 | 396.9 |

Fig. 2 Execution times for sequential and parallel dynamic programming

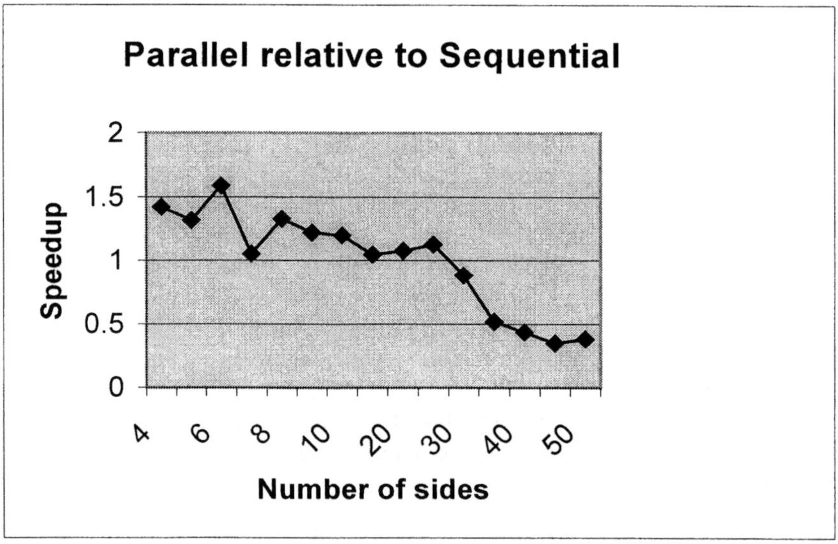


Fig. 3 Speedup of the parallel version of the dynamic programming algorithm

From Fig. 2 and Fig. 3, we recognize that when input size is less than 30, the performance of the parallel version is better than the sequential version. When input size is 30 or above, however, the performance of the parallel version is declining and eventually getting worse than the sequential version. Let's take a closer look at the speedup. According to the dynamic programming algorithm, a two-dimensional array needs to be created for the actors' residence. Initializing the array needs quadratic time and it cannot be parallelized. From the Amdahl's Law:

$$\text{Speedup} = 1 / (f + (1-f)/p)$$

where,
$f \equiv$ fraction of sequential code
$p \equiv$ number of processors

Note that the term $(1-f)/p$ vanishes as $p$ approaches infinity. Now suppose we could have as many processors as we want, then the maximum speedup that can be achieved is: $1/f = 1/(n^2/n^3) = 1/(1/n) = n$. So a priori we may expect the speedup to be at best linear. Apparently, there is no way this maximum speedup can be achieved on the ground that we do not have an infinite number of processors. The empirical result shows that the speedup goes down instead of increasing or remaining constant when the input size exceeds 30. We conjecture that the culprit for this anomaly is granularity. For each actor there is a FOR loop involved in accomplishing its job. Within each FOR loop, only a few assignment and comparison tasks are to be performed and they can be done faster. Parallelizing the computation of the actors incurs the increased consumption of resources for scheduling the competing processes and the added complexity owing to synchronization mechanics (data consistency between the individual copy of working memory within each process and the master copy to which each process has access). Congestion caused by a daunting number of actors in action at the same time and the intense interdependence among them can put a real damper on the speedup.

As noted before, there are some nonsystematic (non-deterministic) components in the relationship between the execution time and input size. Now that we know the dynamic programming algorithm is cubic, we can take one step further to establish a model in the stochastic from:

$$Y_i - \alpha_1 X_i + \alpha_2 X_i^2 + \alpha_3 X_i^3 + u_i$$

where,

$X_i$ number of sides of a polygon,
$Y_i$ expected value of the execution time conditional upon the value of $X_i$,
$u_i$ stochastic disturbance.

To develop the best statistical relationship between the forecast (dependent) variable and the set of predictor (independent) variables, the most commonly used technique is regression analysis.

From the Gauss-Markov Theorem, we know that under the assumptions of the classical linear regression model, the least-square estimators are best linear unbiased estimators. If our interest is not only in point estimation but hypothesis testing, one additional assumption that the error terms are normally distributed can be made and it is thus referred to as a classical normal linear regression model. Although by the Central Limit Theorem we know that the distribution of the sum of independent and identically distributed random variables tends to be normal as the number of such random variables approaches infinity, we should exercise caution in applying it when the sample size is small, as the situation in our case. One may conjure up the queuing theory, two assumptions of which are that the arrival rate is Poisson distributed and that the service rate is exponentially distributed, in grappling with the problem that a priori we do not know how the error terms are distributed. However, if our objective is just point estimation, we can put this sort of issue aside. For the same reason, we can leave out verifying the validity of such assumptions made in the CLRM as multicollinearity, heteroscedasticity, and autocorrelation. Even though these assumptions are violated, the ordinary least square estimators are still unbiased. The problem resulting from the violations of these assumptions is that the variances are no longer dependable in terms of statistical inference.

By using ordinary least square estimators (OLS) command provided in the statistical software package SHAZY we can obtain the OLS estimates. The estimated regression equation therefore is:

$$Y_i = 1.7986X_i - .17898X_i^2 + .0076572X_i^3$$

We have to use the regression-through-origin model because the execution time is zero when input size is zero. Fortunately, most statistical packages provide such an option as to suppress the intercept term. Having the deterministic model in place, we can then plug the various X values into the equation and compute the predicted values. In Fig. 4 the predicted curve is depicted and superimposed on the curve that is drawn based on the actual empirical results (sequential version). Incidentally, we merely take advantage of the estimating power imparted by statistics to suit our needs, but there is no one "true" population in our case. A glance at Fig. 4 suggests that this model does a decent job of estimating the actual curve and, as noted before, there are some random variations. So, without parallelism, the execution time of the sequential version follows a cubic curve in accordance with the mathematical analysis and therefore is roughly predictable. The conclusion we may make out of this outcome is that probably there is not too much room for concurrency in solving the optimal polygon triangulation problem with the dynamic programming algorithm. Be aware that even though when the input size is small the performance of the parallel version is better, we actually do not gain too much benefit in terms of the execution time (seconds).

## References

1. Hao Hsueh, Actor-based Parallel Implementations of the Polygon Triangularization Problem, Master

Thesis, Computer and Information Science Department, University of Massachusetts, Dartmouth, 2000.

2. Sedgewick, Robert. 2nd ed. Algorithms. Reading, MA: Addison-Wesley Publishing Company, 1988.

3. Shatz, Sol M. Development of Distributed Software: Concepts and Tools. New York: Mac Millan Publishing Company, 1993.

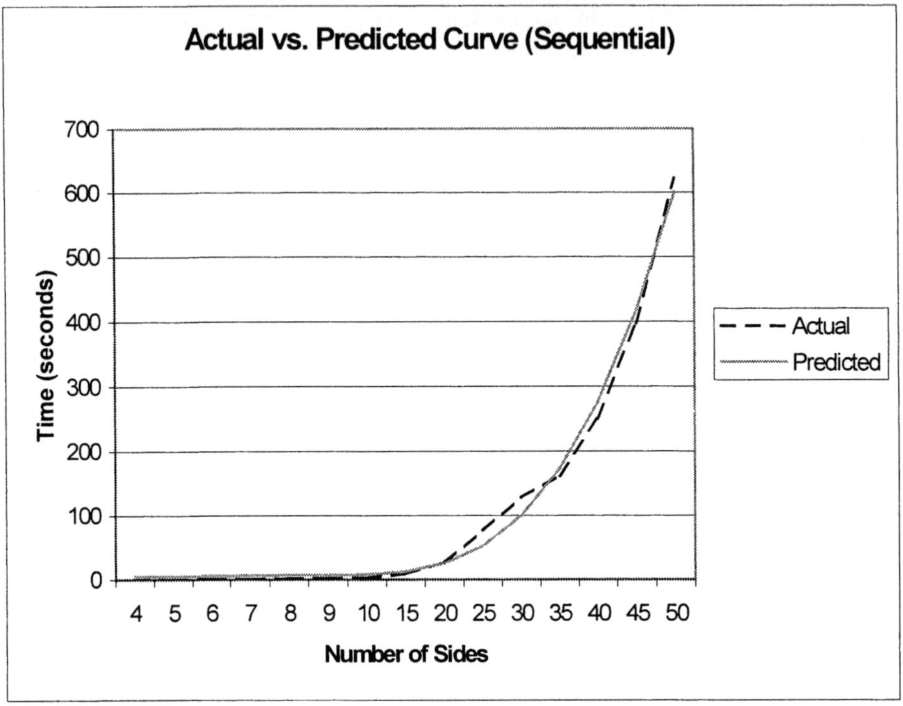


Fig.4. Actual and predicted curves for sequential dynamic programming

# A Model for Extracting a Class of Knowledge Operators, Logic Disjunctions and Logic Alternatives from BDI Agents

**Radosław P. Katarzyniak**

Institute of Control and Systems Engineering, Wrocław University of Technology, Wrocław, Poland

e-mail: radosław.katarzyniak@ists.pwr.wroc.pl

***Abstract:*** *Private knowledge structures of the intentional agent are presented. It is pointed out in what way these structures are used to generate a class of basic knowledge formulas with logic disjunctions and alternatives as their arguments. A knowledge formula is treated as a proper logic-based and externally oriented representation of agent's knowledge if and only if it is true for the overall state of encapsulated knowledge bases. Although the presented solution is based on the idea of possible worlds semantics, it applies an alternative approach to defining truth-values for knowledge operators. In particular, it takes into account the intensional nature of knowledge operators and strictly private nature of possible worlds. The proposed semantics gives a theoretical support for autonomous algorithms that mine disjunctions and alternatives from internal agent's representations of states of ontologically independent and self-contained atom objects.*

*Keywords: intentional agent, possible worlds semantics, intensional semantics, formal epistemology, cognitive science*

## 1. Introduction

The idea of *BDI* models has been introduced and studied in artificial intelligence and cognitive sciences for quite a long time [2,5,17,19,20]. These models are understood as formal counterparts of intentional models of agents [3,18], where intentional modelling is a way of explaining natural and artificial systems' states and behaviour by using anthropomorphic and mentalistic concepts. Some typical statements of intentional models are: *Agent a knows (believes) that a state holds, in which $\varphi$ is true., Agent a prefers the state, in which $\varphi$ is satisfied. Agent a has a goal to create a state of the world, in which $\varphi$ is satisfied. Agent a carries out actions that lead to a state that satisfies $\varphi$.* BDI models are important for practical reasons e.g. they define the relation between informal models of artificial agent systems and their technical implementations [11,15] as well as for theoretical ones e.g. they are in strict relation to formal epistemology [23,24].

The above way of understanding formulas in BDI models is not the only one and can be substituted by intentional statements spoken in the first singular person. In such a case BDI formulas become to be parts of an intentional self - reference model of agent *a*: *I (agent a) know (believe) that a state holds, in which the condition* $\varphi$ *is true., etc.* The fundamental nature of the self - reference mode of interpreting BDI models has a very strong support in the natural order of cognitive processes because in case of each intentionally modelling subject the conceptualisation of its own intentional states is always prior to any conceptualisation of intentional states of other intentionally modelled agents. For further clarification of this issue see the idea of *projection mappings* [4] or levels of anthropomorphizing intentional systems [11,15].

This presentation gives an alternative, non-extensional method for defining semantics of BDI knowledge formulas with logic disjunctions and alternatives, in which the first singular person of natural language interpretations of BDI models is assumed. This method gives a theoretical support for defining a process of semantic communication between artificial intentional agents as well as gives an example of an original way of analysing some concepts traditionally studied by epistemology [23,24] and philosophy of modal logics [7].

## 2. Possible worlds, disjunctions and alternatives in BDI agents

Let us consider knowledge formulas given in Table 1. Formulas $K_a(\phi_1 \vee \phi_2)$ and $K_a(\phi_1 \veebar \phi_2)$ are openly epistemic ones. At the same time $\phi_1 \vee \phi_2$ and $\phi_1 \veebar \phi_2$ formalise statements, in which epistemic operator is only understood but not spoken openly (see open and latent epistemic mood of knowledge communication [15]). The research issue reported below is defined as follows: *What is the state of a private database system encapsulated in an intentional agent that makes it necessary for this agent to use knowledge operator with logic disjunction or logic alternative as an argument for an external, semantic and verbally - oriented representation of this agent knowledge of the world?*

**Table 1.** Atomic knowledge formulas with disjunction and alternative

| Common Language | Formal Abbreviations |
|---|---|
| There is $\phi_1$ or $\phi_2$. | $\phi_1 \vee \phi_2$ |
| There is either $\phi_1$ or $\phi_2$. | $\phi_1 \veebar \phi_2$ |
| I (agent *a*) know that $\phi_1$ or $\phi_2$. | $K_a(\phi_1 \vee \phi_2)$ |
| I (agent *a*) know that either $\phi_1$ or $\phi_2$. | $K_a(\phi_1 \veebar \phi_2)$ |

It is assumed in BDI models [2,5,17,19,20] that the appropriate theoretical model for autonomous algorithms for the generation of $\phi_1 \vee \phi_2$, $\phi_1 \veebar \phi_2$,

$K_a(\phi_1 \vee \phi_2)$ and $K_a(\phi_1 \underline{\vee} \phi_2)$ is given by possible worlds semantics applied to epistemic knowledge operator $K_a$ [16]. In this approach $K_a(\phi_1 \vee \phi_2)$ and $K_a(\phi_1 \underline{\vee} \phi_2)$ are treated as an adequate and external representation of knowledge of agent $a$ if and only if for a given Kripke structure $<s_0,K>$ assigned to agent $a$ formulas $K_a(\phi_1 \vee \phi_2)$ and $K_a(\phi_1 \vee \phi_2)$ are true for $<s_0,K>$ as a model [2,5,17,19,20]. A detailed way of verifying the truth value of $K_a(\phi_1 \vee \phi_2)$ and $K_a(\phi_1 \underline{\vee} \phi_2)$ is carried out according to the following definition:

1. The Kripke structure $<s_0,K>$ is used to yield the set:

   $$U_{\text{Alternative}}(s_0,K)=\{s':<s_0,s'>\in K\}$$

   This set contains of all possible worlds alternative to a chosen world $s_0$.

2. Formula $K_a(\phi_1 \vee \phi_2)$ is true in the sense that it expresses the knowledge stored by agent $a$ in $<s_0,K>$ in a correct way if and only if the alternative $\phi_1 \vee \phi_2$ is true for each possible world belonging to $U_{\text{Alternative}}(s_0,K)$:

   $<s_0,K>\mid=_E K_a(\phi_1 \vee \phi_2)$ iff for each alternative possible world $s\in U_{\text{Alternative}}(s_0,K)$ the relation $s\mid=_{KRP}\phi_1 \vee \phi_2$ holds

3. Formula $K_a(\phi_1 \underline{\vee} \phi_2)$ is true in the sense that it expresses the knowledge stored by agent $a$ in $<s_0,K>$ in a correct way if and only if the disjunction $\phi_1 \underline{\vee} \phi_2$ is true for each possible world belonging to $U_{\text{Alternative}}(s_0,K)$:

   $<s_0,K>\mid=_E K_a(\phi_1 \vee \phi_2)$ iff for each alternative possible world $s\in U_{\text{Alternative}}(s_0,K)$ the relation $s\mid=_{KRP}\phi_1 \underline{\vee} \phi_2$ holds

An important feature of (1-3) is that for each $s\in U_{\text{Alternative}}(s_0,K)$ both symbols $s\mid=_{KRP}\phi_1 \vee \phi_2$ and $s\mid=_{KRP}\phi_1 \vee \phi_2$ are understood as in the traditional semantics for Proposition Calculus or First Order Logic [8,21]. It means that in possible worlds semantics symbols $<s_0,K>\mid=_E K_a(\phi_1 \vee \phi_2)$ and $<s_0,K>\mid=_E K_a(\phi_1 \underline{\vee} \phi_2)$ are treated as a rather direct extension of Tarski's definition of truth [21]. However, some arguments can be raised against the common sense validity of (1-3). In particular, it is impossible to construct an informal explanation of the fact that in (2) and (3) disjunctions $\phi_1 \underline{\vee} \phi_2$ and alternatives $\phi_1 \vee \phi_2$ are evaluated against individual possible worlds $s\in U_{\text{Alternative}}(s_0,K)$. The reason is that it is in conflict with the original meaning of the idea of possible worlds. An informal semantic analysis of this idea proves that the possible world is originally treated and used rather as a complete and self-contained model of an intentional object well known to a subject responsible for possible worlds creation [10]. The consequence for our understanding of the definition given by (1-3) is as follows: If a possible world $s\in U_{\text{Alternative}}(s_0,K)$ is understood as a complete model of an object (perhaps a complex one), there is no acceptable way to relate the content stored in $s$ to a cognitive experience of an alternative or a disjunction. In fact, a cognitive experience of agent $a$ can be understood as cognising a logic disjunction or a logic alternative if and only if agent $a$ refers itself in an intentional stance to at least two different possible worlds from $U_{\text{Alternative}}(s_0,K)$.

This inconsistency between common sense logic of alternatives and disjunctions and its formal logic counterpart given by (1-3) results in rejecting the traditional possible worlds semantics of operator $K_a$ as a theoretical foundation for autonomous processes yielding $K_a(\phi_1 \vee \phi_2)$ and $K_a(\phi_1 \underline{\vee} \phi_2)$ as correct external knowledge descriptions. In consequence, an alternative semantic solution needs to be given in order to relate internal states of agent *a* knowledge and their external and verbally - oriented counterparts. A general outline of such a solution is given below for a particular subclass of formulas (see Table 1).

## 3. Knowledge of objects, cognitive science and phenomenology

The way of relating internal (relational) and external (logic) representations of knowledge that will be given below is strongly related to informal theories of self-contained atom objects proposed by cognitive psychology and phenomenology. In particular, these disciplines help us to resolve at least some problems related to our understanding of internal states of agent *a*, in which a logic disjunction or a logic alternative needs to be spoken out by agent *a* in order to communicate the actual state of its knowledge of the state of two atom properties in a self-contained atom object *o*.

Cognitive psychology (including cognitive neuroscience) has proved that the human agent cognitive abilities of conceptualising the world are originally based on empirical data gathered by this agent from an external world [1]. The very first product of neural processes that take this data as an input is a system of cognitive representations for self-contained atom objects of the world. It is well known that this system is stored (embodied) at a neural level of each human agent. However the detailed way, in which particular representations of concepts appear, is still an open research issue [22]. A fundamental role of the system of embodied concepts of self-contained atom objects is that it makes it possible for a human agent to re-identify existing atom objects over time. Its important feature is, too, that it is not consciously penetrable to human agents and is strongly dependent on their genetic nature [1].

A deeper analysis of BDI models can prove that it is impossible to understand agent *a* as an intentional one without projecting particular representations of self-contained atom objects onto agent *a* internal databases [3,15]. What follows is that there must be a particular process or a structure assumed for an artificial agent that is a counterpart for pre-verbal human abilities of processing cognitive representations of self contained atom objects, and these abilities need to be described in theoretical models of these agents, too.

The theory of the self-contained atom objects that has been proposed by phenomenology, describes the structure of the above system from the perspective of the conscious human agent. It uncovers the ways human agents use and analyse the content stored in particular cognitive systems [9]. An important result from these studies is that from the point of view of the conscious cognition, the concepts of self - contained atom objects need to be treated as conjunctions of atom properties and complex, higher level properties. The atom properties are conceptually impenetrable in this sense that they cannot be analysed by any cognitive process in a conscious way. On the contrary, any complex and higher level property is always a generalised result of cognitive experiences that have been experienced at lower levels of cognition. It is an important phenomenon that these levels of cognitive experience are always present in related complex and higher level properties in a very certain way. In particular, they are „re"-"cognised" and „re"-"activated" by cognitive processes of an agent during a process of analysing the meaning of a generalised property.

In order to simplify this presentation it has been additionally assumed that any higher level and complex property that is included in a concept of self-contained atom objects accessible to an intentionally modelled agent $a$ generalises exactly two atom properties [9]. Below a formal structure of an internal state of an intentional agent will be given, in which a logic disjunction or alternative is required as an external representation of knowledge.

## 4. A simple model for cognitive like semantics of knowledge

Let us now apply the above theories of self-contained atom objects to defining a formal model for a simple intentional BDI agent that is capable of using logic disjunctions and alternatives as external representations of its knowledge. Let the following assumptions be made:

1. World $W$ is given, in which a class of self-contained atom objects exists. Let us denote this class by $N=\{o_1,o_2,...,o_p\}$. W is given in the ontological sense.
2. Agent $a$ is given that is an autonomous subject of knowledge. Agent $a$ is capable of perceiving states of self-contained atom objects in $W$ and is equipped with a system of concepts that makes intentional conceptualisation of states of self-contained atom objects possible.
3. Agent $a$ uses a collection of the so - called characteristic properties $B_1,B_2,...,B_m$ that distinguish self-contained atom objects $o_1,o_2,...,o_p$ to other atom objects of world $W$. Properties $B_1,B_2,...,B_m$ are called characteristic properties that define class $N$ if the following condition holds: For a self-contained object $o_s$ of world $W$ relation $o_s \in N$ holds iff $o_s$ possesses each property $B_1,B_2,...,B_m$.
4. Agent $a$ has already constructed the knowledge of the fact that objects $o_1,o_2,...,o_p$ exist. It means that a cognitive system assigned to agent $a$ (perhaps theoretically) has already developed the whole and preverbal conceptual representation of each object $o_1,o_2,...,o_p$. These representations are all encapsulated in agent $a$ and can be a target of conscious cognition carried out by agent $a$. For simplicity of this presentation it is also assumed that the knowledge of that objects $o_1,o_2,...,o_p$ exist cannot be changed and forgotten.

5. Agent $a$ has already constructed a particular concept to grasp the whole family of self-contained atom objects $o_1,o_2,...,o_p$. According to the phenomenological theory of self-contained atom objects this concept is a conjunction of characteristic properties $B_1,B_2,...,B_m$ and some complex and higher level properties $M_1,M_2,...,M_n$. It has already been assumed that each higher level and complex property $M_i$, i=1.2....,n, can be substituted by one of exactly two lower level properties related to $M_i$. This substitution is carried out by cognitive processes of agent $a$. Formally:

$$M_i \leftarrow \{P_{i,1}, P_{i,2}\},$$

where symbol $\leftarrow$ denotes the fact that during the process of analysing its meaning property $M_i$ can be substituted by and only by properties $P_{i,1}$ and $P_{i,2}$.

Another important idea is a local time counter. If agent $a$ is assumed to actually exist in the world, than there is an idea of a local time history related to and only to this agent $a$. The fact that such a time line has to be considered is the result of a natural order of cognition that always relates a being to the idea of its local time [6]. In consequence, from the point of view of agent $a$ cognitive processes are carried out as related to this particular and fully private line of time points and it needs to be taken into account in our formal approach to modelling. Let $T^a=\{t^a_0,t^a_1,...\}$ be the set of local time points accessible to agent $a$. Let symbols $\rightarrow^{TM}$, $\leq^{TM}$, $<^{TM}$ denote a relation of direct temporal precedence, a general relation of temporal precedence, and a relation of strict temporal precedence, respectively. For each i,j=0,1,2,..., relations $t^a_i \rightarrow^{TM} t^a_j$, $t^a_i \leq^{TM} t^a_j$, $t^a_i <^{TM} t^a_j$ hold iff j=i+1, i≤j and i<j, respectively. The symbol $t^a_0$ is understood as the very starting point from which the local time line is autonomously constructed by agent $a$.

Let us assume that the overall knowledge of agent $a$ about the state of self-contained atom objects $o_1,o_2,...,o_p$ at a particular time point $t^a$ is given, at first, by knowing that objects $o_1,o_2,...,o_p$ exist, at second, by knowing that objects $o_1,o_2,...,o_p$ posses characteristic properties $B_1,B_2,...,B_m$ and, at third, by knowing some results from empirical observations of $o_1,o_2,...,o_p$ regarding properties $P_{i,1}$ and $P_{i,2}$, i=1,2,...,n. In actual world natural constraints exist that make it impossible for agent $a$ to empirically verify at the same time point the state of properties $P_{i,1}$ and $P_{i,2}$, i=1,2,...,n, in each object $o_1,o_2,...,o_p$. What follows is that at a particular time point a lack of knowledge needs to be assigned to agent $a$ as regards to the state of $P_{i,1}$ and $P_{i,2}$, i=1,2,...,n, in objects $o_1,o_2,...,o_p$. The above structure of knowledge state is formalised as the so-called $a$-encapsulated $t^a$-base profile given in the following way [12]:

Definition. For each state of $W$ recognised by agent $a$ as a separate state of $W$, the empirically verified knowledge of $W$ is given as the so-called $a$-encapsulated $t^a$-related world profile:

$$EncProfile(t^a) = < N=\{o_1,o_2,...,o_m\},$$

$B^{+}{}_{1}(t^{a}),B^{+}{}_{2}(t^{a}),...,B^{+}{}_{p}(t^{a})$

$P^{+}{}_{1,1}(t^{a}),P^{-}{}_{1,1}(t^{a}),P^{\pm}{}_{1,1}(t^{a})$ $\quad$ $P^{+}{}_{1,2}(t^{a}),P^{-}{}_{1,2}(t^{a}),P^{\pm}{}_{1,2}(t^{a})$

$P^{+}{}_{2,1}(t^{a}),P^{-}{}_{2,1}(t^{a}),P^{\pm}{}_{2,1}(t^{a})$ $\quad$ $P^{+}{}_{2,2}(t^{a}),P^{-}{}_{2,2}(t^{a}),P^{\pm}{}_{2,2}(t^{a})$

...

$P^{+}{}_{n,1}(t^{a}),P^{-}{}_{n,1}(t^{a}),P^{\pm}{}_{n,1}(t^{a})$ $\quad$ $P^{+}{}_{n,2}(t^{a}),P^{-}{}_{n,2}(t^{a}),P^{\pm}{}_{n,2}(t^{a})$ $\quad$ $>$

The following interpretation and constraints are assumed for *EncProfile*($t^{a}$):

1. For each i=1,...,m, $B^{+}{}_{i}(t^{a})=Universe\mathrm{B}_{i}=N$.
2. For each i=1,...,n, j=1,2, $P^{+}{}_{i,j}(t^{a})\subseteq Universe\mathrm{P}_{i,j}$, $P^{-}{}_{i,1}(t^{a})\subseteq Universe\mathrm{P}_{i,j}$, $P^{\pm}{}_{i,j}(t^{a})\subseteq Universe\mathrm{P}_{i,j}$, where $Universe\mathrm{P}_{i,j}=N$ and the following conditions hold $P^{+}{}_{i,j}(t^{a})\cap P^{-}{}_{i,j}(t^{a})=\varnothing$, $P^{+}{}_{i,j}(t^{a})\cap P^{\pm}{}_{i,j}(t^{a})=\varnothing$, $P^{\pm}{}_{i,j}(t^{a})\cap P^{-}{}_{i,j}(t^{a})=\varnothing$.
3. For each $o_{s}\in N$ the relation $o_{s}\in P^{+}{}_{i,j}(t^{a})$ holds iff from agent *a* point of view $o_{s}$ possesses the atomic property $P_{i,j}$ and this fact has been empirically verified by *a*-encapsulated cognitive processes. The same interpretation is assumed for each $o_{s}$ and each relation $B^{+}{}_{k}(t^{a})_{(k=1,2,...,p)}$.
4. For each $o_{s}\in N$ the relation $o_{s}\in P^{-}{}_{i,j}(t^{a})$ holds iff from agent *a* point of view $o_{s}$ does not posses the atomic property $P_{i,j}$ and this fact has been empirically verified by *a*-encapsulated cognitive processes. This interpretation does not apply to $B_{k}(t^{a})_{(k=1,2,...,p)}$, for each of these properties is realised in advance for each $o_{s}\in N$ before any cognitive and conscious - like conceptualisation starts.
5. For each $o_{s}\in N$ the relation $o_{s}\in P^{\pm}{}_{i,j}(t^{a})=N/(P^{+}{}_{i,j}(t^{a})\cup P^{-}{}_{i,j}(t^{a}))$ defines the scope of *a*-encapsulated $P_{i}$-incompetence as regards to property $P_{i,j}$.

With the profile *EncProfile*($t^{a}$) a set of modal states is related. This set is an output from a process of substituting (filling) incompetence areas $P^{\pm}{}_{i,j}(t^{a})\subseteq Universe\mathrm{P}_{i,j}$, i=1,...,n, j=1,2, with certain atom properties. The scope of this set is given by two factors: the still valid result of the latest empirical verification of the current state of $o_{1},o_{2},...,o_{m}$ (stored in the base profile) and the conceptual space based on a system of concepts used by agent *a*. Formally:

$$ModalStates(t^{a})=$$

$$\{<N,B^{+}{}_{1}(t^{a}),B^{+}{}_{2}(t^{a}),...,B^{+}{}_{m}(t^{a}),$$

$$P^{+}{}_{1,1}(t^{a})\cup Z_{1,1},P^{+}{}_{1,2}(t^{a})\cup Z_{1,2},...,P^{+}{}_{n,1}(t^{a})\cup Z_{n,1},P^{+}{}_{n,2}(t^{a})\cup Z_{n,2}>:$$

$$\text{where } Z_{1,1}\subseteq P^{\pm}{}_{1,1}(t^{a}),\ Z_{1,2}\subseteq P^{\pm}{}_{1,2}(t^{a}),\ ...,\ Z_{n,1}\subseteq P^{\pm}{}_{n,1}(t^{a}),\ Z_{n,2}\subseteq P^{\pm}{}_{n,2}(t^{a})\}$$

Let us now notice that each modal state $s \in ModalStates(t^a)$ can be used as a model structure for traditional semantics of First Order Predicates [8,21].

The overall knowledge of the states of $o_1, o_2, ..., o_p$ recognised by agent $a$ is stored in an $a$-encapsulated temporal collection of all constructed base profiles:

$$KnowledgeProfiles(t^a) = \{EncProfile(t^a_i) : t^a_i \leq_{TM} t^a\}$$

or as the following collection of sets of modal states, equivalently:

$$KnowledgeState(t^a) = \{ModalStates(t^a_i) : t^a_i \leq_{TM} t^a\}$$

$KnowledgeState(t^a)$ is dynamic and changes over the time, for new empirical experiences are collected by agent $a$. It needs to be stressed that in each time point $t^a$ the content of $KnowledgeState(t^a)$ determines the overall scope of the result of agent $a$ cognition realised up to the time point $t^a$. From the point of view of cognitive and phenomenological theory of self contained atom the set $KnowledgeState(t^a)$ is the only source of the subjectively experienced logic relation between $P_{i,1}$ and $P_{i,2}$. In particular, this set is necessary to determine if both properties $P_{i,1}$ and $P_{i,2}$ be combined with either logic disjunction or logic alternative in an external description of an object $o_1, o_2, ..., o_m$. Any formal semantics for knowledge formulas $K_a(\phi_1 \vee \phi_2)$ and $K_a(\phi_1 \underline{\vee} \phi_2)$ both spoken at the time point $t^a$ needs to be in a strict relation with the overall content of $KnowledgeState(t^a)$.

Let us now define an example of a simple logic language that makes it possible to present at least some rules of combining cognitive and phenomenological theories of self – contained atom objects with a simple BDI model. Let us start with the language $L_B$. Its formulas can take individual modal states of the world as their model structures [8,21].

Definition. (Syntax for $L_B$, $L_{B\neg}$ and $L_{B\neg\wedge}$) The basic logic language $L_B$ and its extensions $L_{B\neg}$ and $L_{B\neg\wedge}$ are given as follows. Let the symbols $o_1, o_2, ..., o_p$ denote particular objects from the class $N$, and $p_{i,j(i=1,2,...,n;j=1,2)}$ be predicates related to properties $P_{i,j(i=1,2,...,n;j=1,2)}$, respectively.

R1. For each s=1,2,...,$p$, $i$=1,2,...,$m$, j=1,2, formula $p_{i,j}(o_s) \in L_B$ and $\neg p_{i,j}(o_s) \in L_{B\neg}$.

R2. If $\phi$, $\varphi \in L_B \cup L_{B\neg}$, then $\phi \wedge \varphi \in L_{B\neg\wedge}$.

Definition. (Semantics for $L_B$) Each modal state can be used as a model structure for formulas of $L_B$, $L_{B\neg}$ and $L_{B\neg\wedge}$. Let a particular model structure $state$ be equal to

$$<N, B^+_1(t^a), B^+_2(t^a), ..., B^+_m(t^a), W^+_{1,1}(t^a), W^+_{1,2}(t^a), ..., W^+_{n,1}(t^a), W^+_{n,2}(t^a)>.$$

SR1. For each s=1,2,...,$p$, $i$=1,2,...,$m$, j=1,2, the relation $state \models_B p_{i,j}(o_s)$ holds iff

$o_s \in W^+_{i,j}(t^a)$.

SR2. For any s=1,2,...,$p$, $i$=1,2,...,$m$, j=1,2, the relation $state \models_B \neg p_{i,j}(o_s)$ holds iff it is not true that $state \models_B p_{i,j}(o_s)$.

SR3. For each formula $\phi \wedge \varphi \in L_{B\neg\wedge}$ the relation $state \models_B \phi \wedge \varphi$ holds iff both $state \models_B \phi$ and $state \models_B \varphi$ hold.

It is now possible to give a formal counterpart for $L_B$ extension that includes epistemic formulas with knowledge operators as well as logic disjunctions and alternatives.

Definition. (Syntax for $L_E$) Let a simple epistemic extension $L_E$ of the basic language $L_B$ be given as follows. For each s=1,2,...,$p$, $i$=1,2,...,$m$,

R1. $p_{i,1}(o_s) \vee p_{i,2}(o_s) \in L_E$ and $p_{i,1}(o_s) \underline{\vee} p_{i,2}(o_s) \in L_E$.

R2. $K_a(p_{i,1}(o_s) \vee p_{i,2}(o_s)) \in L_E$, $K_a(p_{i,1}(o_s) \underline{\vee} p_{i,2}(o_s)) \in L_E$,

R3. $L_E$ is the least set of formulas constructed with the rules R1-R2.

Our goal is now to formally describe an internal state of agent $a$ that requires formulas of $L_E$ as a logic representation of agent $a$ knowledge.

For each profile $EncProfile(t^a)$, each pair of properties $P_{i,1}$, $P_{i,2}$ and each object $o_s$, let us define the following sets of modal states of $W$:

$$Z_{Y\text{-}Y}(P_{i,1},P_{i,2},t^a,o_s)=\{s \in ModalStates(t^a): s \models_B p_{i,1}(o_s) \text{ and } s \models_B p_{i,2}(o_s)\},$$

$$Z_{Y\text{-}N}(P_{i,1},P_{i,2},t^a,o_s)=\{s \in ModalStates(t^a): s \models_B p_{i,1}(o_s) \text{ and } s \models_B \neg p_{i,2}(o_s)\},$$

$$Z_{N\text{-}Y}(P_{i,1},P_{i,2},t^a,o_s)=\{s \in ModalStates(t^a): s \models_B \neg p_{i,1}(o_s) \text{ and } s \models_B p_{i,2}(o_s)\},$$

$$Z_{N\text{-}N}(P_{i,1},P_{i,2},t^a,o_s)=\{s \in ModalStates(t^a): s \models_B \neg p_{i,1}(o_s) \text{ and } s \models_B \neg p_{i,2}(o_s)\}.$$

The following remarks can be made: The set $\{Z_{Y\text{-}Y}(P_{i,1},P_{i,2},t^a,o_s), Z_{Y\text{-}N}(P_{i,1},P_{i,2},t^a,o_s), Z_{N\text{-}Y}(P_{i,1},P_{i,2},t^a,o_s), Z_{N\text{-}N}(P_{i,1},P_{i,2},t^a,o_s)\}$ is a partition of set $ModalStates(t^a)$. It can be said at the informal level that members of $Z_{Y\text{-}Y}(P_{i,1},P_{i,2},t^a,o_s)$, $Z_{Y\text{-}N}(P_{i,1},P_{i,2},t^a,o_s)$, $Z_{N\text{-}Y}(P_{i,1},P_{i,2},t^a,o_s)$, $Z_{N\text{-}N}(P_{i,1},P_{i,2},t^a,o_s)$ produces conjunctions $p_{i,1}(o_s) \wedge p_{i,2}(o_s)$, $p_{i,1}(o_s) \wedge \neg p_{i,2}(o_s)$, $\neg p_{i,1}(o_s) \wedge p_{i,2}(o_s)$ and $\neg p_{i,1}(o_s) \wedge \neg p_{i,2}(o_s)$ as the description of its content, respectively.

Let us now notice that in order to very the validity of rules that support the production of logic disjunctions and alternatives these basic profiles are important, for which one of $Z_{Y\text{-}Y}(P_{i,1},P_{i,2},t^a,o_s)$, $Z_{Y\text{-}N}(P_{i,1},P_{i,2},t^a,o_s)$, $Z_{N\text{-}Y}(P_{i,1},P_{i,2},t^a,o_s)$ or $Z_{N\text{-}N}(P_{i,1},P_{i,2},t^a,o_s)$ is equal to $ModalStates(t^a)$. These profiles can be used to prove the real nature of the logic relation between $P_{i,1}$ and

$P_{i,2}$. In these situations the following conditions are true:

$$Z_{Y\text{-}Y}(P_{i,1},P_{i,2},t^a,o_s)=ModalStates(t^a) \text{ iff } o_s\in P^+_{i,1}(t^a) \text{ and } o_s\in P^+_{i,2}(t^a),$$

$$Z_{Y\text{-}N}(P_{i,1},P_{i,2},t^a,o_s)=ModalStates(t^a) \text{ iff } o_s\in P^+_{i,1}(t^a) \text{ and } o_s\in P^-_{i,2}(t^a),$$

$$Z_{N\text{-}Y}(P_{i,1},P_{i,2},t^a,o_s)=ModalStates(t^a) \text{ iff } o_s\in P^-_{i,1}(t^a) \text{ and } o_s\in P^+_{i,2}(t^a),$$

$$Z_{N\text{-}N}(P_{i,1},P_{i,2},t^a,o_s)=ModalStates(t^a) \text{ iff } o_s\in P^-_{i,1}(t^a) \text{ and } o_s\in P^-_{i,2}(t^a).$$

Let us now use the above concepts to define a semantic consistency between formulas of $L_E$ and internal states of agent $a$:

Definition. Relations $KnowledgeState(t^a) \mid=_E p_{i,1}(o_s)\vee p_{i,2}(o_s)$ and $KnowledgeState(t^a) \mid=_E K_a(p_{i,1}(o_s)\vee p_{i,2}(o_s))$ hold iff the following conditions are fulfilled:

1. Relations $o_s\in P^{\pm}_{i,1}(t^a)$ and $o_s\in P^{\pm}_{i,2}(t^a)$ hold.
2. There is at least one object $o_j\in N$ and at least one time point $t^a_1<^{TM}t^a$ such that $Z_{Y\text{-}Y}(P_{i,1},P_{i,2},t_1^a,o_j)=ModalStates(t^a_1)$.
3. There is at least one object $o_j\in N$ and at least one time point $t^a_2<^{TM}t^a$ such that $Z_{Y\text{-}N}(P_{i,1},P_{i,2},t_2^a,o_j)=ModalStates(t^a_2)$.
4. There is at least one object $o_j\in N$ and at least one time point $t^a_3<^{TM}t^a$ such that $Z_{N\text{-}Y}(P_{i,1},P_{i,2},t_3^a,o_j)=ModalStates(t^a_3)$.
5. There is no object $o_j\in N$ and no time point $t^a_4<^{TM}t^a$ such that $Z_{N\text{-}N}(P_{i,1},P_{i,2},t_4^a,o_j)=ModalStates(t^a_4)$.

Definition. Relations $KnowledgeState(t^a) \mid=_E p_{i,1}(o_s)\underline{\vee} p_{i,2}(o_s)$ and $KnowledgeState(t^a) \mid=_E K_a(p_{i,1}(o_s)\underline{\vee} p_{i,2}(o_s))$ hold iff the following conditions are fulfilled:

1. Relations $o_s\in P^{\pm}_{i,1}(t^a)$ and $o_s\in P^{\pm}_{i,2}(t^a)$ hold.
2. There is no object $o_j\in N$ and no time point $t^a_1<^{TM}t^a$ such that $Z_{Y\text{-}Y}(P_{i,1},P_{i,2},t_1^a,o_j)=ModalStates(t^a_1)$.
3. There is at least one object $o_j\in N$ and at least one time point $t^a_2<^{TM}t^a$ such that $Z_{Y\text{-}N}(P_{i,1},P_{i,2},t_2^a,o_j)=ModalStates(t^a_2)$.
4. There is at least one object $o_j\in N$ and at least one time point $t^a_3<^{TM}t^a$ such that $Z_{N\text{-}Y}(P_{i,1},P_{i,2},t_3^a,o_j)=ModalStates(t^a_3)$.
5. There is no object $o_j\in N$ and no time point $t^a_4<^{TM}t^a$ such that

   $Z_{N\text{-}N}(P_{i,1},P_{i,2},t_4^a,o_j)=ModalStates(t^a_4)$.

## 5 Conclusions

This presentation gives an example of an original way of analysing the complex relation of cognition results stored (encapsulated) in an intentional agent and an external logic representation of these results, when the latter comes in the form of disjunction or alternative (sometime with knowledge operator). Formulas that have been considered above are relatively simple. However, even in this case one can see that the nature of the result between internal and external representations of knowledge is realised as a complex network of semantic interconnections.

These results are with strict relation to comments on possible worlds semantics and a need of their further clarification [7] and should be understood as a first step towards the construction of a general non-extensional semantics for BDI knowledge formulas. They can also be understood as a part of the so-called formal analysis of cognition proposed by epistemology [7,23,24]. This text covers only a very narrow part of a broad area of research problems that, at first, are strictly within the theory of intelligent systems and, at second, need to be solved for practical reasons. A natural extension to this research is to consider disjunctions and alternatives of at least three member properties, construct formal semantics for similar belief formulas, apply the same method of analysis to higher level concepts, and integrate other connectives into the model. The foundation for this way of studying the semantics of important BDI and intentional concepts has been given in [12] and partially developed in [11,13,14].

## References


1. Chlewiński, Z.: *Mind. A Dynamic Organisation of the Cognitive System.* Wyd, Nauk. PWN, Warsaw (1999) (in Polish)
2. Cohen, P.R., Levesque, H.J.: Intention is choice with commitment. *Artificial Intelligence*, 42, (1990) 213-269
3. Denett, D.C.: *Kinds of minds. Toward an understanding of consciousness.* Orion Publishing Group Ltd. UK (1996)
4. Fauconnier, G.: *Mappings in thought and language.* Cambridge University Press Cambridge (1997)
5. Halpern, J., Moses, Y.: A guide to completeness and complexity for modal logics of knowledge and belief. *Artificial Intelligence*, 54, (1992) 319-379
6. Heidegger, M.: *Sein und Zeit.* (1927)
7. Hintikka, J.: Epistemic Logic and the Methods of Philosophical Analysis. *Australian Journal of Philosophy,* 46, (1968) 37-51

8. Hunter, G.: *Metalogic. An Introduction to the Metatheory of Standard First Order Logic.* University of California Press, Berkeley Los Angeles (1971)

9. Ingarden, R.: *Formale Ontologie. Teil 1. Form und Wesen.* Max Niemeyer Verlag, Tübingen (1965)

10. Jaskóła, J.: An Alternatives for the Facts - Possible Worlds. An interpretation of the Philosophy by M. Foucault, L. Wittgenstein and E. Husserl. in the Context of the Concept of Possible Worlds. *Filozofia* XXV (1995) 77-90 (in Polish)

11. Katarzyniak, R.: *Defining the relation between intentional and implementation - oriented levels of agents models.* In: Grzech, A., Wilimowska, Z.: Proc. ISAT'2000 Szklarska Poręba Poland, Wroc. Univ. Tech. Wrocław (2000) 208-216

12. Katarzyniak, R.: *A multiagent system for the delegation of management in distributed processing environments.* PhD Thesis. Part 2. *Semantic preliminaries of the model.* Tech, Rep. PRE No. 3, Institute of Control and Systems Engineering Wroc. Univ. Tech. Wrocław (1999) (in Polish)

13. Katarzyniak, R.: *An intentional model of the agent's knowledge of current state of the world.* In: Bubnicki, Z., Grzech, A.: Proc. *IV Konferencja Inżynieria Wiedzy i Systemy Ekspertowe.* Tom 1., Wroc. Univ. Techn., Wrocław (2000) 142-151 (in Polish)

14. Katarzyniak, R.: *Relational and Logical methods of formalizing intentional models of agent's knowledge of the current state of the world.* Tech, Rep. SPR No. 4, Institute of Control and Systems Engineering Wroc. Univ. Tech. Wrocław (2000) (in Polish)

15. Kripke, S.A.: Semantical analysis of modal logic I: normal modal propositional calculi. *Zeitschrift für Math. Logik und Grundlagen der Math.*, 9, (1963) 67-96

16. Lindern, B. van, Hoek, W. van der, Meyer, J.-J. CH.: Formalising abilities and opportunities of Agents. *Fundamenta Informatica*, 34, (1998) 53-101

17. Newell, A.: *The unified theories of cognition.* Harvard University Press Cambridge (1990)

18. Rao, A.S., Georgeff, M.P.: Modelling rational agents within a BDI-architecture. In: *Proc. Knowl. Repr. '91*, San Mateo, CA., 1991, Morgan Kauffman Pub. (1991)

19. Singh, M.: *Multiagent systems: a theoretical framework for intentions, know-how, and communications.* Springer-Verlag Heilderberg (1994)

20. Tarski, A.: Der Warheitsbegriff in den formalisierten Sprachen. *Studia Philosophica*, 1, (1935) 261-405

21. Trąbka, J.: *The Soul of the Brain.* Wyd. WAM, Cracow (2000) (in Polish)

22. Woleński, J.: *Epistemology. Part I. A historical overview and some metatheoretical problems.* Aureus, Cracow (2000) (in Polish)

23. Woleński, J.: *Methamatematics and Epistemology.* PWN, Warsaw (1993) (in Polish)

# Information Dimension of Population's Attractor and Population's Entropy

Paweł Kieś

Institute of Fundamental Technological Research,
Polish Academy of Sciences,
21 Świętokrzyska Str., 00-049 Warsaw, Poland,
phone: (+48)(22)8261281 ext. 144, fax: (+48)(22)8269815,
e-mail: pkies@ippt.gov.pl

**Abstract.** Some tools for description of chaotic dynamics are applied to investigate the work of a binary genetic algorithm ($\mathcal{BGA}$). The method for determining a population's attractor is shown. Attractor's information dimension is taken as a measure of the state of $\mathcal{BGA}$'s activity. The equivalence between the information dimension of a population's attractor and the entropy of related bit positions in the population is proven and confirmed experimentally.

**Keywords.** binary genetic algorithm, optimization, chaotic dynamics, attractor, information dimension, scheme.

## 1 Introduction

The genetic algorithm (GA) is a kind of an evolutionary algorithm. It usually is applied as an optimization method. The reader can find a good explanation of the basic ideas of the GA, as well as many related problems in the Michalewicz's book [8].

Since GAs are known, many researchers try to understand and explain how they work. One knows many papers that present mathematical models of simplified or modified GAs, for example a paper [10] that analyses a behaviour of a GA with a continuous population. Also one can find excellent partial models of elements of GA, for example papers [7] and [3], where models of the generalized crossover operation are proposed. Another well known model of dynamics of GAs uses Markov chains as description of the job of genetic operators: crossover and mutation [12].

In this paper we propose an approach taken from chaotic dynamics analysis. We apply it to the binary GA ($\mathcal{BGA}$). We show that we can treat $\mathcal{BGA}$'s execution as a trajectory composed of strange attractors being subsets of the search space. We can investigate such trajectories using tools from chaotic dynamics in order to measure the $\mathcal{BGA}$'s activity. This approach can explain the role of genetic operators and a selection not only separately but also the way how they cooperate and interact [1].

In Section 2 we explain how we describe the $\mathcal{BGA}$'s execution as a trajectory. Next, in Section 3 we introduce the idea of the population's attractor. In Section 4 we define set's information dimension for continuous and discrete sets. Next, in Section 5 we explain how we can interpret the information dimension of a population's attractor. In Sections 6 and 7 we describe realized experiments and draw our conclusions.

## 2 Genetic algorithm's principles

First, let us state some assumptions about our $\mathcal{BGA}$. Its aim is to find such an element of the discrete search space $X$ that maximizes the fitness function $f : X \to \mathbb{R}$. Each element of $X$ is coded into an $N$-bit chromosome that is an element of the set $\mathcal{B} = \{0,1\}^N$, called the code space. The coding is realized by a bijection $\Psi : X \to \mathcal{B}$ called a coding function. The algorithm operates on $M$-element populations that are vectors from the set $\mathcal{B}^M$.

We assume that the chromosomes from the current population describe the current state of the $\mathcal{BGA}$. So the state is given by the current information content of a population as defined below.

**Definition 1.** Let $G \in \mathcal{B}^M$ be an $M$-element population. An information content is defined as a vector of probabilities $p(G) = (p_{\text{one}}(i|G))_{i=1,\dots,N}$, where $p_{\text{one}}(i|G) = \frac{1}{M}\sum_{j=1}^{M} b_i^j$ and $b_i^j$ is the $i$-th bit in $j$-th chromosome in $G$. □

The information content is an extension of a so-called genetic pool. It describes the "genetic material" contained in a given population, i.e. the probability distribution of chromosomes that we can construct by combining randomly bits from related positions of chromosomes in a given population.

**Definition 2.** For a given chromosome $\underline{b} = (b_1, \dots, b_N) \in \mathcal{B}$ and population $G \in \mathcal{B}^M$ we define the exploration probability as

$$p(\underline{b}|G) = \prod_{i=1}^{N} p_i(b_i|G), \quad \text{where } p_i(b|G) = \begin{cases} p_{\text{one}}(i|G), & \text{for b=1;} \\ 1 - p_{\text{one}}(i|G), & \text{for b=0.} \end{cases} \tag{1}$$

□

Let us notice the we can easily determine the exploration probability for a given point $x \in X$ in the search space and for a given population $G$ as

$$p(x|G) = p(\Psi(x)|G). \tag{2}$$

A $\mathcal{BGA}$ is a probabilistic optimization algorithm, so it does not ensure that each its execution finds the optimum. The algorithm takes many random decisions during its execution. Each such a decision can be treated as a realization of a certain random variable, and each particular execution is fully described by a sequence of values of these random variables. This causes that it is difficult to investigate the $\mathcal{BGA}$'s activity basing on its single execution, because it can vary in a very wide range. Also a simple averaging of many executions is not a good solution because we lose easily synchronization between related stages of executions. The possible solution is to identify somehow the current state of the $\mathcal{BGA}$'s execution and to average measured parameters of related states for many executions.

The introduced above idea of an information content can help us in such an identification. We can treat a single $\mathcal{BGA}$'s execution as a trajectory of populations (see Fig. 2). We have no tools for analysis of trajectories composed of vectors of chromosomes, but for usually used search spaces we can transform each population into a vector of points in $\mathbb{R}^K$. We will investigate such trajectories by tools from chaotic dynamics.

## 3 Population's attractor

We can represent an information content in the domain of the search space $X$ also. In order to do this we apply an idea from Kolonko [7]. He defines the generalized crossover operator as below and shows that it preserves the genetic material contained in parent chromosomes.

**Definition 3.** We define the generalized crossover operator as a mapping $c_u : \mathcal{B}^2 \to \mathcal{B}^2$, where $u \in U$ is a particular crossover operation and $U$ is the set of all possible crossovers. □

For example in the one-point crossover we assume that $U = \{1, \ldots, N\}$ is the set of all possible crossing positions and the value of $u$ is taken randomly from $U$.

```
let A_G := ∅
for w := 1 to W do
    let b_1, b_2 be randomly chosen from G
    let u be randomly chosen from U
    let (b'_1, b'_2) := c_u(b_1, b_2)
    let A_G := A_G ∪ Ψ^{-1}(b'_1) ∪ Ψ^{-1}(b'_2)
end
```

**Fig. 1.** An algoritm that estimates an attractor $A_G$ for a population $G$, where $W$ – number of iterations (higher gives a better estimation), $\Psi^{-1} : \mathcal{B} \to X$ – decoding function, $c_u : \mathcal{B}^2 \to \mathcal{B}^2$ – a generalized crossover operator (see Def. 3).

We construct a simple algorithm based on this idea, shown at Fig. 1. Using it we find a subset $A_G \subset X$ related to the information content of a given population $G$. The received discrete set has similar features to a set well-known form chaotic dynamics: a strange attractor. One can see that its local density depends on the probability of receiving related chromosomes from the generalized crossover and it can be estimated from (2).

The attractor is a basic notion in chaotic dynamics. Recently this branch of knowledge is more and more popular. The reader can find fundamental information on it in many works, e.g. in books [2] and [9].

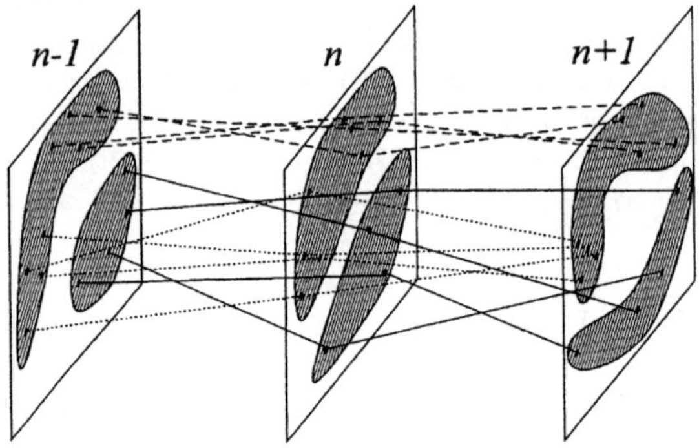


**Fig. 2.** Two population's attractors (lined areas) for three trajectories of a certain $\mathcal{BGA}$, where $n$ is a population number, $M = 4$ – population size and $X \subset \mathbb{R}^2$ – search space. The executions marked by dashed and dotted lines belong to the same attractor. The one marked by a solid line belongs to the other attractor.

We can think of a population's attractor as a Poincaré section of a $\mathcal{BGA}$'s trajectory, while we treat solutions coded by a given population as a set of at most $M$ points in a phase space $X$ and a sequence of such sets resulted from a single execution of the $\mathcal{BGA}$ – as a trajectory. One can see this idea at Fig. 2.

## 4 Attractor's information dimension

The most important feature of a set is its dimension. In the case of an ordinary set the value of a dimension is a natural number. But the dimension of a strange attractor can be a real number.

In the literature one can find many kinds of a dimension of a set (see Baker and Gollub [2]). All of them provide similar information. The main difference between them is their sensitivity to the density distribution of the measured set. We will be especially interested in the capacity and information dimension because they can be most useful for our aims. We define them below for continuous sets (see Falconer [4]). The notion of a dimension of a set can give interesting information when applied in a special way to discrete sets so we show how to do that [2].

**Definition 4.** Let $A \subset X$ and $X \subset \mathbb{R}^K$ be a $K$-dimensional cube. Let us assume that we cover $X$ by $C$ disjoint $K$-dimensional boxes $X_i \subset X$ and $\epsilon$ is the length of an edge of each box. We define the information dimension of $A$ as

$$d_I(A) = -\lim_{\epsilon\to 0} \frac{H(A,\epsilon)}{\log_2 \epsilon}, \tag{3}$$

where

$$H(A,\epsilon) = -\sum_{i=1}^{C} p_i(A,\epsilon)\log_2 p_i(A,\epsilon) \tag{4}$$

is $A$'s entropy for a given $\epsilon$, $p_i(A,\epsilon)$ is probability that a point $x \in X_i \cap A$. □

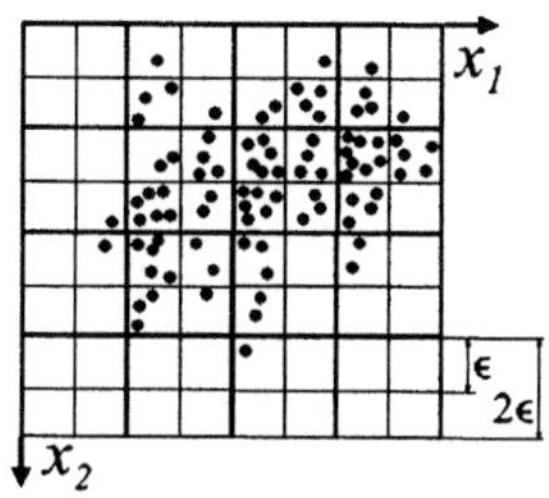


**Fig. 3.** Box covering of an example set $X$ for $K = 2$ for two sizes of a box: $\epsilon$ and $2\epsilon$.

We need to derive a special formula for a discrete set $X$ that approximates the information dimension for a given $\epsilon$. First, we can assume that in Def. 4

$$p_i(A,\epsilon) = \frac{|X_i \cap A|}{|A|}, \tag{5}$$

where $|A| = WM$ (see Fig. 3) and $W$ is the number of iterations of the algorithm at Fig. 1.

After simple calculations [6] we get

$$d_I(A,\epsilon) = H(A,\epsilon) - H(A,2\epsilon). \tag{6}$$

One can notice that the formula (6) can be applied also to continuous sets, but it works differently in both cases, as you can see at Fig. 4.

## 5 Meaning of a set's dimension in the $\mathcal{BGA}$

### 5.1 Coding search space into chromosomes

Now we will show the meaning of set's dimensions in the $\mathcal{BGA}$. First, let us look closer at the way how elements of the search space $X$ are encoded into chromosomes.

We will assume that $X$ is a $K$-dimensional cube, as in Def. 4, i.e.

$$X = \langle x_{1min}, x_{1max}\rangle \times \ldots \times \langle x_{Kmin}, x_{Kmax}\rangle \subset \mathbb{R}^K, \tag{7}$$

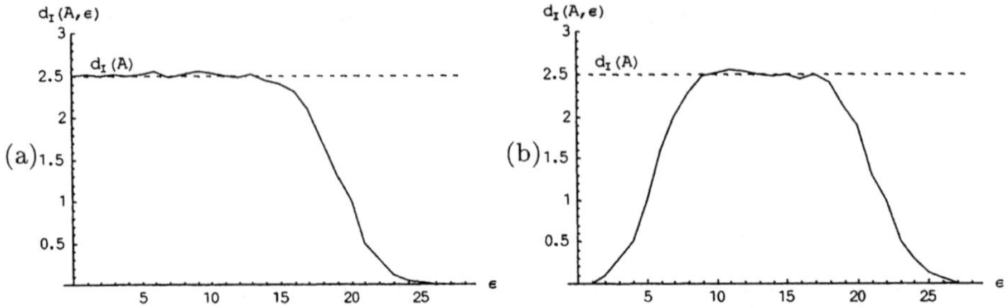


**Fig. 4.** Examplary typical graphs of $d_I(A, \epsilon)$ for a continuous (a) and discrete (b) set $A$. Both graphs have zero for a higher $\epsilon$ when the whole set $A$ is contained in one box. The graph (b) has zero for a lower $\epsilon$ when boxes contain either a single $A$'s element or none.

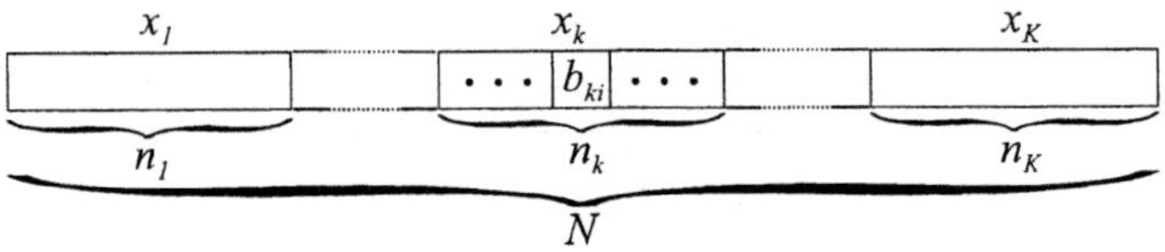


**Fig. 5.** Coding of solutions into chromosomes.

where $k$-th component of $X$ is encoded at $n_k$ bits, so we have

$$\mathcal{B} = \{0,1\}^N = \{0,1\}^{n_1} \times \ldots \times \{0,1\}^{n_K}, \tag{8}$$

and for convenience we introduce a new indexing of bits by a pair of numbers as shown at Fig. 5.

We cover $X$ by boxes using the following rule. We use $r$ most significant bits of the binary code of each component of $X$ as the identificator of a box, thus we got totally $C = 2^{Kr}$ disjoint boxes (see Def. 4), so we can write (8) as

$$\mathcal{B} = \{0,1\}^r \times \{0,1\}^{n_1-r} \times \ldots \times \{0,1\}^r \times \{0,1\}^{n_K-r}. \tag{9}$$

Then each box is equivalent to a scheme

$$\underline{\beta}_i = (\beta^i_{11}, \ldots, \beta^i_{1r}, *, \ldots, *, \ldots, \beta^i_{K1}, \ldots, \beta^i_{Kr}, *, \ldots, *) \in \mathcal{S}, \tag{10}$$

where $\mathcal{S} = \{0,1,*\}^N$ is a set of $N$-element schemes [8]. The value $r$ defines the size of a box as

$$\epsilon_k = \frac{x_{k\,max} - x_{k\,min}}{2^r}, \qquad \text{for} \quad k = 1, \ldots, K. \tag{11}$$

Thus we admit different lengths of box edges for each component of $X$, not influencing the correctness of our reasoning.

### 5.2 Information dimension and bit position's entropy

We will apply (4) to a set $A_G \subset X$ generated by the algorithm at Fig. 1 being an attractor for a given population $G \in \mathcal{B}^M$.

Let us note that the events $x \in X_i \cap A$, mentioned in Def. 4, are cartesian products of $Kr$ independent binary events related to fixed positions in schemes $\underline{\beta}_i$. So using Def. 1 we can write (4) in the form

$$H(A,r) = \sum_{k=1}^{K} \sum_{j=1}^{r} H_p(k,j|G), \tag{12}$$

where

$$H_p(k,j|G) = p_{\mathsf{one}}(k,j|G) \log_2 p_{\mathsf{one}}(k,j|G) + \\ + (1 - p_{\mathsf{one}}(k,j|G)) \log_2 (1 - p_{\mathsf{one}}(k,j|G)) \,. \tag{13}$$

is the entropy of $j$-th bit position of the coding of $k$-th component of $X$ (see Fig. 5) for a population $G$, and the symbol $p_{\mathsf{one}}$ comes from Def. 2.

Finishing, we receive from (6) that

$$d_I(A_G,r) = H(A_G,r) - H(A_G,r-1) = \sum_{k=1}^{K} H_p(k,r|G). \tag{14}$$

**Conclusion 1** *The above result means that the information dimension of a population's attractor for a given $r$ equals to the information contained in $r$-th bits of each component code, and that this information is lost when we reduce the number of bits indexing boxes from $r$ to $r-1$ (see Fig. 6).* □

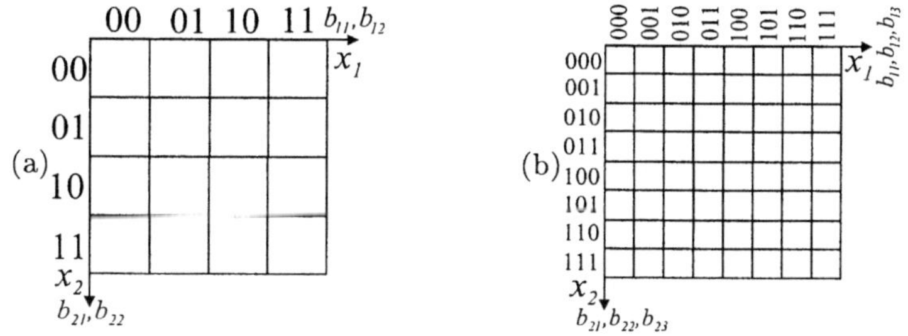


**Fig. 6.** An example of determining $d_I$ for a certain population $G$ and its attractor $A_G$: boxes for $r=2$ (a) and 3 (b), number of $X$'s components $K=2$, and $n_1 = n_2 = 4$, so from (14) we get $d_I(A_G,3) = H_p(1,2|G) + H_p(2,2|G)$.

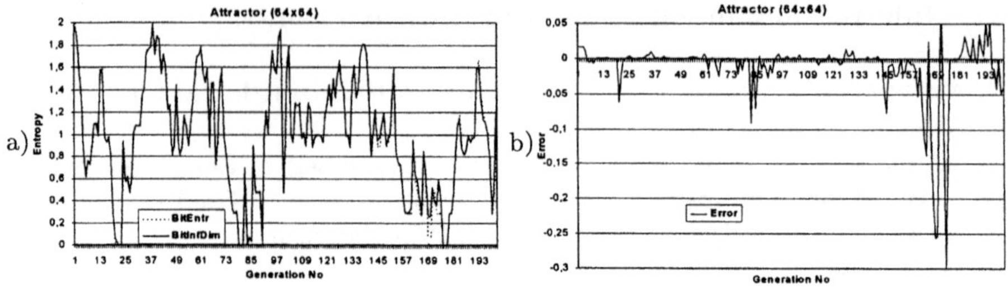


**Fig. 7.** A comparison of the information dimension with the entropy of related bits for a $64 \times 64$ attractor.

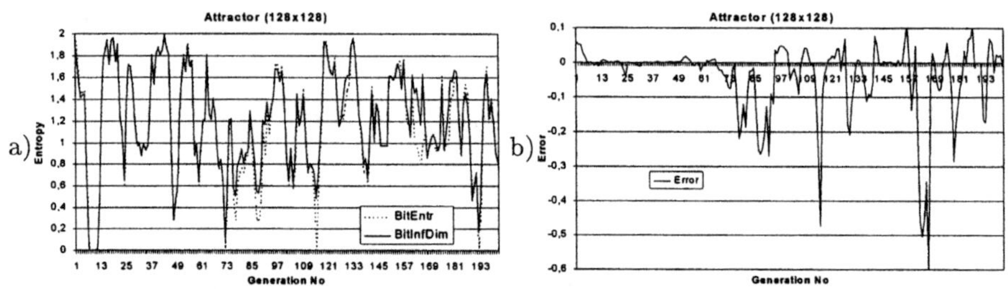


**Fig. 8.** A comparison of the information dimension with the entropy of related bits for a $128 \times 128$ attractor.

## 6 The experiments and results

We investigated a basic $\mathcal{BGA}$ with the elitism [11]. We assumed that the mutation probability $p_m = 0.01$, the crossover probability $p_c = 0.5$, the population size $M = 20$, and a constant number of generations GenNo $= 200$.

The search space was $X = \langle -2, 2 \rangle^2$, and its elements were coded by 32-bit chromosomes. The fitness function was a very simple one:

$$f(x_1, x_2) = -\left[(x_1 - 1)^2 + (x_2 - 0.5)^2\right]$$

with the global maximum at $f(1, 0.5) = 0$.

In order to estimate populations' attractors we determined the union of $W = 10000$ times randomly crossed chromosomes from the measured population, according to the algorithm at Fig. 1. The range of each of two components of the set $X$ was discretized by 64 ($r = 6$) and 128 ($r = 7$) intervals. You can find examplary images with population's attractors in [5].

As a result we present at Fig. 7a and 8a graphs of attractor's information dimension in a function of the generation number determined during a certain $\mathcal{BGA}$'s execution compared with entropy of related bits (6th and 7th). We also present the difference between related values at Fig. 7b and 8b.

The reader can find a detailed discussion on how the attractor's dimension changes during a $\mathcal{BGA}$'s execution in [5].

## 7 Conclusions

The graphs presented at Fig. 7 and 8 confirm our theoretical reasoning realized in Section 5, especially the Conclusion 1. We see that the difference between the two graphs is very small at the begining and increases in finishing populations. The cause of the increase is an error in reconstructing a population's attractor by the algorithm at Fig. 1. We suppose that the value of $W$ should be higher when solutions are concentrated in few boxes only as well as when the number of boxes $C$ is higher.

The received result is very useful because it facilitates an application of tools well known from the chaos dynamics into $\mathcal{BGA}$ examinations. The algorithm at Fig. 1 has a high computational complexity because of intevsive using of the decoding function $\Psi^{-1}$, but thanks to approaches similar to ours we can do much simpler computations in the domain of chromosomes instead. It seems that the presented approach can be useful in investigation of the $\mathcal{BGA}$'s dynamics, but it needs further research.

### Acknowledgements

This material is based upon work supported by the grant 8 T11C 003 16 from the Polish State Committee for Scientific Research (KBN) in 1999-2001.

## References

1. Bäck T.: "The Interaction of Mutation Rate, Selection, and Self-Adaptation within a Genetic Algorithm", *Parallel Problem Solving from Nature* Vol. 2, pp. 85-94, Amsterdam, North Holland, 1992.
2. Baker G.L., Gollub J.P.: *Chaotic Dynamics: an Introduction*, Cambridge Univ. Press, Cambridge, 1996.
3. DeJong K.A., Spears W.M.: "A Formal Analysis of the Role of Multi-point Crossover in Genetic Algorithms", *Annals of Mathematics and AI Journal*, Vol. 5, No. 1, pp. 1-26, J.C. Baltzer AG Scientific Publishing Co., 1992.
4. Falconer K.J.: "Fractal geometry", *Math. Found. Appl.*, John Wiley, Chichester, pp. 15-25, 1990.
5. Kieś P.: "Dimension of attractors generated by a genetic algorithm", *Procs. of the IX-th International Symposium on Intelligent Information Systems*, pp. 40-45, Bystra, Poland, June 2000.
6. Kieś P.: "Meaning of the information dimension of a population's attractor in a binary GA", *IEEE Trans. on Evolutionary Computation*, 2001 (sent to print).
7. Kolonko M.: "A Generalized Crossover Operation for Genetic Algorithms", *Complex Systems*, pp. 177-191, Vol. 9, 1995.
8. Michalewicz Z.: *Genetic Algorithms + Data Structures = Evolution Programs*, Springer-Verlag, Berlin, 1996.
9. Ott E.: *Chaos in Dynamical Systems*, Cambridge Univ. Press, Cambridge, 1996.

10. Qi T., Palmieri F.: "Theoretical Analysis of Evolutionary Algorithms with an Infinite Population Size in Continuous Space, Part II: Analysis of the Diversification Role of Crossover", *IEEE Trans. of Neural Networks*, Vol. 5, No. 1, 1994.
11. Rudolph G.: "Convergence analysis of canonical genetic algorithms", *IEEE Trans. on Neural Networks*, Special Issue on Evolutionary Computation, Vol. 5, No. 1, 1994.
12. Stadler P.F.: "Towards a Theory of Landscapes", *Complex Systems and Binary Networks* edited by Lopez-Pena et al., Springer-Verlag, 1995.

# Quantifier Handling Issues in Computer-Oriented Intuitionistic Calculi

Alexander Lyaletski

Cybernetics Department, Taras Shevchenko Kyiv National University,
2, Glushkov avenue, building 6, 03022 Kyiv, Ukraine,
e-mail: lav@tc.unicyb.kiev.ua

**Abstract.** A new computer-oriented sequent calculus for 1st-order intuitionistic logic is described. The calculus demonstrates the possible method of the optimization of the procedure of quantifier rule applications in the inference search process. Our main objective is to show that by using the original notion of admissible substitutions, a computer-oriented logical inference technique can be created, which does not require analogs of the preliminary skolemization of formulas in intuitionistic logic and which has rather high inference search efficiency. Some results on the soundness and completeness of the calculus are given.

**Keywords**: completeness, quantifier rule, inference, intuitionistic logic, sequent calculus, soundness, substitution

## 1 Introduction

Investigations in computer-oriented reasoning gave rise to the appearance of various methods for the proof search in 1st-order logics. Particularly, Gentzen calculi were suggested. But their practical application as a logical inference technique (without preliminary skolemization) for intelligent systems has not received wide use: preference is usually given to resolution-type methods. This is explained by higher efficiency of resolution-type methods as compared to Gentzen calculi, which is mainly connected with different possible orders of quantifier rule applications and with formula duplications in the calculi while resolution-type methods, due to skolemization, are free of this deficiency.

At the same time, a deduction process in Gentzen calculi reflects sufficiently well natural theorem-proving methods which, as a rule, do not include preliminary formula skolemization so that reasonings are performed within the scope of the signature of an initial theory. This feature of Gentzen calculi becomes still more important when attempts to construct efficient non-classical calculi are made, because a traditional (resolution) approach to the construction of the computer-oriented calculi requires introducing some analogs of skolemization in the calculi that is often impossible to do.

When quantifier rules are applied, the substitution of selected terms for variables is made. To do this step of deduction sound, certain restrictions are put on the substitution. The substitution, satisfying these restrictions, is said to be admissible. Three kinds of the notion of an admissible substitution can be extracted: a Gentzen's standard notion (taken in the form of [1]), a Kanger's notion [2] and a notion suggested in [3]. Note here that the third notion has successfully been used in goal-oriented calculi of so-called a-sequents [4]. But the papers [3,4] have been concerned classical logic only. We show below that the notion of the admissibility from [4] can be easily built-in into standard 1st-order intuitionistic sequent calculi. To concentrate our attention on peculiarities of the notion, we take the Getzen's original calculus $LJ$ (see, for example, [5] or [6]) and construct its certain modification.

## 2 Remarks on the notions of admissible substitutions

Standard quantifier rules, substituting the terms of arbitrary structure when applied "from top to bottom", are usually of the following form [1], regardless of a logic considered ( $G$ [1], $LK$ [5,6], or intuitionistic calculus $LJ$ [5,6]):

*Quantifier Rules*

$(\forall \Rightarrow)_G$-rule:

$$\frac{M, \forall x F \Rightarrow G}{M, F|_t^x \Rightarrow G}$$

$(\Rightarrow \exists)_G$-rule:

$$\frac{M \Rightarrow \exists x F}{M \Rightarrow F|_t^x}$$

where the term $t$ is required to be free for the variable $x$ in the formula $F$. This restriction of the substitution of $t$ for $x$ gives a standard notion of an admissible substitution, which proves to be sufficient for the usual needs of the proof theory. But it becomes useless from the point of view of the efficiency of computer-oriented theorem proving methods. It is clear from the following example (cf. ex. 3(a) from chapter 4 [7]).

Consider the sequent $P_1, P_2, P_3, P_4 \Rightarrow G$, where

$P_1$ is $\forall x_1 \exists b_1 \forall u_1\ (B(u_1, b_1) \supset \exists a B(f(u_1, a), x_1))$

$P_2$ is $\forall x_2 \exists b_2 \forall u_2 \forall y_2\ (B(f(u_2, y_2), b_2) \supset B(u_2, x_2))$

$P_3$ is $\forall x_3 \exists b_3 \forall u_3 \forall y_3 \forall z_3\ (B(f(f(u_3, y_3), z_3), b_3) \supset B(f(f(y_3, z_3), u_3), x_3))$

$P_4$ is $\forall x_4 \exists b_4 \forall u_4 \forall y_4 \forall z_4\ (B(f(f(u_4, y_4), z_4), b_4) \supset B(f(f(u_4, z_4), y_4), x_4))$

$G$ is $\forall a_1 \exists x \forall a_2 \forall a_3 (B(f(a_2, a_3), x) \supset B(f(a_3, a_2), a_1))$

Provability of this sequent in the calculus $LJ$ will be established below, while here we notice that quantifier rules must be applied to all quantifiers occurring in $P_1, P_2, P_3, P_4$ and $G$. Therefore, the standard notion of an admissibility yields 22!/(4!*4!*5!*5!*4!) different orders of the quantifier rule applications to the sequent $P_1, P_2, P_3, P_4 \Rightarrow G$. It is clear that resolution type methods allow to avoid this redundant work.

To optimize the procedure of the application of quantifier rules, S.Kanger suggested [2] his Gentzen-type classical calculus denoted here by $K$. In the calculus $K$ a "pattern" of an inference tree is constructed firstly with the help of special variables, so-called parameters and dummies. At some moments an attempt is made to convert the "pattern" into a proof tree to complete the deduction process. In case of the unsuccessful attempt, the process is continued.

The main difference between $K$ and $G$ (or $LJ$) consists in a special modification of the above quantifier rules and in a certain splitting (in $K$) of the process of the "pattern" construction into stages. In $K$, the $(\forall \Rightarrow)$-rule and $(\Rightarrow \exists)$-rule are as follows:
$(\forall \Rightarrow)_K$-rule:

$$\frac{M, \forall x F \Rightarrow G}{M, F|_d^x \Rightarrow G} \quad t_1, ..., t_n/d$$

$(\Rightarrow \exists)_K$-rule:

$$\frac{M \Rightarrow \exists x F}{M \Rightarrow F|_d^x} \quad t_1, ..., t_n/d$$

where $d$ is a dummy, $t_1, ..., t_n$ are terms, which are free for d and contain only functional symbols from the premises of the rules, and $t_1, ..., t_n/d$ denotes that dummy $d$ must be replaced by one of the terms $t_1, ..., t_n$ when an attempt is made to convert a "pattern" into a proof tree. The replacement of dummies by terms is made at the end of every stage, and at every stage the rules are applied in a certain order.

This scheme of a deduction construction in $K$ leads to the notion of a Kanger-admissible substitution, which is more efficient than the standard one, and it may be used in the intuitionistic calculus $LJ$. Thus, it yields only $6!/2!$ (=360) variants of different possible orders of quantifier rule applications(but none of these variants is preferable) in the above example. Despite this, Kanger-admissible substitutions still do not allow to attain the efficiency comparable with that when the skolemization may be made. It is due to the fact that, as in case of the standard admissible substitution, a certain order of quantifier rule applications is required to select when an initial sequent is deduced. If it proves to be unsuccessful, another order of applications is tried, and so on.

Below we construct a new intuitionistic calculus $mLJ$ based on the calculus $LJ$ and the notion of admissible substitution from [4].

## 3 Calculus $mLJ$

First of all, note that we consider the calculus $LJ$ without the cut rule.

We treat the notion of a substitution as in [8]. Any substitution component is considered to be of the form $t/x$, where $x$ is a variable and $t$ is a term of a substitution. The expression $F|_y^x$ denotes the result of replacing $x$ with $y$.

Let $L$ be a literal. We use the expression $L(t_1, \ldots, t_n)$ to denote that $t_1,...,t_n$ is a list of all the terms (possibly, with repetitions) occupying the argument places in the literal $L$ in the order of their occurrences in $L$.

The basic object of $mLJ$ (as of $gS$ from [4]) is an a-sequent. We consider a-sequents having no more than one object ("goal") in succedents. Also we assume (cf. [4]) that besides usual variables there are two countable sets of special variables, namely unknown variables and fixed variables (dummies and parameters in the terminology of [2]).

An ordered triple $< w, F, E >$ is called *an ensemble* if and only if $w$ is a sequence (a word) of unknown and fixed variables, $F$ is a 1st-order formula, and $E$ is a set of pairs of terms $t_1, t_2$ (equations of the form $t_1 = t_2$).

*An a-sequent* is the expression of a form $< w_1, P_1, E_1 >, \ldots, < w_n, P_n, E_n > \Rightarrow < w, G, E >$, where $< w_1, P_1, E_1 >, \ldots, < w_n, P_n, E_n >, < w, G, E >$ are ensembles.

Ensembles in the antecedent of an a-sequent are called premises, and an ensemble in the succedent of an a-sequent is called a goal of this a-sequent.

Let $W$ be a set of sequences of unknown and fixed variables, and $s$ be a substitution. Put $A(W, s) = \{< x, t, w >$: $x$ is a variable of $s$, $t$ is a term of $s$, $w \in W$, and $x$ lies in $w$ to the left of some fixed variable from $t\}$. Then $s$ is said to be *admissible* for $W$ if and only if (1) the variables of $s$ are unknown variables only, and (2) there are not elements $< x_1, t_1, w_1 >, \ldots, < x_n, t_n, w_n >$ in $A(W, s)$ such that $t_2/x_1 \in s, \ldots, t_n/x_{n-1} \in s, t_1/x_n \in s$ $(n > 0)$.

An initial a-sequent in $mLJ$ is constructed as follows. Suppose that we want to establish the deducibility of the sequent $P_1, \ldots, P_n \Rightarrow G$ in the calculus $LJ$ (without the cut rule). Then an a-sequent $<, P_1, >, \ldots, <, P_n, > \Rightarrow <, G, >$ will be considered as an initial a-sequent in the calculus $mLJ$.

Decomposition of some formula $G$ or $P_i$ by its principal logical connective results in generating new a-sequents.

When proof of an initial a-sequent is searched in $mLJ$, an inference tree is constructed. At the beginning of a search process the tree consists of an initial a-sequent. The subsequent nodes of the inference tree are generated in accordance with the rules below. Inference trees grow "from top to bottom".

1. STRUCTURAL RULES

($Weakening \Rightarrow$)-rule:

$$\frac{M, < w_1, G, E_1 > \Rightarrow < w, F, E >}{M \Rightarrow < w, F, E >}$$

($Contraction \Rightarrow$)-rule:

$$\frac{M, < w_1, G, E > \Rightarrow < w, F, E >}{M, < w_1, G, E_1 >, < w_1, G, E_1 > \Rightarrow < w, F, E >}$$

($Exchange \Rightarrow$)-rule:

$$\frac{M, < w_1, H, E_1 >, < w_2, G, E_2 > \Rightarrow < w, F, E >}{M, < w_2, G, E_2 >, < w_1, H, E_1 > \Rightarrow < w, F, E >}$$

## 2. GOAL SPLITTING RULES

*Propositional rules*

($\Rightarrow\supset$)-rule:

$$\frac{M \Rightarrow < w, F \supset G, E >}{M, < w, F, E > \Rightarrow < w, G, E >}$$

($\Rightarrow \neg$)-rule:

$$\frac{M \Rightarrow < w, \neg F, E >}{M, < w, F, E > \Rightarrow}$$

($\Rightarrow \vee_1$)-rule:

$$\frac{M \Rightarrow < w, F \vee G, E >}{M \Rightarrow < w, G, E >}$$

($\Rightarrow \vee_2$)-rule:

$$\frac{M \Rightarrow < w, F \vee G, E >}{M \Rightarrow < w, F, E >}$$

($\Rightarrow \wedge$)-rule:

$$\frac{M \Rightarrow < w, F \wedge G, E >}{M \Rightarrow < w, F, E > \quad M \Rightarrow < w, G, E >}$$

*Quantifier Rules*

($\Rightarrow \forall$)-rule:

$$\frac{M \Rightarrow < w, \forall x F, E >}{M \Rightarrow < w\overline{x}, F|^{x}_{\overline{x}}, E >}$$

where $\overline{x}$ is a new fixed variable.

($\Rightarrow \exists$)-rule:

$$\frac{M \Rightarrow < w, \exists x F, E >}{M \Rightarrow < wx', F|^{x}_{x'}, E >}$$

where $x'$ is a new unknown variable.

## 3. PREMISE SPLITTING RULES

*Propositional Rules*

($\neg \Rightarrow$)-rule:

$$\frac{M, < w, \neg F, E > \Rightarrow}{M \Rightarrow < w, F, E >}$$

($\wedge_1 \Rightarrow$)-rule:

$$\frac{M, < w_1, H \wedge G, E_1 > \Rightarrow < w, F, E >}{M, < w_1, G, E_1 > \Rightarrow < w, F, E >}$$

($\wedge_2 \Rightarrow$)-rule:

$$\frac{M, < w_1, H \wedge G, E_1 > \Rightarrow < w, F, E >}{M, < w_1, H, E_1 > \Rightarrow < w, F, E >}$$

($\vee \Rightarrow$)-rule:

$$\frac{M, < w_1, H \vee G, E_1 > \Rightarrow < w, F, E >}{M, < w_1, H, E_1 > \Rightarrow < w, F, E > \quad M, < w_1, G, E_1 > \Rightarrow < w, F, E >}$$

($\supset \Rightarrow$)-rule:

$$\frac{M_1, M_2, < w_1, H \supset G, E_1 > \Rightarrow < w, F, E >}{M_1 \Rightarrow < w_1, H, E_1 > \quad M_2, < w_1, G, E_1 > \Rightarrow < w, F, E >}$$

*Quantifier Rules*
($\forall \Rightarrow$)-rule:

$$\frac{M, < w, \forall x F, E' > \Rightarrow < w', G, E >}{M, < wx', F|^{x}_{x'}, E' > \Rightarrow < w', G, E >}$$

where $x'$ is a new unknown variable.
($\exists \Rightarrow$)-rule:

$$\frac{M, < w, \exists x F, E' > \Rightarrow < w', G, E >}{M, < w\overline{x}, F|^{x}_{\overline{x}}, E' > \Rightarrow < w', G, E >}$$

where $\overline{x}$ is a new fixed variable.

4. TERMINATION RULE
($\Rightarrow \#$)-rule:

$$\frac{< w, L(t_1, \ldots, t_n), E > \Rightarrow < w', L(t'_1, \ldots, t'_n), E' >}{< w, \#, E > \Rightarrow < w', \#, E'' >}$$

(Here $E'' = E' \cup E \cup \{t_1 = t'_1, \ldots, t_n = t'_n\}$; $L(t_1, \ldots, t_n)$, $L(t'_1, \ldots, t'_n)$ are atomic formulas.)

5. AXIOMS
Axioms are a-sequents of the form $< w', \#, E' > \Rightarrow < w, \#, E >$ .

Applying the rules "from top to bottom" to an initial a-sequent and afterwards to its "heirs", and so on, we finally obtain an inference tree. A current inference tree $Tr$ is considered to be a *proof tree* if and only if $Tr$ is obtained from an initial a-sequent by inference rule applications, and the following conditions are met: there exists a unifier $s$ of all the pairs of terms (i.e. equations of the form $t_1 = t_2$) from the goals of all leaves of $Tr$; any leaf of $Tr$ is an axiom of $mLJ$; $s$ is the admissible unifier (in the sense of this paper) for the set of all sequences of fixed and unknown variables from the axioms of $Tr$.

Remark. The formulation of the calculus $mLJ$ shows that when automated inference search is being done, the order of quantifier rule applications is immaterial, i.e. it does not influence on a final result. In the calculus $mLJ$, the quantifier rules are needed for revealing quantifier structures of formulas from an initial a-sequent.

**Proposition 1.** *Let $P_1, \ldots, P_n, G$ be formulas of the 1st-order language. The sequent $P_1, \ldots, P_n \Rightarrow G$ is deducible in the calculus $LJ$ if and only if there exists a proof tree for the initial a-sequent $<, P_1, >, \ldots, <, P_n, > \Rightarrow <, G, >$ in the calculus $mLJ$.*

*Proof Scheme.*

*Sufficiency.* Let $Tr$ be a proof tree for the initial a-sequent $<, P_1, >, \ldots, <, P_n, > \Rightarrow <, G, >$ in the calculus $mLJ$, and $s$ be a substitution, which unifies all the equastions of leaves of $Tr$ and is admissible for set $W$ of all sequences of unknown and fixed variables from $Tr$. Without any loss of generality we can assume that the terms of $s$ do not contain unknown variables (otherwise these unknown variables could be replaced by a constant, say, $c_0$) for every unknown variable from $W$ there exists the term $t$ such that $t/x \in s$.

Since $s$ is admissible for $W$, it is possible to construct the following word (sequence) $w$ consisting of unknown and fixed variables which form the sequences of $W$ [9]: (i) every $w' \in W$ is a subsequence of $w$; (ii) the substitution $s$ is admissible for $\{w\}$ (i.e. there is no element $< x, t, w > \in A(\{w\}, s)$ such that $t/x \in s$).

The property (i) of the sequence $w$ permits to prove the following.

The tree $Tr$ can be transformed into the proof tree $Tr'$ (in $mLJ$) satisfying the following conditions: inference rules in $Tr'$ are applied ("from top to bottom") in the order which corresponds to looking through $w$ from the left to the right, i.e. when the first quantifier rule was applied, the first (unknown or fixed) variable of $w$ was generated, when the second quantifier rule was applied, the second variable of $w$ was generated, and so on.

Now it is possible to convert the tree $Tr'$ into proof tree $TR$ for the initial sequent $P_1, \ldots, P_n \Rightarrow G$ in $LJ$. To do this, let us repeat the process of the construction of $Tr'$ in the above order and execute the following transformations.

1) Delete all leaves from $Tr'$. Let us denote the result of this operation by $Tr''$. It is an inference tree that does not contain termination rule applications, and all its leaves have the form $< w, L(t_1, \ldots, t_n), E > \Rightarrow < w', L(t'_1, \ldots, t'_n), E' >$.

2) Suppose that in a processed node of $Tr''$ one of the following rules was applied:

$$\frac{M, < w, \forall x F, E' > \Rightarrow < w', G, E >}{M, < wx', F|^x_{x'}, E' > \Rightarrow < w', G, E >} \qquad \left(\frac{M \Rightarrow < w, \exists x F, E >}{M \Rightarrow < wx', F|^x_{x'}, E >}\right)$$

and $t/x' \in s$ for some term $t$. The term $t$ is free for $x'$ in $F$, because the order of quantifier rules applications of is reflected by $w$, and the property (ii) is satisfied. Therefore, the admissibility in the standard sense will be observed when the above rules are replaced (in $Tr''$) by the following rules of the calculus $LJ$:

$$\frac{M, \forall x F \Rightarrow G}{M, F|^x_t \Rightarrow G} \qquad \left(\frac{M \Rightarrow \exists x F}{M \Rightarrow F|^x_t}\right)$$

and all other occurrences of $x'$ in $Tr''$ are replaced by $t$.

3) In other cases, the rules of the calculus $mLJ$ (except the termination rule) are replaced by their analogs from $LJ$ by a simple deleting the first and third components from these rules.

It is evidently that $TR$ is an inference tree in the calculus $LJ$. Furthermore, the way of converting $Tr''$ into $TR$ allows to conclude that the leaves of $TR$ are axioms of the calculus $LJ$. (Remeber, that every leaf ot $Tr''$ has a form $< w, L(t_1, \ldots, t_n), E > \Rightarrow < w', L(t'_1, \ldots, t'_n), E' >$, and $s$ unifies all equalities $t_1 = t'_1, \ldots, t_n = t'_n$.) Thus, $TR$ is a proof tree for the initial sequent $P_1, \ldots, P_n \Rightarrow G$ in $LJ$.

*Necessity.* Let $TR$ be a proof tree for the initial sequent $P_1, \ldots, P_n \Rightarrow G$ in $LJ$. Convert $TR$ into the tree $Tr$, which, as can be seen bellow, is a proof tree for the initial sequent $<, P_1, >, \ldots, <, P_n, > \Rightarrow <, G, >$ in $mLJ$. For this purpose, first of all repeat (from "top to bottom") a process of the construction of $TR$, replacing in $TR$ every rule application by its analog in $mLJ$ and subsequently generating substitution $s$. (Initially $s$ is the empty substitution.)

1) If an applied rule is one of the following:

$$\frac{M, \forall x F \Rightarrow G}{M, F|_t^x \Rightarrow G} \qquad (\frac{M \Rightarrow \exists x F}{M \Rightarrow F|_t^x})$$

then it is replaced by

$$\frac{M, < w, \forall x F, E' > \Rightarrow < w', G, E >}{M, < wx', F|_{x'}^x, E' > \Rightarrow < w', G, E >} \qquad (\frac{M \Rightarrow < w, \exists x F, E >}{M \Rightarrow < wx', F|_{x'}^x, E >})$$

accordingly with adding $t/x'$ to the existing substitution $s$, where $x'$ is a new unknown variable, and with substituting $x'$ for those occurrences of a term $t$ into "heirs" of the formula $F|_t^x$, which appeared as the result of the applying of a replaced rule "inserting" the term $t$.

2) In all other cases, the replacement of the rules of $LJ$ by the rules of $mLJ$ is evident. ($<, P_1, >, \ldots, <, P_n, > \Rightarrow <, G, >$ is declared as initial sequent of $Tr$).

As a result of the above transformation of $TR$ we obtain the inference tree $Tr'$ in the calculus $mLJ$. It is obvious that the termination rule can be applied to all leaves of $Tr'$, constructing the inference tree $Tr$, and that the finally generated substitution $s$ unifies all equalities from the axioms of $Tr$.

Since $TR$ is a proof tree in the calculus $LJ$ utilizing the standard notion of admissible substitution, so it is clear that the substitution s is admissible (in the sense of this paper) for a set of all sequences of unknown and fixed variables from leaves of $Tr$. Therefore, $Tr$ is a proof tree for the initial sequent $<, P_1, >, \ldots, <, P_n, > \Rightarrow <, G, >$ in $mLJ$.

**Proposition 2 ((soundness and completeness of $mLJ$)).** *A formula $G$ is valid (in Kripke models) if and only if there is a proof tree for an initial a-sequent $\Rightarrow <, G, >$ in the calculus $mLJ$.*

*Proof.* As $LJ$ is the sound and complete calculus (see, for example, [6]), Proposition 2 is the corollary of Proposition 1.

# 4 Examples of Inferences in $mLJ$ and $LJ$

These examples show the advantage of the calculus $mLJ$ in comparison with $LJ$. This advantage contains more obviously when an attempt to prove a uneducable sequent is made (see the remark below).

Note that in the inferences below the exchange rules are used implicitly.

**Proof Tree $Tr$ in $mLJ$:**

Let us consider an initial a-sequent of the form $<, P_1, >, <, P_4, >, <, P_3, >, <, P_2, > \Rightarrow <, G, >$, where $P_1$,$P_2$,$P_3$,$P_4$,$G$ are from Section 2, and construct for it an inference tree $Tr$ in $mLJ$.

1. $<, P_1, >, <, P_3, >, <, P_4, >, <, P_2, > \Rightarrow <, G, >$ (initial a-sequent)

.

.

.

2. $< w_1', P_1', >, < w_3, P_3', >, < w_4, P_4', >, < w_2, P_2', > \Rightarrow < w_5, B(f(\overline{a_2}, \overline{a_3}), x) \supset B(f(\overline{a_3}, \overline{a_2}), \overline{a_1}), >$

(by quantifier rules applied in any order to all the premises and to the goal from 1.)

where:

$P_1'$ is $B(u_1, \overline{b_1}) \supset \exists a B(f(u_1, a), x_1)$,

$P_2'$ is $B(f(u_2, y_2), \overline{b_2}) \supset B(u_2, x_2)$,

$P_3'$ is $B(f(f(u_3, y_3), z_3), \overline{b_3}) \supset B(f(f(y_3, z_3), u_3), x_3)$,

$P_4'$ is $B(f(f(u_4, y_4), z_4), \overline{b_4}) \supset B(f(f(u_4, z_4), y_4), x_4)$,

$w_1'$ is $x_1\overline{b_1}u_1$, $w_2$ is $x_2\overline{b_2}u_2y_2$, $w_3$ is $x_3\overline{b_3}u_3y_3z_3$, $w_4$ is $x_4\overline{b_4}u_4y_4z_4$, $w_5$ is $\overline{a_1}x\overline{a_2}\overline{a_3}$,

$x, x_1, x_2, x_3, x_4, y_2, y_3, y_4, z_3, z_4, u_1, u_2, u_3, u_4$ are unknown variables,

$\overline{a_1}, \overline{a_2}, \overline{a_3}, \overline{b_1}, \overline{b_2}, \overline{b_3}, \overline{b_4}$ are fixed variables.

3. $< w_1', P_1', >, < w_3, P_3', >, < w_4, P_4', >, < w_2, B(f(u_2, y_2), \overline{b_2}) \supset B(u_2, x_2), >, < \overline{a_1}x\overline{a_2}\overline{a_3}, B(f(\overline{a_2}, \overline{a_3}), x), > \Rightarrow < \overline{a_1}x\overline{a_2}\overline{a_3}, B(f(\overline{a_3}, \overline{a_2}), \overline{a_1}), >$

(by ($\Rightarrow\supset$)-rule from 2.)

3.1. $< w_1', P_1', >, < w_3, P_3', >, < w_4, B(f(f(u_4, y_4), z_4), \overline{b_4}) \supset B(f(f(u_4, z_4), y_4), x_4), >, < \overline{a_1}x\overline{a_2}\overline{a_3}, B(f(\overline{a_2}, \overline{a_3}), x), > \Rightarrow < x_2\overline{b_2}u_2y_2, B(f(u_2, y_2), \overline{b_2}), >$

(by ($\supset\Rightarrow$)-rule from 3.)

3.2. $< x_2\overline{b_2}u_2y_2, B(u_2, x_2), > \Rightarrow < \overline{a_1}x\overline{a_2}\overline{a_3}, B(f(\overline{a_3}, \overline{a_2}), \overline{a_1}), >$

(by ($\supset\Rightarrow$)-rule from 3.)

3.3. $< x_2\overline{b_2}u_2y_2, \#, > \Rightarrow < \overline{a_1}x\overline{a_2}\overline{a_3}, \#, \{u_2 = f(\overline{a_3}, \overline{a_2}), x_2 = \overline{a_1}\} >$

(axiom: by termination rule from 3.3.)

3.1.1. $< w_1', P_1', >, <, B(f(f(u_3, y_3), z_3), \overline{b_3}) \supset B(f(f(y_3, z_3), u_3), x_3), >, < \overline{a_1}x\overline{a_2}\overline{a_3}, B(f(\overline{a_2}, \overline{a_3}), x), > \Rightarrow < x_4\overline{b_4}u_4y_4z_4, B(f(f(u_4, y_4), z_4), \overline{b_4}), >$

(by ($\supset\Rightarrow$)-rule from 3.1.)

3.1.2. $< x_4\overline{b_4}u_4y_4z_4, B(f(f(u_4, z_4), y_4), x_4), > \Rightarrow < x_2\overline{b_2}u_2y_2, B(f(u_2, y_2), \overline{b_2}), >$

(by ($\supset\Rightarrow$)-rule from 3.1.)

3.1.3. $< x_4\overline{b_4}u_4y_4z_4, \#, > \Rightarrow < x_2\overline{b_2}u_2y_2, \#, \{f(f(u_4, z_4), y_4) = f(u_2, y_2), x_4 = \overline{b_2}\} >$
(axiom: by termination rule from 3.1.2.)
3.1.1.1. $< w_1', B(u_1, \overline{b_1}) \supset \exists a B(f(u_1, a), x_1), >, < \overline{a_1}x\overline{a_2}\overline{a_3}, B(f(\overline{a_2}, \overline{a_3}), x), > \Rightarrow < x_3\overline{b_3}u_3y_3z_3, B(f(f(u_3, y_3), z_3), \overline{b_3}), >$
(by ($\supset \Rightarrow$)-rule from 3.1.1.)
3.1.1.2. $< x_3\overline{b_3}u_3y_3z_3, B(f(f(y_3, z_3), u_3), x_3), > \Rightarrow < x_3\overline{b_3}u_3y_3z_3, B(f(f(u_4, y_4), z_4), \overline{b_4}), >$
(by ($\supset \Rightarrow$)-rule from 3.1.1.)
3.1.1.3. $< x_3\overline{b_3}u_3y_3z_3, \#, > \Rightarrow < x_3\overline{b_3}u_3y_3z_3, \#, \{f(f(y_3, z_3), u_3) = f(f(u_4, y_4), z_4), x_3 = \overline{b_4}\} >$
(axiom: by termination rule from 3.1.1.2.)
3.1.1.1.1. $< \overline{a_1}x\overline{a_2}\overline{a_3}, B(f(\overline{a_2}, \overline{a_3}), x), > \Rightarrow < x_1\overline{b_1}u_1, B(u_1, \overline{b_1}), >$
(by ($\supset \Rightarrow$)-rule from 3.1.1.1.)
3.1.1.1.2. $< x_1\overline{b_1}u_1, \exists a B(f(u_1, a), x_1), > \Rightarrow < x_3\overline{b_3}u_3y_3z_3, B(f(f(u_3, y_3), z_3), \overline{b_3}), >$
(by ($\supset \Rightarrow$)-rule from 3.1.1.1.)
3.1.1.1.3. $< x_1\overline{b_1}u_1\overline{a}, B(f(u_1, \overline{a}), x_1), > \Rightarrow < x_3\overline{b_3}u_3y_3z_3, B(f(f(u_3, y_3), z_3), \overline{b_3}), >$
(by ($\exists \Rightarrow$)-rule from 3.1.1.1.2.)
3.1.1.1.4. $< x_1\overline{b_1}u_1\overline{a}, \#, > \Rightarrow < x_3\overline{b_3}u_3y_3z_3, \#, \{f(u_1, \overline{a}) = f(f(u_3, y_3), z_3), x_1 = \overline{b_3}\} >$
(axiom: by termination rule from 3.1.1.1.3.)
3.1.1.1.1.1. $< \overline{a_1}x\overline{a_2}\overline{a_3}, \#, > \Rightarrow < x_1\overline{b_1}u_1, \#, \{f(\overline{a_2}, \overline{a_3}) = u_1, x = \overline{b_1}\} >$
(axiom: by termination rule from 3.1.1.1.1.)

All the leaves (3.3, 3.1.3, 3.1.1.3, 3.1.1.1.4, and 3.1.1.1.1.1) are axioms in the tree $Tr$. Denote by $E$ a set of all the equations from the axioms of $Tr$: $E = \{u_2 = f(\overline{a_3}, \overline{a_2}), x_2 = \overline{a_1}, f(f(u_4, z_4), y_4) = f(u_2, y_2), x_4 = \overline{b_2}, f(f(y_3, z_3), u_3) = f(f(u_4, y_4), z_4), x_3 = \overline{b_4}, f(u_1, \overline{a}) = f(f(u_3, y_3), z_3), x_1 = \overline{b_3}, f(\overline{a_2}, \overline{a_3}) = u_1, x = \overline{b_1}\}$.

All the pairs of terms (i.e equations) from set $E$ is unifiable by the most general simultaneous unifier $s = \{\overline{b_1}/x, \overline{b_3}/x_1, \overline{a_1}/x_2, \overline{b_4}/x_3, \overline{b_2}/x_4, f(\overline{a_2}, \overline{a_3})/u_1, f(\overline{a_3}, \overline{a_2})/u_2, \overline{a_2}/u_3, \overline{a_3}/u_4, \overline{a}/y_2, \overline{a_3}/y_3, \overline{a}/y_4, \overline{a}/z_3, \overline{a_2}/z_4\}$.

Let $W = \{w_1, w_2, w_3, w_4, w_5\}$, where $w_1$ is $x_1\overline{b_1}u_1\overline{a}$ and $w_2$, $w_3$, $w_4$, and $w_5$ are from the above sequences. Note that $w_1, \ldots w_5$ are all the sequences from the axioms of $Tr$. Then $A(W, s) = \{< x_1, \overline{b_1}, w_1 >, < x_1, \overline{a}, w_1 >, < u_1, \overline{a}, w_1 >, < x_2, \overline{b_2}, w_2 >, < x_3, \overline{b_3}, w_3 >, < x_4, \overline{b_4}, w_4 >, < x, \overline{a_2}, w_5 >, < x, \overline{a_3}, w_5 >, < x, f(\overline{a_2}, \overline{a_3}), w_5 >, < x, f(\overline{a_3}, \overline{a_2}), w_5 >\}$.

Using $A(W, s)$, it is easy to check the admissibility of the unifier $s$ for $W$ (in the sense of this paper). So, $s$ is admissible for $Tr$, i.e. $Tr$ is a proof tree. Then, the sequent $P_1, P_2, P_3, P_4 \Rightarrow G$ is deducible in $LJ$ by Proposition 1, and the formula $(P_1 \wedge P_2 \wedge P_3 \wedge P_4) \supset G$ is valid (in Kripke models) by Proposition 2.

**Proof Tree** $TR$ **in** $LJ$:

Following the proof scheme of the Proposition 1, it is easy to construct the inference of the sequent $P_1, P_2, P_3, P_4 \Rightarrow G$ in the calculus LJ.

First of all, let us construct the sequence $w$, satisfying the conditions (i) and (ii) from the proof scheme. It can be done by means of the convolution algorithm from [9]. As a result, we have that the sequence $w$ is

$\overline{a_1}x_2\overline{b_2}x_4\overline{b_4}x_3\overline{b_3}x_1\overline{b_1}x\overline{a_2}\overline{a_3}u_1\bar{a}u_2y_2u_3y_3z_3u_4y_4z_4$

In accordance with $w$ we have the following proof tree $TR$ in $LJ$.

1. $P_1, P_2, P_3, P_4 \Rightarrow \forall a_1 \exists x \forall a_2 \forall a_3 (B(f(a_2, a_3), x) \supset B(f(a_3, a_2), a_1))$ (initial sequent)

2. $P_1, P_3, P_4, P_2 \Rightarrow \exists x \forall a_2 \forall a_3 (B(f(a_2, a_3), x) \supset B(f(a_3, a_2), \overline{a_1}))$
(by $(\Rightarrow \forall)_G$-rule from 1: $\overline{a_1}/a_1$)

3. $P_1, P_3, P_4, \exists b_2 \forall u_2 \forall y_2 (B(f(u_2, y_2), b_2) \supset B(u_2, \overline{a_1})) \Rightarrow \exists x \forall a_2 \forall a_3 (B(f(a_2, a_3), x) \supset B(f(a_3, a_2), \overline{a_1}))$
(by $(\forall \Rightarrow)_G$-rule from 2: $\overline{a_1}/x_2$)

4. $P_1, P_3, P_4, \forall u_2 \forall y_2\ (B(f(u_2, y_2), \overline{b_2}) \supset B(u_2, \overline{a_1})) \Rightarrow \exists x \forall a_2 \forall a_3 (B(f(a_2, a_3), x) \supset B(f(a_3, a_2), \overline{a_1}))$
(by $(\exists \Rightarrow)_G$-rule from 3: $\overline{b_2}/b_2$

5. $P_1, P_3, \exists b_4 \forall u_4 \forall y_4 \forall z_4 (B(f(f(u_4, y_4), z_4), b_4) \supset B(f(f(u_4, z_4), y_4), \overline{b_2})), \forall u_2 \forall y_2\ (B(f(u_2, y_2), \overline{b_2}) \supset B(u_2, \overline{a_1})) \Rightarrow \exists x \forall a_2 \forall a_3 (B(f(a_2, a_3), x) \supset B(f(a_3, a_2), \overline{a_1}))$
(by $(\forall \Rightarrow)_G$-rule from 4: $\overline{b_2}/x_4$)

6. $P_1, P_3, \forall u_4 \forall y_4 \forall z_4\ (B(f(f(u_4, y_4), z_4), \overline{b_4}) \supset B(f(f(u_4, z_4), y_4), \overline{b_2})), \forall u_2 \forall y_2\ (B(f(u_2, y_2), \overline{b_2}) \supset B(u_2, \overline{a_1})) \Rightarrow \exists x \forall a_2 \forall a_3 (B(f(a_2, a_3), x) \supset B(f(a_3, a_2), \overline{a_1}))$
(by $(\exists \Rightarrow)_G$-rule from 5: $\overline{b_4}/b_4$)

7. $P_1, \exists b_3 \forall u_3 \forall y_3 \forall z_3\ (B(f(f(u_3, y_3), z_3), b_3) \supset B(f(f(y_3, z_3), u_3), \overline{b_4})), \forall u_4 \forall y_4 \forall z_4\ (B(f(f(u_4, y_4), z_4), \overline{b_4}) \supset B(f(f(u_4, z_4), y_4), \overline{b_2})), \forall u_2 \forall y_2\ (B(f(u_2, y_2), \overline{b_2}) \supset B(u_2, \overline{a_1})) \Rightarrow \exists x \forall a_2 \forall a_3 (B(f(a_2, a_3), x) \supset B(f(a_3, a_2), \overline{a_1}))$
(by $(\forall \Rightarrow)_G$-rule from 6: $\overline{b_4}/x_3$)

8. $P_1, \forall u_3 \forall y_3 \forall z_3\ (B(f(f(u_3, y_3), z_3), \overline{b_3}) \supset B(f(f(y_3, z_3), u_3), \overline{b_4})), \forall u_4 \forall y_4 \forall z_4\ (B(f(f(u_4, y_4), z_4), \overline{b_4}) \supset B(f(f(u_4, z_4), y_4), \overline{b_2})), \forall u_2 \forall y_2\ (B(f(u_2, y_2), \overline{b_2}) \supset B(u_2, \overline{a_1})) \Rightarrow \exists x \forall a_2 \forall a_3 (B(f(a_2, a_3), x) \supset B(f(a_3, a_2), \overline{a_1}))$
(by $(\exists \Rightarrow)_G$-rule from 7: $\overline{b_3}/b_3$ )

9. $\exists b_1 \forall u_1\ (B(u_1, b_1) \supset \exists a B(f(u_1, a), \overline{b_3})), \forall u_3 \forall y_3 \forall z_3\ (B(f(f(u_3, y_3), z_3), \overline{b_3}) \supset B(f(f(y_3, z_3), u_3), \overline{b_4})), \forall u_4 \forall y_4 \forall z_4\ (B(f(f(u_4, y_4), z_4), \overline{b_4}) \supset B(f(f(u_4, z_4), y_4), \overline{b_2})), \forall u_2 \forall y_2\ (B(f(u_2, y_2), \overline{b_2}) \supset B(u_2, \overline{a_1})) \Rightarrow \exists x \forall a_2 \forall a_3 (B(f(a_2, a_3), x) \supset B(f(a_3, a_2), \overline{a_1}))$
(by $(\forall \Rightarrow)_G$-rule from 8: $\overline{b_3}/x_1$)

10. $\forall u_1\ (B(u_1, \overline{b_1}) \supset \exists a B(f(u_1, a), \overline{b_3})), \forall u_3 \forall y_3 \forall z_3\ (B(f(f(u_3, y_3), z_3), \overline{b_3}) \supset B(f(f(y_3, z_3), u_3), \overline{b_4})), \forall u_4 \forall y_4 \forall z_4\ (B(f(f(u_4, y_4), z_4), \overline{b_4}) \supset B(f(f(u_4, z_4), y_4), \overline{b_2})), \forall u_2 \forall y_2\ (B(f(u_2, y_2), \overline{b_2}) \supset B(u_2, \overline{a_1})) \Rightarrow \exists x \forall a_2 \forall a_3 (B(f(a_2, a_3), x) \supset B(f(a_3, a_2), \overline{a_1}))$

(by $(\exists\Rightarrow)_G$-rule from 9: $\overline{b_1}/b_1$)

11. $\forall u_1\ (B(u_1,\overline{b_1})\supset\exists aB(f(u_1,a),\overline{b_3}))$, $\forall u_3\forall y_3\forall z_3\ (B(f(f(u_3,y_3),z_3),\overline{b_3})\supset B(f(f(y_3,z_3),u_3),\overline{b_4}))$, $\forall u_4\forall y_4\forall z_4\ (B(f(f(u_4,y_4),z_4),\overline{b_4})\supset B(f(f(u_4,z_4),y_4),\overline{b_2}))$, $\forall u_2\forall y_2\ (B(f(u_2,y_2),\overline{b_2})\supset B(u_2,\overline{a_1}))\Rightarrow \forall a_2\forall a_3(B(f(a_2,a_3),\overline{b_1})\supset B(f(a_3,a_2),\overline{a_1}))$

(by $(\forall\Rightarrow)_G$-rule from 10: $\overline{b_1}/x$)

12. $\forall u_1\ (B(u_1,\overline{b_1})\supset\exists aB(f(u_1,a),\overline{b_3}))$, $\forall u_3\forall y_3\forall z_3\ (B(f(f(u_3,y_3),z_3),\overline{b_3})\supset B(f(f(y_3,z_3),u_3),\overline{b_4}))$, $\forall u_4\forall y_4\forall z_4\ (B(f(f(u_4,y_4),z_4),\overline{b_4})\supset B(f(f(u_4,z_4),y_4),\overline{b_2}))$, $\forall u_2\forall y_2\ (B(f(u_2,y_2),\overline{b_2})\supset B(u_2,\overline{a_1}))\Rightarrow \forall a_3(B(f(\overline{a_2},a_3),\overline{b_1})\supset B(f(a_3,a_2),\overline{a_1}))$

(by $(\Rightarrow\forall)_G$-rule from 11: $\overline{a_2}/a_2$)

13. $\forall u_1\ (B(u_1,\overline{b_1})\supset\exists aB(f(u_1,a),\overline{b_3}))$, $\forall u_3\forall y_3\forall z_3\ (B(f(f(u_3,y_3),z_3),\overline{b_3})\supset B(f(f(y_3,z_3),u_3),\overline{b_4}))$, $\forall u_4\forall y_4\forall z_4\ (B(f(f(u_4,y_4),z_4),\overline{b_4})\supset B(f(f(u_4,z_4),y_4),\overline{b_2}))$, $\forall u_2\forall y_2\ (B(f(u_2,y_2),\overline{b_2})\supset B(u_2,\overline{a_1}))\Rightarrow B(f(\overline{a_2},\overline{a_3}),\overline{b_1})\supset B(f(\overline{a_3},\overline{a_2}),\overline{a_1})$

(by $(\Rightarrow\forall)_G$-rule from 12: $\overline{a_3}/a_3$)

14. $(B(f(\overline{a_2},\overline{a_3}),\overline{b_1})\supset\exists aB(f(f(\overline{a_2},\overline{a_3}),a),\overline{b_3}))$, $\forall u_3\forall y_3\forall z_3\ (B(f(f(u_3,y_3),z_3),\overline{b_3})\supset B(f(f(y_3,z_3),u_3),\overline{b_4}))$, $\forall u_4\forall y_4\forall z_4\ (B(f(f(u_4,y_4),z_4),\overline{b_4})\supset B(f(f(u_4,z_4),y_4),\overline{b_2}))$, $\forall u_2\forall y_2\ (B(f(u_2,y_2),\overline{b_2})\supset B(u_2,\overline{a_1}))$, $B(f(\overline{a_2},\overline{a_3}),\overline{b_1})\Rightarrow B(f(\overline{a_3},\overline{a_2}),\overline{a_1})$

(by $(\forall\Rightarrow)_G$-rule from 13: $f(\overline{a_2},\overline{a_3})/u_1$)

14.1. $B(f(\overline{a_2},\overline{a_3}),\overline{b_1})\Rightarrow B(f(\overline{a_2},\overline{a_3}),\overline{b_1})$

(axiom: by $(\supset\Rightarrow)_G$-rule from 14)

14.2. $\forall u_3\forall y_3\forall z_3\ (B(f(f(u_3,y_3),z_3),\overline{b_3})\supset B(f(f(y_3,z_3),u_3),\overline{b_4}))$, $\forall u_4\forall y_4\forall z_4\ (B(f(f(u_4,y_4),z_4),\overline{b_4})\supset B(f(f(u_4,z_4),y_4),\overline{b_2}))$, $\forall u_2\forall y_2\ (B(f(u_2,y_2),\overline{b_2})\supset B(u_2,\overline{a_1}))$, $\exists aB(f(f(\overline{a_2},\overline{a_3}),a),\overline{b_3})\Rightarrow B(f(\overline{a_3},\overline{a_2}),\overline{a_1})$

(by $(\supset\Rightarrow)_G$-rule from 14)

14.3. $\forall u_3\forall y_3\forall z_3\ (B(f(f(u_3,y_3),z_3),\overline{b_3})\supset B(f(f(y_3,z_3),u_3),\overline{b_4}))$, $\forall u_4\forall y_4\forall z_4\ (B(f(f(u_4,y_4),z_4),\overline{b_4})\supset B(f(f(u_4,z_4),y_4),\overline{b_2}))$, $\forall u_2\forall y_2\ (B(f(u_2,y_2),\overline{b_2})\supset B(u_2,\overline{a_1}))$, $B(f(f(\overline{a_2},\overline{a_3}),\overline{a}),\overline{b_3})\Rightarrow B(f(\overline{a_3},\overline{a_2}),\overline{a_1})$

(by $(\exists\Rightarrow)_G$-rule from 14.2: $\overline{a}/a$)

14.4. $\forall u_3\forall y_3\forall z_3\ (B(f(f(u_3,y_3),z_3),\overline{b_3})\supset B(f(f(y_3,z_3),u_3),\overline{b_4}))$, $\forall u_4\forall y_4\forall z_4\ (B(f(f(u_4,y_4),z_4),\overline{b_4})\supset B(f(f(u_4,z_4),y_4),\overline{b_2}))$, $\forall y_2\ (B(f(f(\overline{a_3},\overline{a_2}),y_2),\overline{b_2})\supset B(f(\overline{a_3},\overline{a_2}),\overline{a_1}))$, $B(f(f(\overline{a_2},\overline{a_3}),\overline{a}),\overline{b_3})\Rightarrow B(f(\overline{a_3},\overline{a_2}),\overline{a_1})$

(by $(\forall\Rightarrow)_G$-rule from 14.3: $f(\overline{a_3},\overline{a_2})/u_2$)

14.5. $\forall u_3\forall y_3\forall z_3\ (B(f(f(u_3,y_3),z_3),\overline{b_3})\supset B(f(f(y_3,z_3),u_3),\overline{b_4}))$, $\forall u_4\forall y_4\forall z_4\ (B(f(f(u_4,y_4),z_4),\overline{b_4})\supset B(f(f(u_4,z_4),y_4),\overline{b_2}))$, $B(f(f(\overline{a_3},\overline{a_2}),\overline{a}),\overline{b_2})\supset B(f(\overline{a_3},\overline{a_2}),\overline{a_1})$, $B(f(f(\overline{a_2},\overline{a_3}),\overline{a}),\overline{b_3})\Rightarrow B(f(\overline{a_3},\overline{a_2}),\overline{a_1})$

(by $(\forall\Rightarrow)_G$-rule from 14.4: $\overline{a}/y_2$)

14.5.1. $\forall u_3\forall y_3\forall z_3\ (B(f(f(u_3,y_3),z_3),\overline{b_3})\supset B(f(f(y_3,z_3),u_3),\overline{b_4}))$, $\forall u_4\forall y_4\forall z_4\ (B(f(f(u_4,y_4),z_4),\overline{b_4})\supset B(f(f(u_4,z_4),y_4),\overline{b_2}))$, $B(f(f(\overline{a_2},\overline{a_3}),\overline{a}),\overline{b_3})\Rightarrow (B(f(f(\overline{a_3},\overline{a_2}),\overline{a}),\overline{b_2})$

(by $(\supset\Rightarrow)_G$-rule from 14.5)

14.5.2. $B(f(\overline{a_3},\overline{a_2}),\overline{a_1})\Rightarrow B(f(\overline{a_3},\overline{a_2}),\overline{a_1})$

(axiom: by $(\supset\Rightarrow)_G$-rule from 14.5)

14.5.1.1. $\forall y_3 \forall z_3\ (B(f(f(\overline{a_2}, y_3), z_3), \overline{b_3}) \supset B(f(f(y_3, z_3), \overline{a_2}), \overline{b_4})),\ \forall u_4 \forall y_4 \forall z_4\ (B(f(f(u_4, y_4), z_4), \overline{b_4}) \supset B(f(f(u_4, z_4), y_4), \overline{b_2})),\ B(f(f(\overline{a_2}, \overline{a_3}), \overline{a}), \overline{b_3}) \Rightarrow B(f(f(\overline{a_3}, \overline{a_2}), \overline{a}), \overline{b_2})$

(by $(\forall \Rightarrow)_G$-rule from 14.5.1: $\overline{a_2}/u_3$)

14.5.1.2. $\forall z_3\ (B(f(f(\overline{a_2}, \overline{a_3}), z_3), \overline{b_3}) \supset B(f(f(\overline{a_3}, z_3), \overline{a_2}), \overline{b_4})),\ \forall u_4 \forall y_4 \forall z_4\ (B(f(f(u_4, y_4), z_4), \overline{b_4}) \supset B(f(f(u_4, z_4), y_4), \overline{b_2})),\ B(f(f(\overline{a_2}, \overline{a_3}), \overline{a}), \overline{b_3}) \Rightarrow B(f(f(\overline{a_3}, \overline{a_2}), \overline{a}), \overline{b_2})$

(by $(\forall \Rightarrow)_G$-rule from 14.5.1.1: $\overline{a_3}/y_3$)

14.5.1.3. $B(f(f(\overline{a_2}, \overline{a_3}), \overline{a}), \overline{b_3}) \supset B(f(f(\overline{a_3}, \overline{a}), \overline{a_2}), \overline{b_4}),\ \forall u_4 \forall y_4 \forall z_4\ (B(f(f(u_4, y_4), z_4), \overline{b_4}) \supset B(f(f(u_4, z_4), y_4), \overline{b_2})),\ B(f(f(\overline{a_2}, \overline{a_3}), \overline{a}), \overline{b_3}) \Rightarrow (B(f(f(\overline{a_3}, \overline{a_2}), \overline{a}), \overline{b_2})$

(by $(\forall \Rightarrow)_G$-rule from 14.5.1.2: $\overline{a}/z_3$)

14.5.1.3.1. $B(f(f(\overline{a_2}, \overline{a_3}), \overline{a}), \overline{b_3}) \Rightarrow B(f(f(\overline{a_2}, \overline{a_3}), \overline{a}), \overline{b_3})$

(axiom: by $(\supset\Rightarrow)_G$-rule from 14.5.1.3)

14.5.1.3.2. $B(f(f(\overline{a_3}, \overline{a}), \overline{a_2}), \overline{b_4}),\ \forall u_4 \forall y_4 \forall z_4\ (B(f(f(u_4, y_4), z_4), \overline{b_4}) \supset B(f(f(u_4, z_4), y_4), \overline{b_2})) \Rightarrow (B(f(f(\overline{a_3}, \overline{a_2}), \overline{a}), \overline{b_2})$

(by $(\supset\Rightarrow)_G$-rule from 14.5.1.3)

14.5.1.3.2.1. $B(f(f(\overline{a_3}, \overline{a}), \overline{a_2}), \overline{b_4}),\ \forall y_4 \forall z_4\ (B(f(f(\overline{a_3}, y_4), z_4), \overline{b_4}) \supset B(f(f(\overline{a_3}, z_4), y_4), \overline{b_2})) \Rightarrow (B(f(f(\overline{a_3}, \overline{a_2}), \overline{a}), \overline{b_2})$

(by $(\forall \Rightarrow)_G$-rule from 14.5.1.3.2: $\overline{a_3}/u_4$)

14.5.1.3.2.2. $B(f(f(\overline{a_3}, \overline{a}), \overline{a_2}), \overline{b_4}),\ \forall z_4\ (B(f(f(\overline{a_3}, \overline{a}), z_4), \overline{b_4}) \supset B(f(f(\overline{a_3}, z_4), \overline{a}), \overline{b_2})) \Rightarrow (B(f(f(\overline{a_3}, \overline{a_2}), \overline{a}), \overline{b_2})$

(by $(\forall \Rightarrow)_G$-rule from 14.5.1.3.2.1: $\overline{a}/y_4$)

14.5.1.3.2.3. $B(f(f(\overline{a_3}, \overline{a}), \overline{a_2}), \overline{b_4}),\ B(f(f(\overline{a_3}, \overline{a}), \overline{a_2}), \overline{b_4}) \supset B(f(f(\overline{a_3}, \overline{a_2}), \overline{a}), \overline{b_2}) \Rightarrow (B(f(f(\overline{a_3}, \overline{a_2}), \overline{a}), \overline{b_2})$

(by $(\forall \Rightarrow)_G$-rule from 14.5.1.3.2.2. $\overline{a_2}/z_4$)

14.5.1.3.2.3.1. $B(f(f(\overline{a_3}, \overline{a}), \overline{a_2}), \overline{b_4}), \Rightarrow B(f(f(\overline{a_3}, \overline{a}), \overline{a_2}), \overline{b_4})$

(axiom: by $(\supset\Rightarrow)_G$-rule from 14.5.1.3.2.3)

14.5.1.3.2.3.2. $B(f(f(\overline{a_3}, \overline{a_2}), \overline{a}), \overline{b_2}) \Rightarrow B(f(f(a_3, \overline{a_2}), \overline{a}), \overline{b_2})$

(axiom: by $(\supset\Rightarrow)_G$-rule from 14.5.1.3.2.3)

In the tree $TR$ we constructed all the leaves (14.1, 14.5.2, 14.5.1.3.1, 14.5.1.3.2.3.1, and 14.5.1.3.2.3.2) are axioms. So, $TR$ is a proof tree in $LJ$.

Remark. If instead $G$ we would take $\exists x \forall a_1 \forall a_2 \forall a_3 (B(f(a_2, a_3), x) \supset B(f(a_3, a_2), a_1))$ as the goal formula $G_1$ in the initial a-sequent, then "repeating" construction of $Tr$ we would obtain the "copy" $Tr_1$ of $Tr$ with the same mgsu $s$ and with the following set $W_1$ of all sequences of fixed and unknown variables: $W_1 = \{w_1, w_2, w_3, w_4, w_5'\}$, where $w_1, w_2, w_3$, and $w_4$ are not changed, and $w_5'$ is $x\overline{a_1}\overline{a_2}\overline{a_3}$. So, $A(W_1, s) = \{ < x_1, \overline{b_1}, w_1 >, < x_1, \overline{a}, w_1 >, < u_1, \overline{a}, w_1 >, < x_2, \overline{b_2}, w_2 >, < x_3, \overline{b_3}, w_3 >, < x_4, \overline{b_4}, w_4 >, < x, \overline{a_1}, w_5' >, < x, \overline{a_2}, w_5' >, < x, \overline{a_3}, w_5' >, < x, f(\overline{a_2}, \overline{a_3}), w_5' >, < x, f(\overline{a_3}, \overline{a_2}), w_5' >\}$.

Since $A(W_1, s)$ contains $< x_1, \overline{b_1}, w_1 >$, $< x_3, \overline{b_3}, w_3 >$, $< x_4, \overline{b_4}, w_4 >$, $< x_2, \overline{b_2}, w_2 >$, $< x, \overline{a_1}, w'_5 >$ such that $\overline{b_3}/x_1 \in s$, $\overline{b_4}/x_3 \in s$, $\overline{b_2}/x_4 \in s$, $\overline{a_1}/x_2 \in s$, $\overline{b_1}/x \in s$, $s$ is not admissible for $W_1$, and then $Tr_1$ is not a proof tree in $mLJ$.

This shows that $TR$ cannot be transformed into a proof tree in $LJ$ for the initial sequent $P_1, P_2, P_3, P_4 \Rightarrow G_1$ by means of quantifier rules applied in some order. In other words, it is necessary to check 360 different orders of quatifier rule applications if some intuitionistic modification of $K$ is used. In the case of the calculus $LJ$ this number increases up to 22!/(4!*4!*5!*5!*4!).

## 5 Conclusion

The above investigation shows that the new admissible substitution notion may be useful in computer-oriented reconstruction not only of intuitionistic sequent calculi but of classical sequent calculi when an inference search is preferred to be in an initial theory. Besides, it gives an approach to the construction of an efficient theorem-proving technique (without preliminary skolemization) in cases if a problem under consideration requires using non-classical logic, different from $LJ$.

The author thanks referees for useful advice.

## References

1. Gallier J. (1986) Logic for Computer Science: Foundations of Automatic Theorem Proving. Harper and Row, Inc., New York, 513 p.
2. Kanger S. (1963) Simplified Proof Method for Elementary Logic. Comp. Program. and Form. Sys.: Stud. in Logic. North-Holland Publ. Co.
3. Lyaletski A. (1991) Gentzen Calculi and Admissible Substitutions. Actes preliminaries, du Symposium Franco-Sovetique "Informatika-91". Grenoble, France, 99–111
4. Degtyarev A., Lyaletski A., and Morokhovets M. (1999) Evidence Algorithm and Sequent Logical Inference Search. Lecture Notes in Artificial Intelligence, **1705**, 44–61.
5. Gentzen G. (1934) Untersuchungen uber das Logische Schliessen. Math. Zeit., **39**, 176–210.
6. Takeuti G. (1975) Proof Theory. North-Holland Publ. Co., American Elsevier Publ. Co., Inc.
7. Mendelson E. (1963) Introduction to Mathematical Logic. D. van Nostrand Co., Inc.
8. Robinson J.A. (1965) A Machine-Oriented Logic Based on Resolution Principle. J. of the ACM, **12**, 23–41.
9. Lyaletski A. (1981) Variant of Herbrand Theorem for Formulas in Prefix Form (in Russian). Kibernetika, **1**, 112–116

# Verification of the Logic of Plausible Reasoning

Bartłomiej Śnieżyński

Institute of Computer Science, AGH Technical University, Kraków, Poland
e-mail: sniezyn@agh.edu.pl

**Abstract.** Logic of plausible reasoning (LPR) is a formalism which is based on human inference patterns. In the paper the LPR is defined as a labeled deductive system. In this formalism knowledge base consists of formulas representing hierarchies, dependencies and similarities between objects, object-attribute-value triples and implications. Inference patterns are defined as proof rules and are proven to be logically correct. Several examples of inference pattern application are presented.

**Keywords:** logic of plausible reasoning, knowledge representation, handling of uncertainty, labeled deductive system.

## 1 Introduction

There are many theories which deal with uncertainty in knowledge base systems. The most common are: fuzzy logic [11], multiple-valued logic [4], certainty factors [10], Dempster-Shafer theory [9], rough sets [7] and belief networks [8], but there are more of them (see [3]).

In this paper the logic of plausible reasoning (LPR) is considered. It was developed by Collins and Michalski in 1989 [1]. This formalism differs from others theories. Many inference patterns are defined and many parameters estimate certainty.

In [1] LPR is defined using variable-valued logic notation [5]. The knowledge base consists of:

- hierarchies representing the is-a and the part-of relations,
- statements representing values of attributes of objects, which are paths linking nodes in hierarchies,
- similarity, dissimilarity, mutual dependency and mutual implication relations.

Inference patterns are based on human reasoning, hence the inference process is clear and ease to trace for human.

We focus on verification of LPR inference patterns. We show that it is possible to prove the correctness of LPR proof rules. Additionally we propose a reformulation of LPR. It can be defined as a labeled deductive system [2]. We also add new inference pattern based on symmetry of knowledge. Finally, we present some examples of inference rules applications.

## 2 Formalization of LPR

In this section we define LPR as a labeled deductive system. All the knowledge is represented using labeled formulas, where labels are estimates of certainty.

In this paper only positive part of logic is considered, there is no negation symbol and dissimilarity inference pattern is omitted. Negation can be introduced using closed-world assumption and then dissimilarity rule can be defined.

### 2.1 Language

To define a deductive system we need a language. The LPR language consists of a set of constant symbols $C$ (constant symbols represent objects or classes of objects), a set of variable symbols $X$, four relational symbols and logical connectives: $\rightarrow$, $\wedge$.

The relational symbols are: $V, H, S, E$. They are used to represent respectively: statements, hierarchy, similarity and dependency.

Statements are represented as object-attribute-value triples: $V(o, a, v)$ represents a fact that object $o$ has an attribute $a$ equal $v$. Value should be a sub-type of an attribute: if $V(o, a, v)$ is in a knowledge base, there should be also $H(v, a, c)$ there (see below for $H$ description). If object $o$ has several values of $a$, there should be several statements in a knowledge base. We write $o.a = v$ as the abbreviation of $V(o, a, v)$ and $o.a$ as the abbreviation of "attribute $a$ of object $o$".

Relation $H$ represents hierarchy between constant symbols. It can be used to represent type (is-a) and part-of hierarchy. $H(o_1, o_2, c)$ means that $o_1$ is $o_2$ in a context $c$. Context is used for specification of the range of inheritance. $o_1$ and $o_2$ have the same value for all attributes which depends on $o_2.c$.

$S$ is a similarity relation. $S(o_1, o_2, o, a)$ represents a fact, that $o_1$ is similar to $o_2$. Context, as above, specifies the range of similarity. Only these attributes of $o_1$ and $o_2$ have the same value which depends on $o.a$.

To express dependency relation $E$ is used. $E(o_1, a_1, o_2, a_2)$ means that values of $o_1.a_1$ depends on $o_2.a_2$. To represent bidirectional dependency (mutual dependency, see [1]) we need a pair of such expressions. It is more general than one expression, because we can assign different plausible parameters to both of them.

### 2.2 Formulas

Atom formulas are defined as follows:

1. If $o, a, v \in X \cup C$, then $V(o, a, v)$ is an atom formula.
2. If $o_1, o_2, c \in X \cup C$, then $H(o_1, o_2, c)$ is an atom formula.
3. If $o_1, o_2, a, o \in X \cup C$, then $S(o_1, o_2, o, a)$ is an atom formula.
4. If $o_1, a_1, o_2, a_2 \in X \cup C$, then $E(a_1, o_1, o_2, a_2)$ is an atom formula.

Formulas are all atom formulas and clauses of the form $\psi_1 \wedge ... \wedge \psi_n \rightarrow o.a = v$ where $\psi_1, ..., \psi_n$ are atom formulas and $o, a, v \in C \cup X$.

To deal with uncertainty we use labels (see [2]). Hence we need a label algebra: $\mathcal{A} = (A, f_{MP}, f_{SYM}, f_{GEN_o}, f_{SPEC_o}, f_{SIM_o}, f_{GEN_v}, f_{SPEC_v}, f_{SIM_v})$. $A$ is a set of labels which estimate uncertainty. Functions are used in proof rules to generate a label of a conclusion.

Labeled formula is a pair $f : l$ where $f$ is a formula and $l$ is a label. A set of labeled formulas can be considered as a knowledge base.

Variables used in formulas make them more general. Every formula with a variable symbol can be instantiated by replacing all occurrences of the variable by the same constant symbol.

### 2.3 Proof Rules

Proof rules are used to infer new formulas of the form $o.a = v$ from given knowledge base. There are 8 proof rules in LPR, see table 1.

**Table 1.** Proof rules.

$$MP \quad \frac{\begin{array}{l}\psi_1 : p_1 \\ \ldots \\ \psi_n : p_n \\ \psi_1 \wedge ... \wedge \psi_n \rightarrow \varphi : p_0\end{array}}{\varphi : f_{MP}(p_0, p_1, ..., p_n)} \qquad SYM \quad \frac{\begin{array}{l}o.a = v : p_1 \\ H(o, o_1, c) : p_2\end{array}}{v.o_1 = o : f_{SYM}(p_1, p_2)}$$

$$GEN_o \quad \frac{\begin{array}{l}o.a = v : p_1 \\ H(o, o', c) : p_2 \\ E(o'.a, o'.c) : p_3\end{array}}{o'.a = v : f_{GEN_o}(p_1, p_2, p_3)} \qquad SPEC_o \quad \frac{\begin{array}{l}o.a = v : p_1 \\ H(o', o, c) : p_2 \\ E(o.a, o.c) : p_3\end{array}}{o'.a = v : f_{SPEC_o}(p_1, p_2, p_3)}$$

$$SIM_o \quad \frac{\begin{array}{l}o_1.a = v : p_1 \\ S(o_1, o_2, o.c) : p_2 \\ E(o.a, o.c) : p_3 \\ H(o_1, o, a) : p_4 \\ H(o_2, o, a) : p_5\end{array}}{o_2.a = v : f_{SIM_o}(p_1, ..., p_5)} \qquad GEN_v \quad \frac{\begin{array}{l}o.a = v : p_1 \\ H(v, v', c) : p_2 \\ H(v', a, c) : p_3 \\ E(a.o', a.c) : p_4 \\ H(o, o', c') : p_5\end{array}}{o.a = v' : f_{GEN_v}(p_1, ..., p_5)}$$

$$SPEC_v \quad \frac{\begin{array}{l}o.a = v : p_1 \\ H(v', v, c) : p_2 \\ H(v', a, c) : p_3 \\ E(a.o', a.c) : p_4 \\ H(o, o', c') : p_5\end{array}}{o.a = v' : f_{SPEC_v}(p_1, ..., p_5)} \qquad SIM_v \quad \frac{\begin{array}{l}o.a = v : p_1 \\ S(v, v', a.c) : p_2 \\ E(a.o', a.c) : p_3 \\ H(o, o', c') : p_4 \\ H(v', a, c'') : p_5\end{array}}{o.a = v' : f_{SIM_v}(p_1, ..., p_5)}$$

MP is a standard Modus Ponens rule with plausibility added. $GEN_o$ and $SPEC_o$ are generalization and specialization transformations of the object in $o.a = v$ statements. $GEN_v$ and $SPEC_v$ transform values in a similar way. $SIM_o$ and $SIM_v$ are similarity transformations of object and value respectively.

To the set of inference patterns presented in [1] we have added $SYM$ rule. It is based on a symmetry property of the knowledge. For example, if we know, that the sky is blue, we can conclude that one of the blue objects is sky.

Having inference rules, proof can be defined. Proof of a labeled formula $\varphi : p$ from a set of labeled formulas $F$ is a finite sequence of formulas $\alpha_1 : p_1, ..., \alpha_n : p_n$, where $\alpha_n = \varphi$, $p_n = p$ and for every $i \in \{1, 2, ..., n\}$ we have:

1. $\alpha_i : p_i \in F$ or it is an instance of a formula from $F$ or
2. $\alpha_i : p_i$ is a consequence of a proof rule applied to formulas $\alpha_{j_1}, \alpha_{j_2}, ..., \alpha_{j_k}$, where $j_m \in \{1, 2, ..., i-1\}$ for every $1 \leq m \leq k$.

Proof is a formalization of a complex inference process.

## 3 Verification of LPR

In the following section justification of the correctness of the LPR rules is presented. Plausible labels are omitted here. The correctness of the plausible algebra can be considered as a separate problem.

### 3.1 Assumptions

To justify the correctness of the rules we need to list properties of $V$, $H$, $S$ and $E$ relations. First assumption was mentioned in the previous section, it is the *symmetry*:

$$\forall o_1, o_2, a, c, v \in C \cup X : o_1.a = v \wedge H(o_1, o_2, c) \rightarrow v.o_2 = o_1. \quad (1)$$

Second property is the *inheritance of dependencies.* If $o_1$ is $o$ in context $c$ and $o.a$ depends on $o'.a'$, then this dependency should be valid for its descendant $o_1$. It can be written as follows:

$$\forall o, o_1, o', a, a', c \in C \cup X : H(o_1, o, c) \wedge E(o.a, o'.a') \rightarrow E(o_1.a, o'.a'). \quad (2)$$

Third property is similar, it is *inheritance of dependencies II.* Dependency between two attributes of the same object should be inherited by its descendant:

$$\forall o, o_1, a_1, a_2 \in C \cup X : E(o.a_1, o.a_2) \wedge H(o_1, o, a_2) \rightarrow E(o_1.a_1, o_1.a_2). \quad (3)$$

There are more properties of the relations (for example transitivity of $H$, reflexivity of $E$), but they are not necessary for verification of the system and are not considered here.

Next, we have to specify what we exactly mean by $H$ and $S$ relations. Let us assume that $S(o_1, o_2, o.c)$ is equivalent to the following formula:

$$\forall x \in C : E(o_1.x, o.c) \wedge E(o_2.x, o.c) \rightarrow o_1.x = o_2.x. \tag{4}$$

Analogically, $H(o_1, o_2, c)$ is equivalent to the formula[1]:

$$\forall x \in C : E(o_1.x, o_2.c) \rightarrow o_1.x = o_2.x. \tag{5}$$

### 3.2 Verification of the Proof Rules

If we accept assumptions presented above, we are able to prove correctness of the LPR rules. For every rule we can infer its conclusion from its premises[2] using only $MP$.

$MP$ rule does not need verification. Justification for $SYM$ is straightforward because of symmetry property, therefore it is omitted. We start with $GEN_o$. It has the following premises:

$$o.a = v \tag{6}$$

$$H(o, o', c) \tag{7}$$

$$E(o'.a, o'.c) \tag{8}$$

We have (7), so we can use $H$ interpretation (5) and we get

$$\forall x \in C : E(o'.x, o'.c) \rightarrow o.x = o'.a. \tag{9}$$

For $x = a$, having (8) we get $o.a = o'.a$. Hence, because of (6) we have $o'.a = v$, what is a conclusion of $GEN_o$.

We can justify $SPEC_o$ in a similar way. Now we will verify $SIM_o$. The premises are:

$$o_1.a = v \tag{10}$$

$$S(o_1, o_2, o.c) \tag{11}$$

$$E(o.a, o.c) \tag{12}$$

$$H(o_1, o, a) \tag{13}$$

$$H(o_2, o, a) \tag{14}$$

We have $S$ relation, so we can use its equivalent version (4):

$$\forall x \in C : E(o_1.x, o.c) \wedge E(o_2.x, o.c) \rightarrow o_1.x = o_2.x. \tag{15}$$

1 $H$ can be interpreted as a special case of $S$: $H(o_1, o_2, c) = S(o_1, o_2, o_2.c)$ because $E$ should be reflexive ($\forall o, a : E(o.a, o.a)$).

2 Such approach could be used as an alternative proof system with one proof rule – $MP$ and axioms representing knowledge base properties and inference rules. However proof constructed using LPR rules is much more clear and easy to interpret.

From premises (13), (14) and (12) using inheritance of dependencies property (2) we get:

$$E(o_1.a, o.c) \tag{16}$$
$$E(o_2.a, o.c) \tag{17}$$

Therefore we are able to infer $o_1.a = o_2.a$ from (15) given $x = a$. Using (10) we get $o_2.a = v$, a conclusion of $SIM_o$.

Next rule is $GEN_v$. It has the following premises:

$$o.a = v \tag{18}$$
$$H(v, v', c) \tag{19}$$
$$H(v', a, c) \tag{20}$$
$$E(a.o', a.c) \tag{21}$$
$$H(o, o', c') \tag{22}$$

First we apply symmetry property (1) to a statement (18) using (22). In this way we get $v.o' = o$. Now we can use $H$ interpretation (5) for (19) and we have:

$$\forall x \in C : E(v'.x, v'.c) \rightarrow v.x = v'.x. \tag{23}$$

From (20) and (21) using inheritance of dependencies II (3) we get $E(v'.o', v'.c)$, hence for $x = o'$ we infer $v.o' = v'.o'$ from (23). Therefore $v'.o' = o$ and we can use symmetry assumption (1) again to infer conclusion of the $GEN_v$ rule: $o.a = v'$.

Justification of $SPEC_v$ is similar. Therefore now we will verify last rule - $SIM_v$. Its premises are:

$$o.a = v \tag{24}$$
$$S(v, v', a.c) \tag{25}$$
$$E(a.o', a.c) \tag{26}$$
$$H(o, o', c') \tag{27}$$
$$H(v', a, c'') \tag{28}$$

Symmetry property applied to (24) gives $v.o' = o$. Given (25) and using similarity interpretation (4) for quantified variable equal $o'$ we have:

$$E(v.o', a.c) \wedge E(v'.o', a.c) \rightarrow v.o' = v'.o'. \tag{29}$$

Two dependency relations needed we get from (26) using dependency inheritance. Therefore we can infer $v'.o' = v.o' = o$ from (29). Symmetry property applied to this result yields $o.a = v'$, which is conclusion of the rule.

All the rules are logically correct, and we know the assumptions needed to prove it. Now we are able to present examples of rule applications.

# 4 Example of Using LPR

To show how LPR works we need plausible algebra. Its simple version is defined in this section. Next, examples of proof rules applications are presented.

## 4.1 Plausible Algebra

To define plausible algebra $\mathcal{A}$ (see section 2) we need a set of labels and 8 functions. Each label is a tuple of certainty parameters[3] (see table 2).

**Table 2.** Certainty parameters

| Parameter | Description |
|---|---|
| $\alpha$ | Strength of implication and dependency |
| $\gamma$ | Degree of certainty that a formula is true |
| $\tau$ | Degree of typicality in a hierarchy |
| $\sigma$ | Degree of similarity |
| $\phi$ | Frequency of the value in object domain |
| $\delta$ | Dominance of a subset in a set |

For each type of formula specific set of plausible parameters is appropriate. Hence specific label for each type of formulas are defined, see table 3.

**Table 3.** Plausible labels

| Formula | Plausible label |
|---|---|
| $o.a = v$ | $(\gamma, \phi)$ |
| $H(o_1, o_2, c)$ | $(\gamma, \delta, \tau)$ |
| $S(o_1, o_2, a)$ | $(\gamma, \sigma)$ |
| $E(o_1.a_1, o_2.a_2)$ | $(\gamma, \alpha)$ |
| $\psi_1 \wedge ... \wedge \psi_n \rightarrow \varphi$ | $(\gamma, \alpha)$ |

We assume, that a domain of all parameters is $(0, 1]$. Higher values means, that the strength of dependency or similarity (or other property) is high. If value is closer to 0, the value of the property is lower.

Parameter $\alpha$ represents a strength of implication and dependency. It is similar to certainty factor assigned to rules in Mycin [10]. $\gamma$ is a degree of certainty that a formula is true, it is analogy to certainty factor of a fact, but only positive values are used. Parameter $\tau$ in $H(o, o', c) : (\gamma, \delta, \tau)$ specifies how common are the values of appropriate attributes of $o$ in $o'$. In similarity

[3] The idea of certainty parameters was discussed in [1], here we present its realization.

formula $(S)$ $\sigma$ estimates how similar are two objects in given context. Parameter $\phi$ is used in a label of formula $o.a = v$ to specify how common is the value $v$ in the object (or objects) $o$. $\phi = 0.5$ means that half of $o$ has such value. The last parameter $\delta$ shows how big part of object is its descendant.

Now we are able to define plausible functions. They are used in proof rules to define a label of a conclusion. Functions are indexed by rule names. Their definitions are presented in table 4.

**Table 4.** Function definitions

| Function | Arguments | Value |
|---|---|---|
| $f_{MP}$ | $(\gamma_0, \alpha_0)$, $(\gamma_1, \phi_1)$, ..., $(\gamma_n, \phi_n)$ | $\gamma = \min(\gamma_0, \gamma_1, ..., \gamma_n, \alpha_0)$<br>$\phi = \min(\phi_1, ..., \phi_n)$ |
| $f_{SYM}$ | $(\gamma_1, \phi_1)$, $(\gamma_2, \delta_2, \tau_2)$ | $\gamma = \min(\gamma_1, \gamma_2)$<br>$\phi = \phi_1\delta_2/\tau_2$ |
| $f_{GEN_o}$ | $(\gamma_1, \phi_1)$, $(\gamma_2, \delta_2, \tau_2)$, $(\gamma_3, \alpha_3)$ | $\gamma = \min(\gamma_1, \gamma_2, \gamma_3, \alpha_3)$<br>$\phi = \tau_2$ |
| $f_{SPEC_o}$ | $(\gamma_1, \phi_1)$, $(\gamma_2, \delta_2, \tau_2)$, $(\gamma_3, \alpha_3)$ | $\gamma = \min(\gamma_1, \gamma_2, \gamma_3, \tau_2, \alpha_3)$<br>$\phi = \phi_1$ |
| $f_{SIM_o}$ | $(\gamma_1, \phi_1)$, $(\gamma_2, \sigma_2)$, $(\gamma_3, \alpha_3)$, $(\gamma_4, \delta_4, \tau_4)$,<br>$(\gamma_5, \delta_5, \tau_5)$ | $\gamma = \min(\gamma_1, \gamma_2, \gamma_3, \sigma_2, \alpha_3)$<br>$\phi = \phi_1$ |
| $f_{GEN_v}$ | $(\gamma_1, \phi_1)$, $(\gamma_2, \delta_2, \tau_2)$, $(\gamma_3, \delta_3, \tau_3)$, $(\gamma_4, \alpha_4)$,<br>$(\gamma_5, \delta_5, \tau_5)$ | $\gamma = \min(\gamma_1, ..., \gamma_5, \alpha_4)$<br>$\phi = \phi_1$ |
| $f_{SPEC_v}$ | $(\gamma_1, \phi_1)$, $(\gamma_2, \delta_2, \tau_2)$, $(\gamma_3, \delta_3, \tau_3)$, $(\gamma_4, \alpha_4)$,<br>$(\gamma_5, \delta_5, \tau_5)$ | $\gamma = \min(\gamma_1, ..., \gamma_5, \tau_2, \alpha_4)$<br>$\phi = \phi_1$ |
| $f_{SIM_v}$ | $(\gamma_1, \phi_1)$, $(\gamma_2, \sigma_2)$, $(\gamma_3, \alpha_3)$, $(\gamma_4, \delta_4, \tau_4)$,<br>$(\gamma_5, \delta_5, \tau_5)$ | $\gamma = \min(\gamma_1, ..., \gamma_5, \sigma_2, \alpha_3)$<br>$\phi = \phi_1$ |

In $f_{MP}$ definition we assume, that all premises of implication clause are $V$ relations, but it can be generalized. For all types of formulas theirs labels have $\gamma$ parameter so the problem is with $\phi$. We can set $\phi_i = 1$ if premise $i$ is not a $V$ relation.

### 4.2 LPR Rules Applications

Plausible algebra is defined, hence it is possible to show examples of LPR rules applications. They are presented in table 5. Part of them is taken from [1].

## 5 Conclusions and Further Works

It has been demonstrated that LPR can be defined as a labeled deductive system. Also correctness of the inference rules has been confirmed.

**Table 5.** Examples of using proof rules.

$\underline{MP}$
$Patient.Temperature = High : (\gamma = 1, \phi = 1)$
$Patient.Pathogen = Bacteria : (\gamma = 0.9, \phi = 1)$
$Patient.Temperature = High \wedge Patient.Pathogen = Bacteria \rightarrow$
$\quad Patient.Cure = Antibiotic : (\gamma = 1, \alpha = 0.6)$
$\overline{Patient.Cure = Antibiotic : (\gamma = 0.6, \phi = 1)}$

$\underline{SYM}$
$Honduras.Agrucultural\_product = Bananas : (\gamma = 1, \phi = 0.5)$
$H(Honduras, Country, Characteristic) : (\gamma = 1, \delta = 0.001, \tau = 0.02)$
$\overline{Bananas.Country = Honduras : (1, 0.025)}$

$\underline{GEN_o}$
$Chicken.Internal\_organ = Gizzard : (\gamma = 1, \phi = 1)$
$H(Chicken, Bird, Biological\_characteristic) : (\gamma = 1, \delta = 0.1, \tau = 0.9)$
$E(Bird.Internal\_organ, Bird.Biological\_characteristic) : (\gamma = 0.95, \alpha = 1)$
$\overline{Bird.Internal\_organ = Gizzard : (\gamma = 0.95, \phi = 0.9)}$

$\underline{SPEC_o}$
$S.A.Country.Mountains = Andes : (\gamma = 1, \phi = 0.6)$
$H(Uruguay, S.A.Country, Characteristic) : (\gamma = 1, \delta = 0.01, \tau = 0.9)$
$E(Country.Mountains, Country.Characteristic) : (\gamma = 0.9, \alpha = 1)$
$\overline{Uruguay.Mountains = Andes : (\gamma = 0.9, \phi = 0.6)}$

$\underline{SIM_o}$
$West\_Texas.Livestock = Cattle : (\gamma = 1, \phi = 0.9)$
$S(Chaco, West\_Texas, Region.Vegetation) : (\gamma = 0.8, \sigma = 0.6)$
$E(Region.Livestock, Region.Vegetation) : (\gamma = 1, \alpha = 0.7)$
$H(West\_Texas, Region, Livestock) : (\gamma = 1, \delta = 0.0001, \tau = 0.2)$
$H(Chaco, Region, Livestock) : (\gamma = 1, \delta = 0.0001, \tau = 0.2)$
$\overline{Chaco.Livestock = Cattle : (\gamma = 0.6, \phi = 0.9)}$

$\underline{GEN_v}$
$Honduras.Agricult\_product = Bananas : (\gamma = 1, \phi = 0.8)$
$H(Bananas, Tropical\_fruits, Climate) : (\gamma = 1, \delta = 0.2, \tau = 0.95)$
$H(Tropical\_fruits, Agricult\_product, Climate) : (\gamma = 1, \delta = 0.02, \tau = 0.02)$
$E(Agricult\_product.Country, Agricult\_product.Climate) : (\gamma = 1, \alpha = 0.9)$
$H(Honduras, Country, Characteristic) : (\gamma = 1, \delta = 0.001, \tau = 0.02)$
$\overline{Honduras.Agricult\_product = Tropical\_fruits : (\gamma = 0.9, \phi = 0.8)}$

$\underline{SPEC_v}$
$South\_Africa.Minerals = Diamonds : (\gamma = 1, \phi = 0.1)$
$H(Industrial\_diamonds, Diamonds, Characteristic) : (\gamma = 1, \delta = 0.8, \tau = 0.9)$
$H(Diamonds, Minerals, Characteristic) : (\gamma = 1, \delta = 0.001, \tau = 0.005)$
$E(Minerals.Country, Minerals.Characteristic) : (\gamma = 1, \alpha = 0.9)$
$H(South\_Africa, Country, Characteristic) : (\gamma = 1, \delta = 0.002, \tau = 0.02)$
$\overline{South\_Africa.Minerals = Industrial\_diamonds : (\gamma = 0.9, \phi = 0.1)}$

$$\frac{\begin{array}{l}\underline{SIM_v}\\ Wolf.Sound = Howl : (\gamma = 1, \phi = 0.95)\\ S(Bark, Howl, Sound.Means\_of\_production) : (\gamma = 1, \sigma = 0.9)\\ E(Sound.Animal, Sound.Means\_of\_production) : (\gamma = 1, \alpha = 1)\\ H(Wolf, Animal, Characteristic) : (\gamma = 1, \delta = 0.01, \tau = 0.03)\\ H(Bark, Sound, Characteristic) : (\gamma = 1, \delta = 0.01, \tau = 0.03)\end{array}}{Wolf.Sound = Bark : (\gamma = 0.9, \phi = 0.95)}$$

Further research will concern formalism extensions such as adding negation symbol or new proof rules. Modus Tolens inference rule could be added and aggregation of proofs should be examined.

Improving plausible algebra by making plausible labels and functions more sophisticated is the second problem.

Different applications of LPR formalism will be also considered. Using it in intelligent information systems for retrieving information is one field. Second, more interesting, is using it in machine learning algorithms, where abstraction/concretion and generalization/specialization capabilities seems to be very helpful (see [6]).

## References


1. A. Collins and R. S. Michalski. The logic of plausible reasoning: A core theory. *Cognitive Science*, 13:1–49, 1989.
2. D. M. Gabbay. *LDS – Labeled Deductive Systems.* Oxford University Press, 1991.
3. J. W. Grzymala-Busse. *Managing Uncertainty in Expert Systems.* Kluwer Academic Publishers, 1991.
4. J. Łukasiewicz. Many-valued systems of propositional logic. In S. McCall, editor, *Polish logic.* Oxford University Press, 1967.
5. R. S. Michalski. A theory and methodology of inductive learning. *Artificial Intelligence*, 20:111–161, 1983.
6. R. S. Michalski. Inferential theory of learning: Developing foundations for multistrategy learning. In R. S. Michalski, editor, *Machine Learning: A Multistrategy Approach, Volume IV.* Morgan Kaufmann Publishers, 1994.
7. Z. Pawlak. Rough sets. *Int. J. Comp. Inf. Sci.*, 11:344–356, 1982.
8. J. Pearl. Fusion, propagation, and structuring in bayesian networks. *Artificial Intelligence*, 29:241–288, 1986.
9. G. Shafer. *A Mathematical Theory of Evidence.* Princeton University Press, 1976.
10. H. Shortliffe and B. G. Buchanan. A model of inexact reasoning in medicine. *Mathematical Biosciences*, 23:351–379, 1975.
11. L. A. Zadeh. Fuzzy sets. *Information and Control*, 8:338–353, 1965.

# Author Index

GPSR Compliance

*The European Union's (EU) General Product Safety Regulation (GPSR) is a set of rules that requires consumer products to be safe and our obligations to ensure this.*

*If you have any concerns about our products, you can contact us on ProductSafety@springernature.com*

In case Publisher is established outside the EU, the EU authorized representative is:

Springer Nature Customer Service Center GmbH
Europaplatz 3
69115 Heidelberg, Germany

**Batch number: 10577878**

Printed by Printforce, the Netherlands